BENCHMARKS IN DISTANCE EDUCATION

BENCHMARKS IN DISTANCE EDUCATION

The LIS Experience

EDITED BY DANIEL D. BARRON

LIBRARIES UNLIMITED

A Member of the Greenwood Publishing Group

Westport, Connecticut • London

Library of Congress Cataloging-in-Publication Data

Benchmarks in distance education : the LIS experience / edited by Daniel
   D. Barron
     p. cm.
   Includes bibliographical references and indexes.
   ISBN 1–56308–722–7
   1. Library education—United States—Case studies.   2. Distance education—United
States—Case studies.   I. Barron, Daniel D.
Z668.B46   2003
371.3′5—dc21   2003051580

British Library Cataloguing in Publication Data is available.

Library of Congress Catalog Card Number: 2003051580
ISBN: 1–56308–722–7

First published in 2003

Libraries Unlimited, Inc. 88 Post Road West, Westport, CT 06881
A Member of the Greenwood Publishing Group, Inc.
www.lu.com

Printed in the United States of America

∞

The paper used in this book complies with the
Permanent Paper Standard issued by the National
Information Standards Organization (Z39.48–1984).

10 9 8 7 6 5 4 3 2 1

CONTENTS

Preface   ix

Introduction   xi

1. If It's Friday, We're in Gadsden or Mobile: Distance Education at the University of Alabama School of Library and Information Studies   1
Joan L. Atkinson

2. Distance Education at the School of Information Resources and Library Science, University of Arizona   5
Charles A. Seavey

3. Dominican University (River Forest, IL) and the College of St. Catherine (St. Paul, MN) Distance Learning Experience   13
Mary Wagner and Prudence Dalrymple

4. Maintaining High Touch for Effective Distance Education: The Emporia Experience   23
Daniel Roland

5. Distributed Learning in the Florida State University School of Information Studies   29
Gary Burnett, Kathleen Burnett, and Don Latham

6. Distance Learning at the University of Hawai'i: Serving the Underserved in an Island State   53
Violet H. Harada

7. Distance Education at the University of Illinois   63
   Leigh Estabrook

8. The Indiana Virtual Classroom: Interaction through
   Two-Way Video   75
   Daniel Callison, Shirley A. Fitzgibbons, and Edward J. Jurewicz

9. OhioLEARN: Distributed Education in Library and
   Information Science at Kent State University   101
   Danny P. Wallace and Connie Van Fleet

10. The Distance Learning Program at the University of
    Kentucky's School of Library and Information Science   121
    Timothy W. Sineath

11. The School of Library and Information Science at
    Louisiana State University: Distance Education Program   127
    Alma Dawson

12. Distributed Learning: The Development of Courses and
    Programs in LIS at the University of Missouri–Columbia   161
    Thomas R. Kochtanek, Charley Seavey, and John Wedman

13. The University of North Carolina at Greensboro Master
    of Library and Information Studies   169
    Beatrice Kovacs

14. What We Can Learn from Automating the Card Catalog?
    Distributed Learning at the University of North Texas   177
    Philip M. Turner

15. Partnership in Multisite Distance Learning: A Cooperative
    Program for Master's Degrees in Librarianship at North
    Texas   185
    Keith Swigger and Phil Turner

16. "The Spirit of Learning Is a Lasting Frontier": Distance
    Education in Library and Information Studies at the
    University of Oklahoma   199
    Danny P. Wallace

17. The University of Pittsburgh's School of Information
    Sciences Distance Education: Past, Present, and Future   215
    Susan Webreck Alman, Christinger Tomer, and Kara Lizik Pilarsky

18. The University of Rhode Island Regional Program
    Distance Education in New England   233
    C. Herbert Carson

19. The Tortoise May Be Right: The Movement Toward
    Distance Education at Rutgers University   247
    Kay E. Vandergrift and Karen Novick

20. Distance Education at San Jose State University 263
    Blanche Woolls and David V. Loertscher

21. Opening the Door to Distance Learners in South
    Carolina: The College of Library and Information Science
    Story 271
    Daniel D. Barron

22. Distance Education at the School of Library and
    Information Science, University of South Florida 281
    James O. Carey and Vicki L. Gregory

23. The University of Southern Mississippi School of Library
    and Information Science Distance Education History and
    Programs 299
    M. J. Norton

24. A Tradition of Innovation: The Syracuse University
    Experience 313
    Ruth V. Small and Barbara Settel

25. The *Enterprise* Confronts the *Nimitz*: Distance
    Education at the School of Information Sciences, the
    University of Tennessee 325
    Gretchen Whitney and George Hoemann

26. Dimensions of Students' Interactive Video-Based
    Distance Learning Experiences: A Qualitative Study
    Conducted at Texas Woman's University 337
    Patricia Jackson Edwards

27. Distance Education at the University of Wisconsin–
    Madison School of Library and Information Studies 359
    Jane Pearlmutter

28. The Evolution of Distance Learning at the School of
    Information Studies, University of Wisconsin–Milwaukee 365
    Wilfred Fong, Judith Senkevitch, and Dietmar Wolfram

Index 373

PREFACE

This volume has grown from the collective effort of individuals from twenty-eight American Library Association (ALA)–accredited program schools to document the history and growth of distance education for the library and information science (LIS) professions in the United States. Its genesis was the Distance Education in Library and Information Studies Pre-Conference, "A Taste of What's Cooking," which was held at the 1999 Association for Library and Information Science Education (ALISE) annual conference in Philadelphia, Pennsylvania.

The goal of the project was to have a person from each school listed on the ALA Distance Education Opportunities Web site (www.ala.org/alaorg/oa/disted.html) to write a separate chapter on the history and background of their school's experience. In the first Association of American Library Schools (AASL) *Library Education Statistical Report* in 1980, Elspeth Pope reported in the "Curriculum" chapter that 32 AASL members offered 229 courses "off-campus." The name AASL was changed to ALISE and the report to *Library and Information Science Education Statistical Report;* however, each compiler of the "Curriculum" chapter has included data and information on what are now called courses taught away from the "home campus" and includes the use of all of the technologies used to reach distant learners. In the 2002 report, 43 schools reported a total of 1,028 courses taught as distance education courses. Although this information is valuable to the researcher, and there is a growing number of published reports related to studies and assessment of distance education specifically in LIS, the more personal accounts of the history and development of distance education need to be available. No attempt was made to standardize the formats for the papers to let the personality of the author and program come through for readers. This is not the complete record of programs that offer distance learning opportunities. Our international friends and colleagues are noticeably absent; however, those who have worked to create this volume intend to work toward a second edition that will include the stories from all of our schools.

In addition to the special individuals who contributed manuscripts, a sincere thanks goes to the following friends and colleagues who served as advisors, reviewers, and supporters throughout this effort: Chuck Curran, Gayle Douglas, Leigh Estabrook, Bob Grover, Marty Hale, Joe Mika, Jane Robbins, Fred Roper, Donna Shannon, Bill Summers, Lee Shiftlet, Phil Turner, and Linda Walling. Thanks also to Martin Dillon, without whose support and belief in all the authors, this important piece of our professional history would never have been published.

INTRODUCTION

Distance education as a concept is not new to library and information science (LIS) education in the United States. One of the several variations on a common theme, distance education is the latest formal, encompassing descriptor of our efforts to remove the barriers of time and geography from the paths of those qualified to pursue quality education whether it is initial, preservice courses or continuing, in-service activities. The authors have defined distance education as the study and practice of education in environments where the learner and the teacher are separated by time and distance but are connected by technology and commitment. The technology can be mail trucks and airplanes carrying materials for correspondence study or the Internet, linking individuals and groups in an almost immediate interactive environment. The critical elements, however, are the human ones that unite learners and teachers in a learning conversation. LIS educators have been among the first to use the available technologies to reach out and help individuals learn how to make "optimum social utility of the graphic record." This is the beginning of their story.

Distance education can be argued to be a subset of a more comprehensive concept, *distributed education,* a term that is generally accepted as referring to all elements of the academic experience that is enhanced by information technology applications. This broader casting has great importance to those

Substantial portions of this introduction were first published in *Education for Information* (issue 8, 1990, pp. 235–339) and in the *Encyclopedia of Library and Information Science,* "Distance Education in United States Library and Information Science Education." New York: Marcel Dekker, vol. 52, supplement 15, 1993, pp. 72–85.

who study the methods and processes by which we attempt to educate those entering and working in the library and information professions. That, however, is a topic for a separate study.

IN THE BEGINNING

Melvil Dewey at Columbia College opened the doors to the first formal program of library education in the United States, the School of Library Economy, in 1887. Until that time, preparation for library work consisted primarily of apprenticeships in larger libraries and limited coursework, usually for school librarians, available through colleges and state departments of education (White 1976). From the earliest years of Dewey's efforts to the present day, people working in libraries, especially those holding full-time positions and wanting formal education beyond the apprenticeship, have called on educators and administrators to consider their circumstances and needs. From these same early years, there were those who heard those cries and made every effort to accommodate such educational needs without sacrificing the academic credibility of the educational experience.

CORRESPONDENCE STUDY

Correspondence study was one of the first types of distance education used in LIS as well as in education generally. Dewey called for Albany to develop correspondence courses for special library and small library service as early as 1888 (Vann 1971), and the American Library Association (ALA) Committee on Library Training recommended in 1903 that schools and/or "leading libraries" be authorized to offer correspondence work. However, the same committee failed to define standards for such courses in 1905, decided not to suggest standards in 1906, and made "unfavorable" comments on a program sponsored by the International Correspondence University in 1907 (Vann 1971).

In his now-famous reports of 1921 (to the Carnegie Corporation) and 1923 (the published report), Charles Williamson also recommended that library schools adopt the correspondence method of instruction, not "as a substitute for anything else, but merely as the necessary and logical supplement to other methods...the lowest method,...which would lead naturally and easily to other higher steps" (Vann 1971). It appears, as Morehead (1980) posits, that Williamson "became enchanted with correspondence instruction," for some time later he recommended that the Carnegie Corporation fund the development of a school in New York City that "should be expected to develop this work [correspondence study] on a large scale [and] to put into it the best available organizing and teaching ability" (Vann 1971). Williamson was apparently greatly influenced by the very successful education program of the American Bankers Association that relied heavily on correspondence courses (White 1976).

Williamson reported that correspondence study in library science was already ongoing and pointed out that twenty-four lessons in Technical Methods of Library Science were being taught by correspondence by the University of Chicago. He also reported that a cataloging course was taught by correspondence by the California State Library and that the University of Wisconsin Extension Division offered a course in 1920 to "between 250 and 300 students" (Vann 1971, p. 84).

In 1923, the American Correspondence School of Librarianship was established under the direction of H. P. Gaylord at Syracuse University (Linderman 1971). It was transferred in 1928 "with all its assets, good will and students in good standing to Columbia University [renamed from Columbia College] to be administered jointly by the School of Library Service and the Home Study Department" under the direction of C. C. Williamson, then director of the school and libraries (Vann 1971). The program was very popular with practicing librarians and flourished (Linderman 1971) until 1936, when Columbia abolished all correspondence study (Wheeler 1946).

Correspondence study has never enjoyed a very positive reception among LIS educators. In fact, such courses were not spoken of favorably by the ALA Committee on Library Training in the early years of the century (Vann 1971), were "flattened" by resolution of the Board of Education for Librarianship in 1938 (Wheeler 1946), and, from 1951 until today, cannot be used toward meeting the requirements of the master's degree program accredited by the Committee on Accreditation (American Library Association 1990).

Among the fourteen most significant events marking the progress of LIS education attributed to Joseph Wheeler by Jesse Shera (1972), was the "rejection of correspondence courses by the BEL." Reece (1936), discussing the early years of the New York State Library School, claims, "Even if correspondence teaching and college instruction had begun, it is unlikely that they would have exerted material effects upon the curriculum, since they tend to be concerned with segments of library work rather than with its entirety."

At one time, the ALA Standing Committee on Library Education (SCOLE) provided a listing of correspondence courses as a service to the profession. The list came from those courses submitted to SCOLE and went out with the caveat that the association "has not investigated the listed courses as to quality" (American Library Association 1990) and included a warning that the courses might not count toward degree programs. Correspondence study is still not often accepted by accredited program schools.

EXTENSION EFFORTS

Although correspondence study was one of the first, it was not the only early effort in the United States to provide alternative access to education and training in LIS. Either from a sense of concern and responsibility or from a fear for survival, or both, LIS educators have created opportunities for those not able to attend programs fixed in traditional schedules by physically taking instruction beyond the confines of the traditional campus. This is often called *extension education*.

Reece reports on of the earliest efforts: "After the matter had been considered for almost a decade," the New York State Library School offered a summer session in 1896. This was a six-week session, and although it drew from some of the subjects of the school, "it was in fact a separate thing, serving a distinct purpose" (Reece 1936). Summer sessions, weekend sessions, intensive and compacted courses, federally funded institutes, evening classes, and other configurations of time have been used to accommodate learners who work during the regular weekday, teach in schools, or live so far from traditional LIS programs that regular attendance is not possible. These concessions, along with LIS educators' acceptance of part-time students, are noteworthy because they demonstrate that LIS educators have realized the futility of full-time residency among many of those that have been attracted to the profession. Though these efforts are not solely in the domain of distance education, they are important to consider because they represent the fact that almost all LIS programs in the United States have made efforts to accommodate and support the nontraditional learner. This is the first step in legitimating distance education.

LIS educators have also "gone off-campus" or provided other extension courses to meet distant learners, but often they have not heard the stories of their pioneering ancestors who, like the early public librarians, packed up boxes of books in the back of their cars and took information and education beyond the confines of library buildings and college campuses. For example, Louis Shores points out:

Since 1947, the Florida State faculty have carried library education to centers in 37 counties, extending geographically from Pensacola, in the extreme northwest, to Key West 850 miles to the southeast. More than 5000 students have been enrolled in these classes, mostly teachers who have carried the gospel of library learning to their pupils and colleagues. But many good students have been recruited for librarianship, and some have completed their accredited master's requirements, through a combined summer residence-local extension program. (Shores 1972)

LIS programs have offered extension courses and even complete degree programs beyond their home campus. For example Louisiana State University worked with librarians in West Virginia in the 1970s, the University of North Carolina at Chapel Hill worked with a cluster of librarians in Eastern Virginia, Clarion State College took their degree program to Maine, and Emporia has taken their degree programs to Colorado, Nebraska, Iowa, and North Dakota. With the exceptions of the presentations in this volume, little has been written concerning these programs or their relative success. Although extension programs continue, the use of other delivery systems, especially the Web, has found greater appeal among LIS educators than loading up cars, buses, and airplanes (Association for Library and Information Science Education 1989).

TELECOMMUNICATIONS DELIVERY

Educators in the United States have endeavored to make the best use of radio since the 1920s and television since 1930s, but not until the 1960s was their use widespread. Professional groups such as lawyers, pharmacists, teachers, engineers, and health science workers have used telecommunications for academic credits as well as continuing education and conferencing (Vann 1971). Radio has been used (and is still being used) for distance education to a limited extent, but television and telephone delivery have been the primary focus of most educators.

The first use of videoconferencing for continuing education by LIS professionals was the ALA Satellite Teleconference on Copyright, which aired on February 7, 1978 ("Giant Step into the Space Age" 1978). This was followed in 1983 by a videoconference on MARC and AACR2 developed by ALA in cooperation with the Public Service Satellite Consortium. Telephone teleconferencing was used in Oklahoma in 1983 for the delivery of a continuing education experience related to medical reference requests (Wender 1983). David Salt (1987) of the University of Saskatchewan in Saskatoon reported the use of teleconferencing in a continuing education project focusing on the area of technical information use by engineers in 1987. The Association of College and Research Libraries produced two teleconferences related to CD-ROM technology in 1988 and 1989 that, according to the author's personal conversations with the producers, were well received by the professional community. Information Power: Guidelines for School Library Media Programs in 1988 and The Administrator's Guide to Information Power in 1989 were videoconferences that were sponsored by companies from the private sector and produced by the American Association of School Librarians and the Association for Educational Communications and Technology in cooperation with the College of Library and Information Science, University of South Carolina. The latter was also sponsored by the National Association of Elementary School Principals and the National Association of Secondary School Principals.[1]

Separate articles by Wender (1983) and Berk (1982) describe uses of audio (telephone) telecommunications technology in continuing education efforts for health services personnel. Wender reports on four lectures that were delivered via telephone to 110 hospitals in Oklahoma in 1981, and Berk describes an experiment in which the American Medical Library Association offered a continuing education course in management and budgeting in 1982 through the University of Wisconsin's Education Telephone Network. Both positive and negative aspects of the efforts were described, and both authors concluded that the medium was appropriate, was effective, and should be used again by the profession. George Hartje describes his use of telelecture in a library science class at the University of Missouri–Columbia. Though no statistical analysis was reported, the author concluded that the experience was successful and beneficial to the students (Hartje 1973).

The use of television for formal class work in LIS distance education was vaguely referred to by Irving Lieberman (1973) in a part of a collection intended to stimulate research efforts and directions in LIS education. In a list of uses of TV he mentions, "open-circuit television courses for college credit are a reality." Later in the same report he describes telelectures, using telephone technology as a delivery system, but offers no examples in LIS. Actual implementation of television in LIS education appears to have begun at Indiana University, School of Library and Information Science, in the early 1970s and is the focus of one of the few research pieces completed in distance education. Bruce Shuman (1973) describes the use of closed-circuit television for one course at Indiana University and reported that the experience was generally successful except that some students felt as though they were "guinea pigs" in some sort of experiment.

The School of Library and Information Studies, University of Wisconsin–Madison, has been a pioneer in the use of audio (i.e., telephone) teleconferencing in the profession. Darlene Weingand (1984) reported her research comparing student outcomes of those using a traditional classroom setting and those using the audio teleconferencing system for a semester-length class in public library administration. She concluded that the comparison of the two groups was favorable, there was no evidence to support the notion that the classroom is the optimum model for delivery of education, that audio conferencing can be equal if not better than classroom instruction, and that "the absence of face-to-face interaction and the substitution of teleconferencing interaction is not detrimental to the learning process." The school continues to take advantage of one of the most sophisticated audio conferencing systems in the world, the Educational Teleconferencing Network, which links more than 170 sites in the state. With a few recent exceptions, these LIS courses have been offered primarily for continuing education.

Pam Barron describes the development and field testing of Jump Over the Moon: Sharing Literature with Young Children, an award-winning telecourse that was developed in 1982 and continues to be the base for classes available through both state and national delivery systems. She concludes that such a course "should not be used to replace more traditional methods, but it is an effective and viable alternative" (Barron 1987). Jill May (1977) describes the problems involving copyright and the general development and evaluations of a videotaped course in children's media.

Marilyn Ming and Gary MacDonald (1987) report on an innovative effort, the Rural Library Training Project, which provided training for small rural school and public librarians in Alberta, Canada. The project involved the complete design, implementation, and evaluation of a certificate program that relied primarily on print with some videotaped components. The results of their evaluations were very positive, both in the evaluations of students and the program staff.

OTHER HISTORICAL LITERATURE AND RESEARCH

In 1966, Lawrence Allen completed an evaluation of the New York State Library's Community Librarians Training program, an effort to take courses to persons working in public libraries in New York who did not have a professional degree or certification (Allen 1966). He found that the program was successful, and respondents indicated that it should be continued and extended to professional staff as well. Richard Walker described in 1969 the development and use of instructional materials used in an independent study course intended for students located away from his home campus. Though the report is useful, it is awareness and instructional based more than research based (Walker 1964). In 1970, Martha Boaz (1970), then dean of the School of Library Science at the University of Southern California, presented a thought piece in which she commented favorably on the use of off-campus courses in LIS education. Six years later, she reported on an experimental, self-paced, independent learning program offered by the school that she indicated was successful. She recommended that others be undertaken (Boaz 1977). In 1971, Loyola University of Chicago, working with the Western Interstate Commission for Higher Education and the New Mexico State Library, provided correspondence courses and on-site sessions for a project called the Community Librarian Training Program. According to the report of the project, the program was successful (Shubert 1973).

In 1974, a number of authors contributed to a volume intended to explore a wide range of options and philosophical positions in the area of continuing education for library personnel in the Midwestern states. Included among the recommendations is the need for extension courses and cooperative efforts to provide for individual continuing education needs (Tyer 1974). Margaret Monroe (1975) described the British Open University in 1975 and suggested that American librarians might need some of the same skills as their British counterparts if they are to meet the needs of nontraditional adult learners. Some of these skills, she suggests, could be delivered in the same way as that for library clients. Kay Murray (1978) concluded from her 1977 study of American library schools that there was a general acceptance and an increase in the number of off-campus courses being offered. Marylouise Meder (1980) found that of nine variables, the availability of off-campus courses was one of the reasons why students in the sixty-one ALA-accredited program schools choose to enroll in the schools they did. Rogers and Kim (1981) reported on a needs assessment project in Ohio that revealed the critical importance of off-campus education to the continued development of librarians in the state. They not only provide discussion of the needs and rationale for distance education but also propose a consortium model to meet those needs. In 1986, Janice Ostrom (1987) completed a needs assessment of Kansas school library media specialists to determine their preferences, practices, and needs related to continuing education. Among other findings, Ostrom concluded that the respondents felt constrained by time, money, and geography; that they strongly felt the need for continuing education; and that they expressed the desire to have off-campus opportunities brought to them.

A major concern expressed by LIS educators and other educators involved with distance education generally is the lack of available resources to support the classes or courses being brought to the learner. This was the focus of a project of the Clarion State College Library that supported the efforts of the Clarion LIS distance education efforts (McCabe 1986). McCabe's report, although primarily focusing on the project itself, provides a good description of and rationale for LIS schools' efforts in distance education. In a similar descriptive study, Dan Barron surveyed students who had participated in distance education courses from 1976 to 1986 in his college and librarians in libraries on the eight campuses of the University of South Carolina serving those students to determine the use and barriers to use of resources related to distance education courses. His conclusions include strong statements of support for distance education by both students and librarians (the latter supporting distance education in other disciplines as well as LIS), the importance of faculty and librarian communication, and the importance of multitype library networks in meeting local student needs (Barron 1986).

Probably the first study comparing outcomes of distance education efforts in LIS is by Theresa Maggio (1988). She compared the similarities and differences in productivity and status of selected graduates of on-campus and off-campus programs in eight schools with ALA-accredited programs. She concludes that there were more similarities than differences between the groups and that age was a better predictor of future progress in the profession than any of the other variables tested, including on-campus versus off-campus class attendance.

In 1987, a theme issue of the *Journal of Education for Library and Information Science* was devoted to alternative delivery of LIS education. In that issue appears a general overview of distance education (Faibisoff and Willis 1987), a description of the technology available (at the time) to deliver distance education (Wilson 1987), a discussion of the problems and issues related to distance students as part-time students (Curran 1987), and reports of four research projects. Barron surveyed and interviewed the faculty who had provided and students who had taken course work via television and on-site at the College of Library and Information Science, University of South Carolina, to gather their perceptions related to the effectiveness of the various methods of distance education. He concluded that although both groups expressed reservations at the outset and remained partial to the traditional classroom, TV and on-site delivery at a distance are perceived to be as effective as traditional classroom instruction. He also reported on the monitoring of the distance education program in the college and concluded from the data analysis that were no statistically significant differences in test scores, grades, course evaluations, or other output measures available when on-campus students were compared with distance education campus students (Barron 1987). John Olsgaard (1987) concludes from his analysis of the impact of a distance education program in one LIS program that enrollment will be greatly increased, that this increase will be greatest among part-time students, and that class sizes on campus will increase with increased distance teaching. To determine the extent to which advising was provided and how it differed from traditional practices, Nancy Beitz (1987) completed a telephone survey of administrators in LIS programs that indicated that the school provided five or more classes away from the home campus. She concluded that administrators are very much aware of these students' needs and are attempting to meet them. She also provided a list of suggestions for improving advising for distance students.

Barron reported on a survey of chairpersons of curriculum committees in ALA-accredited program schools. He lists the respondents' perceptions of the real or potential barriers to the use of video technologies in LIS education. At the top of the list were concerns of inadequate financial resources need to obtain the necessary hardware and software, lack of courses available that meet the schools' academic needs and standards, logistical complexities involved in supporting the distant learner, a lack of training and education on the part of faculty to use such methodologies, and inadequate rewards for faculty who elect to try these new approaches to education. At the bottom of their list of concerns were feelings of negativity about administrators toward distance education, fear of reprise from accreditation agencies, or feelings of prejudice toward the media used to deliver distance education (Barron 1987).

One research project funded by a Special Research Award from ALISE was completed by Barron, in which he surveyed all faculty and administrators in ALA-accredited program schools to determine their perceptions of problems and concerns that distance and part-time students bring to LIS education programs. The study indicated that although LIS educators are somewhat concerned about the impact that part time and distance students may have on the profession and the discipline, they have a strong commitment to meet their students' needs through distance education. The study also reveals concerns related to the availability of resources to support the distant student locally, the importance of providing quality education rather than stopgap training, the possible threat to established programs, the lack of incentives for individuals and faculties as a whole to participate in distance education, a concern about socialization, and the need to know more about the whole area of adult learning and distance education before educated judgments can be made. The project was the first in a series that will eventually explore the full range of concerns and potential for part-time and distance students in LIS education (Barron 1991).

Dillon, Haynes, and Price (1990) of the University of Oklahoma presented a paper at the Canadian Association for the Study of Adult Education in 1990, later published in the journal of ALISE, on the impact of compressed video on student interaction and learning in a graduate library studies class. The researchers compared the outcomes and attitudes of traditional and distance students participating in a live two-way audio and video telecommunications class. They conclude that the delivery system had no impact on learning at any level, "suggesting that the problem of interaction at a distance does not impede performance on either lower or higher order levels of learning." The authors go on to conjecture that students at the distant sites participated in more student-to-student interactions and peer teaching than those in the on-campus site.

THE ROAD AHEAD

The purpose of this introduction has been to provide the broadest historical perspective possible for the chapters that follow. They take up where this introduction ends. The pictures you are about to see are significant milestones in the use of converging and complementary technologies for learning in the profession. Perhaps more important, they demonstrate the leadership role LIS educators are taking in the larger context of distance and distributed education generally.

NOTE

1. For additional information, contact the American Library Association, 50 E. Huron Street, Chicago, IL 60611.

REFERENCES

Allen, L. 1966. *An Evaluation of the Community Librarians' Training Courses with Special Emphasis on the Entire Training Function in the Library Extension Division of the New York State Library.* New York State Library, New York.

American Library Association, Standing Committee on Library Education. 1990. *Correspondence and Home-Study Courses in Librarianship.* Chicago: American Library Association, p. 1.

Association for Library and Information Science Education. 1989. *Library and Information Science Education Statistical Report.* Sarasota, FL: Association for Library and Information Science Education.

Barron, D. 1986. "Perceived Use of Off-Campus Libraries by Students in Library and Information Science." In *The Off-Campus Library Services Conference Proceedings,* B. Lessin (comp.), Mount Pleasant, MI: Central Michigan University.

Barron, D. 1987. "Faculty and Student Perceptions of Distance Education Using Television." *J. Educ. Lib. Inform. Sci.* 27(4): 257–271.

Barron, D. 1987. "The Use and Perceived Barriers to Use of Telecommunications Technology." *J. Educ. Lib. Inform. Sci.* 27(4): 288–294.

Barron, D. 1991. *Part Time and Distance Students in Library and Information Science Education Programs: Perceptions of Faculty and Administrators.* Sarasota, FL: Association for Library and Information Science Education.

Barron, P. P. 1987. "Production of a Telecourse in Library and Information Science." *J. Educ. Libr. Inform. Sci.* 27(4): 247–256.

Beitz, N. C. 1987. "Academic Advisement for Distance Education Students." *I. Educ. Lib. Inform. Sci.* 27(4): 280–287.

Berk, R. 1982. "The Delivery of Continuing Education: Teleconferencing, An Alternative Mode." *Bull. Med. Libr Assoc.* 70(1): 21–27.

Boaz, M. 1970. *Some Current Concepts About Library Education.* University of Southern California: School of Library Science.

Boaz, M. 1977. *Going Beyond the Rigidities of Formal, Traditional Education: Independent, Self-Paced University Study.* Los Angeles: University of Southern California, School of Library Science.

Curran, C. C. 1987. "Dealing with the Distant Learner as Part-Time Learner." *J. Educ. Lib. Inform. Sci.* 27(4): 240–246.

Dillon, C., K. Haynes, and M. Price, 1990. "The Impact of Compressed Video upon Student Interaction and Learning in a Graduate Library Studies Class." In *Proceedings of the 9th Annual Conference of the Canadian Association for the Study of Adult Education,* B. Stolze Clough (ed.), Victoria, BC: University of Victoria.

Faibisoff, S. G., and D. J. Willis. 1987. "Distance Education: Definition and Overview." *J. Educ. Lib. Inform. Sci.* 27(4): 219–292.

"Giant Step into the Space Age: ALA Satellite Teleconference on Copyright." 1978. *Am. Lib.* 9(4): 192–194.

Hartje, G. N. 1973. *Teaching Library Science and Telelecture.* Columbia: University of Missouri–Columbia, Graduate School of Library and Information Science.

Lieberman, I. 1973. "Relating Instructional Methodology to Teaching in Library Schools." In *Targets for Research in Library Education,* H. Borko (ed.), Chicago: American Library Association.

Linderman, W. B. 1971. Columbia University School of Library Service, *Encyclopedia of Library and Information Science,* vol. 5, New York: Marcel Dekker.

Maggio, T. G. 1988. "On-Campus and Off-Campus Programs of Accredited Library Schools: A Comparison of Productivity and Status of Graduates." Ph.D. dissertation, Florida State University.

May, J. 1977. "Copyright Clearance Problems in Educational Television: Children's Materials." *I. Educ. Librar.* 17(3): 149–160.

McCabe, G. 1986. "Library Services for the Distant Learner: The Clarion State College Libraries' Experience." Paper presented at Annual Conference of the National University Continuing Education Association, Reno, NV. Clarion, PA: Clarion State College.

Meder, M. 1980. "Student Concerns in Choice of Library School." *J. Educ. Lib.* 21(1): 3–24.

Ming, M., and G. MacDonald. 1987. "Rural Library Training: Bridging the Distance Effectively." *Can. Lib. J.* 44(2): 73–78.

Monroe, M. E. 1975. "Implications of the Open University for Changes in Library Education." *Drexel Libr.* 11(2): 54–67.

Morehead, J. 1980. *Theory and Practice in Library Education: The Teaching-Learning Process.* Littleton, CO: Libraries Unlimited, p. 27.

Murray, K. 1978. "The Structure of MLS Programs in American Library Schools." *J. Educ. Lib.* 18(4): 278–284.

Olsgaard, J. N. 1987. "The Impact of a Distance Education Program on Enrollment Patterns." *J. Educ. Lib. Inform. Sci.* 27(4): 272–279.

Ostrom, J. C. 1987. "Continuing Library Education: Practices and Preferences of Kansas School Librarians." Ph.D. dissertation, Kansas State University.

Reece, E. 1936. *The Curriculum in Library Schools.* New York: Columbia University Press, pp. 39–40.

Rogers, R., and M. Kim. 1981. *Alternative Modes for Providing Graduate Education for Librarianship in Ohio.* Washington, DC: U.S. Department of Education.

Salt, D. 1987. "Transmitting Library Instruction via Satellite." *Can. Lib. J.* 44(3): 155–157.

Sherea, J. 1972. *The Foundations of Education for Librarianship.* New York: Becker and Hayes, p. 231.

Shores, L. 1972. *Library Education.* Littleton, CO: Libraries Unlimited.

Shubert, J. 1973. *A Community Librarian's Training Program: A Report on a New Mexico Program and Guidelines for Developing Training Programs Based upon Correspondence Study and Adult Education Techniques.* Boulder, CO: Western Interstate Commission for Higher Education (ERIC Document Reproduction Service no. ED080132).

Shuman, B. 1973. "Teaching a Services and Collections Course via Closed Circuit Television." *J. Educ. Lib.* 14(3): 107–108.

Tyer, T. E. (ed.). 1974. Correspondence and Home-Study Courses in Librarianship Continuing Education, Illinois Libr, 56(6): 432–500.

Vann, S. 1971. *The Williamson Reports: A Study.* Metuchen, NJ: Scarecrow Press, pp. 30–31, 84, 100.

Walker, R. 1964. "Independent Study Materials in Library Science Instruction." *J. Educ. Lib.* 10(1): 1–44.

Weingand, D. 1984. "Telecommunications Delivery of Education: A Comparison with the Traditional Classroom." *J. Educ. Lib. Inform. Sci.* 25(1): 3–12.

Wender, R.W. 1983. "Talkback Telephone Network: Techniques of Providing Library Continuing Education." *Spec. Libr.* 74(3): 265–270.

Wheeler, J. 1946. *Progress and Problems in Education for Librarianship.* New York: Carnegie, p. 84, 85.

White, C. 1976. *A Historical Introduction to Library Education: Problems and Progress to 1951.* Metuchen, NJ: Scarecrow Press, p. 177.

Wilson, S. 1987. "The Sky's the Limit: A Technology Primer." *J. Educ. Lib. Inform. Sci.* 27(4): 233–239.

1

IF IT'S FRIDAY, WE'RE IN GADSDEN OR MOBILE: DISTANCE EDUCATION AT THE UNIVERSITY OF ALABAMA SCHOOL OF LIBRARY AND INFORMATION STUDIES

Joan L. Atkinson

Distance education at School of Library and Information Studies (SLIS) is accomplished in several ways: offering courses via compressed video systems, faculty traveling to off-campus sites, students traveling to weekend classes on and off campus, and professors incorporating Internet instruction into otherwise traditionally offered courses. At this point distance learning or distributed learning is offered exclusively within the state of Alabama, recognizing the obligation the school has to the state as its only ALA-accredited program.

CURRENT PRACTICE

In 2000 the SLIS offered seven courses over the compressed video network, the Intercampus Interactive Telecommunications System (IITS). These courses were Academic Libraries, Information Technologies (offered twice), Digital Libraries, Materials and Services for Adults, Managing Network Information Resources, and Information Resources: Government Publications. Most of the courses originated at SLIS in Tuscaloosa and "traveled" to sites 60 to 200 miles away, the closest being Birmingham and the most distant being Atmore. Approximately fifteen sites may realistically accept SLIS courses if there is local demand. Students probably consider the advantage of IITS courses to be reduction of driving time. Administratively an equally important benefit is curricular: Faculty from other institutions may provide subject expertise that complements that of the SLIS faculty. Science bibliography and government publications, for example, are subjects taught remotely from Auburn University or from the University of Alabama in Huntsville and offered to resident SLIS students and to other sites.

The University of Alabama operates an off-campus center at Gadsden to serve the northeast sector of the state and additionally market to northwest Georgia and middle Tennessee. One of several graduate programs to offer classes in Gadsden, the SLIS delivers a series of twelve courses over a three-year period, making it possible for a student who attends only the Gadsden campus to complete the MLIS degree in three years. At least one course is offered in Gadsden each term, often two. This year the following courses will travel to Gadsden: Information Technologies (required), Materials and Services for Children, Materials and Services for Young Adults, Bibliographic Organization and Control (required), Collection Development, and Information Sources and Services (required).

The Alabama Council on Higher Education (ACHE) strictly controls off-campus activities of state colleges and universities. To gain approval for an off-campus location, a unit must state exactly which classes will be offered and exactly where they will be taught. Currently the SLIS is approved to offer four classes in Birmingham, one each fall and spring, with Bibliographic Organization and Control alternating with Administration and Management in fall semesters and Information Sources and Services alternating with Introduction to Library and Information Studies in spring semesters. These may be taught only at the Birmingham Public Library. Similarly ACHE has approved the SLIS's offering six courses in Mobile. Beginning in fall 1999 there will be one class each fall and spring semester for the next three years, ending in spring 2002, and taught only at the Moorer Branch of the Mobile Public Library.

Weekend and evening courses offered on campus attract students from distant locations as well as those employed full-time. Strictly speaking, these may not be considered distance education; nevertheless, their availability enables nontraditional students to enter the library and information professions. I anticipate that any position the SLIS fills in the future will require faculty to teach at alternative times or with the use of alternative methods of course delivery.

HISTORY

Distance learning became an important focus for the SLIS in the 1980s, when it became clear that many people wished to enter the MLIS degree program who could not attend regular daytime classes in Tuscaloosa. Throughout the decade, SLIS faculty traveled to off-campus sites to teach—Montgomery and Florence in addition to Birmingham. One faculty member offered a course in the Quest program of videotaped instruction but gave it up after one attempt because of the lack of interaction and discussion. Continuing Studies suggested correspondence courses, but that idea never developed.

In the early 1990s the interactive video system emerged, at first as a clunky, slow, and distractingly mechanical delivery method. As technological improvements permitted the use of compressed video and thus more synchronous communication, the system became increasingly desirable. In fact, it was so desirable that competition for the available IITS rooms and time slots resulted in policies that gave first priority to programs that offered a full degree program over the system. SLIS never believed that every course could be adapted for delivery over the system and consequently had to take times and locations that were available after full degree programs made their schedules. At some sites, charges to use the system were also prohibitive. Nevertheless the IITS survived and thrived, and the SLIS continually improved the speed of its network and the quality of equipment, such as projectors, microphones, monitors, and screens, to offer more effective instruction.

In the late 1990s development of the Internet as a vehicle for delivering instruction threatened to outdistance all other technologies. Even though SLIS offers no courses entirely online, professors are incorporating online course delivery into some traditional classes. In the digital libraries course, for example, 30 to 40 percent of the work in the course last semester was conducted via an online discussion forum and e-mail.

THE FUTURE

For the SLIS the major issue is whether the curriculum will be delivered over the Internet in the future. If so, how much and how soon? How will copyright and intellectual property issues be settled? How will interaction among students and faculty in the online environment be facilitated? How will the university support faculty in the transition to Internet course development? What looms in the future for professional education and higher education? How will accreditation of programs be affected?

Last year the University of Alabama provost funded a number of projects to encourage innovation in teaching. A SLIS faculty member received one of the $5,000 grants and purchased a Real Media server (for streaming video). He and other faculty members anticipated its use in offering asynchronous instruction and had a fully online version of certain courses by spring 2001. One of the difficulties at the University of Alabama is that WebCT has been selected as the software package for delivery of online courses. Faculty members who attended workshops about WebCT have returned convinced that the time constraints are overwhelming. Enough faculty effort is needed that the university cannot grant the necessary release time to accomplish the goal. At the moment the campus is experiencing a hiatus from further development. In the SLIS we are poised to participate in this teaching innovation; we are also aware of the difficulty of managing time to add course development to the other demands of teaching, research, and service without an infusion of support services from the university.

2

DISTANCE EDUCATION AT THE SCHOOL OF INFORMATION RESOURCES AND LIBRARY SCIENCE, UNIVERSITY OF ARIZONA

Charles A. Seavey

The School of Information Resources and Library Science (SIRLS; under various names) of the University of Arizona has had long experience with distance education. The school's roots were in programs aimed largely at producing school librarians for the state of Arizona. In the late 1960s and early 1970s the school moved toward becoming a general-purpose library school and toward ALA accreditation. This goal was achieved in the early 1970s with Donald C. Dickinson as the first director. Under Dickinson, ALA accreditation and new quarters in the school's current building all arrived more or less simultaneously.

Once accredited, the school had distance offerings in the sense that coursework was offered in the Phoenix metropolitan area (approximately 100 miles from Tucson) either with traveling regular faculty or Phoenix-area adjuncts hired for the purpose. From the early 1970s through the late 1980s, "distance education" at Arizona meant the Phoenix-area offerings, with occasional summer coursework being offered in Laramie, Wyoming, under the auspices of the Wyoming State Library in cooperation with the University of Wyoming. Both aspects of distance education very much depended on availability of either regular faculty willing to travel or locally based adjuncts willing to teach.

THE FLYING FACULTY

Distance education in a more formal and organized sense started at Arizona in 1989. There is no library school in our neighboring state of New Mexico, but there is a strong need for degreed librarians. During the spring and summer of 1989 the Western Interstate Commission for Higher Education (WICHE) and the school planned for a program to bring library education to New Mexico.[1]

Instruction started in the fall of 1989. Two courses were offered using classroom facilities provided by the College of Education at the University of New Mexico in Albuquerque. The courses were taught on weekends, with three faculty members from the school team teaching the offerings. Faculty members rotated the trip to Albuquerque, each making five trips through the fifteen-week semester. Courses were taught on Saturday, with office hours and advising on Sunday morning and afternoon until the last flight back to Tucson. The faculty involved—John Budd, Charlie Hurt, and Charley Seavey—became collectively known as the "flying faculty."

The same model was continued for the spring semester of 1990. Then, as now, the University of Arizona requires that twelve units of residence credit be applied to a thirty-six-unit MA degree. The summer sessions of 1990 and 1991 saw Tucson heavily populated with New Mexicans earning their residence credits for their MA degrees.

The flying part of the flying faculty model, however, was taking its toll. The school decided that some delivery mechanism that caused a little less wear and tear on faculty members was called for. In addition to using adjunct faculty to teach in New Mexico, we started investigating the possibilities of distance delivery via television. After some discussion the school entered into an agreement with the television cable network Mind Extension University.[2]

THE TV YEARS, 1990–96

The TV years may roughly be divided into the Mind Extension University (MEU) portion in roughly the first half of the period and the latter few years, when we used a direct tape delivery system.

The MEU operation was fairly sophisticated. Classes were held in a university TV studio in Tucson. With permission from all the students in the real classroom, the proceedings were taped and later uploaded via satellite to MEU facilities in Colorado. MEU would then broadcast the class as part of their twenty-four-hours-a-day cable operation. Distance students had the option of either actually watching the tape as originally broadcast or taping it on their home VCRs for later use. Most students opted for the latter, because MEU was putting SIRLS classes on at hours when most people were asleep. The Boston-dwelling daughter of one SIRLS faculty member reported that she could watch her father for twenty minutes or so before going off to work early in the morning.

During the MEU years we operated on a site basis. Rather than individuals taking the class wherever they happened to be, we had designated sites where local librarians acted as site mentors to lead discussions about the content of the tapes, collect assignments, and advise students. Though effective in some instances, it also led to students having to drive considerable distances to get to the site for class. The model worked well in smaller states, but in places like Montana, for instance, there were difficulties, particularly during the winter months. In addition to the site discussions, each class had an e-mail list discussion group in which both distance and Tucson-based students participated. This practice continues today, although with considerably more sophisticated software than existed in the early days.

In the studio/classroom the instructor had a number of visual aids to use to break up the "talking head" problem. Cameras were arranged that could be used to pan the students in the classroom when discussion was under way. Distance students would get to see their Tucson counterparts, although the converse was not true. The instructor also had an overhead "look-down" camera to either pick up handwritten notes, pages from books, or any illustrations the instructor cared to use. In teaching research methods, for instance, the instructor could actually work through a statistical problem using the overhead camera. The studio was also equipped to pick up images from 35mm slides. In addition we discovered a way of using an Excel spreadsheet as a sort of crude PowerPoint presentation package. When PowerPoint itself appeared, we rapidly adopted that program as a graphic aid.

Although there were some severe budget constraints involved, we also were able to do remote shoots and incorporate the footage into the classroom. A session was shot within the university library map collection, for instance, and videotaped presentations by guest speakers, including our football coach, were used as well.

One of the interesting developments of the MEU delivery was that the programs could be viewed by anybody with a cable TV setup and the inclination to flip channels at odd hours of the day or night. This had several unintended consequences, not the least of which was various faculty members receiving some unwanted mail, or, alternatively, being recognized on the street by any number of nonlibrary-related folks in strange cities. In one instance, former undergraduate roommates reconnected while one was confined to a hospital bed with a broken leg and a TV.

There were drawbacks to the MEU operation, however. Not the least of these was that some of the costs involved had to be passed on to the students. The site mentor program, although having many positive aspects, was also somewhat uneven in quality and did present problems for students with long distances to travel, particularly during the winter months. The limitation to areas with cable TV hookups automatically cut out many potential students living in rural areas. Finally, MEU itself started to try to get involved in content issues, rather than acting strictly as a delivery mechanism. The school and MEU parted company.

We needed an alternative delivery mechanism. After some investigation we contracted with a local firm to reproduce, en masse, our master tapes of each session and distribute them via mail to individual students. This got around the requirement that a student have a cable TV hookup; a VCR was a necessity but easier to obtain in rural areas than cable. There were still expenses involved—mailing costs were not inconsiderable, and occasional shipping glitches happened—but largely the years of direct shipment worked well and expanded the potential student base beyond the limitations imposed by the MEU contract. Tape delivery ended some of the media star aspects of teaching but also halted the unwanted correspondence.

THE WORLD WIDE WEB EMERGES

The school had been aware of the development of the World Wide Web from almost the moment that Mosaic was unleashed on the world. As the technology, both hard and soft, of the Web improved over the years, we started thinking in terms of using the Web as a teaching mechanism. Several factors contributed to the eventual decision to use the Web as a course delivery mechanism.

First was hooking the school to the local fiber-optic Ethernet system. As great luck would have it, one of the main lines of the local backbone was to be installed through a parking lot directly behind the school's building. Getting from the backbone to the school, therefore, was a very small cost, and though wiring the building was not cheap, it was certainly doable. The sound of modems connecting over phone lines became a thing of the past.

Second was the rapid development of the Web as a mechanism of disseminating information. Although much of the content on the Web is purely entertainment, the decision of the federal government to move toward an electronic information dissemination system meant that vast amounts of serious material was to be distributed on the Web. It seemed to us that we would wind up teaching Web-based resources, and one way of teaching the system was to use the system itself as a teaching tool. It was obvious that libraries and information agencies were going to use the Web, and we should simply incorporate it into the repertoire of pedagogical tools we employed.

Third, and somewhat coincidentally, we moved from making computer literacy an exit requirement to an *entrance* requirement for admission to the school. We had developed a huge and unwieldy structure devoted to teaching students basic computer skills that were simply not graduate level in nature but necessary in the workplace. We had the luxury of a huge applicant pool, and after a certain amount of grumbling the student body simply realigned itself into computer literacy. We established a basic set of hardware and software requirements necessary for those interested in distance education with the school and made it clear that individual students were responsible for learning the technology involved. The result was that we no longer had to spend time teaching the mechanism and could concentrate once more on content. The emergent computer-literate student body simply took the development of Web-based teaching completely in stride.

After a period of experimentation with various software possibilities we settled on WebCT as the software of choice for our courseware.[3] There are several advantages to WebCT, not the least of which is that it is password-protected, which makes using copyright materials a lot easier. The package also contains its own built-in bulletin board and e-mail systems, along with a chatroom that may or may not be logged for use by students who cannot make the chat. Students may not use pseudonyms, and the program tracks usage, so arguments about participation are easily settled. We still have a public e-mail list, but once students get logged into WebCT we prefer that system because of the privacy of all concerned. There are a few awkward bits about the program, but by and large it serves our needs well.

Developing Web-based courses has involved a good deal of trial and error. We were the first department on campus to start teaching on the Web and had little local expertise to draw on. Early on lectures started off as more or less straight text, with occasional links to other sources, and the odd illustration. By the 1999–2000 academic year, lectures were making far better use of the technology and availability of Web-based sources. They tend to be well illustrated, contain lots of links for reference or further explanation, and, in some cases, have sound clips. All of this requires that the student have the requisite hardware and software, but we state the requirements very clearly and provide links to necessary software—RealPlayer in the case of the course using sound clips.[4] Use of audio streaming software will probably increase, although we do not envision moving to video streaming as long as the great majority of our students are limited by 56K modems.

A THREE-UNIVERSITY EXPERIMENT

During the spring 2001 semester, SIRLS became involved in a three-university experiment in distance education with the Graduate School of Library and Information Science (GSLIS) at the University of Texas–Austin, and the School of Library and Information Studies (SLIS) at Texas Woman's University. All three schools offered sections of a Web-based course dealing with government information. The course was variously numbered and titled at the three institutions, but had its basis in Government Information: Policy and Resources, as taught by a faculty member at the University of Arizona. The faculty member involved has long experience both in the field and teaching the topic. Neither GSLIS nor SLIS had such faculty members, and both were looking for a way of delivering relevant coursework to students registered at their home campuses as well as students taking the course at a distance.

For various reasons, the Texas schools leased the course from SIRLS. Although the technical problems involved in actual course delivery were fairly easily solved, the administrative morass took longer to clear up. In the end twenty-eight students from three universities successfully completed the course. The attrition rate was not abnormally high, and the grades were typical for the course. All students, of course, occupied the same electronic space, and the instructor made no effort to think of students in terms of Austin, Tucson, or Denton. Watching the class bulletin board it became obvious that there was a study group in Austin, and there was probably one in Tucson as well.

Given the nature of the Web, and the fact that niche specialties (such as government information) are not evenly distributed across the LIS faculties, it is entirely possible that this model may serve as the basis for future developments.

LESSONS LEARNED

The style of distance education developed here is the result of a number of factors. The huge distances and rural nature of the Rocky Mountain region that is our natural constituency works against flying faculty or a network of site-based operations. Our model does require that the student be self-sufficient in terms of technology and have the ability to work without daily face-to-face contact with fellow students or the faculty member in question. For some students this works well. For others it does not. Another factor has been cost, to the school and to students. We have developed our distance education program with little technological or pedagogical support, indeed some skepticism, from the university. Through an arrangement with the Extended University office we have been able to provide assistantships for many students who would not otherwise have received financial aid—and not coincidentally, student assistants to faculty members mounting Web-based courses. Basically, however, it has been an in-house operation.

For all that, and for the still experimental nature of a lot of distance education, the Web-based courses have generally worked well. Some classes have cohered far beyond the bonding of a traditional classroom gathering. Normal practice is to kill an e-mail list for a specific class at the end of each semester. Just prior to the adoption of WebCT, we had a fall class that objected to deactivating the list in December, and as late as April of the spring semester there was still traffic on the list. Another class, with students from all over the country, organized their entire summer school experience, including picking a place to stay together and laying out a social schedule prior to arrival in Tucson. They do not always work that well, but some of them do.

We have very little in the curriculum that the school has decided cannot be taught on the Web. After one faculty member successfully experimented with teaching research methods using the Web we have been gradually trying to adapt more courses for the medium. Even "classroom" courses being taught in Tucson now usually have a Web-based component to them. The tool is simply too flexible not to be used. Some courses, like government information, will be taught *only* on the Web because that is the best medium for the content.

Courses that we think probably will not work on the web—or at least nobody has tried them yet—include anything involving children's literature or school librarianship, basic reference, cross-listed courses, and seminars.

The Arizona model works well for our situation. Given smaller distances, a less rural population, or the availability of some new interactive TV system that would work in our region as well as within the borders of the state, we might experiment with different methods of delivering library education over distance. For the time being we feel we have accomplished much with limited resources and to a large degree teach our students by making them learn the technology simply as part of the course.

There are occasionally days when a router is down somewhere, the e-mail messages are piling up, and one cannot get the HTML coding to look right on the screen, and we wish we had never heard of distance education. On the other hand, the school has provided a mechanism for a large number of people in the Rocky Mountain West (and elsewhere) to earn an MA degree they would never have had otherwise and thereby improved the level of library service to an even larger number of folks. That thought makes it all worth it.

NOTES

1. WICHE is a fifteen-state consortium formed in 1953 largely as a resource-sharing enterprise among the member states. All of the states involved are geographically large but sparsely populated, and some cooperation involving specialized education seemed a good idea. The WICHE Web site is www.wiche.edu/home1.htm.

2. Mind Extension University was, at the time we were working with them, a Colorado-based educational TV provider. After we severed our relationship with them they seem to have disappeared into or become Jones International, a corporate entity with many Web-based enterprises, both educational and entertainment. Their Web site is www.jones.com.

3. WebCT was originally developed at the University of British Columbia. It has since migrated to the private sector and is visible online at http://www.webct.com. There are now myriad courseware packages available, but WebCT was among the first, and we have developed along with it. The package has now been adopted for campus-wide use by the University of Arizona, due in no small part to the school's early adoption, use, and development of the program. The only drawback that we see is that we are using a UNIX-based version, and case sensitivity is sometimes bothersome.

4. RealPlayer (www.realplayer.com) is an audio plug-in for a Web browser. It allows the user to listen to audio clips without having to download often large files prior to listening. The entire sound clip is loaded into memory (buffered) and then played. Thus far we have used sound clips of not much more than four minutes, but the students report no problems.

3

DOMINICAN UNIVERSITY (RIVER FOREST, IL) AND THE COLLEGE OF ST. CATHERINE (ST. PAUL, MN) DISTANCE LEARNING EXPERIENCE

Mary Wagner and Prudence Dalrymple

INTRODUCTION

Two metropolitan areas, two private institutions of higher education, one offering an American Library Association (ALA)–accredited masters of library and information science (MLIS) degree and one in a state with no MLIS degree program.

Enter faculty willing to work collegially, enter administrators willing to make changes in systems supporting their work, enter technologies for use in educating students. The result is an ALA-accredited MLIS degree program offered collaboratively by Dominican University (River Forest, IL) and the College of St. Catherine (St. Paul, MN).

This collaboration rests on two comparably developed and equipped campuses with faculty, staff, and students who do not perceive geographical distance as an insurmountable barrier. The uniqueness of this collaboration places student need at its center and recognizes that two institutions can benefit from supporting a single program.

This chapter discusses the place of technology in the collaborative degree program and shows how this program has encouraged development of additional learning opportunities mediated by interactive video technologies.

HISTORICAL BACKGROUND

Dominican University (formerly Rosary College) is a coeducational liberal arts college located in River Forest, a suburb of Chicago. The college traces its beginning to St. Clara Academy, which was chartered by the state of Wisconsin in 1848. The academy was founded at Sinsinawa, Wisconsin, by the

Dominican congregation that had been founded by an Italian missionary, the Very Reverend Samuel Mazzuchelli, O.P. The academy became St. Clara College in 1901. In 1922, at the invitation of George Cardinal Mundelein, archbishop of Chicago, the sisters transferred the college to its present location and incorporated the institution as Rosary College.

In 1930, Rosary College was a recognized liberal arts college for women offering the BA and BS curricula. In September 1930, the curriculum was expanded with the addition of a library education program for both men and women. The goals of the new Library Science Department were the encouragement of scholarship in Catholic institutions through librarianship and service to the Chicago metropolitan community through the development of good libraries. The first director of the department was Sister Reparata Murray, O.P., who served from 1930 through 1949.

In 1938, the program in library science was accredited by the ALA, Board of Education for Librarianship. The board also approved a BS in Library Science for a fifth year of study. Reflecting changes in education for the professions of librarianship, in 1949 Rosary College inaugurated a curriculum leading to an MA in Library Science degree. In 1970, the Department of Library Science became the Graduate School of Library Science, and the title of director was changed to that of dean. To better reflect the growth and scope of its programs, the Graduate School of Library Science became the Graduate School of Library and Information Science (GSLIS) in 1981. In May 1997 Rosary College became Dominican University to recognize the institution's status as a university with three graduate schools and more than nine graduate programs.

In its early years, the master's degree program was one of the few library science degrees available to Roman Catholic religious, including priests and nuns, especially for summer study. From 1944 to 1952 Rosary offered one of the first distance learning opportunities in library science through summer courses offered at the University of Portland in Oregon.

For most of the GSLIS program's existence, there was a nationally recognized master's degree program in library science at the University of Chicago. The program at Dominican has drawn from a more local audience and has been noted in the local library community as a major source of well-qualified library and information professionals. Although most of its alumni remain in the general geographic area of Chicago, where needs for library and information personnel have remained strong, many have achieved national and international reputations and they have worked throughout the world.

A major change in the program occurred in 1992 when the collaborative program with the College of St. Catherine in St. Paul was developed. Like Rosary, the College of St. Catherine (CSC) has a long tradition as a Catholic liberal arts college for women, and it has offered library and information education since 1928. Graduates of its baccalaureate program in library science and information management have achieved recognition, but their opportunities for LIS education at the graduate level have been severely curtailed as a result of the discontinuance of the graduate program at the University of Minnesota.

CSC began its involvement with distance learning in the 1960s. Sister Marie Inez Johnson, CSJ, weekly gathered her carved wooden trolls, Beatrix Potter figurines, and illustrated picture books for use in her Sunrise Semester course in Children's Literature offered through the University of Minnesota. These television courses prompted the college to think about student audiences beyond the traditional eighteen- to twenty-one-year-olds who lived on campus or commuted from the Twin Cities metropolitan area to courses offered between 8 A.M. and 3 P.M. Evening classes became a regular feature of the academic schedule in the 1970s, followed by a weekend-based degree program in 1979.

The Weekend College was designed to meet the higher education needs of working women twenty-five years or older. With the establishment of Weekend College, the time barriers to achieving a degree began to crumble. Since its inception in 1979, over 2,000 women have graduated from twelve programs of study, including a BA/BS degree in Information Management.

The Information Management degree program evolved from a long tradition of library science education. Between 1929 and 1980, students obtained a BA with a library science major and a second subject discipline major. This degree was widely recognized in Minnesota with CSC students competing equally for local library positions with the graduates from the master's program at the University of Minnesota.

Recognizing the changes in information services as a result of technology innovations and the development of the computing environment, the undergraduate library science program evolved into an information management curriculum in the early 1980s. Because the program focused on technology applications in information services, the audience for such a program resided in the business community. The new information management program became the only major offered exclusively in the Weekend College. (There exists an administrative procedure for day students to major in this weekend-only program, although the number doing so is small.)

As the information management curriculum developed to include a growing array of technologies applied to information systems and services, so did the expertise and interest of faculty in how to use these technologies to educate students unable or uninterested in coming to a college campus for classes.

In 1988, three faculty members from the information management department, a former president of the college, and the director of Weekend College explored use of technologies for distance learning, which resulted in a $250,000 grant from the Annenberg CPB Project: New Pathways to a Degree Initiative. The grant funded development of the New Pathways–Electronic

Access to Weekend College program. This program was designed to use computers and e-mail to offer ten courses meeting CSC general education requirements for a degree and seven of the ten courses required for the information management major. In doing so, a student from her home could complete her first two years of an undergraduate degree and then attend campus-based courses to complete a major of her choice in the day or Weekend College format. Students choosing the information management major would need to travel to campus to attend three courses. (For pedagogical reasons the last three courses in the major, including an internship placement, was determined as not suitable for distance learning.)

The New Pathways program served a diverse group of students: disabled students with mobility challenges, single parents without childcare, individuals for whom traditional classroom environments did not meet their learning needs, and students living in rural areas, including a dairy farmer who could not leave the herd to attend college classes.

COLLEGE OF ST. CATHERINE/DOMINICAN UNIVERSITY COLLABORATION

With the Information Management curriculum solidly in place and New Pathways implemented, the Information Management department was poised for growth. The faculty determined that a need existed for an LIS degree program at the graduate level. The University of Minnesota closed its graduate library science program in 1985. The need for librarians and information specialists trained at the graduate level was well documented. During this time, an unsolicited invitation came from the dean of the GSLIS at Rosary College (now Dominican University) to explore a collaborative ALA-accredited master's program.

After consideration by faculty and administration on both campuses, an agreement was reached to offer collaboratively the Dominican University's graduate program on the CSC campus. The program would not be developed as an extension site or a transfer of credit program but rather a program in which the administrative and curricular requirements would integrate the faculty and students on the two campuses. This integration required considerable negotiation and accommodation by administrative departments other than the respective units. Admissions, student accounts, financial aid, housing, and alumni departments were all involved in the planning, implementation, and ongoing support of the collaborative program. Dominican University's GSLIS Faculty Council by-laws required changes to accommodate membership and voting privileges for CSC faculty. CSC faculty sit on faculty committees, including admissions and curriculum. Financial considerations, including revenue streams and cost centers, as well as legal requirements are negotiated and monitored at the vice-presidential level at both institutions.

The focus of this collaborative preservice education program is the student. The learning needs of students guide the development of policy and procedures, most notably in how the curriculum is offered. Barriers exist in relation to time and space. Students in this program must meet a residency requirement and have needs to communicate with faculty on both campuses. Faculty must communicate among themselves in both locations to ensure a quality program of instruction. The use of communication technologies has assisted the teaching faculty, the student advisors, and the students in meeting degree requirements, advising needs, and demands of thorough and ongoing curriculum planning and revision.

Through use of interactive video technologies, classes are offered throughout the year as one option for students to meet the residency requirement. This same technology allows faculty and students to meet "face-to-face" for advising sessions. Students from both campuses are able to form teams and work on projects required in their courses. Faculty meet monthly for council meetings and committee work. Adjunct faculty are able to participate in curriculum planning sessions. The GSLIS dean and the director on the CSC campus use this technology on a regular basis.

In addition to the interactive video, e-mail, Web boards, and the array of communication options offered by technology are used as the tools to connect students, faculty, and administrators to make this program a true collaboration. Students and faculty both have used the technology to turn those at a distance from the "Other" to equal members of the GSLIS program.

The development of the collaborative program essentially introduced a new phase in the history of the Dominican University GSLIS. Beginning in fall 1992, the offering of GSLIS courses on a regular basis in the Chicago Loop or downtown area began to present the program to a more diverse public. In 1996, the Illinois Board of Higher Education approved the offering of the full MLIS degree program by Dominican University in Chicago, and in 1999, it approved offering the MLIS degree program in Lake County, north of Chicago.

Dominican and St. Catherine share a commitment to teaching as a prime responsibility of faculty. Both are on campuses where undergraduate liberal arts education is a central focus. There are advantages to these characteristics, and there are drawbacks. On neither campus do students or faculty have access to a major research library, although that problem may be alleviated as information technologies enhance access to resources. Both the Twin Cities and Chicago areas do provide a range of significant library and information center collections and services, and students are encouraged to tap those resources in addition to those available at their class sites.

The closure of the University of Chicago's Graduate Library School in 1991, followed by the closing of the Northern Illinois University's master's program in 1994, left Chicago with one graduate LIS program accredited by the ALA—the GSLIS at Dominican University. Although the University of

Illinois has for several years offered a "Fridays-only" program geared to enabling students who live and work within a few hours' drive of Urbana to matriculate in their program, the need for access to graduate LIS education in Chicago remains strong. On the other hand, the Chicago area covers a large geographic area, in which commuting to the suburban campus in River Forest poses a significant barrier to graduate students who are frequently able to attend classes only part-time, sandwiched into busy schedules involving work, family, and other activities. The ability to deliver instruction at a time and place that is convenient to students has become increasingly important to the success of the GSLIS. It certainly also contributes to the satisfaction of students who are enrolled in the program.

The primary reason to develop new ways of delivering instruction is to improve access to education and training, not simply because of technological innovation. It is essential to clearly identify the barriers that exist and the most effective ways to go about removing them. Scheduling classes at times that are convenient to a working student population is one step which, although rather obvious, has not been universally adopted, particularly on campuses where the student body is largely residential and full-time. Dominican University's student body is 84 percent part-time. Although evening classes have long been offered, the number of evening classes has steadily increased. Beginning in 1998, weekend classes were offered to enable student from CSC to come to campus while retaining their jobs and family lives in the Twin Cities. Students in the metropolitan Chicago area also have found these courses appealing, as have both full-time and adjunct faculty. In 1998 weekend intensive classes were offered for the first time, consisting of three three-day weekends, again enabling students from St. Catherine to attend classes with Dominican students without disrupting their normal schedules. In fall 1999, the introductory course was scheduled in this three-three format, and St. Catherine's provided transportation from the Twin Cities, enabling students from both campuses to become acquainted, and for the CSC students to visit the Dominican campus at the beginning of their program, rather than at the end. Though this experiment mimicked the initial residency portion of other distance education programs, it was not deemed successful enough to warrant continuation.

In a large metropolitan area such as Chicago, barriers of physical distance may be rather minimal, but traffic congestion steadily increases; the morning and afternoon commuter traffic reports take on greater significance and are often greeted with great dismay. Commute times of two hours each way are not unusual. To address this problem, Dominican has offered classes off-site for several years. One of the long-standing venues was the Chicago Public Library, now located at the handsome Harold Washington Library Center. However, as the public library's commitment to ongoing staff development increased, the competition for classroom space also increased; in 1997,

Dominican moved its Chicago program one block north to the Chicago Bar Association (CBA), where the full degree program is offered. Several classes are taught each term by both full-time and adjunct faculty. Class hours are adjusted to conform to the downtown working student population (5:30–8:30 P.M.). The CBA is located in the Chicago's South Loop area where several other universities have sizable campuses—DePaul and Roosevelt Universities, Columbia College, and Robert Morris College are all located within a few blocks of each other in this area. Five transit lines converge in this area as well. Locating the program in downtown Chicago works because classes are scheduled during blocks of time that would otherwise be spent commuting; when classes end, the evening rush over is over, and students can travel home quickly and safely, whether they reside in the city or in the suburbs.

Suburban locations pose a greater challenge because student population is more widely dispersed and educational facilities are not as readily identifiable or as concentrated as they are in downtown Chicago. For many years, classes have been offered at a variety of sites, but there appeared to be little continuity, resulting in confusion and frustration for students and an inability to establish a "presence" in any particular locale. The classes were taught by both full-time or adjunct faculty, who traveled to the site in typical extension fashion. Technological support was inconsistent at best. In 1992 the Illinois Board of Higher Education created ten educational consortia for the purpose of constructing a videoconference network in support of education. The Chicago metro area contains five consortia, whose purpose is to encourage the use of video-conferencing equipment. State funds were provided to purchase two-way interactive video-conferencing equipment. Each institution receiving such equipment agreed to participate in the educational activities, although the exact nature of this use was left to the individual institution. Sadly, much of this equipment has not been fully utilized; even where it has been used, the applications have not been directly focused on instruction. For example, it has been used for "faculty conversations," which are one to two hours in length and involve three to six faculty members at a few institutions. It is unclear how these benefit the citizens of Illinois, although the faculty conversations do have the spillover benefit of increasing faculty familiarity and comfort with the equipment.

Despite these limitations, the technology and the support staff exist, training for faculty is available, and each consortium has a director responsible for encouraging and coordinating its use. In March 1998, the GSLIS faculty approved two important initiatives. The first was to redefine the residency requirement for CSC. The revised requirement is that students must complete four courses with Dominican faculty. The second was a plan to use two-way interactive video to deliver classes on a systematic and regular basis to identifiable sites in the northern and southwestern suburbs. The first of these was driven by the recognition in the ALA Standards for Accreditation that programs are evaluated "regardless of the location and form of delivery." In the light of this statement in the standards, it no longer seemed logical to insist that students uproot themselves and spend a summer or a semester in River Forest. Both Dominican's and CSC's commitment to video-conferenced classes necessarily increased as a result of this decision, and each semester at least two courses are offered through video-conferencing. In the Chicago area, Dominican has taken advantage of the existing educational consortia to offer classes through video-conferencing.

THE TWO-CLASSROOM MODEL

When classes are sent between CSC and Dominican, the instructor teaches primarily from his or her own campus. The motivation for CSC students to take video-conferenced classes is high, because they may be used to fulfill the four-course "residency" requirement. Increasingly, Dominican faculty travel to CSC once or twice to "teach back" classes from St. Paul to Dominican. Both the faculty and the CSC students enjoy the personal contact, and it does much to remove the feeling that Dominican is the "primary" classroom with CSC the "secondary" classroom.

Student comments on course evaluations demonstrate that the dual classroom mediated by technology works best when instructors are able to meet face-to-face with students at both locations at least once during a term. "After experiencing a video class both with and without you there in person, I would recommend very strongly for traveling teachers, at least once or twice during the term" (St. Paul student).

Another St. Paul student commented,

I think it gets a little better/easier each week. As I said in another message I think it makes a great difference that we know you, and I think the DU students will feel more connected having met you also. I do wish we had the opportunity to meet the DU students at least once in person, however I realized that to do so is not practical....I think people are making comments and asking questions just as they would in a traditional classroom. I would also recommend that DU instructors, who teleconference a class to CSC should come here to teach at least one class.

Students used to face-to-face instruction discovered that with experience and diligence on the part of the instructor and students alike, discussions became more connected and less uncomfortable for the students at the distant site. Several commented on the slight delay caused by the transmission between sites and how that contributed to hesitation to initiate discussion and ask questions from the remote site. One River Forest student commented,

I find class discussion doesn't flow quite as easily using the remote video as it does if the teacher and entire class are in one room. I think the class which has the professor in the room feels more comfortable in asking questions. I have to say, though, that I think the set up we have is pretty much as good as it gets with remote learning. I like the fact that we can see the other class, use the Web discussion board, and communicate through e-mail.

This experience contrasts with the experience in the Chicago area, where video-conferenced classes have also been scheduled and taught using the "two-classroom model" with each classroom having the instructor on site one week out of every two. Neither classroom is designated the "primary" or "sending" site, and neither is consistently the receiving site. Students have been less satisfied with this arrangement, suggesting that unless the barriers to attending class in person are substantial, students are less willing to accept video-conferencing. Furthermore, student services at the off-campus sites are also less available, particularly computer labs and library materials.

In fact, the problem of distance education for LIS offers a peculiar paradox. One might assume that because LIS students are learning to be library and information professionals, they would be skilled in obtaining the library resources to support their education, and indeed many are. One might also assume that because the state of Illinois has a highly developed multitype library system that supports a statewide catalog and reciprocal-borrowing privileges that access to library materials would not pose a significant problem. What is missing from this scenario is that LIS materials are not routinely collected by many libraries. Frequently when they are, they are in professional collections aimed at supporting in-house staff and may not circulate or even be listed in catalogs. Only a small portion of the LIS literature is available electronically. Particularly in more specialized subject areas, such as health sciences librarianship, the number of copies of key texts or journals may be very small statewide. Many libraries still feel squeamish about placing materials on electronic reserve, and faculty are also reluctant to ask students to purchase several texts that may become outdated. Course packs of materials can be used, but they add additional expense for students who are already paying tuition. The small supply of LIS materials and the difficulty in accessing them is a significant liability to providing professional education at a distance from the campus. Even when the distances themselves are not great, as is the case for Chicago, it is somewhat of an anomaly to deliver instruction off-site but require students to come to campus for library and laboratory support.

The availability of library and laboratory facilitates at CSC as well as the support services of an excellent educational facility improve the quality of the collaborative program between these two institutions. When similar collaborative relationships are established between Dominican University and the other educational institutions in and around the Chicago metropolitan area, the student experience will likewise be enhanced.

CONCLUSION

The collaborative model for LIS education developed by the College of St. Catherine and Dominican University is unique in the LIS field. The similarity in institutional profile makes this collaboration both easier and more natural and has resulted in a cohesive program that meets the objectives of the institutions and shares the needs of students and the professional community. Technology has enhanced this partnership, but the fundamental element is personal relationship and collaborative learning.

4

MAINTAINING HIGH TOUCH FOR EFFECTIVE DISTANCE EDUCATION: THE EMPORIA EXPERIENCE

Daniel Roland

The Distance Education Program for the School of Library and Information Management (SLIM) at Emporia State University, Emporia, Kansas, began its Distance Education Program in 1987. The program was initiated by the request of library professionals in areas without local library science schools. The program began at a time when library schools in the western half of the United States were closing and leaving large geographic regions without MLS programs. The challenge to design a program that delivered curriculum to various locations from 200 to 1,800 miles from the home campus while maintaining quality and integrity was formidable and is constant. The result is a flexible program that enables completion of an MLS degree in less than three years for students geographically bound by employment or family responsibilities. Since its inception, more than 800 students have earned the degree through the program without ever needing to attend class on the home campus.

HISTORY

SLIM first offered its MLS curriculum beyond the local campus in Sioux City, Iowa, and pulled in students from Nebraska, South Dakota, and Minnesota as well as Iowa. Soon after its start in Iowa, the SLIM Distance Education Program was invited into Colorado and Nebraska, then later into New Mexico, North Dakota, Oregon, and Utah. SLIM partners with the state library agency in each location and often with an academic institution to secure classroom facilities and other support services. Once a start date has been determined, SLIM works to recruit a cohort of students who will go through the program together in an eight-semester cycle. SLIM started its twenty-first student cohort in fall semester 2002.

SLIM faculty travel from Emporia to distance site locations and teach classes in a weekend intensive format. The basic formula is that a two-credit class is taught over two weekends, about a month apart, rather than the traditional two hours per week for sixteen weeks. Students attend class once every three to four weeks rather than two to three days every week. Although the weekend intensive model requires an adjustment by the faculty from the traditional weekly format, faculty members are quick to see the advantages. For example, they are able to hold the attention of the students for longer periods so that instruction improves qualitatively. They also enjoy the same advantage as students of being able to schedule classes for a semester sequentially rather than concurrently, which allows for more flexibility.

Dialogue among students and with faculty extends beyond the classroom through the online learning environment of WebCT. Each distance program also has a dedicated e-mail discussion list that students use to share information among themselves. The SLIMCAFE e-mail discussion list serves as a virtual student lounge designed to connect students from all locations, and SLIMNEWS serves to facilitate communcication, news, and general announcements.

The program has experimented with live and streaming digital video for several years. This technology was used to facilitate interactions between two sections of students taking the same course, one group in Omaha, Nebraska, and the other in Emporia. Later in the semester, these two groups were able to interact with faculty and participants of a conference in Warsaw, Poland. Two students attended the conference and videotaped interviews with conference attendees, which were then digitized and mounted to a conference Web site for student use. Similar work from a previous conference was made into a CD-ROM that is used as the class textbook.

Such global interactions grow out of an area of the curriculum that focuses on the international nature of modern information systems, and technology is used to initiate and cultivate international experiences. An adjunct faculty member facilitated a summer semester of e-mail interaction between a group of students in Utah and a group of students from a school in Brazil. The faculty member was teaching a course for both schools and groups of students in both countries. It was a valuable exercise in communication and collaboration.

As this technology has developed, SLIM has initiated a program that will allow students in remote locations to participate in classes by way of interactive video. In the fall of 2001, SLIM began delivering MLS curriculum to a small group of students in Boise, Idaho, by way of dedicated ISDN lines between a SLIM classroom in Emporia and the State Library of Idaho office building. Students in Boise and Emporia can see and hear each other in real-time, television-quality video. SLIM has hired a local site coordinator to serve as an advisor to the Boise students and as a team teacher for each course. On several occasions, SLIM faculty have taught the first weekend of a course from Emporia and the second weekend from Boise so that each section of the class experiences the learning environment of the other.

In the fall of 2003, SLIM will have the capacity to deliver curriculum to multiple locations throughout Kansas and the western half of the country with interactive video using Internet protocol. The latest development has been made possible through securing grants to obtain an Internet 2 connection for Emporia State University and for partial purchase of a multiconferencing software server.

THE NEED FOR THE HUMAN TOUCH

SLIM has built its approach to distance education around Naisbitt's notion of high-tech/high-touch,[1] which is that with every introduction of new technology there must also be a counterbalance of human interaction or the technology is rejected.

Galusha qualifies the need for high touch. She notes that "problems and barriers encountered by the [distance] student fall into several categories: costs and motivators, feedback and teacher contact, student support and services, alienation and isolation, lack of experience, and training."[2]

One example of high touch in the SLIM Distance Education Program is the team of six site coordinator/student advisors who work as the local administrators in each program location. In their role as student advisors, they are available for consultation during class weekends, by phone and e-mail, and hold office hours for personal appointments. They each have an average of forty students and will have at least four face-to-face advising sessions with each student over the eight-semester cycle of a program. The site coordinators also encourage student social gatherings, track the return of student work from faculty, and work as advocates in the local area for their students. The SLIM Distance Education Program received the 1997 Outstanding Institutional Advising Program Award from the National Association of Academic Advising.

The local site coordinators also provide high touch for visiting faculty members who may be unfamiliar with the classroom facilities, the local airport, and motel and dining services. A high level of communication is required about faculty needs and resources long before the class weekend arrives. The coordinators also represent SLIM at local library association meetings and maintain the human touch with local alumni. All four of the site coordinators spend several days each year on the Emporia campus for team building, advising training, and general social events so that they, too, receive the high touch necessary for success in their position.

Another example of the high-tech/high-touch approach is the combination of face-to-face and mediated instruction. As SLIM faculty begin to move some of their classes online, most are combining one weekend of face-to-face instruction with the balance of the course taught over the Web. The result is less classroom and travel time for both students and faculty while maintaining a level of human touch.

A final example is the formation of local advisory councils in each of the program sites. Advisory council members are selected from various fields and local association chapters within the profession. Semi-annual council meetings serve as general information-sharing sessions. SLIM keeps members up to date on how the local program is going, and council members advise SLIM on the profession within the local state. Council members are invited to interact with the students to help make students aware of the various associations, career paths, and professional networks available to them. Council members may also be asked to work with the local site coordinator to recommend possible mentors for students.

CURRENT LIMITATIONS

Although the program currently brings the campus to the student by holding classes in Denver, Salt Lake City, Portland, and so on, there still exists the geographical limitation for students who live in such places as Grand Junction, Colorado; Cedar City, Utah; and Ashland, Oregon. Students in these outlying locations may still face journeys of several hours and often over difficult terrain to attend classes. Information gathered through student recruitment indicates that sizable numbers of potential students are still unable to take advantage of the program owing to distance.

Much of the dialogue around distance education is how to overcome such geographical barriers by means of mediated instruction, such as offering classes over the Internet or via satellite TV. However, the reason SLIM has been successful in distance education has been its dedication to the model of face-to-face instruction. For this reason, the SLIM program does not neatly fit the popular definition of distance education in "which teacher and learner are physically separated during the learning process."[3] For SLIM, the student–teacher separation occurs primarily in the interim between weekend classes. E-mail, Web page forums, and toll-free phone numbers help overcome the separation.

Another limitation of the current model is that students at locations other than Kansas are able to start the MLS program only once every two to three years. The time frame may be even longer in smaller markets where it takes longer to recruit enough students to make a program economically feasible. It is problematic for a student to join a program even one semester after it has started because classes in the early semesters of a program are required theory courses and are offered only once in an eight-semester cycle. If a student wants to join a program in the second or third semester, these classes must be taken at another location.

FUTURE DIRECTIONS

SLIM is currently expanding its distance education program on several fronts. The undergraduate degree in information resource studies is currently 80 percent available online and will be 100 percent online by the fall semester of 2004. A graduate degree in legal information management, offered in partnership with the University of Kansas School of Law, will be mostly Internet based.

Participation in the SLIM doctoral program will be available from a distance starting in the fall 2003 semester. Seminar courses will move from meeting for three weekends over the course of a semester to a customizable format to best suit the needs and learning/teaching styles of information professionals. Under the new plan, classes may meet for no more than one weekend or the class time may be broken up into smaller segments and distributed over the course of the semester at the discretion of the instructor. The balance of each course will be highly individualized and interactive, more along the lines of traditional tutorials. The seminar classes will utilize a combination of (1) telephone/video conference calls, (2) Internet chats on WebCT, (3) electronic bulletin board discussions, (4) individual phone conferences between instructor and student, (5) individual e-mails between instructor and student, (6) paper correspondence, and (7) collaboration software.

CONCLUSION

Since 1987, the SLIM Distance Education Program has extended library science education to adult learners by focusing on innovative strategies to bring the curriculum and the campus to the student to minimize geographic distance. The program continues to evolve as technology becomes available, but always maintaining the human touch. The reward for the student is a flexible system that is responsive to student need and that is increasingly available regardless of geographical location. The reward for SLIM comes from the participation and perspective of many more students of multiple backgrounds, cultures, and ways of life than would be possible if the student body were limited only to those able to attend classes on the home campus.

NOTES

1. John Naisbitt. *Megatrends: Ten New Directions Transforming Our Lives.* New York: Warner Books, 1982, p. 39.

2. Jill M. Galusha, "Barriers to Learning in Distance Education." Infrastruction Network, available online at www.infrastruction.com/articles.htm, p. 4.

3. Galusha, p. 1.

5

DISTRIBUTED LEARNING IN THE FLORIDA STATE UNIVERSITY SCHOOL OF INFORMATION STUDIES

Gary Burnett, Kathleen Burnett, and Don Latham

HISTORY

The School of Information Studies at Florida State University (FSU) was founded in January 1948 under the name School of Library Training and Service, or SOLTAS, and from the beginning has emphasized distributed learning as a key component of its overall mission. Just prior to the school's opening, Louis Shores, the first dean, and Sara M. Krentzman, the assistant dean, published an article in *Library Journal* outlining the school's philosophy. The founding of the school represented an attempt to respond to the shortage of trained librarians across the state of Florida, as outlined in the 1947 Florida Citizens' Committee on Education report, *Education and Florida's Future: The Report of the Comprehensive Study of Education in Florida*. Toward that end, Dean Shores and Assistant Dean Krentzman set forth, as one of the principles for the new School, a commitment to distributed learning:

In the interest of recruiting and in-service training, a more liberal policy of extra-campus instruction should be undertaken. Parts of the professional program should be offered at various points in the state where there are need and demand for library education under conditions that will insure the same quality of instruction as on the campus. (Shores and Krentzman, 1947, pp. 1663–1664)

How such a goal would be achieved was made clear in the discussion of the curriculum for the school:

Off-campus instruction will be offered at strategic points in the state—Miami, Jacksonville, Tampa, and elsewhere. One faculty member will be released from campus duty each quarter for field service, including the offering of these courses, thus insuring continuous faculty contact with the needs of the field. (Shores and Krentzman, 1947, p. 1665)

Thus, from the outset significant faculty involvement, as opposed to the use of mostly adjunct instructors, has been an integral part of distributed learning offered through the school.

By fall 1948, less than a year after the school's opening, two faculty members were teaching extension courses in several communities across the state. One of the instructors offered classes in Gainesville and Jacksonville, and the other taught courses in Tampa, Sebring, and Winter Haven (Hunt, 1997, p. 21). In the fall of the following year, the school sponsored extension courses in Miami, Pensacola, and Ft. Myers (Hunt, 1997, p. 23). In 1954, Louise Galloway joined the faculty expressly to teach extension courses as well as on-campus classes (W. Summers, personal communication, August 16, 1999). She quickly became known as the "flying professor," and a profile of her appeared in the June 1955 issue of *Eastern Air Lines Magazine* (Shores, 1956, p. 17). At this time, it was not unusual for a faculty member to be teaching up to four extension classes per week at various places around the state.

The extension program was made possible through the support of the school and the efforts of the General Extension Division. In a 1952 *Florida Libraries* article, Pauline O'Melia, herself an instructor in extension courses, explained how the arrangement worked: "Florida State University has contributed the services of a regular faculty member, while the General Extension Division...has organized the classes and supplied the large materials collections necessary" (O'Melia, 1952, p. 22). The "large materials collections" consisted primarily of materials for children and young people, because most of the students in the extension courses were public school personnel and other children's services workers, such as Sunday school teachers, juvenile court officers, social workers, and Boy Scout and Girl Scout leaders (O'Melia, 1952, p. 23). The library, which was housed in the extension center, included books, records, filmstrips, slides, and films. Because of the demand for materials, the collection was maintained in triplicate, with the happy result that these items could often be shared with children and young people in the community (O'Melia, 1952, p. 22). In addition, music and record stores in the communities where classes were being conducted often donated materials for class review and discussion (O'Melia, 1952, p. 22). The school worked cooperatively with the General Extension Division to select the places where courses would be offered. Communities made requests for courses, and selections were based on identifying "strategic centers throughout the state" that were convenient to as many people as possible and "combinations of centers that [made] a practicable travel schedule" for both faculty and students (O'Melia, 1952, p. 23).

The first course offered in the extension program was in the selection of library materials, with an emphasis on materials for children and young people. Over a period of four years, classes were held at places as far-flung as Pensacola and Jacksonville, Marianna and Miami, De Funiak Springs and Orlando, to name just a few (O'Melia, 1952, p. 22–23). A second course was added in January 1949, in the selection and use of audiovisual materials. By late 1951, a third course, this one in sound film, had been approved for extension (O'Melia, 1952, p. 23).

In the 1950s and 1960s, the extension program thrived. In June 1956, Louis Shores boasted that the school had offered courses in "29 Florida communities extending from Pensacola to Key West to some 3,000 students" (Shores, 1956, p. 17). Fall 1962 saw the school offering extension courses in Tampa, Orlando, Panama City, West Palm Beach, Vero Beach, and Cocoa (Hunt, 1997, p. 31). In the spring of 1965, six extension classes were being taught in Jacksonville, Ft. Lauderdale, Orlando, Pensacola, Palm Beach, and St. Petersburg (Hunt, 1997, p. 32). One imagines that the schedule for these circuit-riding faculty members must have been grueling. It was typical for faculty members to carry key materials with them, in spite of the fact that the General Extension Division furnished most of the materials and supplies. Professor Mary Alice Hunt, for instance, often took to the road (or the air) with a dry-mount press in tow (T. Hart, personal communication, August 17, 1999).

With the 1970s came the oil crisis, and the extension program was shut down for a time. It was no longer economically feasible for the school to send faculty to various places across the state on a regular basis. In addition, the oil embargo kept tourists from visiting Florida, which had a severe impact on the resources the state could allocate to its colleges and universities. However, in the late 1970s, the program was resurrected, due partly to steadily declining enrollment in the school. In fall 1980, overall admissions were at an all-time low (Hunt, 1997, p. 47). The distributed learning program was seen as a way of increasing enrollment while accommodating potential students who could not easily move to Tallahassee. When Dr. F. William Summers became dean of the school in 1985, he announced three strategic long-range plans, one of which was to increase "programs for area-bound students, particularly those in southern Florida" (Hunt, 1997, p. 54). Then in 1989 the Board of Regents, on concluding a five-year review of library education programs in the state, recommended that the school again increase its efforts to offer courses to "place-bound students" across the state. Thus, in fall 1993, the school began operating an ongoing program in southeast Florida (Hunt, 1997, p. 57). This program made use of cohorts, or groups of students who would begin the program at the same time and essentially complete the program at the same pace. Two years later, cohorts were started in Jacksonville and Pensacola.

In spring 1996, FSU President Talbot D'Alemberte solicited proposals from the various schools and colleges on campus for technology-based distributed learning programs. Under the guidance of Dean Jane Robbins, the School of Information Studies submitted a proposal and was subsequently selected to be one of the first units on campus to offer such a program. The school was chosen for several reasons: (1) there was already a statewide clientele because of the school's long-standing tradition of offering face-to-face courses around the state; (2) the school's faculty had made a commitment to both distributed learning and the innovative use of information technology; and (3) the kind of student attracted to library and information studies was seen as being generally able to handle technology-based delivery of information (J. Robbins, personal communication, August 16, 1999 and August 21, 1999). A few months later, in fall 1996, the school began offering a distributed learning program using a combination of interactive television (ITV) technology and the World Wide Web as the mode of delivery (Hunt, 1997, p. 65). Over 180 students at five sites—Miami, Ft. Lauderdale, Orlando, Jacksonville, and Tallahassee—participated in the first course. By fall 1999, there were approximately 275 students in the graduate distributed learning program in the school. Another ninety students had been admitted into the new undergraduate distributed learning program.

TECHNOLOGIES

The goal of the School of Information Studies, in both its on- and off-campus classes, has always been to ensure that technology is used in the service of pedagogy and education rather than allowing it to drive the program. Thus we have utilized several different approaches to providing technological support for courses. We have also conducted experiments to find new ways of using the technology and have pursued ongoing research into the usability of the technologies themselves, into the preferences and information behaviors of the students who use those technologies, and into the educational effectiveness of the classes.

Model One: ITV and the World Wide Web

First Implementation: ITV

In July 1996, one month prior to the beginning of the fall semester, the School of Information Studies received approval to mount a complete master's degree program to students at five sites around the state of Florida. The initial offering of this program, a six credit-hour course titled Foundations of Information Studies, was taught collaboratively by the full faculty of the school. Because a TV studio was housed within the school's Louis Shores building, the initial technological model for the program used ITV as the primary mechanism for content delivery. Though the school simultaneously embarked on a major effort to build a strong set of Web-based resources, such resources were perceived as a supporting rather than a central feature of the school's courses.

ITV was used beginning in fall 1996 to deliver live lectures from Tallahassee to four other sites in Florida. Almost immediately, however, it became clear that several intractable problems were inherent in using this technology this way. For one thing, because ITV is designed to support synchronous interaction between participants at remote sites, it includes a microphone switching system that activates the microphone at any site where there is a sound, disabling it at all others. Thus, whenever students at one site moved in their seats or spoke to one another, the microphone in Tallahassee was silenced; the instructor would continue to speak, but none of the remote sites were able to hear anything but random sounds from whichever site had a live microphone. To overcome this problem, we made the decision to disable the switching mechanism at all of the student sites and allow switching only from Tallahassee. Thus, the interactivity that ITV is designed to support was significantly impeded, and the give-and-take of a verbal discussion session became nearly impossible to sustain. In addition, Florida (particularly in the late summer and early autumn months) is subject to frequent severe thunderstorms and occasional hurricanes, both of which occurred during the first semester. The weather often led to power outages and thus to disruptions in the transmission of the ITV signal between Tallahassee and the remote sites. Fewer than half of the scheduled sixteen synchronous class sessions were, in fact, available to all of the students in the class; most weeks, one or more of the sites were either offline entirely or were only intermittently in contact.

Although the school continued to use ITV for the next few semesters following fall 1996, these problems meant that we began to rely more and more on the Web as the sole technology to support coursework. From the beginning, a core group of faculty had advocated Web-based delivery as superior to ITV technology for pedagogical reasons. In addition, the university determined that the overhead required to upgrade its ITV technology to make it effective for distributed learning was prohibitive in the long run. Thus, in summer 1997, the school, in consultation with the provost, decided that the mode of course delivery should be exclusively Web-based (J. Robbins, personal communication, August 16, 1999 and August 21, 1999). Aside from the fact that this was a more cost-effective mode of delivery, it provided the added advantage of not requiring students to attend class in a particular place. The change meant that students could "attend" class in front of their computers in the comfort of their own homes.

Second Implementation: The Web

From the inception of its distributed master's degree program, the school envisioned using the Web to support at least some aspects of its courses. Thus, the first version of the school's course interface was designed and implemented simultaneously with ITV. From the outset, certain features were in place that continue to be part of the course interface to this day.

However, because it merely supplemented ITV—and because only one month of development time was available—the first version of the school's course interface was limited in functionality, confusingly organized, and difficult for students to use. The initial interface, for example, did not include a course calendar, and students often found it extremely difficult (if not impossible) to determine accurate due dates for their work. In addition, the interface included neither a mechanism for the submission of assignments nor specific guidelines for assignment formatting and submission; this oversight resulted in a deluge of assignments arriving via e-mail in myriad electronic formats (some of which could not be read with the software available to the faculty), as well as hard copies arriving via both the U.S. mail and fax. Throughout the first semester, such limitations led not only to major complaints from students but also to a great deal of frustration among the school's faculty and support staff.

Model Two: The Web

The Course Interface: An Ongoing Developmental Model

Recognizing the limitations plaguing the first implementation of its course Web interface and seeing an opportunity to build continuing improvements into its delivery of distributed courses, the school implemented a research program, including an ongoing series of usability tests, focus groups, and other feedback mechanisms, to study the effectiveness of the design of the interface and of the integration of technological enhancements into its course Web sites. The results of these tests have been integrated into subsequent versions of the interface, beginning with the second version. The following description of the interface reflects this research.

Further development has been governed not only by a strong research base but also by two additional guiding principles:

1. the Web interface will remain consistent across all courses, employing a modular design with a continually present navigation bar, so that changes to one part will not require that the entire system be redesigned, and so that additional functionality and applications can be easily added as they become available, or to meet the pedagogical requirements of specific courses; and

2. course Web sites will be fully functional and will offer the full range of experiences available to students in the classroom.

Guided by these two principles, the distributed courses have undergone a coherent evolution and have become sharply focused on the pedagogical requirements of instructors and the learning needs of students. Although the appearance of the interface has changed dramatically from the second version to the current version, both its structure and its capabilities continue to be governed by these principles. In April 2001, Dr. Kathleen Burnett accepted the FSU President's Award for Exemplary Uses of Technology for Instruction on behalf of the faculty and staff of the School of Information Studies. The award specifically cited the development of this interface.

The Course Interface: Modular Design

The modular design of the school's interface reflects two requirements for a well-designed and effective course Web site. First, information within the site must be usefully organized and accessible to both students and faculty. Second, because students taking distributed courses do not meet face-to-face within a physical classroom, the course site must reconceptualize and make available not only all of the functions of the classroom setting but also the full social and intellectual milieu of the classroom setting. To make such a reconceptualization possible, course sites are organized into sections, each of which supports a particular component of a complete learning environment, including such fundamentals as course work, interaction, and other activities. These sections are accessible via a navigation bar. This navigation bar remains present at the bottom of the monitor no matter what part of a course is displayed and allows access to all of the major content areas available within the course Web site. For a list and description of the major components of a course site, see Appendix I of this chapter.

The Course Interface: Functionality

Because the school uses the Web as the primary delivery mechanism for its distributed courses, it is able to make use of a wide variety of functional capabilities while maintaining both a consistent design and an integrated instructional delivery model. Many of the modules within a course site are built from plain text documents encoded with Hypertext Markup Language (HTML). Others take advantage of the ability of Web browsers to utilize the advanced features made possible through the use of Common Gateway Interface (CGI) applications. For example, almost all of the interaction between faculty and students—as well as all assignment submissions and announcements—takes place through the use of CGI-based Web forms. Such capabilities are commonly available on any computer capable of functioning as a Web server, and they are all available without requiring students to purchase any additional software and without requiring any additional hardware or software support from the university.

The school also has created a range of advanced features by combining other types of Web-compliant software packages and development tools. For a partial list of these functions, see Appendix II of this chapter. All of these functions are available via plug-ins within the standard course interface. Neither students nor faculty need to leave the course environment to take advantage of them. As a result—and with the exception of individual research or writing—all of the school's distributed courses are completely mediated by Web technology.

DISTRIBUTED EDUCATION AT FSU

The School of Information Studies was the first unit on the FSU campus to mount a full degree program using Web technologies. Since the commencement of our master's program, the university has begun to develop larger-scale programs across all academic units for both graduate and undergraduate degrees. Because of the school's experience, its representatives have been involved in several of these programs, although the relationship between the school and the university has sometimes been adversarial rather than cooperative.

Two programs in particular have been closely linked to the school's efforts.

WebMC set out to develop a template for use by faculty who wish to design Web-based course resources without any knowledge of HTML. The school's faculty, with the assistance of several students, helped develop the initial template and a training program for participants in the program.

The 2+2 Program, which was originally intended to follow the materials-based distance learning model originated by British Open University, is an initiative to develop junior- and senior-level courses that will allow students at a distance to obtain bachelor's degrees after receiving AA degrees from two-year institutions in the state of Florida. The first two majors to be offered under the banner of 2+2 are information studies (with collaboration from the College of Communication) and computer science.

Representatives of several units from the FSU campus visited the Open University in 1998 and were introduced to the model. Initially, FSU planned to draw on the Open University's existing materials for its courses. However, at least in information studies, it was found that because of differing cultural and pedagogical assumptions, existing Open University materials were inappropriate for the needs of our faculty and students; thus, the school opted to develop its own materials for its courses. In addition, the school's faculty member who first visited the Open University asked about their use of the Web as a technological support for education. He was told by all but a couple of Open University representatives that the Web "could not" be used for educational purposes in any way. In part, such an answer reflects different economic structures—British citizens must pay by the minute for local telephone calls, making it prohibitive to use modems for extended periods. More important, however, this answer pointed to a fundamental difference in belief about how technologies can be used as supports for pedagogy. Thus, the school has not adapted the Open University distance education model in any significant way but has drawn on its experience in the master's program as it has designed its 2+2 curriculum and courses.

For technological support of the 2+2 program, the initial plan was to develop a Web interface modeled after the School of Information Studies' current design and enhanced with more powerful server capabilities and the input of graphic designers. However, when the work on this new interface was nearly completed, the university decided, for a variety of reasons (and with only minimal consultation from the units that were most deeply involved in the production of online courses), to withdraw their support for on-campus design and testing of interfaces for Web-based courses and to contract with a commercial vendor for all course Web sites.

Because development of its own in-house product involved not only an investment of an immense amount of time and energy but also a significant research effort of a number of its faculty, the school objected to this decision in the strongest possible terms, and a compromise was reached that allowed the school to continue to develop and use its own interface and related instructional support systems.

In fall 2002, the management of the 2+2 information studies major was moved to FSU's Panama City Campus, and two new faculty were hired to supplement the talents of the current faculty member at that campus, Alan Stromberg.

FUTURE DIRECTIONS

As of fall 2001, the school uses its interface for both master's and undergraduate Web-based courses and continues to look for ways to enhance the online learning environment of its students. Although the school currently maintains its online courses on a Windows NT Web Server, almost all of its capabilities can be easily transferred to other platforms, such as UNIX. This adaptability, coupled with the program's modular design and its support of a wide variety of pedagogical approaches and objectives, makes it very flexible. From the beginning of the program, the school's student population has followed a continual growth curve. In addition, the faculty have incorporated many Web-based innovations into on-campus as well as distributed classes. One of the most positive impacts of the introduction of Web-based technologies into all of our instructional situations means that we do not have to make any distinctions between local and distributed students in terms of either instruction or learning.

To ensure that this level of success and innovation is sustained, the school continues to pursue both its research into Web-mediated distributed learning, and its use of an ongoing developmental model for enhancing its courses. Current developmental efforts include, among others, the following:

- the enhanced ability of students to create and submit nontext data (such as statistical data and graphics) into their assignments;

- the integration of robust database capabilities into course sites, allowing us to maintain more useful, more complex, and more secure student achievement data;
- the development of a forms-based course revision tool for faculty and instructional assistants that will not require knowledge of HTML or training in the use of a GUI editor such as Netscape;
- the creation of an online repository of downloadable software that students can use for their coursework; and
- a more robust administrative module, to allow students to manage their own personal information, including calendars for all courses in which they are enrolled, all due dates for assignments, and other features.

PEDAGOGY

Most contemporary discussions of distance education focus on the technology that supports delivery of courses to students geographically separated from the main campus, rather than the pedagogy that is delivered using this technology. Although the master's in LIS was the first FSU degree program delivered using Web-based technology (and was among the first nationally), it has been and continues to be the pedagogy that is the focal point of the school's efforts. Indeed, the school has used its Web-based program as an opportunity not simply to transform existing pedagogical practices but, more important, to develop new pedagogical models and improve its educational offerings in the process. Throughout the development and delivery processes, the school has thought of the technology as a support infrastructure that provides opportunities to reexamine assumptions about how faculty teach and students learn. In the virtual classroom, faculty challenge students, and students often challenge faculty, to question these assumptions during synchronous and asynchronous discussion sessions and, where appropriate, in assignments. Dean Jane Robbins asks the students to question these same assumptions in "Tell the Dean" sessions each semester and during exit interviews. Further examination of these assumptions also takes place in the formal program of applied research conducted by the school (see Appendix III of this chapter).

CHALLENGING ASSUMPTIONS

Assumption 1: Off-campus and on-campus learning occur in isolation from one another. Since 1996, the School of Information Studies has taken an innovative approach to learning regardless of physical location that challenges the assumption that off-campus and on-campus students must learn separately.

From fall 1996 on, all students have been enrolled in a single master's degree program, in one of two majors: library studies or information studies. Since fall 1998, all students have had the option of taking courses in traditional FSU classrooms or from their home computers. Some elective courses are offered only on the Tallahassee campus, and some required courses are routinely offered only through Web-based delivery. Some students begin their studies from their desktops and complete it on campus, as did Winsome Benjamin, who was awarded an ALA Spectrum Scholarship in 1998 that allowed her to relocate from Miami to Tallahassee to complete her degree. Other students begin in the classroom but complete the degree off-campus; for example, Abre Chase, who, as part of his on-campus graduate assistantship helped develop many course Web sites and was able to complete his final semester of coursework after relocating to Orlando to pursue an internship opportunity. Some students complete the entire degree program without coming to campus after the required two- to four-day orientation; others complete it without ever using a computer or facilities outside of those in the Louis Shores Building.

The decision to use ITV beginning in 1996 was made partly because it was thought that this technology would enable the school to bring geographically distributed students together into one "classroom." The fact that the ITV technology did not perform as expected in this regard was at least as responsible for the school's decision to abandon it as was the university's decision not to upgrade the infrastructure. Another major factor in this decision was the conviction of some faculty that virtual learning communities could prove to be even stronger and richer than geographically defined learning communities because they could grow from common interests without the constraints imposed by the need for geographic proximity.

The integration of on- and off-campus students clearly enriches the learning experiences of both groups. Although university and state administrative constraints sometimes make it difficult, the goal is a seamless integration of on- and off-campus learners into a rich, multifaceted learning environment. The evidence of success comes from the students themselves. For example, students enrolled in face-to-face courses on campus frequently request access to the lectures recorded for Web-based courses so that they can review the material, check their understanding of a particular concept, or simply reinforce their knowledge. In some courses, students are deliberately organized into project groups that are geographically distributed. This helps them to develop good communications and management skills that will be essential as they move into work environments that increasingly involve telecommuting. As one student remarked in the evaluation of a course of this type, "At first I thought you were just doing this to make it hard on us, but then I called a couple of friends doing work in this field. They told me that I was gaining invaluable experience that would put me way ahead when I entered the marketplace."

Assumption 2: Face-to-face learning is more interactive than web-based learning. One of the lessons learned from the literature on online learning and confirmed during the initial experience with ITV was that success of the distributed learning program would require a very high level of interaction. In fact, it was the acknowledgment of the importance of interactivity in the classroom that led to the decision to adopt the ITV technology in the first place, and this was one of the primary concerns expressed when the decision to discontinue use of this technology was announced. Ultimately, however, the faculty has realized that, even though ITV transmits images of faces and voices, it merely provides the illusion of interaction rather than true interaction. The Web, however, even though it relies primarily on text-based communication (with some multimedia enhancements), provides a much higher level of interaction between all of the participants in a class.

One of the interesting outcomes of the school's involvement with Web-based delivery has been an increasing realization by many faculty and students that student–faculty interaction is more frequent and more satisfying in Web-based courses than in face-to-face courses. This is demonstrated both in the frequency and quality of interactions. Dr. Elizabeth Logan, Rebecca Augustyniak, and Alison Rees (1999) did a preliminary study comparing the interactions in online discussion groups with those in the classroom for a single course in summer 1998. They found that although there were no significant differences in grades between the Web-based and classroom students, the latter were less likely to ask questions, and those that they did ask tended to be less substantive. Research in computer-based learning has often mentioned that the absence of the visual and auditory cues of face-to-face interaction hinders learning; however, in this study, the absence of such cues did not appear to have much impact on student interaction or outcomes. Dr. Logan did notice, however, that the students interacting online tended to incorporate what she characterized as "hall talk" in their interactions, where students in the classroom left that for the physical hallways. This phenomenon has also been noted in classes where the interactive chat software is used extensively to support class discussions. Although faculty have usually thought of this integration of hall talk as a nuisance, more research needs to be done to determine its effect on learning.

Assumption 3: Face-to-face interaction is required to build learning communities. Another of the lessons learned during the transition from ITV to Web-based delivery was that the establishment of communities of learners would be a key factor in the success of a distributed learning program. Quite early in the ITV experience, the faculty noticed a phenomenon of geographic identity. Each site developed a community persona. In most cases, this was a positive occurrence. For example, the Orlando site developed a study group that met at the public library between sessions. Several of the students from that early group have continued to be involved in the school's activities. One is now a PhD student who serves as a teaching assistant for a master's course and a mentor for an undergraduate course. Another is now a regional coordinator. A third is enrolled in the specialist degree program, is serving as the distributed library graduate assistant, and is also a mentor for an undergraduate course.

Many institutions have responded to the challenge of community-building by increasing the burden of the off-campus student—either by requiring students to make repeated visits to campus or by constraining class size to the point where enrollment becomes highly competitive. The School of Information Studies has taken a different approach, using the technological infrastructure to promote the development of virtual communities, identifying graduates who serve as regional coordinators, and including off-campus learners in graduate assistantships assigned to provide mentoring support for less experienced students in their area.

This approach begins with a required orientation that was initially held on the Tallahassee campus, but as of fall 2002 is available online as well as at the Tallahassee campus. During the orientation, structured opportunities are provided for students to get acquainted with other students who share their interests and will be geographically close to them. In addition, they get acquainted with the regional coordinators, who will help them remain connected throughout the two or more years it will take them to complete the program. Finally, they are introduced to virtual team building through an applied exercise developed by a staff member and a doctoral student. Students have remarked that the orientation increases their technological confidence and makes them feel connected to the school and FSU and that these feelings stay with them throughout their studies. The networks they establish at the orientation—both technical and social—provide a support structure that ensures that they never feel isolated or alone.

The hall talk phenomenon may be an indicator of community-building taking place within the context of the virtual classroom. On-campus students generally restrict such talk to the hallways when faculty are not present, so that faculty members are excluded from some aspects of the development of the learning community.

One of the lessons learned during the initial experiments with incorporating interactive chat software to support interaction and community-building was that the discussion was likely to be substantive only if it was carefully structured. The interactive chat software used by the school was selected because it incorporates a window for the display of presentation slides. Faculty may prepare slides that outline the content to be covered in the discussion, pose discussion questions, and provide examples or illustrations to keep the discussion moving and on track. A phenomenon noted in several courses was that students were logging on before the scheduled time to allow for hall talk without disruption to the course. In some cases, faculty have structured in opportunities for hall talk with great success. For example, one semester a faculty member noticed that students remained "after class" to "talk" with one another. Several times she was drawn into the discussion, and it became known that she put off dinner until very late to lead the class discussions. Toward the end of the semester, the students invited her to a "virtual feast," where they served up a three-course meal complete with dinner conversation.

Another factor in the choice of interactive chat software was the inclusion of so-called emoticons that generate short descriptions of facial expressions and body language indicative of emotional responses. Initially, students tend to use the emoticons inappropriately or overfrequently, but once the novelty wears off, these simple phrases help build a sense of community among the participants.

PEDAGOGICAL MODELS

Developing an integrated and interactive community of geographically distributed learners is a challenge that the School of Information Studies has met head on and with a great deal of success in a very short period of time. One of the reasons for this success was the introduction—in response to faculty requests—of pedagogical models to guide course development. Faculty support was provided through a Web page that included a description of each model and a link to an exemplar course Web site (www.fsu.edu/~lis/forms/models.html). Faculty completed two submission forms: a model submission form assisted in the selection of a model appropriate to the course under development, and a support form helped the faculty member to determine what items from a menu of options they would be expecting to include in their course Web site. Options included audio files, video files, synchronized audio/PowerPoint lectures, asynchronous discussion groups, synchronous discussion groups, collaborative assignments, quizzes, examinations, scanned readings, Web readings, online resources, and so on.

The school identified four pedagogical models: interactive, exploratory, individualized, and collaborative by examining the courses developed by early adopter faculty. Each of these continues to be a viable and supported model for Web course development.

Interactive Model

Interaction is the primary mode of instructional delivery for the interactive model. Types of interaction include one-to-one (e.g., faculty-to-student, student-to-student), one-to-many (faculty-to-entire group, or faculty-to-small discussion group), and many-to-many (student group-to-student group). More than one type of interaction has usually appeared in each of the courses that use this model. Some technologies that support the interactive model include asynchronous discussion groups, interactive discussion groups, and assignment posting and review. A course using the interactive model requires a large ongoing commitment of faculty time to monitor discussion groups, interact with the students, and provide extensive feedback on assignments. It also requires a large ongoing commitment of student time to participate in discussion groups, interact with peers, and prepare assignments. The implementation of certain aspects of this model (such as assignment posting) requires student permission and trust-building, often necessitating a contract between faculty and students.

Exploratory Model

Exploration is the primary mode of instructional delivery for the exploratory model. Characteristics of this mode include directed choice (students select readings, and so on, from a list with many options), directed exploration (links are provided to resources beyond those stored on the school's Web server), and multiple media (a variety of media are used to support learning objectives and styles).

Some technologies that support the exploratory model include hypertext links, resource lists, RealVideo, RealAudio, synchronized audio with slides, animated screen capture, and so on. Implementation of the exploratory model requires significant development time and effort, but the interaction time commitment of the faculty member is more easily controlled than with the interactive model. The exploratory model is most successful when the students are mature, self-motivated, and self-directed learners.

Individualized Model

This model has yet to be implemented as the primary model for a course, though several courses include aspects of the individualized model. The individual is the primary unit to which this model addresses its attention. Web-based technology provides some excellent tools for support of individualized learning, but the commitment in development time tends to discourage its implementation in the school's distributed learning program. In fall 1999 the individualized model was employed to support the learning of a doctoral student who was not resident in Tallahassee during that term. Some kinds of instruction that the interactive model supports include tutorial (directed student reading, including one-on-one interaction time with faculty member), computer-assisted instruction (students complete preprogrammed exercises and receive built-in feedback), and personalized interaction (students are encouraged to personalize what they are learning through setting individual learning objectives, keeping journals, and making explicit personal statements about their progress).

Some technologies that support the individualized model include: the use of CGI and Java scripts and programming, RealVideo, RealAudio, interactive video, synchronized audio presentations, animated screen capture, self-quizzes, and so on.

The individualized model requires significant development time and effort. Depending on the implementation, it may require very little (computer-assisted instruction example) or a lot (read and react, case studies and journals) of faculty interaction time. Similarly, the requirements of students vary depending on the implementation but generally need to be supported by a contract.

Collaborative Model

Collaboration is the primary mode of instructional delivery for the collaborative model. Types of collaborative work include project- or product-oriented groups, support-oriented groups, and discussion-oriented groups. Some technologies that support this model are asynchronous discussion groups, interactive discussion groups, assignment posting and review, journals, and so on. This model requires an ongoing commitment of faculty time to monitor discussion groups, interact with the students, and provide extensive formative and summative feedback on projects and assignments. It also requires an ongoing commitment of student time to participate in discussion groups, interact with peers, and prepare assignments. The implementation of certain aspects of this model (such as assignment sharing and posting) requires student permission and trust-building. Contracts between the members of collaborative groups are useful in keeping the groups focused and productive.

These models can be effectively used to address a range of learning styles, or in Gardner's terms, multiple intelligences (Gardner, 1993). The interactive model, for example, addresses linguistic and interpersonal intelligences, whereas the individualized model may address linguistic, logical-mathematical, spatial, bodily kinesthetic or musical intelligence (depending on the course content) but emphasizes intrapersonal rather than interpersonal intelligence. The exploratory model is rooted in spatial intelligence and may emphasize either interpersonal or intrapersonal intelligence, depending on the specific design. The interpersonal intelligence is put to the fullest test in the collaborative model, which, when most successfully employed, combines aspects of all the intelligences.

The four pedagogical models also address information interaction styles (Brooks and Burnett, 1998, 1999). Developed from two earlier models of identity development by Marcia (1966, 1980) and Berzonsky (1989, 1992), the Information Interaction Styles Model (Figure 5.1) identifies four styles of interaction: diffuse, foreclosed, engaged, and aware. Preliminary data indicate that individuals displaying engaged and aware information interaction styles are more likely to be successful online learners than those displaying diffuse or foreclosed styles. Burnett and Brooks (1998) have proposed that certain pedagogical models may be effective in encouraging those students who display diffuse or foreclosed styles to develop and strengthen information seeking, sifting, sorting, and sharing skills more closely aligned with engaged and aware styles. For example, a student displaying a diffuse information interaction style will have great difficulty coping in a course using the collaborative model, whereas those displaying engaged or aware styles will

Figure 5.1
Information Interaction Styles Model

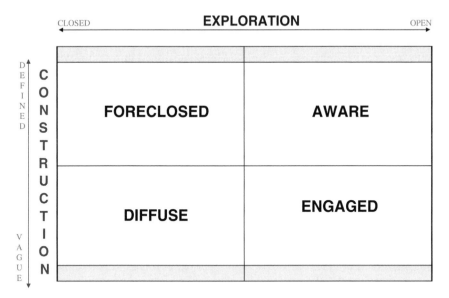

© Robert F. Brooks and Kathleen Burnett, 1998.

cope well in such a course. Intensive work in courses using first the individualized and exploratory models, which are generally favored by diffuse and foreclosed individuals, will help the student strengthen his or her information seeking, sifting, and sorting skills without challenging weaknesses in information sharing. It is hypothesized (and we have some anecdotal evidence) that gradual introduction of elements from the interactive model will help the same student gain the confidence in him- or herself and trust in others sufficient to affect a change in information interaction style to engaged over the course of one or two semesters.

Although the technological infrastructure of Web-based learning is not essential to the deployment of the pedagogical models for learning, it has provided the impetus at the School of Information Studies for reexamination of standard classroom pedagogy. This reexamination has had a healthy effect on classroom as well as Web-based learning. By fall 1998, incorporation of Web-based course materials into the classroom had reached significant levels across all degree programs offered by the school, including doctoral and undergraduate as well as master's courses. Some of this migration was faculty initiated, but much of it grew from student demand. As students gained experience with the new pedagogy, they developed a preference for it over the traditional lecture format. The experience of the School of Information

Studies has been quite the opposite of that predicted by the technology and distance education nay-sayers.

By fall 1999, students from as far away as Switzerland and Guam deliberately chose to pursue their master's degrees in LIS through FSU and at a distance. Some students in other U.S. states have done the same. Still more have relocated to the Tallahassee campus. When questioned during interviews and the orientation as to the reasons for their choice of this program, they consistently named three factors: (1) the program does not require frequent trips to the campus, (2) the out-of-state tuition and fees for FSU are lower than those of many other distance learning programs, and (3) the School of Information Studies master's degree program has a well-deserved reputation for being cutting-edge in its approach to incorporating technology to enhance as well as support learning. To this, students who have been with us for more than a semester add in their evaluation comments that they are impressed with the high level of faculty–student interaction, that they appreciate learning actively rather than passively, and finally that they know the school cares about them as individual learners. As evidence of this, they often cite the responsiveness of the development team—faculty and staff alike—to their suggestions. For a school whose vision statement reads "People and Information: Making Vital Connections," this reaction spells success.

APPENDIX I
MAJOR CONTENT AREAS FOR SCHOOL OF INFORMATION STUDIES' COURSE WEB SITES

Each course site, whether designed for a graduate or an undergraduate course, contains the following major areas:

1. **Calendar.** The course calendar was the first feature to be added to the school's course Web site as a result of our usability studies and feedback from students. It contains, in one location, all relevant dates for course activities, readings, and work, with active links to appropriate materials. The calendar is designed as a "one-stop shop" for courses, a place where students can obtain a unified overview of the course. It is the page that functions as the course home page and is displayed first each time students visit the course site.

2. **Syllabus.** The syllabus contains all of the standard materials for the administration of a course, including course description and objectives, contact information, and so on.

3. **Resources.** The resources section of a course site is the primary repository for materials containing the course content, including any readings for which we have received copyright clearance, links to other Web resources, and audio files of course lectures.

4. **Discussions.** Course sites support a variety of options for class discussions and communication between faculty and students, each of which recon-

structs a particular type of interaction available in a more traditional class-room setting. These options include:

- A *Faculty Office,* which is a place where students can ask content- or process-related questions of the instructor or the teaching assistants.
- Optional *Small Group Discussions,* which can be used to divide students into smaller groups to discuss specific topics.
- A *General Class Discussion Area,* which is typically used for other types of interaction, including the kinds of informal discussions that may take place in a hallway outside the classroom or before the class starts. Students often use this discussion area to ask each other questions about their readings or their assignments.
- A *Technical Discussion Area,* which is available to all classes and is a place where students can ask technical rather than content- or course-specific questions. This area is not monitored by faculty but by the school's technical staff.

All of the discussion forums are asynchronous and can be used at the students' leisure. Questions may be asked one day and answered the next, and they will remain available for anyone to see (or to respond to) throughout the semester.

In addition to these asynchronous discussion groups, the discussion area of a course may also include synchronous chatrooms that can be used to gather students together at the same time for the kinds of free-wheeling conversations that can take place in the classroom in those situations for which immediacy and spontaneity are desirable. The school uses ichat software to support these sessions.

All of these options are available for all courses; faculty may mix and match them according to their specific needs.

5. **Assignments.** All assignments for a course are found here. With rare exceptions, all assignments are designed to be submitted electronically, via Web forms, each of which is customized to meet the specifications of the assignment. In most courses, assignments are submitted as plain-text files via these forms.

6. **Announcements.** This section contains any timely announcements of changes in the course calendar, cancellations of synchronous discussions, and so on. Students are asked to look at these announcements first whenever they visit the course site, to be sure that they are aware of any late-breaking news.

7. **Communication.** Although at one time the school considered including the discussion groups within the more general communication area, usability studies indicated that students found it difficult to locate them unless they were immediately accessible from the navigation bar. Thus, the two areas have been separated. The communication area contains contact information, a "mailroom" containing e-mail addresses for all students, and a variety of e-mail utilities.

8. **Help.** A library of help files covering technological issues, typical procedures for submission of assignments, and so forth, can be found here. The current contents of these help files can be found at www.fsu.edu/~lis/distance/help/index.html.

9. **Home.** Because each course is part of the larger context of the School of Information Studies, this button provides a link to the school's home page.

APPENDIX II
ADVANCED WEB SITE FUNCTIONS

Course Web sites typically include some of the following advanced features.

Streaming audio files for lectures, combined with either text or Power-Point lecture notes. The use of RealAudio capabilities available through Real-Networks products allows us to synchronize notes with the audio for simultaneous delivery and allows students to download files for viewing and listening at their leisure.

Portable Document Format (PDF) files for the delivery of print readings. Using PDF files for readings, rather than simple HTML, allows us to retain the layout and appearance of readings that have been published in print. Documents that originate on the Web are typically provided via hyperlinks; in those cases in which we import Web documents into the course site, we use HTML.

A fully functional Course Administration Utility functions both as an interface for grading assignments online and as a database for maintaining records of all student work within a course. As a grading interface, this utility contains a standardized set of comments, grade options, and a text box that can be used for further comments. Instructors can customize it to meet their specific grading requirements and practices. As a database, this utility stores copies of all comments and grades for each assignment; students can see their own records (but not those of other students), and faculty can see the records of all students, sorted either by student name or by assignment. Further capabilities are being added to this utility regularly as needed.

APPENDIX III
RESEARCH AND WEB DEVELOPMENT

Research

Research on distributed learning at the School of Information Studies is divided into three areas: theoretical frameworks, learning evaluation, and program evaluation.

Theoretical Frameworks

Investigation of theoretical frameworks includes development of models of technology interaction, identity, and information contexts (Kathleen Burnett and E. Graham McKinley, Rider University), development of the Information Interaction Styles model (Robert F. Brooks and Kathleen Burnett), development of a typology of information behaviors and information exchange within virtual communities (Gary Burnett), and the application of critical hermeneutics theory to the analysis of virtual communities, including learning communities (Gary Burnett).

Learning Evaluation

Learning evaluation focuses on self-identity development and performance. The purpose of research into self-identity development is to better understand the relationship between technology use and individuals' changing views of identity within the context of distributed learning. Based on the theoretical frameworks, the position is taken that learning is an alteration of self that takes place as individuals interact with information; in this context, learning involves behavioral, emotional, and cognitive aspects. Projects in this area include investigations by Robert F. Brooks, Kathleen Burnett, Laurie Bonnici, Elizabeth Logan, Rebecca Augustiniak, Aimee Reist, and Joyce Kincannon.

Program Evaluation

Program evaluation focuses on four areas: student valuation and success, course assessment, interface assessment, and support services and resources assessment. The purpose of the student valuation and success area is to (1) understand changes in values and information-seeking behavior of individuals who are enrolled in a Web-based distributed learning program, and (2) understand factors important to distributed learning students' perceptions of success in a Web-based distributed learning program. Data collected thus far indicate that students seek more information about the online program after enrollment in an online learning program than they do before enrollment, that they mostly seek that information from fellow students, and that they change their valuation of distance learning as better than traditional learning. Each of these three results were statistically significant comparing before enrollment to after enrollment. This investigation is being conducted by Robert F. Brooks, Kathleen Burnett, and Sharon Edwards.

Course Assessment

The purpose of course assessment is to better understand factors that distributed learning students consider important to course design and support in a Web-based distributed learning program. Evaluation of this area depends on developing a method for collecting data from students that is comparable to or the same as the State University Student Assessment of Instruction and Student Instructional Rating System (SUSSAI/SIRS Evaluations). The Office of Distributed and Distance Learning began providing such an instrument in fall 2000.

Interface Assessment

The purpose of interface assessment is to better understand factors important to computer interface design in a Web-based distributed learning program. The focus in this area is on developing a standard gateway into each course that conceptually and functionally simplifies and improves students' navigation of the course Web site and maximizes students' learning. Several student projects under the direction of Myke Gluck provided initial data for this area. A usability study conducted in 1999 by Boryung Ju, Robert F. Brooks, Kathleen Burnett, and Sharon Edwards was awarded the ALISE Methodology Paper Award in 2001.

Support Services and Resource Assessment

The purpose of support services and resources assessment is to better understand factors external to the computer interface that contribute to the student success in a Web-based distributed learning program. The focus in this area is in assessing student needs for resources and developing support services and resources to meet those needs. Stephanie Maatta and Marilia Painter have developed and continue to develop resources.

Web Development

The effort to develop and maintain Web resources for courses at the School of Information Studies has from the very beginning been a collaborative effort involving faculty, staff, and students. The initial course interface was designed and implemented, under tremendous time pressure, by former students Kevin Harrington and Blair Monroe. Subsequent conceptualization, design, and development has been supported by more people than can be mentioned. Key staff members in this effort have been Blair Monroe, Robert Riley, Lisa Fisher, and Ryan Miller; primary faculty input has come from Kathleen Burnett and Gary Burnett; in addition, many students been instrumental in furthering the goals of the school. Finally, instructional design support has been provided by Joyce Kincannon, Laurie Bonnice, Rita-Marie Conrad, and Anthony Chow, among others.

REFERENCES

Berzonsky, M.D. (1989) "Identity style: Conceptualization and measurement." *Journal of Adolescent Research*, 4, 268–282.

Berzonsky, M.D. (1992) "Identity style and coping strategies." *Journal of Personality*, 60, 771–788.

Brooks, R.F. & Burnett, K. (1998) Exploring alternatives and constructing knowledge to sustain self in a communication-rich environment: Information interaction styles. Unpublished manuscript.

Burnett, K. & Brooks, R.F. (1998, 1999) Information interaction styles and web-based distributed learning. Unpublished manuscript.

Gardner, H. (1993) *Multiple intelligences: The theory in practice, a reader.* New York: HarperCollins.

Hunt, M.A. (1997) *Transitions: The informal history of a school in celebration of its 50th anniversary 1947–1997.* Tallahassee, FL: School of Library and Information Studies, Florida State University.

Logan, E., Augustyniak, R., & Rees, A. (1999, January) *Distance education as different education: Student-centered investigation.* Paper presented at the ALISE 1999 National Conference. Philadelphia, PA. Available online at www.alise.org/nondiscuss/conf99_paper_Logan.htm.

Marcia, J.E. (1966) Development and validation of ego-identity status. *Journal of Personality and Social Psychology,* 3, 551–558.

Marcia, J.E. (1980) Identity in adolescence. In J. Adelson (Ed.), *Handbook of adolescent psychology* (pp. 159–187). New York: Wiley.

O'Melia, P. (1952) "The school of library training and service on the road." *Florida Libraries,* 2(10), 22–23.

Shores, L. (1956) "Portrait of a library school: Florida State University." *Florida Libraries,* 7(1), 17.

Shores, L., & Krentzman, S.M. (1947) "Florida U. plans library training course." *Library Journal,* 72(21), 1660–1665.

6

DISTANCE LEARNING AT THE UNIVERSITY OF HAWAI'I: SERVING THE UNDERSERVED IN AN ISLAND STATE

Violet H. Harada

Distance learning at the University of Hawai'i provides opportunities for quality higher education to students who are unable to attend the university campus offering their program of choice. A state-supported system of higher education, the University of Hawai'i is comprised of three university campuses, seven community colleges, an employment training center, and five education centers distributed across six islands throughout the state. The Library and Information Science (LIS) Program resides on the largest of the campuses, the University of Hawai'i at Manoa.

The university currently offers over 630 distance learning credit and noncredit courses, resulting in more than 7,300 registrations a year (University of Hawai'i, 2002b). Fifty certificate endorsement and bachelor's and master's degree programs utilize a variety of distance learning options. They include (1) telecommunications-assisted instruction (synchronous or asynchronous interaction) supported by interactive television, cable, Internet-based delivery, telephones, fax machines, teleconferencing, and mail service; and (2) off-site instruction where faculty fly to or are hired at sites distant from the campus conferring the credit or credential. Distance learning may take place in state or out of state and be credit or noncredit (University of Hawai'i, 2000).

Among the technology-assisted courses, use of the Internet and interactive television have been the most popular modes of delivery. The university's LIS Program was one of the first departments on campus to use interactive television.

HAWAI'I INTERACTIVE TELEVISION SYSTEM

The Hawai'i Interactive Television System (HITS) Services provides full-motion analog video services, with four outgoing channels from the Manoa campus to all sites, and a signal return channel from each neighbor island campus. It uses both point-to-point microwave and Instructional Television Fixed Signals (ITFS) to connect the origination and receive classrooms, with all sites connected to the university complex at the hub of the network (University of Hawai'i, 2002a).

The state legislature and the Federal Communications Commission agreed to jointly fund and license the system on the basis of the university's interest in using HITS to distribute scarce resources around the state and to ensure education equity in the state (Young, 1986). Toward this end, the legislature appropriated $4.3 million in the late 1980s to construct a microwave network of electronic pathways to each of the major islands. The network permitted low-cost transmission of telephone communications and TV programming between islands, allowing for two-way audio and visual communication (Nahl, 1993).

ADMINISTRATION AND COORDINATION

Distance learning within the University of Hawai'i system is a collaborative enterprise requiring partnerships between and among campuses and units. At the university, the Office of the Vice President for Academic Affairs provides overall coordination of the system-wide distance learning effort. The special assistant for distance learning assigned to this office facilitates the work of the Master Scheduling Group (MSG), which develops a rolling three-year master schedule of programs. The group also addresses other issues related to distance learning, such as needs assessments, the expansion of technical and physical facilities, faculty training and curriculum development, funding opportunities, instructional quality, and student outcomes (*Ku Lama*, 1999). MSG members represent or work closely with other units who share major responsibility for distance learning, including Information Technology Services, the University of Hawai'i Community Colleges Distance Education Committee, the University Centers, the Distance Learning Academic Support Group, and Outreach College on the Manoa campus (*Ku Lama*, 1999).

Outreach College is the administrative point of contact for all distance learning programs originating from Manoa. The college works with faculty to broker the courses and guide students to the appropriate support services. Information Technology Services is responsible for the overall design, development, maintenance, and support of the system-wide telecommunications infrastructure that supports the university's distance learning program. This unit is also responsible for developing system technical standards to ensure the efficient and effective operations of all distance learning technologies.

INFRASTRUCTURE AND SUPPORTING TECHNOLOGIES

HITS classes originating from the Manoa campus involve six other sites, including two on the island of Hawai'i and one each on Oahu, Kauai, Molokai, and Lanai. All sites have both video and audio capabilities.

Several communications and educational support technologies are used in HITS to promote a highly interactive learning environment. Cable, satellite, and microwave technologies are used to provide a four-channel statewide band for instructional and teleconferencing transmissions (Young, 1986). The ITFS signal is broadcast from a tower on the ridge of Manoa Valley overlooking the campus and is retransmitted via high-frequency microwave relays. A single ITFS transmitter services a number of sites, and the receiving sites use a down-converter to display the signals on a TV set. Although the University of Hawai'i can originate on C band using a satellite dish, it can also receive C and Ku band programs via satellite from other sources.

The studio classrooms at the remote sites are often located in the library or media center of the institution. Some of the origination sites are better equipped, especially the Manoa studio classrooms, which have monitors for each of the sites so that the instructor and students may see the participants at two-way video receive sites throughout the entire class period.

The transmission of classes is live and interactive, requiring that each studio classroom have microphones or telephones, cameras, and video monitors, as well as a control room for one or two technicians. Each student has a microphone, which must be activated individually to enable the instructor and students at the other sites to hear questions and comments. There are at least two cameras, and an overhead camera used for showing visuals, graphics, and three-dimensional objects. Instructors may also transmit computer images via HITS with the studio's computers (Nahl, 1993).

Supporting technologies used include fax, e-mail, and telephones. There are fax machines located at every site; however, at the remote sites they may be in an office, the library, or the media center rather than in the studio classroom. A UNIX-based network allows for personal e-mail communication between students and between students and instructors. Each HITS student receives an account, is trained on the system, and has access to computer terminals in his or her library that connect to the university's Manoa Computing Center, which coordinates and provides training at all sites. The network permits access to the University of Hawai'i library online catalogs and databases, other libraries on the network, and electronic bulletin boards. In addition, the University of Hawai'i Manoa Bookstore also has a toll-free number that off-campus students can call to place orders, with most orders filled within forty-eight hours.

LIS PROGRAM

As the only accredited library education program in Hawai'i, the LIS Program currently provides over 70 percent of the professional workforce in school, public, and academic libraries in the state. Moreover, at a time when there is a shortage of underrepresented ethnic groups in our profession, over 50 percent of our student population are Asians, Asian Americans, or Pacific Islanders (Library and Information Science Program, 1999).

Founded in 1965 as the Graduate School of Library Studies, the program has undergone a period of reorganization that culminated in 1997 with the merger of the LIS Program and the Department of Information and Computer Sciences. Faculty and students feel that the restructuring effort strategically positions the program to prepare graduates for an increasingly technical library and information science environment while continuing to imbue students with the core concepts and humanistic values critical to the field. The LIS Program currently offers a master's in library and information science (MLIS) and a Certificate in Advanced Library and Information Science. It also participates in an interdisciplinary doctoral program in communication and information sciences.

As a campus pioneer in providing distance education, the LIS Program was one of the first campus units to commit to a regular schedule on HITS. In 1989, following guidelines established by the Western Association for Accreditation of Schools and Colleges, the LIS Program conducted a needs analysis on each neighbor island. Two hundred people responded to the survey, indicating that there was a sufficient population of potential students (Nahl, 1993). Many of the respondents were teachers seeking school library specialist certification, and others wanted the MLIS degree or continuing education opportunities. The majority indicated they could not afford the cost of travel to Oahu to do their assignments or to attend classes. They also said they could not give up their jobs to pursue advanced degrees on the Manoa campus.

COURSE OFFERINGS

In response to the demand on the neighbor islands, two courses were first offered in spring 1991: Basic Cataloging and Classification (LIS 605) and Media Technology and Resources (LIS 642). At that time, the faculty agreed that eighteen to twenty-one credits (six or seven courses) might be offered on a rotating schedule over HITS. Today, two courses are offered each semester via HITS; sixteen different courses totaling forty-eight credit hours are offered over a four-year cycle.

A residency requirement that all LIS students enroll for a minimum of twelve credits on the Manoa campus was rescinded in 1998. This has made it possible for students living on the neighbor islands to complete almost all of their forty-two credit hours for the MLIS degree through enrollment in HITS courses. Although the program offers a variety of courses via HITS, many of its computer-intensive courses, which require hands-on experience and exposure to a number of licensed databases, and its specialized reference courses, which require contact with the research library's collection on the Manoa campus, are not readily available through HITS. Therefore, academic advisors carefully counsel students interested in taking most of their degree work via HITS so they are aware of some of the existing limitations.

In 2001 HITS offerings included the following—all of these courses, except for LIS 615 and LIS 670, were taught by the six full-time faculty:

LIS 601, Introduction to Reference and Information Services

LIS 605, Basic Cataloging and Classification

LIS 610, Introduction to Library and Information Science

LIS 612, History of Books and Libraries

LIS 615, Collection Development

LIS 647, Systems Approach to Library Operations

LIS 650, Management of Libraries and Information Centers

LIS 664, Indexing and Abstracting for Information Services

LIS 665, Teaching Information Technology Literacy

LIS 670, Introduction to Information Storage and Retrieval

LIS 672, Library Automation

LIS 681, Books and Media for Children

LIS 682, Books and Media for Young Adults

LIS 683, Services in Libraries

LIS 684, Administration of School Library Media Centers

LIS 686, Information Literacy and Learning Resources

ENROLLMENT

The LIS Program has experienced fluctuation in enrollment in the last five years with the largest numbers in years when required core courses (e.g., basic reference services, cataloging, and classification) have been offered and lowest registration in semesters when electives with prerequisite courses have been scheduled (e.g., abstracting and indexing, library automation). Neighbor island students comprised 34 percent of HITS enrollments from 1997 through 2002 (Table 6.1).

INSTRUCTIONAL PRACTICE

Distance learning is first and foremost an academic endeavor. As with conventional courses, faculty are responsible for maintaining the integrity of program coherence, individual courses, and content and for using appropriate pedagogy in course delivery (University of Hawai'i, 2002b). The quality of the course work is the same as that for students enrolled on campus, and a

Table 6.1
Registration Count for HITS Courses, 1997–2001

	1997	1998	1999	2000	2001
Hawai'i	12	5	7	8	9
Kauai	4	5	9	8	10
Lanai	0	3	0	0	0
Maui	20	24	16	14	9
Molokai	0	1	0	0	0
Oahu	59	69	69	79	38
Total	95	107	101	109	66

majority of the students give high ratings on their evaluations to the intellectual challenge of these courses.

Although much has been done in distance technology to simulate traditional face-to-face instruction, faculty members agree that teaching over interactive television requires a number of adjustments in the design of instruction and in the style of teaching (Ho, 1991). Physical, psychological, and technical differences present new challenges for the distance learning teacher not encountered before in the traditional classroom. Instructors have found that the key to planning an effective course for interactive TV is to identify the needs of students and develop learning experiences based on measurable outcome objectives. Through class observations and course surveys, LIS faculty have discovered that our typical distant learner is an older, nontraditional student whose needs and learning attributes may be quite different from the traditional, young adult student who is campus-based.

Some approaches that have been effectively employed include:

- Providing a detailed syllabus that describes course activities, assignments, and deadlines so that students have ample time to prepare and schedule their career and personal activities.
- Designing course projects that motivate students to explore and use resources in their work and community environment and that accommodate a wide range of learner preferences and interests.
- Encouraging regular student-to-student and student-to-instructor networking using e-mail or the phone.
- Allowing for ongoing assessment from students regarding their own progress in the course and their feedback about the course itself.

As part of their teaching repertoire, LIS faculty use lectures, demonstrations augmented with PowerPoint visuals and multimedia, videotapes, and presentations by guest lecturers. A critical component of effective learning has been the use of cooperative and collaborative instructional methods in interactive distance learning (Bard, 1996). The technology allows the creation of electronic groupings for small group online discussion between two different sites. This facilitates integrating students from various sites into one cohesive class cohort. Use of e-mail and fax, along with class time for some of the initial planning and scheduled progress reports, makes it possible for students to collaborate more effectively across distances. Students report that group participation helps them feel less isolated at their remote sites and more a part of a single, integrated class that just happens to meet at different locations (Bard, 1996).

Students and faculty report other mutual advantages in distance education. The large-screen monitors at some of the sites, coupled with roving cameras, provide close-ups of student communication and allow for clear observation. For students, the high-resolution monitors often provide a better view of demonstrations and graphics than in the traditional classroom.

Distance learning students at remote sites also receive the same quality of faculty advising as on-campus students. Each classified student has a faculty advisor who keeps in touch using e-mail, fax, and telephone. The HITS arrangement often schedules three hours of studio time for the LIS classes. This includes twenty minutes of "online office hours" at the end of class sessions for individual or group conferences with the instructor.

LOGISTICS AND PREPARATION

Each class session is videotaped and archived until the end of the semester, when all sessions are erased and the tapes are reused. Students who miss classes may view the tapes later. Faculty use the tapes to review class sessions and find it a valuable form of feedback on their teaching performance, student involvement, and class activities.

Instructors must work closely with the producers and technicians, who actually run the equipment and coordinate with the remote site technicians during the broadcast. The producer requires a copy of the syllabus and needs to know how the instructor plans to run each session (e.g., small group discussion, lecture, demonstration, class discussion) and whether there will be guest presenters. Courses with a mix of teaching modes require more planning with the producer than straight lecturing. First-time instructors attend an orientation meeting with the producer before they appear on camera, and the producer also gives continual feedback and helpful suggestions to instructors throughout the semester.

The experience thus far has revealed that preparation is almost doubled for HITS classes, especially if instructors are teaching them for the first time. To assist instructors with the additional work, clerical student support is available to help with photocopying, distribution of materials, and other tasks related to course preparation.

FUTURE

Distance learning has helped the LIS Program update and adapt its practices in an ever changing social and technological milieu. The program has been able to reach traditionally underserved regions of the state and has produced a greater number of qualified graduates for the local, national, and international job markets.

In addition to the HITS offerings, the LIS Program is developing Web-based courses. The first course offered in spring 2000, LIS 686 (Information Literacy and Learning Resources), was a hybrid using both interactive TV and Web-enhanced components. Students engaged in forum discussions and posted their final products using WebCT. The first totally asynchronous course, LIS 605 (Basic Cataloging and Classification), was offered in spring 2001. Students accessed slide shows with lecture voice-overs and printed versions of the lecture notes in PDF format. They also participated in chatroom discussions and had e-mail contact with the instructor for specific individual questions.

Other LIS instructors are currently creating Web-supported additions to their courses, including class discussions using electronic distribution lists, threaded Web discussions, guest presenters on the Internet, virtual field trips, student products shared on the Internet, electronic links to other resources, and Web-based assessment and evaluation measures.

As an institution, the University of Hawai'i is committed to a "vigorous distance learning and instructional effort to equalize higher educational opportunity in all parts of the state" (University of Hawai'i, 1998, p. 2). Toward this end, the University of Hawai'i envisions increased use of multiple technologies in courses and a proliferation of Web-based instruction. Distance learning is explicitly linked with the university's overall strategic plan as articulated:

The emergence of the Internet and convergence among computing and telecommunications are profoundly changing assumptions about populations to be served with distance learning technologies and the time and space in which they are served. Technology-assisted learning will increasingly involve all students—day, evening, on-campus, and off-campus. Advances in telecommunications, multimedia, and integrated instructional technologies that make education available any time, anywhere may ultimately blur distinctions between "distance" and "on-campus" students. (University of Hawai'i, 1998, p. 2)

As the university's distance learning programs and services continue to expand, the LIS Program will remain a major participant in efforts to deliver quality academic programs to citizens of our state and the Pacific Rim.

REFERENCES

Bard, T. B. (1996) "Cooperative activities in interactive distance learning." *Journal of Education for Library and Information Science,* 37 (1), 2–10.

Ho, C.P. (1991) "Instructional strategies for interactive television." *Journal of Special Education Technology,* 11 (2), 91–98.

Library and Information Science Program. (1999) *Library and Information Science Program, University of Hawai'i at Manoa: Program Presentation to the Committee on Accreditation.* Honolulu: University of Hawai'i.

Ku Lama. (1999, February 19) "'MSG' spices up system-wide distance learning." *Ku Lama: Newsletter of the University of Hawai'i System,* pp. 1, 7.

Nahl, D. (1993) "Communication dynamics of a live, interactive television system for distance education." *Journal of Education for Library and Information Science,* 34 (3), 200–217.

University of Hawai'i. (1998) *University of Hawai'i distance learning plans, policies, and procedures.* Honolulu: University of Hawai'i.

University of Hawai'i. (2000) *University of Hawai'i strategic plan for information technology 2000.* Honolulu: University of Hawai'i. Available online at www.hawaii.edu/spit2000/spit2000.html.

University of Hawai'i. (2002a) *University of Hawai'i distance learning plans, policies, and procedures.* Online document available at www.hawaii.edu/dl.

University of Hawai'i. (2002b) *University of Hawai'i 2001 distance learning offerings and enrollment report.* Office of the Vice President for Planning and Policy. Honolulu: University of Hawai'i.

Young, J.B. (1986) *Windows of opportunity: Information technology at the University of Hawaii.* Honolulu: University of Hawai'i.

7

DISTANCE EDUCATION AT THE UNIVERSITY OF ILLINOIS

Leigh Estabrook

CONTEXT FOR DISTANCE EDUCATION

Outreach and extension have, from their early days, been essential to the mission of the Graduate School of Library and Information Science (GSLIS) at the University of Illinois. Originally founded at the Armour Institute in Chicago in 1893 by Katharine Sharp,[1] the school moved, four years later, to the University of Illinois. While in Chicago "[Sharp] and her cohorts were involved in summer training classes, library extension services, and other forms of outreach."[2] The school's move to the land-grant institution of the state ensured that extension would remain a vital component of the school's mission. These "people's colleges" were intended to serve all the people.

Exploration of the early historical materials tells one that the land grant idea is not about a specific institutional arrangement, but is a set of beliefs about the social role of the university in society. It was not about agriculture as such, despite much rhetoric to that effect. Thus, the original 19th century beliefs were that the land grant university exists to:

1. Provide broad access to higher education, irrespective of wealth or social status,
2. Educate and train the professional cadres of an industrial, increasingly urban society, and to
3. Strengthen and defend American democracy by improving and assuring the welfare and social status of the largest, most disadvantaged groups in society—which in the 19th century were farmers and industrial workers (then called mechanics).[3]

Such a commitment is embodied today in the University's Partnership Illinois, UI-Online, and the Great Cities Program (based at the University of

Illinois, Chicago)—each directed to extending the university to the broader Illinois community.

HISTORICAL DEVELOPMENT OF EXTENDED DELIVERY AT THE UNIVERSITY OF ILLINOIS

In her survey of extension teaching at GSLIS,[4] Leslie Edmonds identifies three periods of time in which the school was most involved in extension: its first decade under Sharp, the mid-1940s to mid-1960s under the leadership of Alice Lohrer, and recent initiatives begun in the mid-1980s extending to today.

As noted, Sharp was strongly committed to extension service. Her thesis at the New York State Library School was on the relationship of university extension and public libraries. When she arrived in Illinois, Sharp developed extension courses for Cleveland Public Library and in collaboration with the University of Chicago. After the school moved to the University of Illinois, university librarians offered extension courses on theory and practice.[5] Sharp was motivated not only by a desire to improve the skills of working librarians but also by a strong interest in creating new libraries in the state. An early budget request to the president of the university from Sharp asked for funding for just such initiatives.

Edmonds notes (p. 197) that the faculty meeting minutes of the Library School throughout the first forty years of the twentieth century reflect a strong demand for extension, particularly short courses. She attributes much of the demand to the development of school libraries and growth in children's book publishing. Although there appear to have been extensive debates about admissions criteria and ways in which the school should be responsive, Edmonds concludes "there was more discussion of extension teaching than there were actual courses offered. Faculty acknowledged that this was a service needed in Illinois, but resources were often unavailable to meet this need" (p. 197).

This all changed when Alice Lohrer joined the faculty in 1941. A woman passionately committed to youth services and to extension, Lohrer taught extension courses from 1944 through the 1960s. Her early experiences involved driving ninety miles each way to Springfield, Illinois, once a week to teach extension courses for the Illinois State Library. She recalls

This was during the war, when food and gas rationing added their spice to our weekly ventures. The most memorable night was in late winter, when we ran out of gas at...about 11:30 P.M. Someone had forgotten to check the gas gauge. No cars had passed us going either way on the trip home. With snow all around us, with no heat in the car, no lights anywhere, it was a long cold wait for help. (Slanker, p. 94)

In 1947, the school expanded its service to the state in response to requests from Morrison, Illinois. The idea to develop in-service training programs throughout the state for teachers and librarians faced significant obstacles, but "my protests that Morrison was over 200 miles away, that library facilities were limited, that winter was approaching, and that post-war travel restrictions were a handicap were of no avail" (Slanker, p. 96). The university chose the following solution:

The weekly journey started early Friday morning with reservations on the Panama Limited to Chicago. My luggage was always heavy since there were no library facilities available for many of my students and I carried as many books as possible each trip. For this reason I took a Parmalee bus from the 12th Street I.C. station to the Northwestern depot to pick up reservations on a through train to Denver, Colorado. The first stop was Clinton, Iowa. There I disembarked to wait for a bus to take me back to Morrison, Illinois. The four-hour class met from 4:30 to 6:30 with an hour for dinner and then from 7:30 to 9:30. After class one of my students drove me to Sterling, Illinois, where I had hotel reservations for the night. Early in the morning I took a taxi to...pick up the City of Denver on its way back to Chicago. I arrived too late to take the Illinois Central morning train to Champaign. So the day was spent in downtown Chicago waiting for the later afternoon train to return to campus.

Under these conditions, it is not surprising that Lohrer instigated and inaugurated the university's "flight" extension program in 1948 in which university planes were used to transport faculty directly to remote teaching sites. For Lohrer this cut her travel time from thirty-seven to nine hours. In that same year the school appointed its first full-time extension instructor, Viola James, and began to offer graduate-level courses by extension.

At this time, professional library education was moving from the fifth-year baccalaureate to the master's degree. During that period, the University of Illinois taught extension courses at both levels in locations around the state. Another experience Lohrer reports in "A Quarter Century of Extension Teaching, 1944–1968" is the following:

The faculty were amused and skeptical at my weekly reports. So one week I asked if anyone wanted to go with me on a trip. There was room for one more passenger on the plane. Rose B. Phelps accepted the invitation. We started off as usual, but ran into rain and sleet before we reached the...airport. We finally landed safely but were told we could not take off that night nor the next day....We had no overnight bags and no assurance of getting on the morning train for Chicago. I did have a letter I carried with me from the University to railroad officials asking that I be allowed on the train even if it were overcrowded. They finally let us sit in the washroom since there were no vacant seats. (Slanker, p. 97)

With Lohrer's retirement, the level of extension activity lessened significantly. In the 1970s and early 1980s a small number of faculty taught in Peoria and Springfield, Illinois. They were paid as an overload by University Extension services, but for almost twenty years extension was not a priority for the school. Full courses were offered, but a student could not complete the entire program without coming to Champaign-Urbana.

TRYING TO GET TO CHICAGO

In 1986, Northern Illinois University was in the process of closing its library school, and the University of Chicago was threatening to do the same. With an eye to establishing a presence in Chicago and in the process saving Chicago's Graduate Library School, the University of Illinois offered a merger with Chicago. Discussions between provosts at each institution did not, however, end in such a merger, and Chicago closed the Graduate Library School. This left only two ALA-accredited programs in Illinois:, Rosary College (now Dominican University) and the University of Illinois at Urbana-Champaign.

For the next ten years GSLIS activities in distance/extension education were shaped by struggles between the University and the Illinois Board of Higher Education (IBHE), the state body charged with approving the sites at which programs are offered. In 1986 and 1987 the University of Illinois received strong pressure from librarians around the state who wanted LIS education brought to their geographic regions. One of my first visitors after I assumed the deanship in 1986 was Alice Lohrer, now retired, pleading the case for extension and attention to youth services.

In 1987, GSLIS faculty proposed to teach their full master's degree program in Chicago in "executive" format. Courses were to be taught by regular GSLIS faculty every other weekend at Loyola University's Water Tower campus. With the approval of the University of Illinois, students were recruited with notices that the beginning of the program was "subject to IBHE approval." That approval never came, despite a letter-writing campaign from librarians, assistance from then commissioner of the Chicago Public Library John Duff, and a bill introduced into the state legislature that would have allowed GSLIS to offer the program in Chicago without IBHE approval. The IBHE never formally decided *not* to give site approval, but it refused to act, saying there was insufficient demand for the program. Political pressures against approval from the LIS dean and a member of the board of Rosary College also played an important role in IBHE nonaction.

When it became clear that GSLIS would not be given authority to begin offering its master's degree in Chicago in fall 1988, the school began a "scheduling option" called Fridays Only. Still in existence, this option schedules courses on the Urbana-Champaign campus such that students can attend on Fridays only and be assured the courses will be offered that will enable them to complete the MS degree. Not strictly "extension," Fridays Only has nonetheless allowed many Illinois residents who would not otherwise be able to do so complete the degree.

One particularly successful use of Fridays Only was an initiative by Sharon Hogan, director of the University of Illinois at Chicago (UIC) library. Concerned about increasing the number of minorities in professional positions, Hogan provided a van for up to four paraprofessionals in her library to attend the Fridays Only program. Attendees were also given time off from work and were guaranteed a professional position in the library on graduation. In return, graduates of the GSLIS were expected to work for two years at UIC. Two cohorts completed the program in this way.

In the early 1990s the school also experimented with technology to support teaching at multiple sites. Jana Bradley (at Indiana) and Geoffrey Bowker (at Illinois) taught a course jointly, with students on each campus enrolled and working together on projects. Judith Weedman (Illinois) and Maurita Holland (Michigan) also taught a course jointly using two-way video.

In early 1995, with expected personnel changes in the IBHE, GSLIS once again initiated a proposal to teach its master's degree program in Chicago. It may be apocryphal that University of Illinois President Stanley Ikenberry said to Rosary President Donna Carroll, "You cannot keep the University of Illinois LIS program from going north of I-80." It is true that the two presidents met and argued and that, in the end, state politics led to a formal denial by IBHE of GSLIS's proposal.

Within days of this second refusal to grant site approval to teach LIS courses in Chicago, faculty of the GSLIS had approved and sent to the provost a proposal for an open access (i.e., site-independent) model for delivering the degree. The proposal from GSLIS Dean Leigh Estabrook to Provost Larry Faulkner, dated November 8, 1995, stated:

We believe it would be possible to begin the program this coming summer if we could hire support and technical staff by January and had approvals in hand. This may be too quick for you; but I wanted you to know of our willingness to try to seize the opportunity to take significant leadership both in the University and in the nation.

The proposed LEEP3 (now LEEP) program was shaped by the values of the faculty expressed in electronic and face-to-face discussion before voting approval to go ahead. Among these were:

If they are always seen as separate programs because of the tuition difference or political considerations, then I think we will have shot ourselves in the foot, in terms of taking our present master's curriculum forward into the 21st century.
                                   Pauline Cochrane, e-mail to faculty, 10/27/95

The human-contact high that Bryan describes, or the creation of a third voice through interaction between a first and second, is what I'm most concerned about injecting into the electronic program.
                                    Betsy Hearne, e-mail to faculty, 10/31/95

It does help to see people once in a while, too. I like the part about coming to campus for a few days or a week....There has to be a way, too, for student-to-student communication.... Group projects are important parts of courses—we work in groups in life.
                            Kathryn Luther Henderson, e-mail to faculty, 11/3/95

In all discussions there was an insistence that whatever the faculty did, it must be of the highest quality. The school was scheduled to be reviewed for reaccreditation in fall 1997, and the faculty did not want to jeopardize either ALA accreditation or the reputational quality of the school.

The proposal *Using New Information Technologies to Support Delivery of the UIUC Master's Degree in Library and Information Science* is essentially the LEEP program as it is offered today. Like Fridays Only, it was designed (and continues to be treated) as a scheduling option. It is not separate from the face-to-face option, except for delivery mode. Students on campus, in LEEP, and in the Fridays Only option enroll in each other's sections if there is space available. Tuition is the same. It also reflects Professor Hearne and others' concerns about the human connection. Students begin the course of study with a required on-campus session during which they are taught one course (Libraries, Information, and Society) and given the technological background necessary to work effectively once they leave Champaign-Urbana. Internet-based classes include synchronous sessions and asynchronous communication, with each faculty member determining how these modes are used. All students are required to come to Champaign-Urbana for a long weekend once a semester. This face-to-face session provides opportunities to use materials that may otherwise be unavailable, do presentations, interact with guest speakers, and continue to build a sense of community.

The courses emphasize group work and projects for which it is important that these students build relationships that enable them to work effectively together electronically. During the times they are not on campus, students work together in chatrooms, on Web-based bulletin boards, and even face-to-face when several live near one another in remote regions. In addition to instructor-authored Web pages, students make use of textbooks, course packs, electronic reserves, and materials available at libraries near their homes or obtained with the assistance of the Academic Outreach Library. To ensure quality, the school planned that faculty would receive release time before and during the first time they taught a new LEEP course, that the school would invest heavily in its own technology staff, and that a faculty member would have administrative responsibility for the program. We requested $700,000 in start-up funds from the University of Illinois.

By early January 1996, the school had received the strong support of Provost Larry Faulkner, who wrote to University of Illinois Vice President Sylvia Manning as follows:

Dean Leigh Estabrook is proposing to adapt the curriculum leading to the Master of Science in Library and Information Science to utilize multiple technologies and delivery formats including the Internet.... I strongly support the concept.... In reviewing the IBHE policies for off-campus programs, it appears that *only campus approvals will be necessary* [emphasis added] in order to implement the curriculum....

Financial elements need appropriate approvals. First, this curriculum is to be largely self-supporting. In this regard, the tuition generated by the enrollments in the curriculum will need to be dedicated to the Graduate School of Library and Information Science. I will be authorizing the addition of up to five faculty positions based on this assumption....

Second, the technology needs are such that a course technology fee is proposed. I request that the addition of such a fee be considered in the development of the FY98 budget next fall. During the pilot year of FY97, the technology expenses will be underwritten with campus funds....

The master's program curriculum adapted to the Internet and combined with on-campus intensive sessions in the summer promises to be an important pioneering step for the University in utilizing our knowledge about networks and the World Wide Web in meeting the educational goals of both the University and of the students we can serve. (Larry Faulkner to Sylvia Manning, 1/9/96)

The LEEP proposal pleased the university on a number of counts. It successfully avoided the control of IBHE, control that places constraints on innovation. The program promised to use the university's high-technology orientation to the benefit of Illinois residents. It provided the opportunity to engage the university fully in Internet-based distance education at a time when the promises of new technology for education were just beginning to be realized. Illinois administrators were pleased at the idea of being early adopters. So, too, were the GSLIS faculty, who desired to exert leadership in this area.

By March 1996, GSLIS had received a commitment for $600,000 in start-up funds, and it began recruiting a class of twenty-five students, twenty in-state, the goal set by the university. In July 1996, the first LEEP class began with a total of thirty-one. Although most students were in state, the fact that one was from Alaska added to the program's cachet. During spring 1997, as GSLIS concluded its first year offering the master's degree in this mode, faculty, students, and staff were interviewed for a PBS special titled "NetLearning."

In July 2002, the school began its sixth year of LEEP with over 200 students enrolled, more than half from out of state. The goal of being fully self-supporting through tuition income (all of which is returned to the school) has been met.

Publicity and recruitment for LEEP have been accomplished through Web pages describing the program, announcements placed in relevant e-mail lists, entries in directories of distance learning programs, and targeted mailing of brochures to employing organizations who may have staff seeking to earn a professional degree.

By spring 2003 the school was offering fifteen LEEP courses per semester during the academic year and seven additional courses during summer session. Expanding the concept of extension, adjunct faculty from around the country contribute significant expertise to the program. Several teach on a regular basis. Because the school allows students from different scheduling options to cross-register, these adjuncts have also allowed the school to offer courses to on-campus students for which campus-based instructors were not available. With few exceptions, LEEP and a number of on-campus students are being educated together.

The program has benefited from an extraordinary staff. In 1997, Professor Linda Smith agreed to become associate dean with primary responsibility for LEEP. A retention rate of over 95 percent and the reputation for quality of LEEP can be attributed directly to her attention to the students, commitment to quality, and recognition of the importance of attending to all aspects of technology support and administration. Early in LEEP development, Vince Patone, a former doctoral student with a background in psychology, assumed responsibility for technology. He now heads the Instructional Technology Office. It is supported by one full-time Computer-Assisted Instruction Specialist (Jill Gengler, formerly a LEEP student) and five graduate assistants. The size of the staff is in part due to the way LEEP has become integrated into the fabric of the school. In spring 1999, Patone became director of all instructional technology at a time when it was no longer easy to maintain the boundary between LEEP3 teaching and technology and that of the rest of the school. Beginning in August 2000, LEEP graduate and doctoral student Rae-Anne Montague joined the staff as a half-time LEEP coordinator.

Early in the program's development, we also discovered the critical role that front-office staff and staff in the campus Academic Outreach office play in recruitment and retention of LEEP students. Distance students do not have the option to walk across campus to argue with the financial aid office or to read in the *Daily Illini* about registration dates. Moreover, campus support staff are only beginning to recognize their responsibilities for distance students.

One of the school's greatest struggles has been to coordinate student support with the campus. We have insisted that LEEP students should have status and support equal to that of other students enrolled in our programs, but it has not always been easy to accomplish. The University of Illinois has separate registration systems for distance students. This has implications for course enrollment, grade rosters, and network ID assignments, among other things. GSLIS staff have created a number of work-arounds to solve the problems. It has been one of the prices of taking the lead for the campus on offering a full degree Internet-based program.

LEEP has done much more than educate students who otherwise might not be able to gain the LIS master's degree. It has, as Professor Cochrane suggested it might, helped the school make numerous other changes to meet the dynamic growth of this field. Because all GSLIS faculty teach in LEEP, all are learning how to use new technologies to assist instruction. Increasingly the methods of LEEP instruction have been imported into on-campus instruction. The technology competencies initially intended only for LEEP students are now mandated for all GSLIS master's students.

The budgeting system for LEEP also contributes significantly to the school. Five new faculty lines, all of the educational technology support, and support for faculty development time were funded by LEEP tuition income. LEEP was implemented at a time of budget reform across the campus that allocates all graduate tuition back to units, but even without that change, the school had the guarantee of full recovery of LEEP tuition.

LEEP is still held up as an example on the UIUC campus. Linda Smith has been recognized as Distinguished Teacher/Scholar, in part because of her leadership with LEEP. She and other faculty are frequent presenters at university conferences on distance education. They also meet with visitors to the campus from other universities who wish to learn more about how to design and deliver distance education programs. Other departments have been eager to understand how LEEP is designed and managed. The visibility of the program on campus also has positioned the school as a leader in use of new information technologies. In November 2001, LEEP was recognized with the Sloan-C Award for the Most Outstanding Asynchronous Learning Network Program, marking five years of successful program development.

Part of LEEP's initial design involved having an outside evaluator review the program. Stephen Gill, an independent consultant who has done work for the W. K. Kellogg Foundation, was hired to evaluate the first cohort of LEEP students. Among his findings were the following:

- The two-week and on-campus sessions facilitated communication and helped build group cohesion;
- The LEEP option is the only way most of the students could have earned the degree;
- LEEP had an immediate positive and direct effect on professional careers of students;
- LEEP requires the development of strong written communication and teamwork; and
- Technology became secondary to content.

No such assessment has been done for students entering after 1996, but all faculty use standardized teaching evaluation tools and LEEP has been the subject of faculty retreats and ongoing discussion. These relatively informal mechanisms are supplemented by several research projects designed to understand LEEP as one example of distance learning.

Caroline Haythornthwaite's research on LEEP looks at patterns of collaboration and information exchange among these computer-supported learners—who talks to whom, about what, and via which media. These studies explore the way in which the available communication media and the structure of class activities facilitate or constrain interactions among students. The general premise from the collaborative learning perspective is that students can (and should) learn from each other. Her studies explore how this is played out in the LEEP environment, that is, when students are distributed and computer-supported.

A second aspect of Haythornthwaite's research looks at how students develop and sustain a sense of community when distributed and computer-supported, that is, exploring the virtual community of these learners (with it being about 90 percent virtual). This work explores what's important both inside and outside LEEP that makes it possible for them to complete the program and have a satisfactory experience with the program.

Professor Karen Ruhleder's research involves detailed analyses of the actual interactions among LEEP students to understand how they work and support one another in the process of learning. She also makes significant contributions to our understanding of how to conduct research in a virtual environment. These and other research on LEEP are listed in an online bibliography (available at www.lis.uiuc.edu/gslis/degrees/leep.bib.html).

The future of extension/distance education at the University of Illinois is discussed frequently by faculty and staff. At the present staffing level and as presently designed LEEP does not easily scale up, although the Certificate of Advanced Study is now available in LEEP format. Moreover, faculty are committed to expanding the doctoral program and an undergraduate minor in information technology studies. Current discussions center around developing several professional development sequences (twelve credit hours) that could be offered using LEEP technologies but would not entail campus visits or administrative overhead at the level of the master's degree program. These may include sequences on information and knowledge management or school media and youth services.

With support from the Provost's Initiative on Teaching Advancement, GSLIS held the first LEEP retreat in August 2002 for faculty, students, and graduates. This provided an opportunity to determine what teaching strategies, methods, and supporting technologies have been more advantageous to learning. It is beginning to inform future Illinois initiatives in distance education.

NOTES

Linda Smith and Rae-Anne Montague provided invaluable help in preparing this chapter.

1. Melvil Dewey considered her the woman who was "the best man in America to start the...library school."

2. Laurel Grotzinger, "Remarkable Beginnings: The First Half Century of the Graduate School of Library and Information Science," in *Ideals and Standards: The History of the University of Illinois Graduate School of Library and Information Science, 1893–1993*. Champaign, IL: Graduate School of Library and Information Science, 1992, p. 8.

3. From James T. Bonnen, "Land Grant Universities Are Changing" (November 1996). Available online at www.adec.edu/clemson/papers/bonnen1.html.

4. Much of this section is drawn from Leslie Edmonds, "Extension Teaching: A Century of Service," in *Ideals and Standards: The History of the University of Illinois Graduate School of Library and Information Science, 1893–1993.* Champaign, IL: Graduate School of Library and Information Science, 1992.

5. It is important to recall that the library and library school were one academic unit at this time. Both were directed by Sharp.

SUGGESTED READINGS

Allen, Walter C. and Robert F. Delzell, editors. (1992) *Ideals and Standards: The History of the University of Illinois Graduate School of Library and Information Science, 1893–1993.* Champaign, IL: Graduate School of Library and Information Science. Written in honor of the school's centennial, this collection of essays provide a historical overview of the school supplemented by essays on special topics, such as the school's physical facilities, teaching of different areas, and ancillary units like the Library Research Center.

Estabrook, Leigh. Assorted papers and presentations. Former dean of GSLIS, Estabrook frequently speaks about LEEP. Among her presentations are "Will Distance Education Destroy the University?" (Lazerow Lecture, September 17, 1999, Florida State University) and "New Forms of Distance Education: Opportunities for Students, Threats to Institutions." Full text for many of these are available from her home page (www.lis.uiuc.edu/~leighe).

Grotzinger, Laurel Ann. (1966) *The Power and the Dignity: Librarianship and Katharine Sharp.* New York, Scarecrow Press. Grotzinger's knowledge of Katharine Sharp is unsurpassed. This biography provides detail about Sharp's interest in extension and the way she shaped the Library School for decades after her directorship.

LEEP Bibliography, available online at www.lis.uiuc.edu/gslis/degrees/leep.bib.html (a source for articles about LEEP and for research findings related to LEEP).

Slanker, Barbara Olsen, editor. (1968) *Reminiscences: Seventy-five Years of a Library School,* Urbana, Illinois: University of Illinois, Graduate School of Library Science. As the title suggests, this is another collection of essays honoring a milestone in the history of the school. Of particular note is Alice Lohrer's essay, "A Quarter Century of Extension Teaching, 1944–1968."

Smith, Linda C. *Pedagogy in Educating Information Specialists: Lessons Learned from Internet-Based Distance Education.* Paper presented at a conference on Information Specialists for the 21st Century, Hanover, Germany, October 14–15, 1999. Available online at http://Conference99.fh-hannover.de/fulltext/smith-f.htm. Smith is interim dean at GSLIS and has held administrative oversight for the program since 1997. She is a rich source of information about the program and has published several papers on the subject.

University of Illinois Library School Association, editor. *Fifty Years of Education for Librarianship: Papers presented for the celebration of the fiftieth anniversary of the University of Illinois library school, March 2, 1943.* Urbana: University of Illinois Press, 1943.

8

THE INDIANA VIRTUAL CLASSROOM: INTERACTION THROUGH TWO-WAY VIDEO

Daniel Callison, Shirley A. Fitzgibbons, and Edward J. Jurewicz

The Virtual Indiana Classroom (VIC) Network connects all eight Indiana University (IU) campuses as well as the IU centers in Columbus, Elkhart, and Schereville, with two-way interactive video. Using TI digital telephony, the system allows for point-to-point as well as multipoint classes and meetings.

The VIC system was launched in 1995. Selected courses from the IU School of Library and Information Science (SLIS) have been taught over the VIC since the first semester of the network. The school currently offers a regular selection of courses through two-way video across Indiana that allow students to complete most of the credits necessary for certification in school or public librarianship at the graduate level. This chapter examines the evolution of course planning and presentation from one-way video broadcast to two-way video interaction enhanced with a variety of additional telecommunications tools. Information presented in this chapter may also confirm or reject some of the proposed benefits of the VIC Network (see Table 8.1) and two-way video instruction in general. In addition, this chapter contains basic entry-level introductions to the operation of a two-way audio/video system as well as a glossary of key terms and acronyms.

COMPONENTS OF THE VIC VIDEO CONFERENCING NETWORK

Two types of rooms make up the network's physical facilities. Video Teleconferencing Classrooms (VTCs) contain off-the-shelf equipment systems that allow instructors and students to present information and interact with a minimum of technical knowledge. The Interactive Classroom Studios (ICSs)

Table 8.1
Benefits of the Virtual Indiana Classroom Network

Faculty and students will find that the VIC Network
- brings the resources of the university to a wider audience
- encourages interaction by providing a variety of classroom resources and activities
- makes it possible for students to learn from each other as well as from their instructors
- allows outside experts to participate in classes, thereby adding variety and interest
- allows local programs and resources to be shared statewide and beyond

Administrators and staff will find that the VIC Network
- allows them to share research and resources with colleagues and experts
- allows them to meet when it is most convenient
- saves time and money
- increases communication and support
- promotes partnerships among people who might not otherwise be able to meet

allow instructors to use high-end TV production equipment to present classes. The physical location for delivery of IU SLIS distance education courses now originates from one of the VTC units with connections that vary according to the instructional goals and plans of the instructor. Most SLIS courses originate from Bloomington and are received at Indianapolis (Indiana University, Purdue University at Indianapolis, or IUPUI); IU campuses at Gary, South Bend, Fort Wayne, and Richmond; as well as the Evansville Public Library. Nearly 85 percent of the total Indiana population is within a one-hour drive of a receiving site and a majority of the population is within thirty minutes. Instructors often travel to different VIC locations so that at least one class session originates from each site during the ten to fifteen sessions for the semester.

GROWTH IN SLIS DISTANCE EDUCATION

Diana Zepp (2000) documented the growth in distance education offerings found in schools of library and information science. She found that 16 percent of the accredited LIS programs used distance education in some electronic or telecommunications format in 1989. In ten years this had grown to 75 percent with nearly 20 percent offering the option to complete a degree over distance education in 1998. By the end of the 1990s, Zepp found that 22 percent of the thirty-six accredited library science programs offering distance education were using only an Internet-based technology to deliver classes, and 50 percent of those programs were using both the Internet and the audio/video technologies in combination.

Faculty members at Indiana University have experimented with various distance education formats over the past two decades. Since 1994, a combination of distance delivery modes has been used to meet demands in various areas of the graduate program. A regular annual cycle of courses totaling twenty-four credits is now delivered over interactive TV from the Indianapolis campus to statewide receiving sites. The primary purpose of this set of courses is to meet the basic certification requirements for school and public librarianship certification. Reception is within Indiana only and currently serves over 200 students. The full MLS degree is not offered with the expectation that students come to either the Bloomington or the Indianapolis campus to demonstrate interpersonal skills in the balance of their coursework. Thus, student experience both the modern interactive and traditional interactive environments as a basis for education, communication, and leadership in a variety of settings. The mode of the distance education delivery is tailored to meet the purpose of the course, needs of the students, and innovative abilities of the instructor (Cronin, 1997).

Within the past few years greater use of online systems to support interactive TV have evolved. Web-based discussion is often a part of the televised course. Electives in support of the school media program have been developed that are delivered completely online. These include courses developed by Carol Tilley, lecturer at IU Indianapolis, in grant writing, school media research, and advanced study of nonfiction resources for young adults. New full-time faculty joining the SLIS at the Indianapolis campus are hired with the expectation that they will accept development and delivery of one distance education course annually.

Howard Rosenbaum, associate professor in Information Science, has developed the first online course for IU SLIS that has reached international audiences. By 2002, Rosenbaum was delivering his course, the Information Industry: Electronic Commerce, beyond the United States to Great Britain, Scotland, Australia, and Germany. Participating schools included programs in information science, computing, and business. Total student population was more than 400 involved in coursework and e-commerce services (http://ebiz.slis.indiana.edu/ebizp).

The SLIS at IU Indianapolis is now part of a plan to develop future coursework in a learner-centered environment that can be accessible to students seven days a week and twenty-four hours a day (Plater, 2002). The goal is to target the needs of over 80 percent of the Indianapolis-based students who are employed part-time or full-time in library settings across Indiana and adjacent states.

INTERACTIVE STUDIOS AT ALL SITES

The VIC system is composed of four major components: the classrooms, the network, a bridging hub, and the conference scheduling system. The VTC is based on either a conference room, seating approximately twelve students, or standard classroom layout, seating up to thirty students. A typical room is equipped with a basic package of conferencing equipment including a codec, the network connection, a couple of large monitors, and a camera. Some of the VTCs are equipped with additional monitors and up to three cameras.

All classrooms contain a document camera and have Internet connections as well. The VIC system is used for full-semester classes, special educational events, and mini-classes as well as administrative teleconferencing. Approximately forty full-semester classes utilize the current network. Courses from the SLIS constitute about 10 percent of the current regular course offerings.

The ICS is usually made up of a classroom with an adjacent control room and production studio. In addition to the codec and network transport, the ICS has a complex installation of video and audio production equipment. Some ICS installations have the ability to route video with campus cable, satellite, and local community school systems. There are twenty-four ICS and VTC sites throughout the Indiana University statewide campus system.

The video network transport is T1-based. All T1s converge to an Ameritech video bridging center in Indianapolis. The bridging hub is what connects multiple sites in a conference. Two or more sites can be joined together. The hub controls who sees what and keeps the present "talker" always displayed on far-end monitors.

INDIANA HIGHER EDUCATION TELEVISION SYSTEM

The VIC Network has been constructed within an umbrella system for televised education that has been recognized nationally and internationally for the quality of its programming since 1967. The Indiana Higher Education Television System (IHETS) originated as a single-channel closed-circuit microwave TV network limited to reaching sites within the state. Today, IHETS provides its member institutions an eight-channel satellite TV network accessible across the nation, a statewide long-distance telephone network, and a data network through which members of the consortium connect to the Internet. Nearly 300 public schools, community libraries, universities, cooperative extension services, hospitals, industries, and government offices are connected to the network, allowing for extensive distribution of college credit and continuing education courses. Courses offered over VIC can be a part of the greater IHETS schedule as well, but IHETS-delivered courses are limited to only one-way video communication with options for phone-in audio response.

IHETS is a dynamic hub for collaboration among Indiana's colleges and universities to deploy and use information technologies in support of their missions of teaching, research, and public service. The IHETS Vision Statement for 2001 is based on a rich history of innovation and leadership in telecommunications (see Table 8.2). Through the consortium, the member institutions attempt to reach these goals:

Table 8.2
Milestones in Development of the Indiana Higher Education Television System

March 1967	IHETS-enabling legislation signed into law
February 1968	Inauguration of State Universities Voice Network (SUVON)
May 1969	Installation of fully switched statewide video network
September 1969	Completion of first Instructional Television Fixed Service station
June 1980	Inauguration of IHETS Conference Network services
August 1980	IHETS members join in project with public television for tele-courses
March 1985	Intelenet project started
August 1986	Completion of multiplexing project to expand video network
April 1987	IHETS legislation amended to include videotape courses
June 1987	Beginning of transfer of SUVON and IHETS TV networks to Intelnet fiber-optic backbone network
May 1991	Indiana's first Internet backbone and connections proposed for colleges and universities
August 1992	Creation of Indiana Partnership for Statewide Education (IPSE)
January 1993	Inauguration of Indiana's Internet Data Network (INDnet) and Beginning migration of IHETS TV to satellite
April 1994	Approval of IPSE Home Institution Concept
October 1995	Approval of IPS Learning Center Model
January 1996	Major expansion of Indiana's Internet (INDnet) capacity IHETS/IPSE

- maximize the return on their investment in information technologies by sharing resources among themselves and with others;
- employ the most efficient and effective technologies available for the ubiquitous delivery of education;
- engage in joint ventures with other major technology users and providers;
- extend their individual capabilities to provide traditional and nontraditional life-long learning;
- commission and publish research on educational uses of and needs for technology;
- provide a clearinghouse for information about their resources, expertise, and activities in technology and technology-based education.

As a result, residents of Indiana, wherever they live or work, have ready access to a variety of lifelong learning opportunities to enrich their lives and improve their economic well-being. Learners across the country and around the world also choose to take advantage of Indiana's educational resources because of their competitive quality and convenience. The 2001 IHETS

Vision Statement concludes, "The availability of such post-secondary educational access is a significant advantage to the State for economic development." The Indiana College Network has more than twenty degree programs offered by satellite TV, interactive video, cable TV, videotape, or the Internet.

LIMITATIONS OF ONE-WAY VIDEO

Until the VIC, the only option for video transmission at IU was one-way presentation over IHETS. Although this system allowed for wide distribution of a course, advantages quickly became the disadvantages. The one-way system focused complete attention on the instructor and made it very difficult for the instructor to share or facilitate learning experiences. Although a portion of the students, usually about a third of the class, could be present in the same studio, it was not possible to gain immediate verbal feedback. Call-in comments were delayed, often by more than five minutes. Students waited to come on the air to deliver comments on issues that were often resolved or past the point of relevance at the time the student could be aired across the system. The result was often embarrassment for the students and a growing reluctance to attempt to participate again. Though a situation or problem could be posed for discussion and call-in responses could be scheduled from around the state, such student feedback often became cumbersome and usually did not create further discussion or wide interest.

Delivery of the course without travel to distance sites was appealing to the instructor. Some instructors had taught at a variety of IU campuses, some as much as a ten-hour round-trip drive from Bloomington. However, it became apparent within just a few weeks that students at remote sites did not feel as involved in class as those at the home site with the instructor. Face-to-face communication at least once during the semester was desired. One-way video transmission was restricted to originating the course from a single site. The instructor was held to the home base without the opportunity to meet all students in the class. In some cases, students could call the instructor for additional information immediately following class. In the mid-1990s, those who had access to e-mail could make contact for purposes of gaining clarification on assignments, adding comments to class discussion, or seeking advice on future classes in the program. The communication process was lacking in many respects: For example, common concerns could have been addressed over the TV system if students had had a more immediate method to communicate. Two-way video and the growing use of e-mail and online discussion groups eventually met these problems.

One-way video tends to focus on the instructor to the extent that the presentation style takes on aspects of TV news reporting. Though the content may be enhanced with guest speakers or video clips, the instructor remains the "anchor" with nearly all events still centering on his or her presence. The technical operation of the one-way system also requires a great deal of on-site technical assistance, often with two professional support personnel in the studio with the instructor. With these technicians on board, the presentation begins to take on the feel and impression of a formal TV production. Tapes are precued, switches are thrown, and timing becomes very tight. Formality sets in, and an informality that should lead to open invitations for student participation becomes more difficult. Even graphics are designed in a professional manner to be legible and visually effective; however, they add to the impression that the presentation is so scripted and organized that student interaction will cause problems and disrupt the instruction.

From 1992 to 1995, several IU SLIS courses were offered through one-way video. To spark discussion and to add field experts to the class, video interviews were compiled of various educators and other professionals. These interviews were conducted at national and state conferences or taped when the individual was a guest speaker in class. These interviews were edited to provide brief clips of four to ten minutes in which the expert raised issues or discussed trends. The end result through one-way video, however, was that these clips became part of the news-delivery format. The instructor tended to move from one video clip to another, to a set of graphics predesigned to summarize points, to a final set of conclusions focused on his or her thoughts.

The end result of the instructor-focused environment was the unwillingness of most students to engage the instructor in content questions and a hesitation on the part of all students to interject meaningful observations in an immediate manner. Interactions, when they did take place, seemed staged between student and instructor, and seldom was there a flow among students across various sites. Discussion among students, especially at a graduate education level, is extremely important. Although steps could be taken to improve interaction through the one-way system, the development of two-way video delivery at Indiana University in 1995 created a welcome new approach to distance education interaction.

INCREASED INTERACTION WITH TWO-WAY VIDEO

Instructors who desire a lot of synchronous interaction among class participants often choose two-way video. Although many teaching strategies may adapt to two-way video, one that emphasizes participant interaction works especially well. In addition to facilitating interaction, two-way video, or interactive video, allows instructors to demonstrate points visually. They can focus the camera on activities they are performing, provide close-ups of illustrations or diagrams, and quickly add comments or illustrations offered by students. If at least one document camera is available at each site, students can become engaged in sharing information both orally and visually. Equipment can be managed by instructors and students, thus providing a flow of information exchange seen and heard at all participating sites.

Nancy Franklin, Michael Yoakam, and Ron Warren described some key instructional considerations for two-way video in Distance Learning: A Guide to System Planning and Implementation (1995). This guide was an award-winning publication in 1996, recognized for excellence by the University Continuing Education Association. The guide has been recently revised with Yoakam as the lead author (Yoakam, Franklin, and Warren, 2001). The team designed the guide specifically for development of the VIC Network, and the 1995 edition provides a useful discussion of the advantages and disadvantages of several modes of distance learning (see Table 8.3). Those preparing to teach in a two-way video environment for the first time should become familiar with the major differences between this mode of learning and a face-to-face situation. Instructional considerations include the following (pp. 3–16):

- Because of less spontaneity than face-to-face instruction, participants will likely feel a greater sense of distance and may be less comfortable volunteering information. The instructor will want to consider a variety of approaches to facilitate interaction, including assigning students responsibility for leading various portions of the discussion (see Table 8.4).
- The downside of having audio and video capability at each site is that participants may distract others from the instruction, inadvertently or consciously, by saying or doing things at inappropriate times, and this will be picked up by microphones and cameras. Everyone will likely need to go through an adjustment period to understand the ramifications of having cameras and microphones positioned to capture all sound and movement. The result might be a set of communication protocols that facilitate interaction in this kind of environment.
- The successful instructor will need to focus on ways to reach out to students so that they will have a sense of personalized contact with the instructor. These techniques may include collecting and sharing biographies, frequently using names, the instructor visiting remote sites when possible, gathering all students at one location periodically, and continually motivating and rewarding students as they become involved in class interactions.

Personal visits to remote sites add time and expense to the instructional package but have important benefits as well. Students gain personal contact with the instructor, even if it is for just one class session out of a dozen or more. The instructor gains an understanding of the classroom structure and support services available to the student. More in-depth program advising also takes place.

Advising and counseling often require attention to issues that are unique to distance learners (Paulet, 1988). The obligations that compel students to take distance courses might carry job- or family-related pressures such that students may need special counseling or help with managing time and coping with varied responsibilities. Because distant learners are often returning to school after years of absence, significant pauses in their education might need to be assessed and remedied. Distance students must also take responsibility

Table 8.3
Advantages and Disadvantages of One-Way and Two-Way Video (Franklin, Yoakam and Warren, 1995)

One-Way Video	
Advantages	*Disadvantages*
Permits students at many distance sites to receive instruction	Heavily instructor focused in terms of instructional presentation
Instructor may focus attention on a very specific aspect or issue	No nonverbal feedback cues and oral responses may be restricted
Readily accommodates lecture format	May encourage students to become passive rather than active learners
Instructor must focus on delivery presence and style so as to maintain student attention	
Requires strong technical support	

Two-Way Video	
Advantages	*Disadvantages*
Most closely approximates face-to-face contact	May be costly if many sites are involved and instructor travels
Allows all participants to see and hear each other	Restricts room layout and student seating Requires instructor to manage video and audio inputs from several sites
Works particularly well for small groups at each site, thus encouraging small group discussion as well as large class interaction	Some sites may not connect or have technical problems and local support staff may not be immediately available, especially on weekends
Camera and monitor control can be managed locally or remotely	Students attending class at central campus may resent loss of contact with full-time faculty who travel to originate class from remote sites
Visuals as well as oral comments may be shared from any site across all sites	
Encourages student interaction if such is motivated and rewarded	Requires significant extra effort from instructor to make sure class administrative tasks are handled and may require extra time to coordinate access to reserves or other materials which cannot be provided on line
Students learn operation of basic video and audio technologies if placed in the role to do so	
Instructor may originate class from any site in the network	
Wider geographic distribution often results in greater diversity of student backgrounds and experiences to share	

Table 8.4
Steps in Interactive Discussion of Issues over Two-Way Video

1. *Select an issue or topic.* This may be an issue or topic that has been broached in assigned readings for the class session or has clearly become an area of interest for the students as well as being relevant to the course content. The topic can be left broad and open, for example: Censorship. The issues can be stated as a resolution or hypothesis: Library media specialists who have a recent, board-approved collection development policy are more likely to retain controversial materials in their school library collection. Or pose a question: What are the most critical factors associated with censorship of instructional materials in public schools?

2. *Brainstorm.* Encourage "intra-active" brainstorming, meaning that small groups at each site are given 10 to 15 minutes to consider their own ideas and to place them on cards or paper to be shared later with the rest of the class across all sites in interactive discussion. At sites where just one or two students are present, allow them to connect and discuss as a group, while sites with large student populations divide into teams of four or five.

3. *Record and cluster.* Quick three-minute reports can be made from each site, with the instructor or a selected student illustrating the shared comments by listing them as they are presented. These comments may be clustered or associated in some manner to show relationships that the instructor wants to emphasize or to have students comment on further.

4. *Explore in-depth.* Key issues will become apparent. These may depend on definition of terms, variance of situations, evidence from research studies, and personal experiences. Allow time for students to interact and react to students from various sites. The instructor must facilitate the discussion, not dominate it.

5. *Elaborate.* Students should be encouraged to elaborate on some key issue they select during the days prior to the next class session. Through electronic mail or a Web-based conference system, the students may share insights in detail and document them with evidence whenever possible. MUD, MOO, and MAUD tools (see "Teleconferencing and Distance Education Glossary") allow for very creative ways to extend conversations and debate.

6. *Introduce experts.* Field experts may be added to the class online discussion group to examine student contributions to the discussion, which may serve as a background to the expert's participation in a future class. The field expert may participate in a future class by attending any of the sites or by telephone conference. The expert does not need to be present at the same site as the instructor.

7. *Analyze and prioritize.* During a class session following the online discussion group elaborations, raise the topic again. Usually about two weeks need to pass between the initial brainstorming and this final step. At this point, again through use of both "intra-" and "inter-" active sessions, request that student teams make a final analysis of the issues, and indicate those that seem to be most critical and why.

8. *Reward.* Evaluate and reward constructive participation in these activities. A portion of the student's grade and performance feedback should pertain to the degree of active participation in sharing comments over the video system, presenting in-depth evidence during e-mail elaboration, and defending critical choices to prioritize actions.

themselves in addressing their own needs. This may need to be explicitly communicated to these learners. For example, distance learners must assume greater responsibility for their own learning, become more active in asking questions and obtaining help, be respectful of the flexibility required by other students, and be prepared to deal with technical difficulties in the two-way flow of information.

An important advantage in two-way video, however, is the opportunity to mix diverse groups in the same virtual classroom. It is not unusual for the student population at the central campus, Bloomington, to be composed of mostly full-time students who are young and/or inexperienced in professional library work or teaching responsibilities. In general, the student population outside of Bloomington is employed and/or has several years of professional experiences, which may or may not fit neatly with the theory and scenarios presented in class. The result is a blending of questions and insights from those who have new technical skills and those who have real-world expertise. Discussions can become rich with multileveled perspectives. The successful instructor capitalizes on this diversity and facilitates a process that will allow students to discover critical evidence and key issues (see Table 8.4).

Video interviews of selected content experts, which had been produced for the one-way video medium, were introduced in the two-way system. The extent of follow-up interaction was dramatically different in the two-way system as students reacted to issues and trends. As students became accustomed to the audio and video controls at their own site, contributions began to flow more naturally. Often student feedback, comments, and questions exceeded the class time of the original expert video interview. Video interviews that had been produced to consume some instructional time in the one-way setting were now edited to be shorter and more focused so that more class discussion time could be provided. Two-way video provided the means to manage quick student interaction from all sites around the state.

E-mail discussion lists or Internet Web boards allow for elaboration of discussions outside of class. In addition, field experts (practicing professionals related to the content of the course) are added to the e-mail list so they may react to issues as well. This enhances the spectrum of opinions and observations so students learn from the course professor, each other, and from individuals close to the issues while on the job. Profiles of the field experts may include individuals within the geographic location of many of the students so personal visits can be arranged and may also include field experts in international settings to provide even greater perspectives on trends and issues from different cultures. Professional experience backgrounds may vary as well, so perspectives of professionals new to the job can be compared to those who have been in the profession for several decades. Because student contributions can be noted in class as well as logged over e-mail, instructors should provide a clear means of evaluating and rewarding student interactions. A sample rubric is given below:

Outstanding Achievement. Student performance demonstrates full command of the course materials and evinces a high level or originality and/or creativity that far surpasses course expectations. Frequent (at least twice each week) contributions to class and e-mail discussions are made based on use of documents and professional literature which have been assigned. The student further supports his/her interactions with professional materials which are in addition to those assigned. The student takes a leading role in identification of issues and may offer insights as to trends based on an analysis of comments from other students, the instructor, and field experts. Thus the superior student demonstrates skills in information analysis, linkage of issues, and analysis leading to prediction of likely future trends in research and practice.

Excellent Achievement. Student performance demonstrates thorough knowledge of the course materials and exceeds course expectations. The student provides evidence of reading and considering assigned literature and frequently adds comments to class and e-mail discussions.

Very Good Work. Student demonstrates above-average comprehension of assigned readings and participates as a member of discussion teams. The student contributes some comments to the course e-mail discussion.

Marginal Work. Student attends class but seldom offers comments and infrequently, less than once every two weeks, offers any form of contribution to the class e-mail discussion.

PROTOCOLS FOR THE INTRODUCTION OF TWO-WAY VIDEO OPERATION

The following list of skills is a synthesis of expert opinion and the literature on distance teaching that has relevance today, even though it was compiled during the early years of teleconferencing (Boone, 1984). Each skill is illustrated by particular behaviors resulting from analysis of actual teleconferences. Teachers in teleconferencing and other distance contexts should have the ability to

- provide structure—use authority, control verbal traffic
- provide socio-emotional support—integrate late group members, encourage humor
- establish a democratic atmosphere—share authority, ask for participation
- create a sense of shared space—describe environment, create a sense of shared history
- model appropriate behavior—model conciseness, use variety of presentation modes
- repair sessions going awry—bring fragments together into relevant summary
- set an appropriate pace—seek conciseness and clarity, direct questions specifically

Teachers need to become aware of their roles in orienting students to the delivery medium and in linking them to resources other than the instructor. To maximize distance education's potential for interaction, instructors must make participants comfortable with the technology by modeling comfort with the system and by providing an early orientation, including hands-on practice, to whatever technology is being used (McMann, 1994). Such orientation and shared practice should take place during the first class meeting and may consume as much as thirty to forty-five minutes. Practice should include student use of cameras (see Table 8.5) as well as an understanding of effective audio communications (see Table 8.6).

In addition, students should be informed orally as well as in writing through the course syllabus, both print and Web-based, of support services. All phone numbers for each site should be given along with names, positions, and likely expertise that can be provided. Students should actually phone to make contact during the first session to be assured that help is within reasonable reach if necessary. Such contacts need to be tested and enforced to be certain they can be reached, especially for evening and weekend classes. Although more resources can be made available over the Internet, specific means to access materials on reserve at various site library collections as well as names of individuals responsible for reserves at each site are also important to provide to all students. In some cases, interlibrary loan procedures will make it possible for students to share resources across sites when necessary.

IU LIBRARY EDUCATION CERTIFICATION PROGRAM VIA DISTANCE LEARNING

In 1997, the Indiana University SLIS formalized its distance education efforts into an effort to provide the courses leading to basic school media or public library certification. The Library Education Certification Program was designed to provide the key courses for the twenty-four-credit minor in school librarianship and the twelve credits necessary for entry level certification in public librarianship. Although faculty would have some flexibility as to specific sites where they would deliver instruction, in general the schedule called for two courses each semester to be presented over VIC at six locations.

The Indiana State Library Certification Board has outlined the requirements for minimum library education to include a bachelor's degree, completion of the undergraduate course Computer-Based Information Tools, and at least nine graduate credit hours to include Management of Information Environments, Information Sources and Services, and Collection Development and Management. Completion of the next certification level, intermediate, can be accomplished with such courses as Library Materials for Children and Young Adults and Library Automation.

Courses packaged for the VIC Network, which would lead to a large portion of the school library services minor, included Information Inquiry for School Teachers, School Media Specialist, as well as the courses in the intermediate public library certification offerings. In 1999, eighty part-time students were enrolled in courses offered through VIC at sites beyond the central campuses of Bloomington and Indianapolis. Courses are placed in a

Table 8.5
Sample Hands-On Exercise with Video Cameras

Select among cameras #1, #2, and #3 at local and remote sites, using the control tablet (see Figure 8.1).

- Ensure that the control tablet is on by pressing the tablet one icon at the lower right with the electronic pen. If there is no response, you can assume it is off. Simply press the icon again and you will know it is on.
- Select local camera #1.
- Select remote camera #1 and repeat the exercise.
- Switch back to local camera #1.
- Select local camera #2.
- Select remote camera #2.
- Switch back to local camera #1.
- Frame and focus camera #1 using control tablet features: move (tilt and pan), zoom, iris, focus.
- Make sure local camera #1 is selected.
- Tilt up and tilt down with the up and down move arrows.
- Pan right and pan left with the right and left move arrows. Note the result on the monitor to be certain the movement is what you desire.
- Zoom in and zoom out. Which views, long or close-up, seem best for showing you and/or your students on the monitor?
- Open the iris and close it. How much brightness is necessary?
- Try this: make a name tent from a folded index card with letters printed about two inches high. All students should have such identification cards. Move the camera to focus on one name and one student. Can the student's name be easily read by students at other sites? Position, frame, and focus graphics on the document camera.
- Switch to camera #2 or #3, whichever is linked to the document camera.
- Check to be certain the power switch for the document camera is turned on.
- Using the controls on the document camera's base, zoom in, zoom out, and focus.
- Experiment with positioning different visuals, including illustrations from books, under the document camera.
- Experiment with reception of different colors.
- Ask students at other sites how well the visuals are being received.
- Consider how a chain of visuals might be presented: size of the visual and the font chosen may affect how much must be adjusted from one visual to the next; consider advantages of recording these visuals through more advanced practice with the table and document camera.
- Note that printed messages work best over the document camera when they
    are arranged in landscape orientation (wider than tall) same as the standard monitor screen, rather than in portrait orientation.
    are composed of only a few lines and concepts; usually no more than three lines in 36-point type with a space between lines.
    are in a sans serif font such as Arial, Verdana, Helvetica, or Geneva.
    include little or no use of italic and underlines, although some use of bold will help with emphasis.
    are on a light blue paper to reduce glare with black print.
    avoid low-contrast colors such as blue on green or orange on yellow.
    are supported by handouts if contents include a great deal of data displayed in charts or tables.

Figure 8.1
Sample Control Tablet

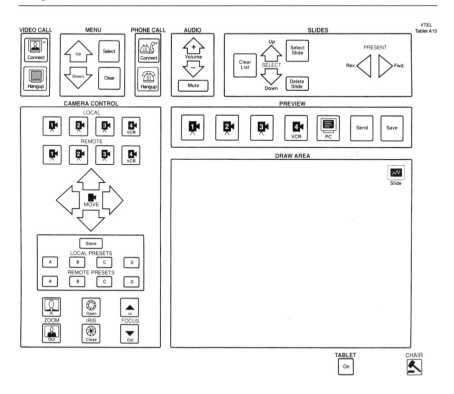

long-range schedule providing for up to a two-year advance notice of offerings. In addition, to accommodate the nearly universal student characteristic as a full-time employee in a library system or public school, courses are offered during later afternoon, evening, and weekend hours.

Courses are also offered during summer months as well as the regular academic year. Class meetings are usually for a three-hour block, once a week for fifteen weeks. However, some experimentation has been successful in offering the management class in a weekend series with classes in session for several three-hour blocks over three or four weekends. Two courses in the school media track are offered annually on Saturday mornings from 9 A.M. to 12:30 P.M. and meet on a twelve-week schedule along with two weeks at field locations to visit exemplary school facilities.

Table 8.6
Student Protocol for Audio Communication

- Keep the control tablet (see Figure 8.1) on mute until you need to ask a question or participate in a discussion across the system.
- If you can't see or hear what is being transmitted, raise your hand and wave or raise your hand holding a bright-colored paper to gain the instructor's attention. If you can't be seen, call out the instructor's name and use your name and location to introduce the need for assistance.
- Use time identified by the instructor for advisement and other questions outside of the content of the specific class. Usually these questions can be raised during break or during time allotted after class.
- Don't be afraid to communicate or appear in front of the camera. The more you get involved, the easier interaction becomes.
- Speak in a normal voice. You shouldn't have to reposition or pick up the microphone.
- Keep table noise to a minimum. Rustling of paper, jingling of keys or bracelets, and other extraneous noise can be picked up and cause both visual and aural disturbance.
- Don't hesitate to ask for repetition if you missed something important.
- Introduce yourself with your first name and location prior to offering a comment, as this allows students at other sites to learn who you are.
- If the audio fails, do one of the following:
    write your concern on the wall-mounted board and maneuver a camera to show the written message.
    write the message on a sheet of paper and place it under the document camera, then switch to the document camera to display the message.
    use the class telephone to call the instructor's site.
    if available, use fax to send a written message to the instructor's site.
- Attention can usually be gained by having the local camera focus on you in close-up and then opening the local microphone by turning off Mute; the instructor may request that you wait a few moments to add your comment or question but will be aware of your need to communicate.

STUDIES OF TWO-WAY VIDEO AT IU SLIS

Four courses from the IU SLIS distance education schedule have been used as subjects in recent studies and evaluations at Indiana University. Results and conclusions from these studies are still being compiled, but three specific efforts provide some insight as to the issues and techniques related to the use of the VIC Network to deliver quality graduate education in library and information science.

Issues of Self-Efficacy

Research on student satisfaction in distance education has examined factors such as the need for control, learning styles, perception of social presence, and levels of interaction. One researcher suggests that adult learners' characteristic need for autonomy means that to be satisfying, a learning situation must allow students to control the balance between independence, competence, and support in the learning transaction between instructor and students (Baynton, 1992). Others believe that social factors also influence student satisfaction in distance education. Social presence, the degree to which an individual is perceived or experienced as a "real" person, is a significant factor in instructional effectiveness and student satisfaction. An instructor's ability to create a high level of social presence is related to increased satisfaction with both the instructor and the course (Gunawardena, 1994). Satisfaction may also be related to levels of personal and overall interaction (Fulford and Zhang, 1993; Chandler and Hanrahan, 2000; Machtmes and Asher, 2000; Simonson, 2000).

Research data indicate that student attitudes toward technology often evolve as student familiarity with the technology increases. Students new to a particular technology may initially exhibit some concern about the role of technology in the learning experience. If this occurs, these students typically demonstrate a reluctance to actively participate in the distance classroom (Barron, 1987; Smith and McNelis, 1993). Student attitudes toward distance learning are frequently affected by the teaching methods used. Research suggests that teachers who know how to make the most of the available technology are judged as more successful than those who approach technology as an add-on to a traditional class. Students prefer engaging in small group discussion or interactive question and answer sessions to viewing lectures (Bland, Morrison, and Ross, 1992).

Julie Reinhart of Indiana University and Paul Schneider of the University of Illinois surveyed 222 students in two-way audio/video distance classes in 1997 and presented their findings at conferences in 1998. Forty percent of the students were graduate students in courses offered over distance education by the Indiana University SLIS. Reinhart and Schneider attempted to measure a relationship between students' perceptions of the two-way audio/video distance classroom and their perceptions of self-efficacy, where self-efficacy is defined as self-assessment of one's ability to be successful in a two-way audio/video classroom.

For most people, two-way audio/video distance education environments are new experiences. New experiences by nature can provoke anxiety. The coupling of a new experience with new technology provides an even greater potential for increased anxiety. Support for two-way audio/video's ability to provide a medium that is equivalent to face-to-face in terms of interaction has also been supported by findings in communications research. When examining interactions between people over two-way audio/video versus face-to-face situations, researchers in this area found that people tend to communicate equally well in either situation (Sellen, 1995).

Reinhart and Schneider (1998) reported that they found a significant positive relationship between students' perception of environmental aspects (physical elements, layout, and management of the distance learning experience) and students' anxiety level and their satisfaction with the learning experience. Furthermore, students' perception of the physical elements in the environment and the management of the distance learning experience explain a significant portion of the variance of their anxiety. The team concluded that at the very least designers should consider students' perceptions of environmental elements and their relationship to students' self-efficacy when designing a two-way audio/video classroom.

Interaction and Learning Community

In the mid-1950s, Ned A. Flanders pioneered research in the observation and charting of interaction in the classroom (1965). Flanders established ten categories for sorting interactions. Seven were assigned to teacher talk, two to student talk, and a tenth to classify pauses, short periods of silence and talk that is confusing and noisy. His work has established samples of several matrices, which may be used to plot frequencies of instructional and noninstructional interactions. Similar techniques have been applied to interactions observed over two-way video distance education (Murphy, 1995; Jurewicz and Callison, 1999). Findings include:

- there is no significant difference in frequency and type interactions between two-way audio/video telecourses and traditional face-to-face courses.
- student talk, teacher talk, cognitive talk, and noncognitive talk did not differ greatly between the two instructional modes.
- students at remote sites in two-way audio/video, however, were more likely to engage in requests and conversations that were not cognitively linked to the course content than students located at the originating site.

Murphy found that student talk occupied about 10 percent of classroom time, and 60 percent of that was cognitive talk or related to class content with the balance concerning small talk and general questions not related to the instruction tasks of the day. Additional items of interest from Murphy's study include:

- the average percentage of statements from instructors that could be classified as giving praise or encouragement to students was 1.7 percent, under the 3 to 10 percent normally found in traditional face-to-face instruction; and
- the average percentage of communication from instructors in the form of a question was 4.1 percent, within the lower range of the 3 to 12 percent reported in studies of face-to-face instruction.

Edward J. Jurewicz plotted instructor and student interaction in two of the two-way audio/video distance education offerings from IU SLIS and compared his observations to those previously recorded concerning the one-way video medium for the same classes. He concluded that:

- movement to compressed video resulted in less instructional formality;
- less formality allowed for a greater range of student and teacher input;
- student control of media resulted in increased involvement;
- increased involvement resulted in increased sharing of knowledge and experiences.

Jurewicz and Callison (1999) contend that the presence of the instructor at a given site is a factor that affects the interaction of students during on-air discussions. Reactions of students at remote sites seem to remain similar, and students will increase their on-task participation when the instructor is present at their respective site. Thus the instructor needs to be sensitive to the communication needs of remote site groups regardless of his or her location for originating the class.

The Jurewicz observations were also supported by the off-air interactions represented on the class online discussions. Content analysis of these e-mail interactions indicated frequent on-task communication connected to class discussions in two-way audio/video. Discussions were enhanced with the addition of field experts and classroom speakers added to the class e-mail list. It was evident that there was a dramatic increase in the frequency of student talk founded on interviews with field experts and that these comments were offered more frequently as the course progressed both in class discussions and in e-mail messages during the rest of the week. Jurewicz further concluded that a fifth type of interaction could be identified based on inclusion of several field experts and the expectation that students gather and share information based on field interviews. The four established types of interaction include:

- learner–content interaction
- learner–instructor interaction
- learner–learner interaction
- learner–interface interaction

Jurewicz contends "learner–learner community interaction" has evolved because of the geographic separation of the members of the classes, and yet they come together in class and over a common online discussion on a frequent basis. Thus the interaction stems from a community of learners as they exchange ideas on issues and gain from interaction with a professional community willing to be interviewed at their schools or libraries and to monitor electronic discussions.

Professional Development

The Indiana University School of Continuing Studies and the Faculty Colloquium on Excellence in Teaching (FACET) have collaborated on a mission of enhancing excellence in teaching by analyzing and assessing the role and impact of technology in the classroom (Wertheim, Bender, and Fraenkel, 1999). Specifically, this effort has involved a three-year project concerning observation of teaching techniques in the use of distance education delivery. The goals for the Closing the Distance project have been to:

1. Refine traditional teaching methods
2. Introduce innovative methods of teaching and learning
3. Define how such methods can be used to improve the sharing of information and ideas
4. Explore new approaches to improve teaching and learning
5. Encourage communication and collaboration among colleagues representing eight campuses university-wide.

Three IU SLIS courses from the certification program offered over two-way video were observed and documented by senior faculty members selected by FACET for their leadership in instructional and academic expertise (Gray, 2001). Two of the authors, Fitzgibbons and Callison, participated in the FACET project. Fitzgibbons also was a faculty participant in a second professional development project, the Alliance for Continuing Professional Education. She, along with two other SLIS faculty members, attended an intensive one-week interactive distance education workshop. A management plan, along with student evaluations, was required for completion of the professional development projects. In both projects, the help with technology training, the small stipends for enhancing course planning, and the intensive evaluation efforts—both formative and summative—provided extensive professional development that is not usually available to faculty. The change to a distance education format for several courses necessitated an enormous amount of time, energy, and anxiety. The professional development opportunities created by the university-funded projects turned a burden into a new challenge.

One innovation that several of the SLIS faculty implemented was the faculty member moving among each of the distance education sites, meeting students individually as well as face to face in the classroom. Students have an initial fear of the technology and feel isolated with the loss of weekly face-to-face contact both in the classroom and individually. However, as they learn to control the technology, and become a part of the teaching process, they become more comfortable and some even forget "seeing themselves on TV." Through the on-site visits by the instructor, some of the discomfort is alleviated. Students on the main campus, who have moved to that campus to receive a full-time educational experience, seem to become the group least comfortable with the new learning experience and may resent a greater "sharing" of the faculty with students at remote sites. Students at the main campus, however, are often inexperienced in the library profession, and they may not realize that many students at remote sites have valuable professional expertise to share. As the semester progresses, main campus students grow to appreciate the insights offered by their more experienced classmates. In course evaluations, three-fourths of the student respondents strongly agreed that interaction with other students in the course was important. Over 90 percent greatly appreciated the fact that the instructor had been available for consultation and responsive to their needs on a personal basis.

Moving into any new mode of teaching without being fully prepared and sharing this preparation and orientation with students is risky. With the help of similar professional development activities on campus or as part of professional conferences, a faculty member can feel more fully prepared. Those entering this teaching mode should consider preparing themselves by observing an experienced distance education teacher several times and discuss issues with that teacher as well as attend the growing number of distance education training opportunities now offered both locally and regionally through universities.

REFERENCES

Barron, D. 1987. "Faculty and Student Perceptions of Distance Education Using Television." *Journal of Education for Library and Information Science,* 27:4. 257–271.

Baynton, M. 1992. "Dimensions of Control in Distance Education: A factor analysis." *American Journal of Distance Education,* 6:2. 16–31.

Bland, K. P., G. R. Morrison, and S. M. Ross. 1992. Student Attitudes Toward Learning Link: A distance education project. ERIC Document ED 356 766.

Boone, M. E. 1984. "Examining Excellence: An analysis of facilitator behaviors in actual audio teleconferences." In L. Parker and C. Olgren, eds., *Teleconferencing and Electronic Communications* 111. Madison, WI: University of Wisconsin, pp. 218–222.

Chandler, G., and P. Hanrahan. 2000. "Teaching Using Interactive Video: Creating Connections." *Journal of Nursing Education,* 39:2. 73–80.

Cronin, B. 1997. *Distributed Education and Indiana University: Strategic Pathways and Windows of Opportunity.* Bloomington, IN. Final Report of the President's Advisory Committee on Distance Education. Indiana University.

Flanders, N. A. 1965. *Interaction Analysis in the Classroom.* Ann Arbor, MI: The University of Michigan, School of Education.

Franklin, N., M. Yoakam, and R. Warren. 1995. *Distance Learning: A guide to system planning and implementation.* Bloomington, IN: Indiana University School of Continuing Studies. Available online at www.indiana.edu/-iudisted/diresources/dlprimer.html.

Fulford, C. P., and S. Zhang. 1993. "Perceptions and Interaction: The critical predictor in distance education." *American Journal of Distance Education,* 7:3. 8–21.

Gray, D. 2001. *Advancing Learning, Closing the Distance: Evaluation of Distance Education Course L551 Information Inquiry for School Teachers.* Bloomington, IN. Faculty Colloquim on Excellence in Teaching and the School of Continuing Studies. Available online at www.indiana.edu/~iude/casebook/callison.htm.

Gunawardena, C. N. 1994. "Social Presence Theory and Implications for Interaction and Communication in Telecommunications-Based Distance Education." In *Proceedings of the Distance Learning Conference*. College Station, TX: Texas A&M University, Department of Educational Human Resource Development, pp. 119–127.

Jurewicz, E. J., and D. Callison. 1999. Interaction in Distance Education. Paper for the Indiana Partnership in State Education Conference, Ball State University, October 25.

Machtmes, K., and W. J. Asher. 2000. "A Meta-Analysis of the Effectiveness of Tele-courses in Distance Education." *American Journal of Distance Education*, 14:1. 27–46.

McMann, G. W. 1994. "The Changing Role of Moderation in Computer Mediated Conferencing." In *Proceedings of the Distance Learning Research Conference*. College Station, TX: Texas A&M University and the Department of Educational Human Resource Development, pp. 159–166.

Murphy, T. 1995. *A Quantitative Analysis of Instructor-Student Verbal Interaction in a Simultaneous Two-Way Audio-Video Distance Education Setting*. Doctoral dissertation. Texas A&M University.

Paulet, R. O. 1988. "Factors Influencing Successful Counseling in Selected Distance Education Programs." *Journal of Research and Development in Education*, 21:3. 60–64.

Plater, W. 2002. IUPUI Online: A Concept Paper. Indianapolis, IN. Dean of the Faculties Office, Indiana University Purdue University Indianapolis.

Reinhart, J., and P. Schneider. 1998. Foundations for Creative Effective Two-Way Audio/Video Distance Education Environments: Issues of self-efficacy. ERIC Document ED 421 504. Paper presented at the Annual Meeting of the American Educational Research Association, San Diego, CA, April 13–17, 1998.

Sellen, A. J. 1995. "Remote Conversations: The effects of mediating talk with technology." *Human-Computer Interaction*, 10. 401–444.

Simonson, M. 2000. "Myths and Distance Education: What the Research Says and Does Not Say." *Quarterly Review on Distance Education*, 1:4. 277–279.

Smith, D. L., and M. J. McNelis. 1993. Distance Education: Graduate student attitudes and academic performance. ERIC Document ED 345 716.

Wertheim, J., E. Bender, and K. L. Fraenkel. 1999. *Closing the Distance Casebook*. Bloomington, IN: Indiana University, School of Continuing Studies.

Yoakam, M., N. Franklin, and R. Warren. 2001. *Distance Learning: A Guide to System Planning and Implementation*. Bloomington, IN: Indiana University School of Continuing Studies. Available online at www.indiana.edu/~iude/dltoc.html.

Zepp, D. 2000. "Distance Education in Library and Information Science Education: Trends and Issues." Master of Library and Information Science research paper. Kent State University.

TELECONFERENCING AND DISTANCE EDUCATION GLOSSARY

Analog vs. digital. The terms *analog* and *digital* refer to the way information is stored electronically. Analog representation is a continuous waveform that varies by time and intensity, whereas digital representation codes everything into a binary language of ones and zeros. Today's distance learning technology is a mix of analog and digital technologies. Telephone and video technologies have traditionally been analog, whereas computer technology has been digital. However, the convergence of these technologies will eventually lead to all-digital technology. Telecommunications are still a mix of analog and digital signaling, but they will continue to upgrade to all-digital facilities. The challenge is to strike a balance between what exists today and what will exist in the digital future.

Asynchronous. Communication between a sender and a receiver that does not happen in real time.

Audiographics. Audiographics combines the telephone for vocal interactions and computer-based visual materials accessible via dial-up networking or the Internet. Sessions are held in real time, connecting people to multiple sites via conference bridge technology.

Bridge. A device, often leased through a phone company, that links three or more telephone lines together for audio teleconferencing.

Codec or compression decomposition. An electronic device that converts standard TV signals into compressed digital signals for transmission. The same device can convert incoming compressed digital signals back into viewable TV signals. A codec allows motion images to be transmitted through special telephone lines.

Compressed video. System by which a vast amount of information contained in a TV picture and its accompanying audio signal is squeezed or compressed into a fraction of its former bandwidth and sent onto a smaller carrier, with some information sacrificed in transmission, resulting in some diminishing of color, clarity, and some "ragged" motion. It can be delivered over land lines or broadcast satellite but results in many more signals being sent more economically. The compression ratio of 234:1 can make a matchable picture deliverable at 384 kilobytes per second, which is 0.043 percent of the original information in the signal.

Collaborative groupware. The term *groupware* describes applications that provide an electronic work space for collaborative work and sharing of ideas. Groupware can store, sort, and organize learners' and instructors' input, as well as support such group processes as idea generation, evaluation, and consensus building.

Compression. Digital signal processing techniques that are used to reduce the amount of information in a video signal. This allows the video signal to be sent through telephone data lines.

Convergence. Although the telephone, computer, and video industries have traditionally been separate, today's changing technologies are blurring the distinctions among them. Their common denominator, digital information, makes it possible for phone networks to deliver video and computer services and for cable companies to deliver phone service. Computers that handle all these applications are on the market.

Demodulation. Process of converting analog signals sent over a telephone line into digital form so that they can be processed by a receiving computer, or in telecommunications, where digital signals can be processed by an analog television receiver.

Distance learning. The process of connecting learners to remote educational resources. Distance learning uses such communication technologies as teleconferencing, videoconferencing, satellite broadcast, and computer-based training (including CD-ROMs and the Internet) to enhance an organization's instructional strategies and to allow the strategies to reach a broader audience with more flexibility.

Duplex, full. A communications system, circuit, or component capable of transmitting in both directions simultaneously.

Duplex, half. A communications system, circuit, or component capable of transmitting in two directions alternatively, not simultaneously.

E-mail. E-mail (electronic mail) allows learners and instructors to communicate across time and space by sending typed messages over local/global computer networks. Many e-mail systems allow users to attach documents to their messages, thus providing a way to distribute instructional materials. Group messaging strategies—such as distribution lists, electronic bulletin boards, and online discussion lists—allow mass mailing strategies.

E-mail discussion list. An electronic mailing list maintained by a specialized software program that allows subscribers to share ideas, generally on a particular topic, with everyone on the list. Can be managed by the instructor and used as an enhancement for continued discussion of issues outside of class, allowing students to elaborate on ideas for which there was not time in class.

Graphics tablet. A computer device that converts hand-drawn images into digital information that can be displayed on computer screens.

Interaction. The level of learner–instructor interaction provided by distance learning systems varies. Correspondence courses allow one level of interaction, satellite programs another, and interactive TV yet another. Interaction does not always take place in real time. Voice mail and e-mail are good examples of interaction outside of real time.

Interactive video. The transmission of video and audio signals between two or more sites so that students at remote locations can interact orally and visually with their instructor and each other.

Interactive Voice Response Systems (IVRS). IVRS are telephone systems that allow learners to retrieve and store information held on a data network via a touch-tone telephone from anywhere in the world in real time. Learners may request instructional and administrative materials to be sent by e-mail or fax.

MUD, MOO, MAUD. Internet-based conferencing tools that provide users with Internet spaces to access, objects to act upon in the spaces, and opportunities to converse with other users visiting the spaces. Stands for Multi-User Domain, MUD Object Oriented, and Multi-Academic User Domain.

One-way video. The transmission of video signals in one direction, generally from an instructor's site to one or more distance sites. Common methods of delivering one-way video include videotape distribution, broadcast over TV or cable, satellite transmission, or streaming video over the Internet.

Point-to-point and multipoint connections. As the names imply, point-to-point connections involve interaction between two locations and multipoint connections provide interaction among three or more locations. The two terms describe all types of conferencing such as audio, computer, and video. Multipoint connections are created using a bridge in audio systems or a multipoint control unit (MCU) in video systems. Multipoint services can be obtained commercially, or the technology can be installed as part of a distance learning system.

Resolution. The clarity of the image on a video display screen. Three factors influence resolution: lines of resolution, vertical and horizontal; scan rate, or the number of times per second the image on a video screen can be refreshed or lit up again; and bandwidth.

Simplex. A communication system, circuit, or device capable of transmission in one direction only.

Synchronous. Communication between a sender and a receiver that occurs in real time.

T1 line. A special type of telephone line that transmits digital information at a high rate.

T3 line. A telephone line that is capable of transmitting digital information at rates even higher than those of a T1 line.

Two-way interactive video. Two-way interactive video allows video and audio communication in both directions between (and among) learners and instructors. All sites in a two-way system are equipped with cameras, monitors, and microphones. Increasingly, each site will also have a document camera and computer to allow live sharing of illustrations, outlines, and Web sites. The sites are linked by point-to-point (two sites) or multipoint (more than two sites) connections so that learners and instructors can see and hear each other. These connections use various communication circuits that deliver varying levels of picture and sound quality.

Web board. An electronic discussion managed over the Internet allowing for posting and sorting or categorizing of participant input. May be used to continue group discussions as well as link to special visuals, charts, or articles students may add or link to on the Internet as a portion of their supporting resources.

Definitions are based on information from the following resources:

Barron, Ann E., and Gary W. Orwig. *New Technologies for Education: A beginner's guide*. Englewood, CO: Libraries Unlimited, 1997.

Franklin, Nancy, Michael Yoakam, and Ron Warren. *Distance Learning: A guide to system planning and implementation*. Bloomington, IN: Indiana University School of Continuing Studies, 1995.

Patton-Bennington, Elaine. "Glossary of Distance Education Terms." Indiana Higher Education Television System. 1998. Available online at www.inets.org/distance-ed/ipse/disted.html.

Yoakam, Michael, Nancy Franklin, and Ron Warren. *Distance Learning: A Guide to System Planning and Implementations*. Bloomington, IN: Indiana University School of Continuing Studies. 2001. Available online at www.indiana.edu/~iude/dltoc.html.

ACKNOWLEDGMENT

Several faculty members from Indiana University reviewed this chapter. Elin Jacob, Holly Crawford, and Tom Nisonger, who have also taught classes over VIC, provided insightful feedback. Carol Tilley and Catherine Collins, doctoral students who have taught for IU over the VIC system, helped shape the content of this chapter.

9

———◆•◆———

OHIOLEARN: DISTRIBUTED EDUCATION IN LIBRARY AND INFORMATION SCIENCE AT KENT STATE UNIVERSITY

Danny P. Wallace and Connie Van Fleet

THE CLIMATE FOR LIBRARY EDUCATION AND TRAINING IN OHIO

Ohio is a particularly library-rich state. The state's public libraries are among the best funded in the United States. The OHIOLINK system, which provides network services to all the state's public universities and many privately supported institutions of higher education, is a model for resource sharing. The Ohio Public Library Information Network (OPLIN) provides network services to every branch of every public library system. INFOhio extends network services to the state's elementary and secondary school library media centers. Regional library systems provide essential resources and services to specific geographic subareas of the state. The State Library of Ohio plays a fundamental leadership role and administers state and local funding opportunities. Membership associations—such as the Ohio Library Council, the Academic Library Association of Ohio, and the Ohio Education/Library Media Association—serve as a focus for professional interaction. Each of these agencies plays a role in education and training for library workers. An abundance of learning experiences is provided to employees of the state's libraries, from hands-on technical training for support staff to postprofessional continuing education for seasoned professionals.

A BRIEF HISTORY OF THE KENT STATE UNIVERSITY SCHOOL OF LIBRARY AND INFORMATION SCIENCE

Undergraduate education in library science was first offered at Kent State University in 1946. The Department of Library Science, academically part of the College of Education, was functionally attached to the University Library, with the university librarian as department chair. The department operated from space in the University Library. By 1949, a decision had been made to move the program to the graduate level, and a master of arts degree was authorized. The first eight graduates completed the master's program in 1950.

The program grew slowly during the 1950s. The master's program was first accredited by the ALA in 1963, becoming the thirty-third accredited master's degree program. By 1966, the Department of Library Science had become the School of Library Science, headed by a dean rather than a chairperson.

Program growth during the late 1960s led to a significant space crunch, which was eventually solved, at least temporarily, by moving the school to a newly constructed main library building. That move, scheduled for sometime in 1970, was delayed by the event for which Kent State University is best known to most people—the May 4, 1970, incident in which four people were killed by armed National Guardsmen on the university's Blanket Hill. Following the closing of the campus, students and faculty continued to meet in an "underground university" environment, but enrollment in the university as a whole suffered thereafter, and the school was not unaffected.

By 1971, enrollment in the school had again begun to increase, and growth continued throughout the 1970s. A slight decline in enrollment during the very early 1980s was countered by rapid growth during the remainder of the decade. Between 1982 and 1992, headcount enrollment increased by 250 percent, with more than 500 students enrolled by 1992; fall 1999 enrollment was 550 master's students, the largest in the school's history. By 1989, the school had the highest enrollment among ALA-accredited master's programs, a status it retained until surpassed by San Jose State University in 1997. The decade of the 1980s had, however, seen a major shift from full-time to part-time students that continues to characterize the school.

THE BEGINNINGS OF DISTANCE AND DISTRIBUTED LEARNING

During the first quarter century of its history, enrollment in the Kent State University School of Library Science was confined to students who could study at the school's facility in northeast Ohio. In 1975, after Ohio universities were authorized by the Ohio Board of Regents to offer courses away from their home campuses, the school began to offer courses in the Cleveland and Columbus metropolitan areas. Cleveland courses were and are offered at the rate of one or two per semester and relieve residents of Cuyahoga County, the county where the greatest number of students actually resides, of the approximately one-hour commute to Kent.

The Columbus program, originally designed to provide a limited number of extension courses in central Ohio, eventually became a site at which students could complete a somewhat limited version of the full master's degree program. By 1996, the Columbus campus, housed in space leased from the Ohio State University, was home to 3 full-time faculty, 1 full-time systems specialist, 1 half-time clerical staff member, and approximately 140 graduate students. During the early 1980s, an instructional program was initiated in the Dayton area to serve as a "feeder" for the Columbus program. This program failed after less than two years.

In 1996, in response to expressions of interest and support from the dean of Libraries and Learning Resources at Bowling Green State University and other members of the professional community in northwest Ohio, the school launched the Northwest Ohio Project, later renamed the Northwest Ohio Program, offering courses on the campus of Bowling Green State University. This program initially operated as a traditional extension program, with courses taught by Kent- or Columbus-based regular faculty or by adjunct faculty members recruited from northwest Ohio. The Northwest Ohio Program was designed to make it possible for students to complete the MLS program's four required core courses and a carefully selected set of electives in Bowling Green. Northwest Ohio Program students must travel to Kent and/or Columbus to complete a substantial portion of the program; the need to enroll in Kent or Columbus depends in large part on the student's chosen area of specialization. Since 1996, more than fifty students have enrolled in courses offered as part of the Northwest Ohio Program.

The immediate success of the Northwest Ohio Program was coupled with expressions of interest from other institutions. In his fall 1997 State of the University address, the president of Ohio University suggested that an initiative would be undertaken to create a library and information science program at that institution. Although this was actually a misstatement, it led to an extended dialog of possible interinstitutional collaboration involving the provost's office, chief information officer, and library administration at Ohio University and the dean of the College of Fine and Professional Arts and director of the School of Library and Information Science at Kent State University. During the same time frame, a discussion of the potential for collaboration began involving the director of the school and the dean of Libraries at the University of Cincinnati. These transactions led to "A Statewide Vision for Library and Information Science Education for Ohio," which was approved by the faculty of the School of Library and Information Science in February 1997. This was the first of several discussion and planning documents that eventually led to the OhioLEARN Infrastructure Project.

THE BEGINNINGS OF TRUE DISTANCE AND DISTRIBUTED LEARNING

In 1997, Bowling Green State University Dean of Libraries and Learning Resources Linda S. Dobb and School of Library and Information Science

Director Danny P. Wallace wrote a proposal for the Ohio Board of Regents Technology Initiative grant program to support acquisition of a digital video-conferencing system to be housed at the school. This system was to be connected to a compatible system in Bowling Green State University's Jerome Library to provide a mechanism for delivering courses at a distance. The grant was funded; this success was a major step toward what became the OhioLEARN Infrastructure Project. A distributed learning classroom was installed at the Kent campus, in space provided by Kent State University's Library and Media Services, during 1998. Plans to offer a distributed learning course in the fall semester of 1998 were derailed by delays in installation of the equipment. The school's first distributed learning course, taught by Richard Rubin, was offered to students in Kent and Bowling Green in spring 1999.

THE OHIOLEARN INFRASTRUCTURE PROJECT

Building on the success of the Ohio Board of Regents Technology Initiative grant and grounded in the series of planning documents that had been developed, in 1998 Wallace wrote a Library Services and Technology Act (LSTA) grant proposal to support the OhioLEARN Infrastructure Project. This proposal was based in part on a plan developed by Wallace, Connie Van Fleet, and Assistant to the Director Julie A. Gedeon for OhioLEARN, the Ohio Libraries Education, Access, and Resource Network (the original working plan is reproduced as an appendix to this chapter). OhioLEARN was originally developed as a model for multilevel education and training for library and information science in the state of Ohio. An adjunct to the OhioLEARN model was a proposed structure for a "focused MLS program" designed to be delivered through distributed learning technology.

The OhioLEARN Infrastructure Project, a $339,000 initiative funded by LSTA via the State Library of Ohio, is an effort to provide a core platform for shared library education and training in the state of Ohio. The major partners in the project are the Kent State University School of Library and Information Science; Kent State University Libraries and Media Services; OHIOLINK, the statewide network for college and university libraries; Bowling Green State University; the University of Cincinnati; Ohio University; OPLIN, serving Ohio's public libraries; and INFOhio, the state's network for school library media centers. In addition to grant support from LSTA, the OhioLEARN Infrastructure Project has received financial support from the School of Library and Information Science, OHIOLINK, Bowling Green State University, the University of Cincinnati, and Ohio University. OHIOLINK, by purchasing its own videoconferencing equipment, contributed most of the required 25 percent matching funds for the LSTA grant. OPLIN and INFOhio are primarily contributors of content.

OHIOLEARN GOALS

As the original working plan notes:

OhioLEARN is envisioned as a long-term project involving the greatest possible representation and involvement of the Ohio library community. The goals of the project are clearly too comprehensive to be met by any one agency or institution. The Kent State University School of Library and Information Science, as the only agency in the state charged exclusively with the education of library and information professionals, will play a central role in the development of the programs proposed by the model. Some aspects of the model, such as professional-level education leading to an accredited master's degree, are obviously the province of the School. Other aspects, such as preprofessional and postprofessional education and training, may be achieved through a wider variety of experiences. Success in achieving program goals will require participation by the State Library of Ohio, the state's professional associations, statewide library networks, regional consortia, and individual libraries.

OhioLEARN Infrastructure Project Sites

OHIOLEARN OBJECTIVES

The OhioLEARN Infrastructure Project seeks to build the basic platform from which geographic barriers to education and training can be overcome, diverse agencies can collaboratively deliver education and training experiences, and new technology can be used to support a broad-based library and information science education and training program. Specific objectives of the Infrastructure Project include:

1. Acquisition, installation, and implementation of the hardware, software, and telecommunications links necessary to support a videoconferencing network linking five geographically diverse sites.

2. Design, development, and implementation of a coordinated, collaborative education and training program consistent with statewide needs and the goals and objectives of participating agencies.

3. Design, development, and delivery via the teleconferencing network of education and training experiences consistent with statewide needs and the goals and objectives of participating agencies.

The first of these goals has been achieved via the LSTA grant and contributions from the project's partner institutions. The second and third objectives are ongoing targets that have been met in part by the OhioLEARN MLS Program.

OHIOLEARN PRIORITIES

A fundamental aspect of the OhioLEARN Infrastructure Project is its dedication to education and training for library and information science. OhioLEARN is a network of library and information agencies, not one of academic institutions. The digital videoconferencing systems acquired with LSTA funding were deliberately located in the main libraries of the three partner universities—Jerome Library at Bowling Green State University, Langsam Library at the University of Cincinnati, and Alden Library at Ohio University. Planning for the project was carried out primarily through interaction between Wallace and library administrators at the three universities— Linda Dobb, dean of Libraries and Learning Resources at Bowling Green State University (as of this writing, Dobb is interim provost at Bowling Green State University); David F. Kohl, dean of Libraries at the University of Cincinnati; Hwa-Wei Lee, dean of University Libraries (retired in 1999) and Gary Hunt, associate dean of University Libraries at Ohio University; and Tom Sanville, executive director of OHIOLINK.

The focus on LIS education and training is reflected in the priorities for use of the network agreed on by the four university partners. The digital videoconferencing facilities funded by the OhioLEARN Infrastructure Project are to be used in the following priority order:

1. Networked, collaborative library education and training, including but not restricted to the OhioLEARN MLS program. It is anticipated that, in addition to the programs of the School of Library and Information Science, agencies (such as OHIOLINK) and state associations (such as the Ohio Library Council) will use the network to distribute training opportunities throughout the state.

2. Other networked, collaborative uses linking libraries and information agencies, such as meetings of committees of the state's library networks or professional associations. The ability to conduct committee meetings and related events in a dis-

tributed manner is a major focus of OHIOLINK's interest in the network; it can be expected that other state library and information agencies will follow OHIOLINK's lead.

3. Other needs of the partner libraries, such as conducting staff meetings and training sessions linking branch campuses. Each of the partner institutions operates at multiple sites. Ohio University, for instance, operates five regional campuses in addition to the main campus in Athens. The regional campuses are distributed throughout the geographically challenging Appalachian section of Ohio, and the greatest distance between campuses is less than 200 miles.

4. Uses by the host university for purposes that do not relate to libraries, such as delivery of learning experiences in other academic areas.

THE OHIOLEARN MLS PROGRAM

The OhioLEARN MLS Program is a specialized version of the Kent State University MLS program designed for delivery via the OhioLEARN digital videoconferencing network. The OhioLEARN MLS Program makes it possible for students in southeast Ohio (at the Athens campus of Ohio University), southwest Ohio (at the University of Cincinnati), northwest Ohio (at Bowling Green State University), and northeast Ohio (at Kent State University) to complete a structured version of the school's ALA-accredited master's degree program. A Columbus section of the OhioLEARN MLS Program was canceled as a result of technical limitations and administrative concerns.

A fundamental aspect of the OhioLEARN MLS Program is the provision of nearly all of the degree program at the remote sites. The program is highly structured, with thirty of the thirty-six semester hours required for the degree prearranged. The remaining six semester hours can be completed through a combination of School of Library and Information Science courses and credit workshops, graduate course credit transferred from another university, or completion of Individual Investigation (independent study) or practicum experiences. The need to travel to Kent or Columbus was by design limited to a two-day, one-semester-hour experience in Kent.

Thirty-eight students entered the OhioLEARN MLS program in fall 1999. Students successfully continued throughout the program and graduated in December 2001. OhioLEARN MLS students attended a one-semester-hour workshop in Kent during late August 1999. This workshop was designed to provide an orientation to the OhioLEARN MLS program, familiarize students with the basic principles and structures of the library and information professions, introduce students to the literature of library and information science, provide a basic understanding of distributed and distance learning, and foster a team/cohort group commitment to the OhioLEARN MLS experience. An unanticipated outcome of the workshop is a concerted expression of desire to repeat the experience the following year.

THE OHIOLEARN MLS TEAM

In fall 1998, Van Fleet drafted a proposal for special university funding to support a team approach to developing the first four courses to be taught as part of the OhioLEARN MLS Program. This proposal was approved and funded by the provost's office. During summer 1999, the OhioLEARN MLS Team, consisting of Bill Caynon, Mary Stansbury, Van Fleet, and Don A. Wicks, worked to address structural, curricular, and instructional issues, such as training in the use of the digital videoconferencing equipment, handling of library reserve materials and textbooks, on-site student orientations, and teaching techniques. The efforts of the team resulted in production of a manual of policies, procedures, and tips for teaching in the distributed learning environment. The team's work was augmented by a one-day workshop taught by an experienced trainer/facilitator.

IMPLEMENTATION AND THE FUTURE

The OhioLEARN MLS Program and the OhioLEARN collaborative network were celebrated with a September 1999 virtual ribbon cutting and reception involving administrators of the partner institutions, the faculty of the school, the thirty-eight pioneering OhioLEARN MLS Program students, and the professional communities of the state of Ohio. Leading up to the virtual ribbon cutting were many hours of work on the part of professional and technical staff members at the partner institutions.

A key component in making the OhioLEARN education and training network functional was the identification of local support personnel and the development of clear lines of authority and responsibility. Although the major players in the planning process were the chief administrative officers of the school and the partner university libraries, it was recognized that those individuals could not assume continuing hands-on responsibility for the project. Technical contacts and scheduling/local arrangements contacts were identified at each site and involved in appropriate planning and implementation activities. The technical contacts are responsible for coordination of on-site telecommunications and technological issues. The scheduling/local arrangements contacts are responsible for such issues as parking arrangements, library and computer lab privileges, local events, helping coordinate calendars, and ensuring that rooms are available when needed. The OhioLEARN MLS program also benefits from substantial support from the professional community, with notable expressions of interest in serving as adjunct faculty members, guest lecturers, and practicum experience hosts from a large number of people in the areas served by the program.

In addition to the OhioLEARN MLS Program as currently constituted, the School of Library and Information Science will continue to explore other approaches to delivering professional library and information science education at a distance. The success of the Northwest Ohio Program suggests potential for a Southwest Ohio Program and a Southeast Ohio Program exploiting a variety of approaches to instructional delivery, including regular faculty traveling to remote sites, courses taught by local adjunct faculty members, courses delivered via the digital videoconferencing network, and courses delivered via media as yet unexplored by the school, such as courses for which the Web is the primary delivery medium.

The OhioLEARN MLS Program is one aspect of the total OhioLEARN project. Based on enrollment, the OhioLEARN MLS Program can be termed a success. Evaluation of programmatic success will be a continuing effort. The 1999–2000 academic year saw increased attention to building awareness of the potential of OhioLEARN among the state's library training providers, encouraging development of education and training activities that make use of the system, and examining ways in which the school could use the network to support learning activities that transcend the OhioLEARN MLS Program.

APPENDIX 1

The OhioLEARN Model

Kent State University
School of Library and Information Science
(330) 672-2782
Fax (330) 672-7965
P. O. Box 5190, Kent, Ohio 44242–0001

OhioLEARN: A Model for Collaboration

A discussion document prepared by
Danny P. Wallace, Connie Van Fleet, and Julie Gedeon
Kent State University School of Library and Information Science
Center for the Study of Librarianship
February 16, 1998

The model described here under the working title Ohio Libraries Education, Access, and Resource Network (OhioLEARN) is an attempt to represent a broad range of needs of the Ohio library community. The model responds to a variety of converging forces, including but not limited to expanded opportunities for grant funding for library-related projects, recognition of the need to improve diversity in the library workforce, evolution of the technological environment that supports libraries, the increasing maturity of Ohio's major library networks, higher education initiatives such as the most recent Ohio Board of Regents master plan, new standards and measures for public library performance, the move to develop a process for certification of public library directors, court-sanctioned changes in elementary and secondary school funding, and the introduction of new licensing standards and procedures for school library media specialists. At the center of these converging influences is one enduring goal: to provide equitable access to information, instruction, and support for patrons of all Ohio libraries, regardless of such factors as geographic location and personal or community income.

The model is multitype, but not comprehensively so. In its current form the model represents public libraries, academic libraries, and school library media centers, but not special libraries and information centers. This is a matter of focus, not of exclusion; the model can easily be extended. The model emphasizes direct patron services and the preparation of staff to deliver those services. Other collaborative efforts, such as cooperative collection building, interlibrary reference, and other forms of resource sharing are not included in the model but are clearly related to the intent of the model.

The fundamental thrust of the model is those services that can be supported collaboratively to the benefit of library patrons. The model does not address services or products that are most appropriately developed and provided purely at the local level. Education and training of library staff are at the heart of the model. It is the conviction of the framers of the model that adequate and appropriate staff preparation are critical to the effective delivery of library services and that staff education and training represent an area of universal concern with regard to equitable access to library services. Although a considerable wealth of education and training opportunities is offered to Ohio's library community, there is at present no effective coordination of those activities. By looking at education and training holistically, the OhioLEARN model provides a framework for collaboration, coordination, and sharing. The model also recognizes the need for collaboration in the preparation, testing, and use of materials, products, and services for providing direct patron access to shared resources and the essential nature of effective education and training for library patrons.

OhioLEARN is envisioned as a long-term project involving the greatest possible representation and involvement of the Ohio library community. The goals of the project are clearly too comprehensive to be met by any one agency or institution. The Kent State University School of Library and Information Science, as the only agency in the state charged exclusively with the education of library and information professionals, may play a central role in the development of the programs implied by the model. Some aspects of the model, such as professional-level education leading to an accredited master's degree, are obviously the province of the School. Other aspects, such as preprofessional and postprofessional education and training, may be achieved through a wider variety of experiences. Success in achieving program goals will require participation by the State Library of Ohio, the state's professional associations, statewide library networks, regional consortia, and individual libraries.

Funding for the project will be sought from a variety of sources, including state agencies, federal grants, corporate partnerships, and foundation support. Two grant proposals directly related to achieving OhioLEARN goals are currently being developed by the KSU SLIS Center of the Study of Librarianship. The first, a proposal for an Institute of Museum and Library Services (IMLS) Leadership Grant, will seek funding for development and initial implementation of new professional and postprofessional programs in the School of Library and Information Science. The second, related proposal will seek LSTA funding to support a pilot project to establish a distributed education and training network based on desktop videoconferencing technology. Success with these two proposals will be a starting point for development of the entire range of programs represented by the OhioLEARN model and will provide an impetus for the development of additional grant proposals.

OhioLEARN (Ohio Libraries Education, Access, and Resource Network):

A COORDINATED MULTILEVEL EDUCATION AND TRAINING PROGRAM FOR OHIO LIBRARIES

OVERVIEW

Goal: To bring together a broad array of converging forces, trends, initiatives, and influences to ensure equity of access to information, instruction, and support for patrons of all Ohio academic libraries, public libraries, and school library media centers.

Premise: Providing equity of access requires a coordinated, multilevel, interinstitutional effort that addresses issues of direct patron access, patron education and training, and education and training for library staff.

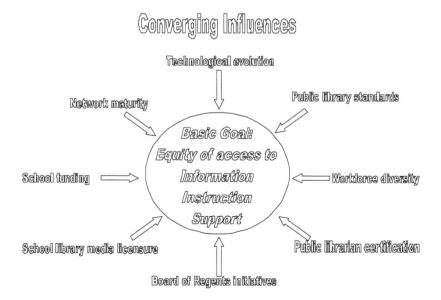

Four levels of service: Patron Service

Preprofessional Education and Training

Professional Education and Training

Postprofessional Education and Training

The emphasis at the Patron Service level is on providing the information, products, and services needed to patron success.

Information: The currently developing models of shared access to catalogs, collection sharing, database access, and related information sources serves as a major focus of the need for a coordinated multilevel education and training program.

Products: A major outgrowth of the coordinated program will be an array of customizable Web-based tools designed to facilitate both mediated and self-guided learning.

Services: Human contact is essential for solving individual problems; the program will emphasize education and training for staff members to maximize their abilities to provide quality patron service.

Learning experiences: A critical element of the program is development of a combination of meaningful learning experiences for library patrons, including on-site live training, distributed interactive electronic training, and asynchronous Web-based training.

The emphasis at the Preprofessional Education and Training level is on ensuring fundamental technical and technological skills for staff members directly or indirectly involved in patron service.

Learning experiences: On-site live training will be the primary mechanism for noncredit training, supported by appropriate asynchronous Web-based training and distributed interactive electronic training; credit education and training will be largely campus-based.

Noncredit programs: Noncredit training will be the emphasis of the Preprofessional level, although a limited credit program option will be available.

Level I Workshops: Level I workshops will be base-level noncredit training experiences, designed in a coordinated, collaborative process and delivered primarily by individual libraries, with assistance from regional consortia and statewide networks.

Level II Workshops: Level II workshops will be continuing training experiences, designed in a coordinated, collaborative process and delivered primarily by regional consortia, statewide networks, the State Library, and SLIS; Level II workshops may carry CEU credit or, if developed by an accredited college or university, undergraduate or graduate credit.

Credit programs: Undergraduate and graduate credit at KSU will be awarded through the interdisciplinary New Media Certificate program.

The emphasis at the Professional Education and Training level is on ensuring professional competence, with added emphasis on management and technology.

Learning experiences: On-campus classroom experiences will be augmented by flexibly scheduled courses, live distributed learning, interactive electronic distributed learning, and asynchronous learning.

Noncredit programs: The Professional level will emphasize credit programs, but noncredit opportunities will be developed, delivered, and promoted.

Level III workshops: Level III workshops, which may carry graduate credit, will be designed and delivered primarily by SLIS.

Credit programs: The primary emphasis will be the Master of Library Science degree program offered by SLIS.

The comprehensive MLS program, already in existence, will be enhanced by program development for the Focused MLS program. The Focused MLS program is designed to overcome geographic and time restraints that act as deterrents to professional education. Previous managerial or technological experience will be a requirement for admission to the Focused MLS program. The role of the professional in facilitating education and training will be a fundamental aspect of the Focused MLS program; students enrolled in the Focused MLS program will be required to complete a practicum experience centered on the design, development, and delivery of a staff training workshop.

Graduate credit at KSU may be awarded through the interdisciplinary New Media Certificate program.

The emphasis at the Postprofessional Education and Training level is on continuing professional education and skill-building, with an emphasis on management and technology.

Learning experiences: On-campus classroom experiences will be augmented by flexibly scheduled courses, live distributed learning, interactive electronic distributed learning, and asynchronous learning.

Noncredit programs: The Postprofessional level will provide a shared emphasis on noncredit and credit programs.

Credit programs: The primary emphasis will be on a redesigned version of the Post-Master's Certificate of Advanced Study offered by SLIS. The streamlined Certificate program will employ a multidisciplinary, interdepartmental, potentially interinstitutional approach to providing advanced education in management or information technology. The role of the professional in facilitating education and training will be a fundamental aspect of the Post-Master's Certificate program; students enrolled in the program will be required to complete a practicum experience centered on the design, development, and delivery of a staff training workshop.

Graduate credit at KSU may be awarded through the interdisciplinary New Media Certificate program.

Table 9.1 OhioLEARN
A Coordinated Multilevel Education and Training Program for Ohio Libraries

	Patron Service	*Preprofessional Education and Training*	*Professional Education and Training*	*Postprofessional Education and Training*
Focuses	Equity of access	Technical Technological	Comprehensive Management Technology	Management Technology
Delivery Mechanisms	Products On-site Distributed electronic Asynchronous	On-campus (credit only) On-site Distributed live Distributed electronic	On-campus Distributed live Distributed electronic Asynchronous	On-campus Distributed live Distributed electronic Asynchronous
Noncredit Programs	None	Level I and II workshops New Media Certificate	Level II and III workshops New Media Certificate	Level I and II workshops New Media Certificate Post-master's Certificate
Credit Programs	None	Level II workshops	Comprehensive MLS Focused MLS Level II and III workshops	Level II and III workshops
Entrance Requirements	Patron of Ohio library	**Noncredit:** Employed in an Ohio library **Credit:** Admitted to KSU	**Noncredit:** Employed in an Ohio library **Credit:** Admitted to KSU MLS	**Noncredit:** Employed in an Ohio library **Credit:** Admitted to KSU post-master's

114

Primary Development Responsibility	KSU Statewide networks State Library Regional consortia Individual libraries	**Noncredit:** SLIS Statewide networks State Library Regional consortia Individual libraries **Credit:** SLIS	**Noncredit:** SLIS Statewide networks State Library Regional consortia **Credit:** SLIS	**Noncredit:** SLIS Statewide networks State Library Regional consortia **Credit:** SLIS
Primary Delivery Responsibility	Statewide networks State Library Regional consortia Individual libraries	**Noncredit:** KSU SLIS Statewide networks State Library Regional consortia Individual libraries **Credit:** KSU SLIS	**Noncredit:** SLIS Statewide networks State Library Regional consortia **Credit:** SLIS	**Noncredit:** SLIS Statewide networks State Library Regional consortia **Credit:** SLIS

APPENDIX 2
OhioLEARN Press Release

Kent State University
School of Library and Information Science
(330) 672-2782
Kent, Ohio, September 16, 1998

FOR IMMEDIATE RELEASE
SCHOOL OF LIBRARY AND INFORMATION SCIENCE TO BUILD STATEWIDE NETWORK

For more information, contact
Dr. Danny P. Wallace, (330) 672-2782
The Kent State University School of Library and Information Science is the center of a $339,381 [grant] to build a statewide library and information science education and training network. The OhioLEARN (Ohio Libraries Education, Access, and Resource Network) Infrastructure Project will be funded by $252,689 from the federal Library Services and Technology Act (LSTA) and $86,692 from a coalition of Ohio educational institutions. OhioLINK, the state's college and university library network, will contribute $70,582 to the project.

The OhioLEARN partnership includes Kent State University, OhioLINK, Bowling Green State University, Ohio University, and the University of Cincinnati. The OhioLEARN Infrastructure Project will create an electronic distributed learning network using digital videoconferencing technology. The network will be used to provide workshops and courses, including the Kent State University Master of Library Science degree, the only professional library and information science program in Ohio. The project will begin in October 1998, and the first workshops and courses will be delivered during the late spring and summer of 1999.

LSTA funding is administered by the State Library of Ohio. The grant to Kent State University was the third largest of 18 grants awarded to Ohio libraries in the first year of LSTA funding, and the only grant to support higher education. Only 31% of proposed LSTA projects were funded.

APPENDIX 3
OhioLEARN Recruiting Brochure

Kent State University
School of Library and Information Science
Introducing the
OhioLEARN MLS Program

WHAT IS IT?

The OhioLEARN MLS Program is a specialized version of the Kent State University Master of Library Science (MLS) degree program tailored for delivery via the OhioLEARN (Ohio Libraries Education, Access, and Resource Network) distributed learning system. Students will experience most courses in the program through the digital videoconferencing network made possible by the OhioLEARN Infrastructure Project, a collaborative effort funded by a federal Library Services and Technology Act grant.

WILL THE DEGREE BE ACCREDITED BY THE AMERICAN LIBRARY ASSOCIATION?

Yes. In January 1998 the American Library Association re-affirmed accreditation of the Kent State University MLS under the 1992 *Standards for Accreditation of Master's Programs in Library and Information Studies,* including all instructional sites.

WHO MAY ENROLL?

Students enrolled in the program will work toward the MLS degree conferred by Kent State University. Applicants must meet all normal admission criteria for unconditional admission to the MLS degree program. The basic requirement for unconditional admission is completion of a bachelor's degree from an accredited institution with a cumulative grade point average of 3.0 on a 4.0 scale (a B average). Enrollment will be limited to no more than fifteen students per site. Applications will be evaluated and accepted in the order in which they are received. OhioLEARN MLS courses will be available only to students enrolled in the OhioLEARN MLS Program.

WHAT WILL IT ENTAIL?

Students enrolling in the program will have an opportunity to complete the Kent State University MLS program in a structured manner. Students in the OhioLEARN MLS Program will not have access to the range of electives and specializations available at the Kent and Columbus campuses. Students beginning in the fall 1999 cohort who make acceptable progress can expect to receive the degree at the fall 2001 commencement.

WHAT IS THE CURRICULUM?

The OhioLEARN MLS Program curriculum consists of an initial one semester-hour orientation, nine courses (27 semester hours) delivered through the OhioLEARN system, the Master's Research Paper required of all MLS students, and six semester hours of approved student-selected electives. Open electives may include practicum, individualized investigation, courses completed at the Kent or Columbus campuses, graduate credit workshops, special courses delivered via the OhioLEARN system, or graduate courses transferred from an institution other than Kent State University.

FIRST YEAR SCHEDULE

Summer 1999

LSCI 50693   Workshop in Library and Information Science: Distance and Distributed Learning in Library and Information Science (required for OhioLEARN MLS students)

Fall 1999

LSCI 60600   Foundations of Library and Information Science
LSCI 60001   Access to Information

Spring 2000

LSCI 60002   Organization of Information
LSCI 60604   Research for Decision Making in Library and Information Science

WHEN WILL IT BEGIN?

Students admitted to the OhioLEARN MLS Program will enter as a cohort group, with the first group admitted for study beginning in the fall semester of 1999. The program will begin with an intensive two-day orientation in Kent approximately two weeks prior to the beginning of the semester, which all students in the program will be required to attend. Site-specific orientation sessions, conducted during the week immediately preceding the beginning of the semester, will also be required.

WHO ARE THE FACULTY?

Most courses, including all core courses, will be taught by full-time faculty of the Kent State University School of Library and Information Science. Selected elective courses in specialized areas may be taught by experienced adjunct faculty.

WHERE WILL COURSES MEET?

The instructional sites for the OhioLEARN MLS Program will be the main facility of the Kent State University School of Library and Information Science in the Library Building on the Kent Campus, the OHIOLINK Training Center in Columbus, Jerome Library at Bowling Green State University, Alden Library at Ohio University, and Langsam Library at the University of Cincinnati.

ARE THERE ANY SPECIAL REQUIREMENTS?

Communication between faculty and students will rely heavily on the use of electronic mail and the Internet. Some courses may be delivered in part via the World Wide Web. Students must have reliable access to these resources and be familiar with their use. Explicit instruction in the use of electronic mail and the Internet will not be provided as part of the OhioLEARN MLS curriculum.

HOW MUCH WILL IT COST?

Graduate resident tuition at Kent State University is $242.50 per semester hour during 1999–2000. Tuition is subject to change. Some courses carry additional special fees. Students are responsible for purchasing textbooks and other instructional materials.

APPENDIX 4
MEMO TO PROSPECTIVE STUDENTS

INTERDEPARTMENTAL COMMUNICATION
KENT STATE UNIVERSITY
School of Library and Information Science
DATE: January 14, 2003
TO: Individuals Interested in the OhioLEARN MLS Program
FROM: Danny P. Wallace, Director, School of Library and Information Science
RE: The OhioLEARN MLS Program

Thank you for your interest in the OhioLEARN MLS Program. The OhioLEARN (Ohio Libraries Education, Access, and Resource Network) MLS Program is a highly focused version of the Master of Library Science (MLS) degree program designed for completion through the OhioLEARN distributed learning system. Students will experience most courses in the program through the digital videoconferencing network made possible by the OhioLEARN Infrastructure Project, a collaborative effort funded by a federal Library Services and Technology Act grant.

OhioLEARN MLS students will have the opportunity to graduate in two-and-one-half years. Enrollment is limited to fifteen students at each of five sites: Kent, Athens, Bowling Green, Cincinnati, and Columbus. Students must select an instructional site at the time of application and will not normally be allowed to transfer among sites. OhioLEARN MLS students are expected to enroll for two courses per fall and spring semester beginning in the fall of 1999; students who cannot make this commitment should consider options other than the OhioLEARN MLS Program. Although this is an experimental program, the School is committed to supporting the first student cohort to completion. The next cohort of OhioLEARN MLS students will begin the program no earlier than the fall of 2001.

The OhioLEARN MLS Program curriculum consists of an initial one semester-hour orientation, nine courses (twenty-seven semester hours) delivered through the OhioLEARN system, the Master's Research Paper required of all MLS students, and at least five semester hours of approved student-selected electives. Open electives may include practicum, individualized investigation, courses completed at the Kent or Columbus campuses, graduate credit workshops, additional courses delivered via the OhioLEARN system, or graduate courses transferred from an institution other than Kent State University.

All OhioLEARN MLS students must attend a one semester-hour orientation workshop in Kent. The orientation workshop is scheduled for August 26 and 27, 2003. Registration information for the orientation workshop and for OhioLEARN courses will be sent to OhioLEARN MLS students following admission to the program. Students who do not attend the orientation workshop will be dismissed from the OhioLEARN MLS Program.

Applicants must meet all normal admissions criteria for *unconditional* admission to the MLS degree program. The basic requirement for unconditional admission is completion of a bachelor's degree from an accredited institution with a cumulative grade point average of 3.0 on a 4.0 scale (a B average). Enrollment will be limited to no more than fifteen students per site. Applications will be evaluated and accepted in the order in which they are received.

OhioLEARN MLS courses will be available only to students enrolled in the OhioLEARN MLS Program. Additional information regarding the OhioLEARN MLS Program can be found in the enclosed brochure.

To apply for admission to the OhioLEARN MLS Program, please complete the enclosed application materials and submit them as directed.

Thank you for your interest in the OhioLEARN MLS Program. If you have any further questions about the program or about other offerings of the School of Library and Information Science, please contact me.

Enclosures:

Introducing the OhioLEARN MLS Program
Biographical Sketch Form
Application for Admission
Student Handbook

10

THE DISTANCE LEARNING PROGRAM AT THE UNIVERSITY OF KENTUCKY'S SCHOOL OF LIBRARY AND INFORMATION SCIENCE

Timothy W. Sineath

BRIEF HISTORY

Library science education began at the University of Kentucky in 1911 with a single course in the English Department. During the period from 1911 to 1928, the curriculum was expanded and focused primarily on the preparation of school librarians. By 1930, the first full-time faculty member—Mildred Semmons—was employed, and by 1932 the Department of Library Science was established in the College of Arts and Sciences. Semmons built the department and added several new faculty members, including Azile Wofford and Laura K. Martin, both of whom achieved national reputations and focused attention on the department from the beginning of their tenures, which lasted twenty-four and thirty-one years, respectively.

Soon after the department was organized, the Southern Association of Colleges and Secondary Schools accredited it, and in 1934 an invitation was extended to the Board of Education for Librarianship of the ALA to visit the University of Kentucky for the purpose of accrediting the program. However, because the thirty-hour program was only in it first year and, apparently, because of the high unemployment among librarians, the ALA Board was reluctant to encourage the development of more training programs. As a result, the visit was not made until 1937. After meeting board recommendations on strengthening the program's financial support, it was accredited under the 1933 standards following a second visit in 1942 by two members of the Board of Education for Librarianship, Ralph Munn and Helen Harris. The accreditation was for a Type III school—one that could offer undergraduate courses as part of its program, with special emphasis on library services to schools and colleges. From the time of initial accreditation until 1951, the department offered the bachelor's degree as a fifth year.

By fall 1949, two programs in library science were offered: an undergraduate program for those seeking school library certification, and the graduate program. The graduate program consisted of twenty-four hours of library science, a foreign language, and an oral examination on an accepted thesis. The Department of Library Science was reaccredited in 1955 under the new Standards of Accreditation developed in 1951. These standards, first applied in 1953 and continued until 1971, dropped the former classification of schools according to type and set up standards that applied only to programs leading to a master's degree. The master's degree programs were reaccredited in 1975 under the 1972 standards and, in 1997, under the 1992 standards.

The organization of the department underwent significant changes over the years. By 1968, the department had grown not only in size and stature but also in relationship to the university structure. Accordingly, the department was established as an autonomous Graduate School of Library Science with Lawrence A. Allen as it first dean. As part of a university reorganization, the school became the College of Library Science, placing it on the same level as other colleges within the university. This action created the first college of library science in the United States. Timothy W. Sineath was appointed dean in 1977. His tenure began with major overhaul of the curriculum; the faculty proposed in 1982 that the College of Library Science change its name to the College of Library and Information Science in recognition of the expanding scope of the college's teaching and research program.

In 1993, responding to the president's call for innovative organizational ideas for the university, the faculties of the Colleges of Library and Information Science and of Communications developed a proposal to create a new College of Communications and Information Studies. The new college combined four previously existing departments and two colleges in a single college with three units: the Department of Communication, the School of Library and Information Science (SLIS), and the School of Journalism and Telecommunication. An informal collaboration that had existed for a number of years thus became formalized. Also, by this time, the school had recruited Donald O. Case as director; his doctoral degree is in communications research from Stanford. Increasing levels of collaboration are being pursued. An important result has been the development of a doctoral program in information studies as a track in the existing doctoral program in communication. With the addition of a new faculty member in health information systems, SLIS will be developing joint research projects with the well-established health communication emphasis in the Department of Communication and with the medical informatics program in the University of Kentucky's Medical Center.

INVOLVEMENT IN DISTANCE EDUCATION

In the early 1970s SLIS offered off-campus courses in six locations around the state. By 1974, they were concentrated into two centers: one in Covington (northern Kentucky/greater Cincinnati area) and one in Louisville. The university created a Graduate Center on the campus of Northern Kentucky University, and courses were offered through this Center staffed by UK employees. The school continues to offer much of its program at that site. In 1982, the university established tuition reciprocity for the greater Cincinnati counties whereby residents of those Ohio counties could take courses offered though the Graduate Center at Northern Kentucky University (NKU). Since that time and continuing to date, that program is the largest off-campus program offered by SLIS.

Instruction has been typically face to face using regular UK faculty and adjuncts or compressed video. By the early 1990s it was clear that by virtue of the number and variety of courses offered at NKU, students were earning a complete off-campus degree, which we were not authorized to provide. The school was authorized to offer no more than 75 percent of the master's degree off-campus. To bring the program into compliance and ensure that students' programs included appropriate technology components (not available off campus), off-campus students must now come to campus for three of the four required courses and for the advanced technology requirement.

In the 1980s SLIS offered courses in Ashland, Kentucky/Huntington, West Virginia utilizing the facilities of the UK Community College System. This location assisted commuting students from West Virginia, with which UK has a Common Market Tuition agreement for study in LIS. In 1982, at the invitation of the West Virginia Board of Regents, the school provided distance learning courses in Charleston. Considerable planning went into determining the courses that could be offered with minimal library support. Wayne A. Wiegand, then an associate professor in the school, taught two courses a semester that met during weekends. Although a number of students were able to begin study toward the master's degree, the demand for courses had been overestimated and the program soon ceased.

CURRENT ACTIVITY

The school continues its substantial distance learning program through NKU and in 1998 began offering a limited number of courses on the Internet and started a cohort group at the University of Louisville. The Louisville program resulted from a collaboration between the school, the University of Louisville, Jefferson County Public Schools, and the Louisville Free Public Library to help address serious recruiting problems. The Public Library Foundation has provided funds for any employee of the system who wishes to pursue the master's degree. The program combines face-to-face instruction, compressed video, Internet, and alternative on-campus scheduling.

For nearly thirty years, SLIS has been involved in delivering graduate education to off-campus constituencies to serve the needs of the commonwealth and region for professionally educated information professionals. This has been done successfully through face-to-face instruction at a distance, by compressed video, and by satellite technologies. These efforts and alternative scheduling have minimized commuting to campus and made the programs more broadly accessible. Building on that experience, the school began to utilize the Internet in its delivery of graduate education in spring 1999. Beginning in 1999–2000, four courses were delivered totally or in part via the Internet. Of these, one is required for all master's degree students, and one is required for those seeking school media certification. Each year the number of courses that have major Internet components has increased by two new courses per year.

FUTURE DIRECTIONS

The faculty continues to update the school's distance learning plan. Approximately thirty semester hours were available by fall 2002. We expect to provide instruction for these courses primarily through Internet technologies along with important components of on-campus instruction. Our goal, however, is to utilize a variety of information technologies that are the most appropriate to the achievement of the goals of the individual courses and program while maintaining high-quality graduate education. This is accomplished using a hybrid mix of Internet, compressed video, and face-to-face meetings with a variety of intensive scheduling formats. We have targeted especially the needs for preparing school media librarians because we have solid information on that market. As part of this effort, the school received a U.S. Institute of Museum and Library Services National Leadership Grant in the amount of $329,427 to develop a model for recruiting and training school media librarians. In collaboration with Jefferson County (KY) Schools, certified teachers are job sharing while completing the MLS degree. Much of this program is delivered at a distance.

As part of its distance learning plan, the faculty has developing statements of principles that will guide the further utilization of Internet-based instruction. We are also guided by the principle that information technologies are not only tools for the delivery of course content but also *are* course content in many cases. This adds a special need to model various technologies for the storage and retrieval of information and to have maximum flexibility in design and delivery of instruction.

Established in 1997, the Kentucky Commonwealth Virtual University (KCVU) is a technology-based system for coordinating delivery of postsecondary education in the state. The KCVU has targeted LIS education as a priority, and although a support system exists within the University of Kentucky, the school is exploring collaboration with the KCVU as a vehicle for providing Internet-based courses. A number of university policy issues, including variable tuition and capital investment, are currently being addressed.

As part of the system, KCVU has developed the Kentucky Commonwealth Virtual Library, which envisions providing complete library support for distance learners. Whether or not the school's courses are offered directly through the KCVU, the virtual library is a major support service for distance learners.

NOTE

The summary of the history of the school is in part from Timothy W. Sineath, "University of Kentucky School of Library Science," *Encyclopedia of Library and Information Science Supplement*, vol. 37, suppl. 2. New York: Marcel Dekker, 1984, pp. 179–186.

11

THE SCHOOL OF LIBRARY AND INFORMATION SCIENCE AT LOUISIANA STATE UNIVERSITY: DISTANCE EDUCATION PROGRAM

Alma Dawson

HISTORICAL OVERVIEW

The Louisiana State University (LSU) School of Library and Information Science celebrated its seventieth anniversary fall semester 2001. Organized in 1931 as the Graduate School of Library Science (GSLS), the purpose of the program was to meet the demands for library training in the central South and Southwest, especially Louisiana. It should be noted that from 1926 through 1931, under the direction and supervision of the university librarian, LSU offered library science courses during summer for practicing librarians and library assistants, including those persons who had an interest in some phase of library work and met admissions standards.[1] As of fall 2001, the school had graduated more than 3,000 students with a master's degree in Library and Information Science (MLIS). In addition to the MLIS degree and the Certificate of Advanced Studies (CLIS), the school offers several joint degrees, including a joint degree in Library and Information Science and Systems Science.

Several developments contributed to the formation of the program in library science at LSU. The State Library Commission, the Louisiana State Library Association, and the Southeastern Library Association gave encouragement, support, and recommendations regarding the need for trained librarians in the state and region and for the location of the school. In 1926 the State Library Commission of Louisiana adopted a project that supported the "establishment of a training course for librarians in the State" as a result of a 1925 demonstration grant received for public library development from the Carnegie Corporation of New York. In the same year, the Louisiana Library Association appointed its Committee on Library Training to "promote training facilities for librarians in our State and to have appointed only trained librarians in the various libraries."[2] In 1929, the Southeastern Library Association made a recommendation to the ALA's Board of Education for Librarianship that the whole library school situation in the South be studied. The survey, conducted in 1930 by Sarah C. N. Bogle of the ALA and Tommie Dora Baker, then director of the Carnegie School (Atlanta, Georgia), made the recommendation that "in view of the demand for library workers of all types, and in view of the fact that in Louisiana the State University is already offering summer courses, a library school of graduate grade offerings in the academic year is needed there."[3]

According to announcements issued by LSU for the period 1926–31, the summer courses offered between 1926 and 1931 were also for the purpose of cooperating with the Louisiana Library Commission "to meet the demand for librarians equipped with some knowledge of technique and to support the State Department in its endeavor to have a librarian in every accredited high school in the state."[4]

According to Florrinell Morton (director of the school from 1944–71), the recommendation of this survey, the interest in the area in library development, and the combined efforts of the university, the State Library Commission, and the State Department of Education resulted in LSU being selected as a recipient of a $60,000 grant from the General Education Board of New York in spring 1931 to be expended over a five-year period for the development of a library school with the university assuming a larger portion of the burden each year until 1936, when the university would assume the full cost.[5] Consequently, the school was established June 8, 1931, by the Board of Supervisors of the Louisiana State University and Agricultural and Mechanical College as the Graduate School of Library Science, a subdivision of the university. The school opened in September 1931 and offered a full professional curriculum that led to the degree of bachelor of science in library science. The school was provisionally accredited in 1932 and fully accredited in 1933 as a Type II graduate library school.

Margaret Herdman (director of the school from 1937–41) recalled that at the time the school opened, there were only five librarians in the state public school system with twenty-four to thirty semester hours of training, and thirty-five with six semester hours or less. However, there were many more schools in the state system that required trained librarians to meet the Southern Association of Colleges and Secondary Schools or state standards. It was a time of active development of school libraries as well as a great need for training of school librarians. Therefore, the enrollment expanded at the school from an average of 24 students each semester during the first five years to an enrollment of 150 students by summer term 1938.[6]

In addition to course offerings, the GSLS and the Louisiana State Department of Education jointly sponsored conferences and workshops for school librarians and held them at LSU. Three conferences provided example. The school and the State Department of Education jointly sponsored the Working Conference: The School Library and Audio-Visual Materials, on June 17–19, 1947; Conference on School Library Problems: Looking Toward a Blue Print for Louisiana School Libraries, on June 12–30, 1951; and Elementary Materials Workshop, held June 11–30, 1951.[7] At the beginning, school librarians made up the largest number of graduates, followed by college and university librarians. Parish and regional library development became the next major area of development in the state, and therefore a demand for public librarians was created.

Although distance education course records for the period 1937–47 are archived in university registration records in a format currently unavailable to the author, Florrinell Morton recorded a specialized course on County and Regional Library Service offered in 1939 and taught by Edith Gantt, Essae M. Culver, Tommie Dora Barker, Alfred Rawlinson, Mary Walton Harris, and Mary Mims, lecturers. In 1940, she identified an institute on County and Regional Library Service offered at LSU and taught by Harriet Long, Loleta Fyan, Mary Rothrock, Essae M. Cover, Mary Mims, and Lois Shortess, lecturers. The institute was held in cooperation with the State Library Commission of Louisiana.[8]

Between 1932 and 1958, the bachelor's degree was awarded to 725 students for the successful completion of this program. At the opening of the 1951–52 year, the GSLS began its program leading to the master's of science degree. The bachelor of science degree program was discontinued for new students. The MS was initially accredited in 1955 by the Committee on Accreditation of the ALA under the 1951 standards adopted by the ALA. On August 3, 1973, the LSU Board of Supervisors approved a degree title change from master of science to master of library science. In 1981, the name was changed from Graduate School of Library Science to the School of Library and Information Science (SLIS). In 1983–84, the school added the library and information science–systems science joint degree and for the first time during fall 1986, the master of library and information science degree was awarded. During 1987–88, the CLIS was implemented. In 1998, the SLIS and the LSU Department of History introduced a dual degree with an emphasis on archives, in which students could earn both an MLIS and an MA in history within three years. A grant from the Institute on Museums and Library Services funded an LSU Institute on Archives for twenty librarians in summer 1999, which included the first LSU course on archives management. Instruction was offered through interactive, compressed video from Arkansas to six locations in Louisiana. Participants also completed a 120-hour field experience in a museum or library archive, applying classroom knowledge in a project involving preservation, organization, and/or retrieval resources. Archives management is a new focus for the school, and a new faculty member was employed beginning spring 2000 to develop the archives curriculum. During 2001–02, the school added cooperative programs with the departments of Spanish and Public Administration. The school has a structure in place to add other dual degrees with other academic units as needs are identified.

The LSU program of study in LIS has been continuously accredited by the appropriate accrediting agency throughout its history; the MLIS program is currently accredited by the ALA. SLIS is an independent administrative unit of the university, and the dean reports to the executive vice chancellor and provost of the university. Students admitted to the SLIS are also admitted to the Graduate School. During its seventy-year history, the school has had eight directors and deans: James A. McMillen, 1931–37 and 1941–44; Margaret A. Herdman, 1937–41; Florrinell F. Morton, 1944–71; Donald Foos, 1971–77; Jane Robbins Carter, 1979–81; Kathleen Heim McCook; 1983–1990; Bert Boyce, 1990–2000; and Beth Paskoff, fall 2000–present. Sister Marie Cairns, O.P., served twice as acting dean from 1977–79 and again from 1981–83; Dr. Francis Miksa did so from May 19, 1983 to August 15, 1983.

HISTORY OF DISTANCE EDUCATION AT LSU SLIS

The University Extension Division was created at LSU in 1924 to offer correspondence and credit classes to students who were unable to attend classes on campus and to extend higher education throughout the state. Historically, the Division of Continuing Education provided both credit and noncredit programs through the departments of Independent Study and Evening School. The division's name has changed through the years from Extramural Teaching, to Evening School, to Continuing Education. Evening School was known as Extramural Teaching until 1992. The SLIS has offered all courses to remote locations via the university's Extension Division through Extramural Teaching or Evening School. When compressed video courses were first offered by LSU in 1995–96, it became a joint effort of the academic departments, Evening School, and the Division of Instructional Support. Evening School's role was admission, registration, marketing, fee collection, and instructional support. However, "general responsibility for the University's distance education initiatives was vested in the Division of Instructional Support (DISD) working in concert with the various academic departments."[9]

Both traditional core and specialized courses have been offered by SLIS traveling faculty, faculty from other locations around the state, and, on one occasion, faculty from Arkansas State University to sites in Louisiana. The school has also utilized the campus audio graphics telelearning system and the compressed video system to deliver courses around the state. The SLIS became the first academic unit at LSU to offer a course via the compressed video system and also the first academic unit at LSU to develop and have approved a five-year plan (1996–2001), which included all core courses and selected electives. Core courses were first offered off-campus during the fall semester 1978 and included LIS 7002, Information Services, in Shreveport and LIS 7004, Principles of Management for Librarians and Information Specialists, in New Orleans. In March 2000, the school added the full curriculum to the five-year plan (spring 2000–fall 2005). In its sixth revision, spring 2002–fall 2007 (see Appendix D of this chapter) the plan now enables students to complete all requirements for the MILS degree by distance education. The Curriculum Committee reviews the five-year plan annually in March and makes adjustments in course offerings or faculty appointments as needed. Web-based courses (LIS 7002, Information Services, and LIS 7008, Information Technologies) were offered for the first time in summer 2000.

Significant developments, course delivery methods, and locations in the SLIS distance education program from 1931–2001 are outlined chronologically. A descriptive narrative of these events follows in Table 11.1.

EARLY DEVELOPMENT TO 1960

It is interesting to note that prior to the formal organization of the school in 1931, "Library Science I, History of the Book" appeared in the university catalog with other courses offered via extension. James McMillen, director of both the University Library and the Library School, is listed as instructor for the Baton Rouge–based course for the years 1929–30[10] and 1930–31.[11] After the GSLS was organized, the first extension course offered was in 1937. According to Director Morton:

In 1937 the first extension course was offered, and, although limited by the size of its staff in the amount of extension courses it can make available, the School attempts to comply with requests for classes, and has offered courses in various sections of the state.[12]

In 1938, three former graduates were identified as assisting with courses for school librarians. Those graduates included Cathleen Fletcher, who taught at Louisiana Polytechnic Institute in Ruston; Frances Flanders, who taught at Southwestern Louisiana Institute in Lafayette; and Helen Maestri, who was located at Loyola University in New Orleans.[13] The GSLS both offered courses in the regular curriculum while also responding to special requests for classes from different locations around the state. An early example is provided through the work of Norris McClellan, an associate professor who specialized in school librarianship and taught for the GSLS from 1939 to 1971. Her work was critical to the delivery of off-campus courses in school librarianship around the state. Records indicate that McClellan taught twenty off-campus courses between 1947 and 1965 while continuing to teach a full load on campus. For example, she taught LIS 115, Children's Books, at Opelousas, Louisiana, during fall 1947, followed by two off-campus courses

Table 11.1
Distance Education at Louisiana State University, 1929–2001

Date	Significant Events/Developments	Course Delivery Method	Location(s)
1931	LSU Graduate School of Library and Information Science opened		
1937–1947	School librarianship courses/in-service training workshops offered	Traveling LS faculty	North and South Louisiana
1947–1950	Organized approach to DE began and included school librarianship course taught by Ms. Norris McClellan; Ms. McClellan also taught courses scheduled according to Strawberry Parish school terms	Traveling and remote faculty	Opelousas, Natchitoches, New Roads, New Orleans, Hammond, Monroe, Baton Rouge, and Covington
1950–1960	Cooperative Programs implemented in School Librarianship with College of Education, State Department of Education, and State Library	Traveling and remote LS faculty	New Orleans, Franklinton, Amite, Bastrop, Jena, St. Joseph, Bogalusa, and Gretna
1960–1970	School Librarianship and other public and academic library courses offered; Jefferson Parish Public Library courses for employees; USL and LSU proposal developed	Traveling and remote LS faculty	Chalmette, New Orleans, Shreveport, Monroe, Quachita Parish, Winnsboro, Alexandria, Harahan, Lafayette, Baton Rouge, Gretna, Mandeville, Reserve, and Covington
1970–1980	Selected courses offered	Traveling LS faculty	Shreveport, Lafayette, and New Orleans
1973–1979	Resident Centers established	Adjunct faculty	USL Lafayette, LSU Shreveport
1973–1980	Health Sciences program—Grade 1 Medical Certification	Adjunct faculty	LSU Medical Center—New Orleans and Shreveport
1980–1985	Identified qualified adjunct faculty throughout the state; expansion of Resident Centers	Traveling and remote LS faculty	Alexandria, New Orleans, Shreveport, Pineville, Thibodaux, Lafayette, and Baton Rouge

Year	Event	Method	Location
1981	First course taught overseas	Study abroad	British Isles
1983–1984	Dr. Lee Shiflett named coordinator of SLIS extension		
1985–1986	Resident Centers expanded	Traveling faculty	Baton Rouge, Eunice, Shreveport, New Orleans, and Lafayette
1987–1991	First SLIS interactive course offered	Telelearning/Audio-Graphics system	Baton Rouge, Shreveport, and Alexandria
1987	Two overseas courses	Study abroad	England
1987–1991	Interactive and select other courses taught by traveling faculty	Telelearning/Audio-Graphics system	Baton Rouge, Shreveport, Alexandria, and Eunice
1991–1992	North Louisiana Program approved and announced	Adjunct faculty approved by LSU Graduate School	Shreveport, Ruston, Baton Rouge, Eunice, Alexandria, and Lafayette
1992–1994	North Louisiana Program implemented	Adjunct faculty	Monroe, Natchitoches, Ruston, and Shreveport
1993–1996	South Louisiana Program implemented	LS traveling and remote faculty	New Orleans and Lafayette
1995	SLIS offered first LSU compressed video course	Compressed video	Baton Rouge to Shreveport
1996	SLIS developed first five-year program plan at LSU (approved 3/18/96). Incorporated North and South Louisiana Programs into Compressed video system; Dr. Patsy Perritt named Master DE Teacher for LSU Campus	Compressed video and adjunct faculty	LSU-Eunice, Alexandria, Shreveport, and New Orleans
1997	SLIS developed second five-year plan; all DE courses offered via compressed video only	Compressed video	Baton Rouge, New Orleans, Shreveport, Alexandria, and Eunice
1998	SLIS faculty members received DISD stipends to develop compressed video courses	Compressed video	Baton Rouge, New Orleans, Shreveport, Alexandria, Eunice, and Monroe

Table 11.1
Distance Education at Louisiana State University, 1929–2001 (*continued*)

Date	Significant Events/Developments	Course Delivery Method	Location(s)
1999	SLIS revised five-year plan to include the entire curriculum in its compressed video system. SLIS professors David Robins and Dana Watson developed proposal for Web-based courses, LIS 7002 and LIS 7008. SLIS Archives course offered from Arkansas State University at Jonesboro	Compressed video	Baton Rouge, New Orleans, Shreveport, Alexandria, Eunice, Monroe, and Lake Charles; Archives course delivered from Jonesboro
2000–2001	SLIS received grant from LA Board of Regents for development of Web-based courses. SLIS offered Web-based courses. SLIS continued to deliver all core courses and electives via compressed video	Web/Internet Compressed video	Web/Internet courses hosted by SLIS–LSU; Compressed video courses are delivered from Baton Rouge to New Orleans, Alexandria, Shreveport, Eunice, Monroe, Lafayette, Thibodaux, and Lake Charles

in spring 1948. She taught Children's Books and Library Work with Children in New Roads, Louisiana, February 24–May 29, 1948, and LIS 118, School Library Administration, in Hammond to serve teachers in the Strawberry Parishes (Tangiphoa, St. Helena, and Livingston) from April 10 to June 10, 1948, to coincide with the Strawberry School Term, although the Strawberry School Term (April 1 to July, 1948) overlapped with the LSU semester.[14] School librarianship courses were offered in both north and south Louisiana and included new faculty members.

During the 1960s and 1970s, the school expanded its offerings through residence centers set up by the university to allow courses to be offered to residents not available through their local campus. As enrollments grew and more demands were received for off-campus courses, the school began to make use of adjunct/and or off-campus faculty to assist in the delivery of courses. Significant among off-campus faculty during the 1960s and 1970s were John Richard, director of the Louisiana State University Library at Alexandria; Collen Salley, professor of library science at Louisiana State University in New Orleans (now University of New Orleans); and Genevieve Aillet, librarian, Baton Rouge High School. The types of courses offered included those that supported careers in public librarianship and college and university libraries. The school responded to the requests of area librarians and to large systems, and this was evidenced by the courses offered for Jefferson Parish Library employees.[15] Other courses specific to youth and adult services in public libraries were taught by Shirley Stephenson (1943–72) and Ruth Baldwin (1956–77) at different locations around the state, including Shreveport, Monroe, Lafayette, Natchitoches, and New Orleans.

SPECIAL PROGRAM FOR HEALTH SCIENCES

Through the school and the LSU Division of Continuing Education, the school offered a Health Sciences Program at the LSU Medical Centers in New Orleans and Shreveport from 1970 to 1980. On completion of the program and the MLS degree, students received the Grade I Medical Library Certificate from the Medical Library Association.[16] Instructors who taught in this program included Kay Haas, Nancy Hardy, Robert Berk, Virginia Algermissen, Pauline Angione, and Jane Pool.

DEVELOPMENT OF REGIONAL PROGRAMS

At different periods throughout the history of the school, several attempts were made to meet the needs of librarians throughout the state through development of programs in the communities. Florrinell Morton, director of the Library School, and Kenneth Toomb, director of the library at the University of Southwestern Louisiana, developed one early proposal for delivery of the library science courses to an off-campus site. In 1964, the two developed a "Proposal for Cooperative Action by the University of Southwestern Louisiana (USL) and Louisiana State University to meet the needs of students in the Lafayette area for graduate courses and/or programs in library science." LSU Library School proposed offering courses at USL that would count toward a minor and/or a master's degree in library science (twelve hours and eighteen hours, respectively). Courses were offered in the Lafayette area based on sufficient enrollment in courses until the compressed video system was implemented in 1995–96.

During the latter part of the 1980s and the early 1990s, the school planned extension offerings that entailed three-year cycles for students by geographical area. For example, the northern Louisiana program and the southern Louisiana program were developed under the leadership of Deans Kathleen Heim McCook (1983–90) and Bert Boyce (1990–2000). The northern Louisiana program was in a program track so that students could acquire twenty-one credit hours within a three-year cycle. In that this was a major drain on faculty, adjunct faculty consisting of library directors or others with earned doctorates and an appropriate publication record were recruited for the different areas. Those who passed the LSU Graduate School Review were employed to teach two courses per year in a three-year cycle. The SLIS dean and associate dean held faculty meetings with these adjunct faculty.[17]

From spring 1992 through fall 1994, the LSU SLIS provided a three-year curriculum for northern Louisiana that covered the areas of Monroe, Natchitoches, Ruston, and Shreveport. Students choosing this curriculum could acquire twenty-one hours of credit toward the master's degree. Two classes per semester during spring and summer and one course during summer term were offered through the LSU Division of Continuing Education. Both core and elective courses were offered. (See Appendix A of this chapter.) From 1992 to 1996, the school extended the three-year curriculum to include southern Louisiana. Both core and elective courses were offered (see Appendix B of this chapter).

SYNCHRONOUS COURSES TO MULTIPLE SITES

From 1987 to 1991, LSU SLIS offered seven different courses to multiple sites via an audiographics telelearning system. The first course offered was the basic reference course, LIS7002, Information Services, taught by Lee Shiflett, and was delivered from Baton Rouge to LSU–Shreveport, LSU–Alexandria, and LSU–Eunice.[18] According to Danny Wallace, who taught on two different occasions using this technology, "The system provided fully interactive audio via a telephone connection and microphones. In addition to the two way voice link, there was a very primitive graphics system that allowed for display of text and limited graphics." Wallace used the graphics system exclusively and prepared disks far enough in advance to mail them to remote sites. He then controlled the computers at all sites to advance the images.[19] Shiflett taught using the lecture method almost entirely and reported that he found better student interaction using the telelearning system than the compressed video system.[20] Michael Carpenter prepared course materials in advance of classes and delivered them to the sites for use on given days. He had students videotape presentations and mail them to him. He then made copies of these video tapes and redistributed them to the different sites so that all students could view the presentations and participate at the same time.[21] Shiflett taught the first telelearning class in 1987, and Carpenter taught the last tele-learning class in 1991.

Predating the compressed video era, Charles Patterson (1972–93) experienced a different version of distance education. He was among SLIS faculty members who not only traveled by car to the different locations but also was flown to a distant campus (Shreveport in particular) with other campus faculty on the LSU airplane, which was dedicated to transporting faculty back and forth to classes during the 1970s and early 1980s. When he drove, Patterson often carried library materials to supplement course materials not available in the local libraries. The days were long and challenging, but the instructors made it work.[22] Rachel Green's letter to Dean Kathleen Heim (1983–90) is an example of many letters from distance students. Green wrote,

With a full time job and other responsibilities here in Shreveport, being a student here on the Baton Rouge campus for an extended period of time, was impossible. However, even though I was far removed from the campus for the majority of my program, I was always able to get my questions answered with a phone call to the Library School. The extension students were made to feel just as much a part of the program as the Baton Rouge students.[23]

In fall 1995, Dr. Patsy Perritt offered the first compressed video course at LSU, connecting to one site in Shreveport.[24] She recalls that the video system allowed the instructor more flexibility than the system that is in place today, and she enjoyed teaching using the technology. From the control panel in Baton Rouge, she could control the cameras at the distant site, generally see what activities were going on, and vary the instructional modes more easily by engaging students in small group work during the class period. In addition, the system was programmed to rotate cameras automatically every three to five minutes between sites, so that the instructor could observe student reactions. As the statewide network grew, it was necessary to go to contracted services and automatic control of some operations.[25] The system installed provides for camera control at local sites and voice-activated system for viewing of sites. That is, only when a student at a distant site turns on a microphone to ask a question or to respond to a question from the instructor is the system activated. There is a sixty-second delay in the time the student speaks and the system responds. With advanced planning, it is very possible to vary the instructional modes utilizing the assistance of proctors located at each site to ensure active learning for all enrolled students.

In spring 1996, the school projected and received university approval for the first five-year plan (1996–2001) at LSU for courses to be offered around the state of Louisiana. In addition during 1996, Perritt was named the master teacher for distance education at LSU. In this capacity, she provided statewide distance education training for teachers and made presentations to the Board of Regents and college presidents. In addition she made three instructional videos for the university, as well as served on the LSU Advisory Council for Distance Education.[26]

By spring 1997, students were receiving instruction at five sites: Baton Rouge, New Orleans, Alexandria, Shreveport, and Eunice. In spring 1998, the Monroe site was added, giving potential students access to six sites around the state. With the addition of the new sites, the LSU Division of Support Services increased its assistance to individual instructors by providing teaching stipends to selected faculty members to purchase teaching materials (excluding educational software). SLIS faculty members Dana Watson, Alma Dawson, and Patsy Perritt secured teaching stipends from the DISD to support development of their distance education courses and also took advantage of DISD's assistance with Web design, presentation software, and courseware. (DISD was renamed the Centers for Excellence in Teaching in 2001.) SLIS continued to lead the campus in program offerings through distance education and was the only LSU academic department to offer a distance education course in summer 1998.

During 1999, the Lake Charles site was added, and SLIS developed its second five-year plan. The second plan (1998–2002) established a pattern for at least one course to be offered each semester on a weekday evening and expanded to include one or two Saturdays as well. During summer term 1999, the program included a course in archives management, which was taught by Dr. Brady Banta, an adjunct professor at Arkansas State University. The course was taught from Arkansas and delivered to six sites in Louisiana. The LSU Institute on Archives funded twenty librarians who took the course along with other regularly enrolled SLIS students. Increased demand for SLIS courses prompted the school to include all courses in the MLIS program with the fifth revision of the five-year distance education plan, 2000–05. During summer and fall 2001, SLIS added compressed video sites in Lafayette and Thibodaux, respectively. The school now delivers its distance education schedule via compressed video from Baton Rouge to eight other sites around Louisiana.

ASYNCHRONOUS COURSES

During November 1999, Dana Watson and David Robins secured a Louisiana Board of Regents Grant in the amount of $64,033 for their proposal "Streaming Towards the Future: A Unique Academic Program Incorporates Web-Based Technologies." The goals of the project were to investigate the viability of technologies that address concerns regarding deficiencies of communication modes for participants in distance education and to create a model of and documentation for migrating traditional classroom courses to rich, interactive Web-based courses that would include state-of-the-art technologies. Watson and Robins developed/migrated two core courses (LIS 7002, Information Services, and LIS 7008, Information Technologies) to Web-based courses, which they taught summer 2000. LIS 7002, Information Services, was offered again in fall 2000, and LIS 7008 again during summer 2002.

THE FUTURE

When asked about the future of distance education in the LSU SLIS, Dean Beth Paskoff observed that she expects the school to continue to offer different educational options for students pursuing the MLIS and CLIS degrees. As the only accredited LIS program in the state, it is important for LSU to try to meet the needs of both those students who come to Baton Rouge and those whose work and personal lives make it impossible for them to do so. "The statewide compressed video system has been quite successful, and we have received requests from students to expand the number of locations," she said.

There have also been requests from prospective students in Louisiana, across the nation, and from around the world for either compressed video or Web-based courses from LSU. Response to the Web-based courses that have been offered has been enthusiastic by the students in distant locations, but many of the students who have made the effort to come to the LSU campus for their graduate education have been disappointed with this option. Paskoff anticipates that blended courses with several face-to-face meetings during the semester and a large percentage of the course content delivered through the Internet may be an effective blending of traditional and contemporary methodologies.

For a chronological listing of courses offered in the LSU SLIS distance education program, see Appendix C of this chapter.

NOTES

1. Louisiana State University, Baton Rouge. "Announcement of Summer Courses in Library Science. 1926."

2. Abramson, Debra. "The Louisiana Library Association: Its History." *LLA Bulletin* 15 (March 1952): 71.

3. "School of Library Science: Report of the First Five Years, 1931–1936." *University Bulletin, Louisiana State University* 29 N.S. no. 3 (March 1937): 1.

4. Louisiana State University, Baton Rouge. "Announcement of Summer Courses in Library Science, 1926–1931." [This announcement with course listings appeared in all bulletins from 1926 to 1931.]

5. Morton, Florrinell F. "Twenty-Five Years in the Life of a Library School; Louisiana State University, 1931–1955." *LLA Bulletin* 18 (fall 1955): 129.

6. Margaret Herdman. "The Library School of Louisiana State University." *Bulletin of the Louisiana Library Association* 2 (December 1938): 10.

7. Sources are conference programs for these dates and circular no. 3559, dated April 24, 1951, to parish superintendents re: elementary materials workshop by Shelby M. Jackson, State Superintendent of Education.

8. Morton, "Twenty-Five Years in the Life of a Library School," p. 141.

9. LSU Distance Advisory Council. "A Long Range Plan for Distance Education at Louisiana State University." May 20, 1997, Appendix A, p. 15.

10. Extension Work, Session 1929–30. *University Bulletin, LSU Agricultural and Mechanical College.* XXII-N.S. Catalogue Issue 1929–30. No. 4 (April 1930): 154.

11. Extension Work, Session 1930–31. *University Bulletin, LSU Agricultural and Mechanical College.* XXIV-N.S. Catalogue Issue 1931–32. No. 4 (April 1932): 156.

12. Morton. "Twenty-Five Years in the Life of a Library School," p. 132.

13. "Important Dates in the Development of Library Education at Louisiana State University." *Louisiana State University Library School Newsletter.* 25th anniversary edition. (March 1956): 2.

14. Correspondence from Florinnell Morton to J. W. Brouillette, director, General Extension Division, re: course in library science for teachers in the Strawberry Parishes. March 17, 1948.

15. Courses offered at Jefferson Parish Library (Letter, Maurice D. Walsh Jr., December 2, 1969, which included a formal request for courses other than LS 123, LS 127, LS 115, LS 112, and LS 222).

16. Donald Foos, May 14, 1975, report to Fritz McCameron, director of Continuing Education, on State Certification of Instructors.

17. Includes the correspondence of Kathleen Heim McCook and Bert Boyce to instructors in northern and southern Louisiana and this memo: "Approval for Instructors for use in extension courses in northern Louisiana, September 9, 1991, from Bert Boyce, dean of the School of Library and Information Science to Kathleen Heim, dean of the LSU Graduate School.

18. Lee Shiflett, ed. "SLIS Extension Courses Serve the State." *Alumni Association Newsletter, School of Library and Information Science, LSU* 14 (spring 1987): 2.

19. Danny P. Wallance to Alma E. Dawson, May 30, 2000, e-mail, re: Teaching Off-Campus Courses through the Telelearning Program at LSU SLIS.

20. Lee Shiflett, interview with Alma Dawson, May 15, 2000.

21. Michael Carpenter, interview with Alma Dawson, May 17, 2000.

22. Charles Patterson, telephone interview with Alma Dawson, August 25, 2000.

23. Rachel Green to Dr. Kathleen Heim, School of Library and Information Science, letter dated 20 August 1987.

24. Beth Paskoff and Lee Shiflett, eds. "SLIS Launches LSU's Two-Way Interactive Video Instruction." *LSU School of Library and Information Science Newsletter* 24 (fall 1995): 1.

25. Joe Hutchinson (Director of DISD), interview by Alma Dawson, July 28, 2000.

26. Patsy Perritt, interview by Alma Dawson, December 6, 2000.

SUGGESTED READING

Carter, Jane Robbins. "News Release—Graduate Resident Center Courses in Library Science." LSU, Graduate School of Library Science, 1980.

Koenig, Paul E. *Report of the Committee on Extramural Resident Graduate Credit.* Louisiana State University: Division of Continuing Education, 1–8, n.d.

"Library Personnel Conference." *LSU Library School Newsletter* (May 1960): 2.

LSU Library School News Bulletin (October 1938): 1.

Morton, Florrinell. "Extension Services." *LSU Library School Biennial Report* (1956–58): 3–4.

———. "Extension Services." *LSU Library School Biennial Report* (1958–60): 3.

———. "Progress." *LSU Library School Biennial Report* (1962–64): 1.

———. "Progress." *LSU Library School Biennial Report* (1964–66): 1–2.

———. "Resident Instruction." *LSU Library School Biennial Report* 1966–68): 2–3.

———. "Service to the Public." *LSU Library School Biennial Report* (1960–62): 1–2.

———. "Off Campus Courses." *LSU Library School Biennial Report* (1954–56): 3–4.

———. "Off Campus Courses." *LSU Library School Biennial Report* (1968–70): 7.

———. "Other Significant Information." *LSU Library School Biennial Report* (1950–52): 4.

Powell, John B. III. *A History of Louisiana State University Division of Continuing Education 1924–1973.* PhD dissertation. Louisiana State University, 1977.

Shyler, Marsha. "Distance Learning: TV Degrees." *Sunday Advocate* (Baton Rouge), January 30, 2000.

APPENDIX A
PROJECTED THREE-YEAR CURRICULUM FOR NORTHERN LOUISIANA
SPRING 1992–FALL 1994

	Spring 1992	Summer 1992	Fall 1992	Spring 1993	Summer 1993
Monroe/Ruston			7203—Sources of Government Inf. Martha Lawson Alternating Sat.	7003—Collection Development Walter Wicker Louisiana Tech Saturdays	7700—History of Books and Libraries Walter Wicker Louisiana Tech Saturdays
Natchitoches/ Shreveport	7405—Public Libraries Jeffery Salter LSU-Shreveport Sat. 9 A.M.–12 P.M.	7002—Inf. Services Alda Jarred Northwestern State Univ. Saturdays	7101—Media Servs. for Children Mattie Mosley LSU-Shreveport Thurs. 5:30–8:30 P.M.	7005—Foundations of Lib. and Inf. Science Brady Banta Thurs. 5:30–8:30 P.M.	

	Fall 1993	Spring 1994	Summer 1994	Fall 1994
Monroe/Ruston	7403—Special Libs. & Inf. Ctrs. Martha Lawson Alternating Sats.			
Natchitoches/ Shreveport	7608—Cat. and Classification Mattie Mosley LSU-Shreveport Thur. 5:30–8:30 P.M.	7807—Lib. User Inst. Alda Jarred Northwestern State Univ. Alternating Sats.	7807—Lib. User Inst. Alda Jarred Northwestern State Univ. Alternating Sats.	7405—Public Libraries Jeffrey Salter LSU-Shreveport Saturdays 7200—Resources for the Humanities Orella Brazile Southern-Shreveport Thurs. 5:30–8:30 P.M.

142

APPENDIX B
PROJECTED CURRICULUM FOR SOUTHERN LOUISIANA
SPRING 1993–FALL 1996

	Spring 1993	Summer 1993	Fall 1993	Spring 1994	Summer 1994	Fall 1994
New Orleans	7005—Foundations John Budd UNO Wed. 6–9:00 P.M.	7004—Management Don Wilson UNO Sat. 9 A.M.–3 P.M. 6/12–7/24	7404—Health Sci. Librarianship Judith Caruthers UNO Wed. 6–9 P.M.	7201—Social Sci. Lee Shifflett UNO Sat. 9 A.M.–12 P.M.	7400—Sch. Med. Ctrs. Brenda Hatfield UNO MTWThF 9 A.M.–12 P.M. (2½ weeks)	7700—History of the Book Florence Jumonville UNO Sat. 9 A.M.–12 P.M.
Lafayette	7809—Research Danny Wallace USL Thurs. 6–9:00 P.M.		7005—Foundations Gary Rolstad USL Wed. 6–9:00 P.M.	7003—Collection Development CANCELED		7002—Information Services Staff USL

	Spring 1995	Summer 1995	Fall 1995	Spring 1996	Summer 1996	Fall 1996
New Orleans	7606—Abstracting and Indexing Carol Barry UNO Tues. 6–9:00 P.M.	7101 CANCELED	7002—Information Services Dana Watson Sat. 9 A.M.–12 P.M.	7209—Special Collections Florence Jumonville UNO Sat. 9 A.M–12 P.M.	7405—Public Libraries Don Wilson UNO Sat. 9 A.M–12 P.M.	
Lafayette	7700 CANCELED		7004 CANCELED			

APPENDIX C
A CHRONOLOGICAL LISTING OF COURSES OFFERED IN THE DISTANCE EDUCATION FORMAT BY THE LSU SLIS

1937: First extension course offered
1937–1947: Specific course records not available

1947

Fall
LS 115—Children's Books
Opelousas, LA
Ms. Norris McClellan, GSLS

Fall
LS 125—Book Selection for Teachers
Natchitoches, LA
Ms. Leo Carnahan

1948

Spring (2/24–5/29)
LS 115–Children's Books and Lib.
   Work with Children
New Roads, LA
Ms. Norris McClellan, GSLS
Spring (4/10–6/10)
LS 118—School Libraries
Hammond, LA
Ms. Norris McClellan, GSLS

Fall
LS 115 E—Children's Books and Lib.
   Work w/Children
Hammond, LA
Ms. Norris McClellan, GSLS

1949

Spring
LIS 115 E—Children's Books and Lib.
   Work with Children
Hammond, LA
Ms. Norris McClellan, GSLS
Spring
LIS 118—School Libraries
Hammond, LA
Ms. Norris McClellan, GSLS

Fall
LS 115 E—Books and A-VI Materials for
Children
Monroe, LA
Ms. Norris McClellan, GSLS

1950

Spring
LS 112 E—Selection and Use of Materials
   for School Libs.
Baton Rouge, LA
Ms. Norris McClellan, GSLS
Fall
LS 115—Books and Audio-Visual
   Materials for Children
Baton Rouge, LA
Ms. Mildred Harrington, GSLS

Fall
LS 115—Books and Audio-Visual Materials
   for Children
Covington, LA
Ms. Norris McClellan, GSLS

1951

Fall
LS 115—Books and Audio-Visual
   Materials for Children
New Orleans, LA
Ms. Norris McClellan, GSLS

1952

Spring
LS 115 E—Books and Audio-Visual Materials for Children
New Orleans, LA
Ms. Norris McClellan, GSLS

1953

Fall
LS 127—Libraries as Information Centers
Franklinton, LA
Ms. Norris McClellan, GSLS

1954

Spring
LS 115—Books and Audio-Visual Materials for Children
Amite, LA
Ms. Norris McClellan, GSLS

1956

Spring
LS 115—Books and Audio-Visual Materials for Children
Ms. Norris McClellan, GSLS

1957

Spring
Books for Young People (noncredit)
Bastrop, Jena, and St. Joseph, LA
Ms. Norris McClellan, GSLS

1960

Spring
LS 127—Libraries as Information Centers
Gretna, LA
Ms. S. Metella Williams, GSLS
Spring
LS 226—Problems in Sel. and Use of
    Library Materials
Monroe, LA
Ms. Norris McClellan, GSLS
Fall
LS 115—Books and Audio-Visual Materials
    for Children
Bogalusa, LA
Ms. Norris McClellan, GSLS

Fall
LS 127—Libraries as Information Centers
Jefferson Parish Library, LA
Ms. S. Metella Williams, GSLS
Fall
LS 222—Guidance of Young People's Reading
Monroe, LA
Dr. Shirley Stephenson, GSLS

1961

Spring
LS 123—Sel. and Use of Books and
    Audio-Visual Materials
Jefferson Parish—Gretna, LA
Dr. Ruth Baldwin, GSLS
Spring
LS 222—Guidance of Young People's
    Reading
Shreveport, LA
Dr. Shirley Stephenson, GSLS

Fall
LS 118—School Libraries
Chalmette, LA
Ms. Norris McClellan, GSLS
Fall
LS 123—Sel. and Use of Books andl
    Audio-Visual Materials
Jefferson Parish, LA
Dr. Ruth Baldwin, GSLS

1962

Spring
LS 118—Schools Libraries
New Orleans, LA
Ms. Norris McClellan, GSLS
Spring
LS 224—Guidance of Adult Reading
Shreveport, LA
Dr. Shirley Stephenson, GSLS
Fall
LS 117—Acquisition and Org. of Lib. Materials
St. Bernard, Chalmette, LA
Ms. Norris McClellan, GSLS

Fall
LS 224—Guidance of Adult Reading
Monroe, LA
Dr. Ruth Baldwin, GSLS
Fall
Noncredit Course—Northern Parishes
    Librarians
Quachita Parish, Winsboro, LA
Dr. Shirley Stephenson, GSLS

1963

Spring
LS 222—Guidance of Young People's Reading
Alexandria, LA
Dr. Shirley Stephenson, GSLS

Fall
LS 225—Problems in School Librarianship
Alexandria, LA
Ms. Norris McClellan, GSLS

1964

Spring
LS 115—Books and Audio-Visual Materials
    for Children
Harahan, LA
Dr. Shirley Stephenson, GSLS
Spring
LS 127—Libraries as Information Centers
Baton Rouge, LA
Ms. Genevieve F. Aillet
Spring
LS 225—Problems in School Librarianship
Ms. Dorothy Nickey

Fall
LS 222—Guidance of Young People's
    Reading
Lafayette, LA
Dr. Shirley Stephenson, GSLS
Fall
LS 226—Problems in Selection and Use of
    School Library Materials (resident credit)
Alexandria, LA
Ms. Norris McClellan, GSLS

1965

Spring
LS 118 Sel. and Use of Materials for
    School Libraries
Gretna, LA
Ms. Gladys Ward, visiting assistant professor
Spring
LS 179—History of Books and Libs.
Lafayette, LA
Ms. Florrinell Morton, GSLS
LS 205—Library Org. and Administration
Lafayette, LA
Dr. Ruth Baldwin, GSLS

Fall
LS 205—Library Org. and Administration
Alexandria, LA
Mr. John Richard
Fall
LS 226—Prob. in Sel. and Use of School
    Lib. Materials
Alexandria, LA
Ms. Norris McClellan, GSLS

1966

Spring
LS 203—Library Resources
Lafayette, LA
Dr. Shirley Stephenson, GSLS
Spring
LS 224—Guidance of Adult Reading
Natchitoches, LA
Dr. Ruth Baldwin, GSLS

Fall
LS 127—Libraries as Information Centers
Baton Rouge, LA
Ms. Genevieve F. Gibbs
Fall
LS 203—Library Resources
Alexandria, LA
Mr. John Richard

Fall
LS 118
Mandeville, LA
Ms. Colleen Sally

Spring
LS 118—School Libraries
Mandeville, LA
Ms. Colleen Sally
Spring
LS 118—School Libraries
Baton Rouge, LA
Ms. Genevieve F. Aillet
Spring
LS 204—Library Resources
Alexandria, LA
Mr. John Richard
Spring
LS 207—Reference Services
Shreveport, LA
Mr. Charles Harrington
Spring
LS 224—Guidance of Adult Reading
Harahan, LA
Dr. Ruth Baldwin, GSLS

Spring
LS 118
Baton Rouge, LA
Ms. Genevieve Aillet
Spring
LS 127
Covington, LA
Ms. Colleen Sally

Spring
LS 224—Guidance of Adult Reading
Shreveport, LA
Dr. Ruth Baldwin, GSLS

Fall
LS 224—Guidance of Adult Reading
Lafayette, LA
Dr. Ruth Baldwin, GSLS

1967
Fall
LS 112—Sel. and Use of Materials for School Libs.
Mandeville, LA
Ms. Colleen Sally
Fall
LS 179—History of Books and Libraries
Alexandria, LA
Ms. Florrinell Morton, GSLS
Fall
LS 204—Library Resources
Lafayette, LA
Dr. Shirley Stephenson, GSLS
Fall
LS 205—Library Org. and Administration
New Orleans, LA
Dr. Ruth Baldwin, GSLS

1968
Spring
LS 205—Library Org. and Administration
Shreveport, LA
Dr. Ruth Baldwin, GSLS
Fall
LS 115
Reserve, LA
Ms. Colleen Sally

1969

1970: No extension courses

1971

Spring
LS 179—History of Books and Libraries
Lafayette, LA
Ms. Florrinell Morton, GSLS

1972

Fall
LS 205—Principles of Lib. Mgt. and Automation
Shreveport, LA
Dr. Ruth Baldwin, GSLS

1973: No extension courses identified

1974

Spring
LS 205—Principles of Lib. Mgt.and Automation
Lafayette, LA
Dr. Donald Foos, GSLS
Summer
LS 201—Cataloging and Classification
Lafayette, LA
Dr. Francis Miksa, GSLS
Summer
LS 235—Inf. Resources of the Health Sciences
New Orleans, LA
Ms. Kay Haas

Summer
LS 244—Health Sciences Librarianship
New Orleans, LA
Ms. Hay Haas
Fall
LibS 7002—Reference and Bibliography
Lafayette, LA
Dr. Charles D. Patterson, GSLS
Fall
LibS 7104—Media for Adults
Shreveport, LA
Dr. Donald D. Foos, GSLS

1975

Spring
LibS 7001—Selection of Lib. Materials
    and Collection Dev.
Shreveport, LA
Dr. Patsy H. Perritt, GSLS
Spring
LibS 7001—Selection of Lib. Materials
    and Collection Dev.
Lafayette, LA
Dr. Robert K. Dikeman, GSLS
Summer
LibS 7204—Inf. Resources of the
    Health Sciences
New Orleans, LA
Dr. Nancy Hardy
Summer
LibS 7303—Health Sciences Librarianship
New Orleans, LA
Dr. Nancy Hardy

Summer
LibS 7402—Systems of Libraries
Shreveport, LA
Dr. Donald D. Foos, GSLS
Fall
LibS 7006 Cataloging and Classification
Shreveport, LA
Dr. Francis L. Miksa, GSLS
Fall
LibS 7402—Systems of Libraries
Lafayette, LA
Dr. Donald D. Foos, GSLS

1976

Spring
LibS 7002—Reference and Bibliography
Shreveport, LA
Dr. Charles D. Patterson, GSLS
Spring
LibS 7102—Media for Young Adults
Lafayette, LA
Dr. Patsy H. Perritt, GSLS
Summer
LibS 7204—Inf. Resources of the
    Health Sciences
Shreveport, LA
Dr. Robert Berk

Summer
LibS 7303—Health Sciences Librarianship
Shreveport, LA
Dr. Robert Berk
Summer
LibS 7900—Research Methods in Library Sci.
Lafayette, LA
Dr. Donald D. Foos, GSLS
Fall
LibS 7004—Principles of Lib. Mgt. and
    Automation
Shreveport, LA
Dr. Donald D. Foos, GSLS

1977

Spring
LibS 7004—Principles of Lib. Mgt.and
    Automation
Lafayette, LA
Dr. Ruth Baldwin, GSLS

Summer
LibS 7303—Health Sciences
    Librarianship
New Orleans, LA
Dr. Virginia L. Algermissen

Spring
LibS 7102—Media for Young Adults
Shreveport, LA
Dr. Patsy H. Perritt, GSLS
Summer
LibS 7204—Inf. Resources of the Health
   Sciences
New Orleans, LA
Dr. Virginia L. Algermissen

Fall
LibS 7001—Selection of Lib. Materials and
   Collection Dev.
Shreveport, LA
Dr. Patsy H. Perritt, GSLS
Fall
LibS 7605—Documents and Inf. Retrieval
New Orleans, LA
Dr. Robert K. Dikeman, GSLS

1978

Spring
LibS 7004—Principles of Lib. Mgt. and
   Automation
New Orleans, LA
Dr. Jane Robbins, GSLS
Spring
LibS 7006—Cataloging and Classification
Shreveport, LA
Dr. Francis L. Miksa, GSLS
Spring
LibS 7104—Media for Young Adults
Lafayette, LA
Dr. Donald D. Foos, GSLS
Spring
LibS 7202—Resources in Sciences and Technology
New Orleans, LA
Dr. Robert K. Dikeman, GSLS

Summer
LibS 7204—Inf. Resources of the Health
   Sciences
Shreveport, LA
Dr. Pauline Angione
Fall
LibS 7001—Selection of Lib. Materials
   and Collection Dev.
New Orleans, LA
Dr. Patsy H. Perritt, GSLS
Fall
LibS 7002—Reference and Bibliography
Shreveport, LA
Dr. Charles D. Patterson, GSLS

1979

Spring
LibS 7004—Principles of Lib. Mgt. and
   Automation
Shreveport, LA
Dr. Donald D. Foos, GSLS
Spring
LibS 7607—Online Lib. Systems and Services
New Orleans, LA
Ms. Judith Caruthers
Summer
LibS 7204—Resources of the Health Sciences
New Orleans, LA
Dr. Pauline Angione

Summer
LibS 7404—Health Sciences Librarianship
New Orleans, LA
Dr. Pauline Angione
Fall
LibS 7200—Resources for the Humanities
New Orleans, LA
Dr. Charles D. Patterson, GSLS

1980

Spring
LibS 7405—Public Librarianship
New Orleans, LA
Dr. Eugene Wright
Summer
LibS 7404—Health Sciences Librarianship
Baton Rouge, LA
Dr. Jane Pool

Fall
LibS 7209—Resources in Special Libraries
New Orleans, LA
Dr. David Combe
Fall
LibS 7400—School Librarianship
Alexandria, LA
Dr. Mary Chaudoir

Summer
LibS 7204—Resources for the Health Sciences
Baton Rouge, LA
Dr. Jane Pool

1981

Spring
LibS 7607—Online Lib. Systems and Services
New Orleans, LA
Ms. Judith Caruthers

Spring
LibS 7800—Art and Practice of Storytelling
Lafayette, LA
Dr. Patsy H. Perritt, SLIS Faculty

Summer
LibS 7204—Resources for the Health Sciences
Shreveport, LA
Dr. Robert Berk

Summer
LS 7209
British Isles
Dr. Eloise Norton

Summer
LibS 7404—Health Sciences Librarianship
Shreveport, LA
Dr. Robert Berk

Fall
LibS 7400—School Librarianship
Thibodeaux, LA
Dr. Sara Buckmaster

Fall
LibS 7505—Media and Services for Young Adults
Pineville, LA
Dr. Mary Chaudoir

Fall
LibS 7505—Analysis of Library and Inf. Systems
New Orleans, LA
Dr. Anthony Tassin

Fall
LibS 7908—Special Topics in Lib. and Inf. Sci.
Lafayette, LA
Dr. Jean Kreamer, Adjunct Professor

Fall
LibS 7102—Media and Services for Young Adults
Alexandria, LA
Dr. Mary Chaudoir

1982

Spring
LibS 7908—Special Topics in Lib. and Inf. Systems
Lafayette, LA
Dr. Jean Kreamer, Adjunct Professor

1983

Summer
LibS 7908—Special Topics in Lib. and Inf. Systems
Alexandria, LA
Dr. Mary Chaudoir Edwards

1984

Spring
LibS 7006—Organization of Information-
  Description
Alexandria, LA
Dr. Francis Miksa, SLIS Faculty

Spring
LibS 7501—Management of Lib. and
  Inf. Systems
New Orleans, LA
Dr. Lee Shiflett, SLIS

Summer
LibS 7003—Lib. and Inf. Agencies and
Resources
Shreveport, LA
Dr. Mary Edwards

Fall
LibS 7002—References and Bibliography
Alexandria, LA
Dr. Charles Patterson, SLIS

Fall
LibS 7004—Principles of Library Mgt
Shreveport, LA
Dr. Joy Lowe

Fall
LibS 7106—Problems in Sel. and Eval.Their
  of Lib. Res.
Baton Rouge, LA
Dr. Patsy Perritt, SLIS

Summer
LibS 7004—Principles of Library Managemen
Alexandria, LA
Dr. Mary Edwards

Fall 1984
LibS 7403—Special Librarianship
New Orleans, LA
Dr. Tillie Krieger

1985

Spring
LibS 7003—Lib. and Inf. Agencies and
    Their Resources
Alexandria, LA
Dr. Sara Buckmaster

Spring
LibS 7405—Public LibrarianshipL
New Orleans, LA
Dr. Elfreda Chatman, SLIS

Spring
LibS 7603—Organization-Document
    Systems-Description
Shreveport, LA
Dr. Mattie Mosley

Summer
LibS 7101—Media and Services for Children
Alexandria, LA
Dr. Mary Edwards

Summer
LibS 7102—Media and Services for Young Adults
Shreveport, LA
Dr. Patsy H. Perritt, SLIS

Summer
LibS 7603—Org. of Document
    Systems-Description
New Orleans, LA
Dr. Leslie Morris

Fall
ibS 7002—Reference and Bibliography
Lafayette, LA
Dr. Sara Buckmaster

Fall
LibS 7202—Resources for Sci. and Tech.
New Orleans, LA
Dr. Eleanor S. Elder

Fall
LibS 7209—Resources for Law Librarianship
New Orleans, LA
Dr. David Comb

Fall
LibS 7405—Public Librarianship
Shreveport, LA
Dr. Julia K. Avant

1986

Spring
LibS 7004—Principles of Library
    Management
New Orleans, LA
Dr. Kathleen Heim, SLIS

Spring
LibS 7401—Academic Librarianship
Shreveport, LA
Dr. Joy Lowe

Spring
LibS 7605—Information Science
Lafayette, LA
Dr. Danny Wallace, SLIS

Summer
LibS 7002—Information Services
New Orleans, LA
Dr. John Budd

Summer
LibS 7209—Inf. Resources for Special Subjects
Shreveport-Baton Rouge, LA
Dr. Patsy Perritt, SLIS

Fall
LibS 7201—Resources for the Social Sciences
Shreveport, LA
Dr. Ada Jarred

Fall
LibS 7506—Automation of Bibliographic
    Control Systems
New Orleans, LA
Dr. Danny Wallace, SLIS

1987

Spring
LibS 7002—Information Services
    (Telelearning)
Shreveport, LA
Dr. Lee Shiflett, SLIS

Summer
LibS 7907—Special Topics in Lib. and
    Inf. Science
England
Dr. Patsy Perritt, SLIS

Spring
LibS 7003—Lib. and Inf. Agencies and
  Their Resources
New Orleans, LA
Ms. Anna Perrault
Spring
LibS 7401—Academic Libraries
New Orleans, LA
Dr. John Budd
Summer
LibS 7209—Inf. Resources for Special Subjects
Shreveport, LA
Dr. Patsy Perritt, SLIS Faculty
Summer
LibS 7809—Research in Library and Inf. Science
New Orleans, LA
Dr. John Budd

Summer
LibS 7909
England
Dr. Patsy Perritt, SLIS
Fall
LibS 7003—Lib. and Inf. Agencies
  and Their Res. (Telelearning)
Alexandria and Shreveport, LA
Dr. Lee Shiflett, SLIS
Fall
LibS 7405—Public Libraries
New Orleans, LA
Dr. Dan Wilson and Dr. Pat Coady

1988

Spring
LibS 7004—Principles of Library Management
Natchitoches, LA
Dr. Ada Jarred
Spring
LibS 7608—Cataloging and Classification
New Orleans, LA
Dr. Mark McKnight
Summer
LibS 7907—Special Topics in Lib. and Inf. Science
New Orleans, LA
Drs. Kathleen Heim, SLIS, and Lee Shiflett, SLIS

Fall
LibS 7404—Health Sciences Information Centers
New Orleans, LA
Ms. Judith Caruthers
Fall
LibS 7605—Inf. Science (Telelearning)
Alexandria and Shreveport, LA
Dr. Danny Wallace, SLIS

1989

Spring
LibS 7102—Med. & Serv. Young Adults
  (Telelearning)
Alexandria and Shreveport, LA
Dr. Patsy Perritt, SLIS
Spring
LibS 7907—Special Topics in Lib. and
  Inf. Science
New Orleans, LA
Dr. Danny Wallace, SLIS
Summer
LibS 7103—Med. & Servs. for Young Ad
  (Telelearning)
Alexandria, Shreveport, and Monroe, LA
Dr. Patsy Perritt, SLIS

Summer
LibS 7605—Information Science
New Orleans, LA
Dr. Danny Wallace, SLIS
Fall
LibS 7004—Principles of Library
  Management
New Orleans, LA
Mr. Gary Rolstad
Fall
LibS 7400—School Media Centers
  (Telelearning)
Alexandria, Shreveport, and Monroe, LA
Dr. Patsy Perritt, SLIS

1990

Spring
LibS 7003—Lib. & Inf. Agencies and Res.
  (Telelearning)
Alexandria, Shreveport, LA
Dr. Connie Fleet, SLIS

Summer
LibS 7907—Special Topics in Lib. and
  Inf. Science
Shreveport, LA
Dr. Patsy Perritt, SLIS

Spring
LibS 7209—Inf. Resources for Special Subjects
New Orleans, LA
Mr. Gary Rolstad
Fall
LibS 7809—Res. in Lib. and Inf. Sci. (Telelearning)
Alexandria, New Orleans, and Shreveport, LA
Dr. Danny Wallace, SLIS

Fall
LibS 7002—Information Services
Lafayette, LA
Dr. Charles Patterson, SLIS

1991

Spring
LibS 7002—Information Services
Harvey, LA
Dr. Danny Wallace, SLIS
Spring
LibS 7004—Principles of Mgt. (Telelearning)
Baton Rouge, Alexandria, Lafayette, and
    Shreveport
Dr. Michael Carpenter, SLIS
Spring
LibS 7209—Inf. Resources for Special
    Subjects (Sources in African American
    History and Culture)
New Orleans, LA
Dr. Keith Winsell

Fall
LIS 7002—Information Services
Alexandria, LA
Dr. Charles Patterson, SLIS
Fall
LIS 7405—Public Libraries
New Orleans, LA
Dr. Dan Wilson
Fall
LIS 7908—Special Topics: Use of Media
in Libraries
Lafayette, LA
Dr. Jean Kreamer, adjunct faculty

1992

Spring
LibS 7405—Public Libraries
Shreveport, LA
Mr. Jeff Salter
Spring
LibS 7608—Cataloging and Classification
New Orleans, LA
Dr. Lee Shiflett, SLIS
Summer
LibS 7002—Information Services
Natchitoches, LA
Dr. Ada Jarred
Fall
LibS 7002—Information Services
New Orleans, LA
Dr. Charles Patterson, SLIS

Fall
LIS 7005—Foundations in Lib. and Inf. Science
Lafayette, LA
Mr. Gary Rolstad
Fall
LIS 7101—Media and Services for Children
Shreveport, LA
Dr. Mattie Mosely
Fall
LibS 7203—Sources of Government Information
New Orleans, LA
Drs. Lee Shiflett, SLIS, and Martha Lawson

1993

Spring
LIS 7003—Principles of Collection Management
Ruston, LA
Dr. Walter Wicker
Spring
LIS 7005—Foundations of Library
    and Inf. Science
Shreveport, LA
Dr. Brady Banta

Summer
LibS 7004—Principles of Management
New Orleans, LA
Dr. Dan Wilson
Summer
LibS 7700—History of Books and Libraries
Ruston, LA
Dr. Walter Wicker

Spring
LIS 7005—Foundations of Library and
    Inf. Science
New Orleans, LA
Dr. John Budd, SLIS

Spring
LIS 7809—Research in Library and Inf. Science
Lafayette, LA
Dr. Danny P. Wallace, SLIS

Fall
LIS 7404—Health Sciences Information
    Centers
New Orleans, LA
Ms. Judith Caruthers

Fall
LIS 7607—Cataloging and Classification
Shreveport, LA
Dr. Mattie Mosley

1994

Spring
LIS 7200—Resources for the Humanities
Shreveport, LA
Dr. Orella Brazile

Spring
LIS 7201—Resources for the Social Sciences
New Orleans, LA
Dr. Lee Shiftlett, SLIS

Summer
LIS 7004—Principles of Mgt. in Inf. Agencies
Shreveport, LA
Dr. Brady Banta

Fall
LIS 7700—History of Books and Libraries
New Orleans, LA
Ms. Florence Jumonville

1995

Spring
LIS 7606—Abstracting and Indexing
(compressed video)
Dr. Carol Barry, SLIS

Fall
LIS 7002—Information Services
New Orleans, LA
Dr. Dana Watson, SLIS

Fall
LIS 7400—School Media Centers
(compressed video)
Dr. Patsy Perritt, SLIS

1996

Spring
LIS 7107—Use of Media in Libraries
(compressed video)
Dr. Dana Watson, SLIS

Spring
LIS 7202—Resources for Sci. and Tech.
(compressed video)
Dr. Beth Paskoff, SLIS

Spring
LIS 7209—Special Collections
New Orleans, LA
Dr. Florence Jumonville

Summer
LIS 7201—Res. for the Social Sciences
(compressed video)
Dr. Lee Shiflett, SLIS

Summer
LIS 7405—Public Libraries
New Orleans, LA
Dr. Dan Wilson

Fall
LIS 7400—School Media Centers
(compressed video)
Dr. Patsy Perritt, SLIS

1997

Spring
LIS 7008—Computer Fundamentals for
    Inf. Mgt.
(compressed video)
Dr. Carol Barry, SLIS

LIS 7005—Foundations of Lib. and Inf. Science
    video)
Dr. Lee Shiflett, SLIS

Summer
LIS 7203—Sources of Government
    Inf.
(compressed video)
Dr. Lee Shiflett, SLIS

LIS 7400—School Media Centers(compressed
(compressed video)
Dr. Patsy Perritt, SLIS

1998

Spring
LIS 7002—Information Services
(compressed video)
Dr. Dana Watson, SLIS

Spring
LIS 7003—Principles of Collection
   Management
(compressed video)
Dr. Alma Dawson, SLIS

Spring
LIS 7908—Legal Bibliography
(compressed video)
Carla Pritchett and Marie Erickson

Summer
LIS 7205—Business Inf. Resources
(compressed video)
Dr. Beth Paskoff, SLIS

Fall
LIS 7400—School Media Centers
(compressed video)
Dr. Patsy Perritt, SLIS

1999

Spring
LIS 7012—Bibliographic Org. and Res. Dev.
(compressed video)
Dr. Michael Carpenter, SLIS

Spring
LIS 7201—Res. for the Social Sciences
(compressed video)
Dr. Robert Ward

Spring
LIS 7608—Cataloging and Classification
(compressed video)
Dr. Lee Shiflett, SLIS

Summer
LIS 7013—Evaluation of Information Systems
(compressed video)
Dr. Carol Barry, SLIS

Summer
LIS 7910—Special Topics; Archives
(compressed video)
Dr. Brady Banta

Fall
LIS 7011—Inf. Needs Analysis
(compressed video)
Dr. Lee Shiflett, SLIS

Fall
LIS 7403—Special Libraries
(compressed video)
Dr. Beth Paskoff, SLIS

2000

Spring
LIS 7008—Information Technologies
Web-based
Dr. David Robins, SLIS

Spring
LIS 7401—Academic Libraries
(compressed video)
Dr. Alma Dawson, SLIS

Spring
LIS 7901—Issues in Library and Inf. Science
(compressed video)
Dr. Beth Paskoff, SLIS

Fall
LIS 7002—Information Service
Web-based
Dr. Dana Watson, SLIS

Fall
LIS 7005—Foundations of Lib. and Inf. Science
(compressed video)
Mr. Jason Holmes, SLIS

Summer
7002—Information Resources
Web-based
Dr. Dana Watson, SLIS

Summer
LIS 7004—Principles of Inf. Management
(compressed video)
Dr. Michael Carpenter, SLIS

Summer
LIS 7008—Information Technologies
Web-based
Dr. David Robins, SLIS

Fall
LIS 7607—Electronic Information Resources
(compressed video)
Dr. Carol Barry, SLIS

Fall
LIS 7807—Library User Instruction
(compressed video)
Dr. Alma Dawson, SLIS

2001

Spring
LIS 7002—Information Services
(compressed video)
Dr. Elizabeth Dow, SLIS

Spring
LIS 7011—Information Needs Analysis
(compressed video)
Dr. Lee Shiflett, SLIS

Spring
LIS 7107—Use of Media in Libraries
(compressed video)
Ms. Sharon Southhall

Spring
LIS 7403—Special Libraries and Information
 Centers
(compressed video)
Dr. Beth Paskoff, SLIS

Fall
LIS 7203—Sources of Government
 Information
(compressed video)
Ms. Charlene Cain

Summer
LIS 7003—Principles of Collection Management
(compressed video)
Dr. Alma Dawson, SLIS

Summer
LIS 7012—Bibliographic Org. and Resource Dev.
(compressed video)
Dr. Michael Carpenter, SLIS

Summer
LIS 7910—Archives
(compressed video)
Dr. Elizabeth Dow, SLIS

Fall
LIS 7004—Principles of Management in
 Inf. Agencies
(compressed video)
Dr. Michael Carpenter, SLIS

Fall
LIS 7606—Abstracting and Indexing
(compressed video)
Mr. John Anderson

Note that library science faculty are identified by GSLS or SLIS. Instructors who taught class for the school have names listed only.

APPENDIX D
PROJECTED DISTANCE EDUCATION SCHEDULE (SPRING 2002–FALL 2007)

Semester, Year, Day, and Time	Course #	Probable Instructor
SPRING 2002: Saturday 12:30–3:30 P.M.	LIS 7013 EVALUATION OF INFORMATION SYSTEMS	DR. BERT BOYCE
SPRING 2002: Tuesday 4:00–7:00 P.M.	LIS 7200 RESOURCES FOR THE HUMANITIES	DR. MARGIE THOMAS
SPRING 2002: Thursday 4:00–7:00 P.M.	LIS 7202 RESOURCES FOR SCIENCE & TECHNOLOGY	DR. BETH PASKOFF
SPRING 2002: Saturday 8:30–11:30 A.M.	LIS 7608 CATALOGING AND CLASSIFICATION	MS. BOBBY FERGUSON
SPRING 2002: Thursday 7:00–9:00 P.M.	LIS 7901 ISSUES IN LIBRARY AND INF. SCIENCE	DR. BETH PASKOFF
SUMMER 2002: Tues. & Thurs. 4:00–7:00 P.M.	LIS 7005 FOUNDATIONS OF LIBRARY & INF. SCIENCE	DR. ALMA DAWSON
SUMMER 2002: INTERNET	LIS 7008 INFORMATION TECHNOLOGIES	DR. CAVAN MCCARTHY
SUMMER 2002: Mon. & Wed. 4:00–6:40 P.M.	LIS 7404 HEALTH SCIENCES INFORMATION CENTERS	MS. ETHEL MADDEN
SUMMER 2002: Saturday 8:30 A.M.–2:30 P.M.	LIS 7911 RECORDS MANAGEMENT	MS. WENDY MCLAIN
FALL 2002: Tuesday 4:00–7:00 P.M.	LIS 7002 INFORMATION SERVICES	DR. ELIZABETH DOW
FALL 2002: Saturday 8:30–11:30 A.M.	LIS 7400 SCHOOL MEDIA CENTERS	DR. MARGIE THOMAS
FALL 2002: Thursday 4:00–7:00 P.M.	LIS 7807 LIBRARY USER INSTRUCTION	DR. ALMA DAWSON
SPRING 2003: Tuesday 4:00–7:00 P.M.	LIS 7004 PRINCIPLES OF MGT. FOR LIBRARIANS	DR. MICHAEL CARPENTER
SPRING 2003: Thursday 4:00–7:00 P.M.	LIS 7107 USE OF MEDIA IN LIBRARIES	STAFF
SPRING 2003: Saturday 8:30–11:30 A.M.	LIS 7401 ACADEMIC LIBRARIES	DR. ALMA DAWSON
SPRING 2003: Saturday 12:30–3:30 P.M.	LIS 7405 PUBLIC LIBRARIES	DR. ROBERT WARD
SPRING 2003: Thursday 7:00–9:00 P.M.	LIS 7901 ISSUES IN LIBRARY AND INF. SCIENCE	DR. CAROL BARRY
SUMMER 2003: Mon. & Wed. 4:00–7:00 P.M.	LIS 7005 FOUNDATIONS OF LIBRARY AND INF. SCIENCE	DR. ALMA DAWSON
SUMMER 2003: Tues. & Thurs. 4:00–7:00 P.M.	LIS 7101 MEDIA AND SERVICES FOR CHILDREN	DR. MARGIE THOMAS
SUMMER 2003: Saturday 8:30 A.M.–2:30 P.M.	LIS 7608 CATALOGING & CLASSIFICATION	DR. MICHAEL CARPENTER

Semester, Year, Day and Time	Course #	Probable Instructor
FALL 2003: Tuesday 4:00–7:00 P.M.	LIS 7008 INFORMATION TECHNOLOGIES	DR. CAVAN MCCARTHY
FALL 2003: Thursday 4:00–7:00 P.M.	LIS 7402 COOPERATIVES, CONSORTIA, AND NETWORKS	DR. ROBERT WARD
FALL 2003: Saturday 8:30–11:30 A.M.	LIS 7403 SPECIAL LIBRARIES & INF. CTRS	DR. BETH PASKOFF
SPRING 2004: Thursday 4:00–7:00 P.M.	LIS 7011 INFORMATION NEEDS ANALYSIS	DR. CAROL BARRY
SPRING 2004: Tuesday 4:00–7:00 P.M.	LIS 7102 MEDIA AND SERVICES FOR YOUNG ADULTS	DR. MARGIE THOMAS
SPRING 2004: Saturday 12:20–3:30 P.M.	LIS 7202 RESOURCES FOR SCIENCE AND TECHNOLOGY	DR. BETH PASKOFF
SPRING 2004: Saturday 8:30–11:30 A.M.	LIS 7*** RECORDS MANAGEMENT	MS. WENDY MCLAIN
SPRING 2004: Thursday 7:00–9:00 P.M.	LIS 7901 ISSUES IN LIBRARY AND INFORMATION	DR. CAROL BARRY
SUMMER 2004: Tues. & Thurs. 4:00–7:00 P.M.	LIS 7002 INFORMATION SERVICES	DR. ELIZABETH DOW
SUMMER 2004: Mon. & Wed. 4:00–7:00 P.M.	LIS 7005 FOUNDATIONS OF LIBRARY & INF. SCIENCE	DR. ALMA DAWSON
SUMMER 2004: Saturday 8:30 A.M.–2:30 P.M.	LIS 7606 ABSTRACTING AND INDEXING	DR. CAROL BARRY
FALL 2004: Thursday 4:00–7:00 P.M.	LIS 7012 BIBLIOGRAPHIC ORG. & RESOURCE DEV.	DR. BERT BOYCE
FALL 2004: Saturday 8:30–11:30 A.M.	LIS 7203 SOURCES OF GOV'T DOCUMENTS	STAFF
FALL 2004: Tuesday 4:00–7:00 P.M.	LIS 7400 SCHOOL MEDIA CENTERS	DR. MARGIE THOMAS
SPRING 2005: Thursday 4:00–7:00 P.M.	LIS 7013 EVALUATION OF INFORMATION SYSTEMS	DR. BERT BOYCE
SPRING 2005: Saturday 12:30–3:30 P.M.	LIS 7700 HISTORY OF BOOKS & LIBRARIES	DR. MICHAEL CARPENTER
SPRING 2005: Saturday 8:30–11:30 A.M.	LIS 7*** PRINCIPLES OF ARCHIVES MANAGEMENT	DR. ELIZABETH DOW
SPRING 2005: Tuesday 4:00–7:00 P.M.	LIS 7*** DIGITAL LIBRARIES	DR. CAVAN MCCARTHY
SPRING 2005: Thursday 4:00–7:00 P.M.	LIS 7901 ISSUES IN LIBRARY AND INF. SCIENCE	DR. CAROL BARRY
SUMMER 2005: Saturday 8:30 A.M.–2:30 P.M.	LIS 7002 INFORMATION SERVICES	DR. ELIZABETH DOW
SUMMER 2005: Mon. & Wed. 4:00–7:00 P.M.	LIS 7003 PRINCIPLES OF COLLECTION MANAGEMENT	DR. ALMA DAWSON

Semester, Year, Day and Time	Course #	Probable Instructor
SUMMER 2005: Thursday 4:00–7:00 P.M.	LIS 7608 CATALOGING & CLASSIFICATION	DR. MICHAEL CARPENTER
FALL 2005: Thursday 4:00–7:00 P.M.	LIS 7005 FOUNDATIONS OF LIBRARY AND INF. SCIENCE	DR. ALMA DAWSON
FALL 2005: Tuesday 4:00–7:00 P.M.	LIS 7607 ELECTRONIC INFORMATION RESOURCES	DR. CAROL BARRY
FALL 2005: Saturday 8:30–11:30 A.M.	LIS 7800 ART AND PRACTICE OF STORYTELLING	STAFF
SPRING 2006: Saturday 12:30–3:30 P.M.	LIS 7004 PRINCIPLES OF MGT. FOR LIBRARIANS	DR. MICHAEL CARPENTER
SPRING 2006: Saturday 8:30–11:30 A.M.	LIS 7200 RESOURCES FOR THE HUMANITIES	DR. MARGIE THOMAS
SPRING 2006: Tuesday 4:00–7:00 P.M.	LIS 7501 MANAGEMENT OF INFORMATION SYSTEMS	DR. ROBERT WARD
SPRING 2006: Thursday 4:00–7:00 P.M.	LIS 7605 INFORMATION SCIENCE	DR. CAROL BARRY
SPRING 2006: Thursday 7:00–9:00 P.M.	LIS 7904 ISSUES IN LIBRARY AND INF. SCIENCE	DR. CAROL BARRY
SUMMER 2006: Mon. & Wed. 4:00–7:00 P.M.	LIS 7008 INFORMATION TECHNOLOGIES	DR. CAVAN MCCARTHY
SUMMER 2006: Tues. & Thurs. 4:00–7:00 P.M.	LIS 7103 MEDIA AND SERVICES FOR YOUNG ADOLESCENTS	STAFF
SUMMER 2006: Saturday 8:30 A.M.–2:30 P.M.	LIS 7606 ABSTRACTING AND INDEXING	DR. CAROL BARRY
FALL 2006: Saturday 8:30 A.M.–2:30 P.M.	LIS 7011 INFORMATION NEEDS ANALYSIS	DR. CAROL BARRY
FALL 2006: Tuesday 4:00–7:00 P.M.	LIS 7201 RESOURCES FOR THE SOCIAL SCIENCES	DR. ROBERT WARD
FALL 2006: Thursday 4:00–7:00 P.M.	LIS 7*** DESCRIPTION OF ARCHIVAL MATERIALS	DR. ELIZABETH DOW
SPRING 2007: Saturday 8:30–11:30 A.M.	LIS 7005 FOUNDATIONS OF LIBRARY AND INF. SCIENCE	DR. ALMA DAWSON
SPRING 2007: Saturday 12:30–3:30 P.M.	LIS 7205 BUSINESS INFORMATION RESOURCES	DR. BETH PASKOFF
SPRING 2007: Tuesday 4:00–7:00 P.M.	LIS 7809 RESEARCH IN LIBRARY AND INFORMATION SCIENCE	DR. CAROL BARRY
SPRING 2007: Thursday 4:00–7:00 P.M.	LIS 7*** RECORDS MANAGEMENT	STAFF

SPRING 2007: Thursday 4:00–7:00 P.M.	LIS 7901 ISSUES IN LIBRARY AND INFORMATION SCIENCE	DR. CAROL BARRY
SUMMER 2007: Saturday 8:30 A.M.–2:30 P.M.	LIS 7012 BIBLIOGRAPHIC ORGANIZATION AND RESOURCE DEVELOPMENT	STAFF
SUMMER 2007: Mon. & Wed. 4:00–7:00 P.M.	LIS 7406 LITERATURE AND METHODS FOR READERS ADVISORY SERVICE	STAFF
SUMMER 2007: Tues. & Thurs. 4:00–7:00 P.M.	LIS 7801 ILLUSTRATOR AS STORYTELLER	STAFF
FALL 2007: Saturday 8:30–11:30 A.M.	LIS 7013 EVALUATION OF INFORMATION SYSTEMS	STAFF
FALL 2007: Tuesday 4:00–7:00 P.M.	LIS 7502 NETWORKS OF INFORMATION CENTERS	DR. ROBERT WARD
FALL 2007: Thursday 4:00–7:00 P.M.	LIS 7*** PRESERVATION	DR. ELIZABETH DOW

*Tentative; Subject to Change

*Initial Distance Education Site: Louisiana State University, Baton Rouge, LA

*Also at http://slis.lsu.edu/courses/distance_schedule.shtml

160

12

DISTRIBUTED LEARNING: THE DEVELOPMENT OF COURSES AND PROGRAMS IN LIS AT THE UNIVERSITY OF MISSOURI–COLUMBIA

Thomas R. Kochtanek, Charley Seavey, and John Wedman

Thomas R. Kochtanek, Charley Seavey, and John Wedman

BRIEF HISTORY OF THE MLS PROGRAM AT THE UNIVERSITY OF MISSOURI

In 1839 the University of Missouri was chartered as one of the first land grant institutions west of the Mississippi River. The university was established primarily to serve as a residential undergraduate degree granting educational institution. As research activities and graduate education expanded in the twentieth century, so did the University of Missouri. In the early 1950s, Dr. Ralph H. Parker, University Librarian, began to offer courses leading to an undergraduate minor in Library Science through the College of Education. He recruited several new faculty members to the university (Frances J. Flood, Helmut Lehman-Haupt) and expanded the curriculum to include courses in Libraries and Librarianship, Collection Development, Cataloging and Classification, Reference Materials, Management, and Library Information Systems. In 1966 he succeeded in creating a new School of Library and Informational Science (SLIS), which had at the outset two departments: one in library science (LS) and another in information science (IS). The school would attract students from throughout the state of Missouri, offering them an advanced professional degree program of study centered in Columbia. Parker's goal was to develop a cadre of professional librarians in the state, and he felt that a separate department was the most effective tool for promoting this goal. The school, on receiving ALA accreditation in 1968, was thus one of the first MLS-granting programs that incorporated the words *information(al) science* in its title.

Professor Jim Flood served as the first LS chair of the newly accredited school, with Dr. Donald A. B. Lindberg as the first chair of the IS Department. Parker served as dean until his retirement from administration in 1972. He continued to be a member of the SLIS faculty until his retirement from the university in 1977. The SLIS continued as an autonomous unit on campus for the next two decades. During that time period the curriculum moved from a thirty-credit hour program to a thirty-six-hour program, to the present forty-two-credit hour graduate degree program.

As the program grew in terms of numbers of students, demand for coursework outside Columbia became an issue. Many individuals across the state, primarily those in the metropolitan areas of St. Louis, Springfield, and Kansas City, sought to improve their professional credentials by completing the ALA-accredited program. As the only ALA-accredited program in the state, the Columbia campus was charged with the task of supporting demand from a dispersed student base. Residency requirements were strict, and the number of courses offered off campus was limited to those that could be offered by the resident faculty and a few selected adjunct faculty. The courses were primarily delivered on a site off campus, arranged through the Extension Division of the University of Missouri–Columbia, and delivered using a face-to-face model. Students still had to travel to an appointed site at a specific time to receive graduate coursework. This delivery model had limitations of scale and was accompanied by quality control and logistical problems.

In 1996 the SLIS joined the College of Education and merged with an existing Educational Technology program in 1997 to become the School of Information Science and Learning Technologies (SISLT). This merger with a larger unit has extended the resources made available to the program and, among other things, has stimulated growth in the delivery of courses to students at a distance.

Survey results, recent experience, and pressures from the profession all pointed to the same conclusion: *There is a demand across the state of Missouri for graduate education in LIS.* Besides statewide demands for distributed learning opportunities, nearby states lacking an accredited MLS program were interested in gaining the same opportunities for their potential students.

HISTORY OF DEVELOPMENT OF DISTRIBUTED EDUCATIONAL EXPERIENCES

During the first decade of its existence as an ALA-approved MLS-granting program, the SLIS offered its courses primarily in the Columbia area on the MU campus. Occasional courses that were in high demand were offered "in extension" by SLIS faculty in the metropolitan areas of St. Louis, Kansas City, and Springfield. Many students started their MLS careers in extension courses, taught by traveling faculty as a course overload. Typically two or three courses per year, based on faculty availability, were offered in these areas. Because distance courses were considered "course overloads" for individual faculty members, extra compensation was offered to cover the cost of course delivery. The course credit hours were channeled through the Extension Division of the University of Missouri–Columbia, and student head count was not reflected in the statistics of the SLIS.

In 1981 the MLS curriculum was revised, and certain courses were "bundled" together into five-credit-hour blocks of offerings. The then basic core of information technology, cataloging, and reference were offered in these five-hour blocks. This effectively reduced the ability to offer such courses in a distant setting by faculty associated with the SLIS. After five years this curriculum reverted to "standard" three-credit hour core courses, and the offering of courses in extension was again instigated. At this point, extension courses were viewed as a feeder for students being recruited into full-time study at the Columbia campus. Many students in the metropolitan areas (primarily St. Louis and Kansas City) began their program of study in extension and later made the commitment to complete the thirty-six-hour MLS program by taking up residence in Columbia or by commuting to campus to take selective courses that fit with their schedules. Up to half of the curriculum (eighteen credit hours) could be taken off campus, with the remaining required to be taken on campus. "On campus" simply meant that the student was resident in Columbia or visited the campus to take coursework. More often than not students were inconvenienced with the time commitment and travel arrangements for them to meet these residency requirements. Student demand for more offerings resulted in the exploration of the use of adjunct faculty to teach selected courses at off-campus sites.

The use of adjuncts presented yet another problem of coordination. Logistics such as classroom locations and computer labs was one part of this equation. The training and development of a cadre of adjuncts were another. Ownership of courses, syllabi, objectives, and content had to be clearly communicated. Differences between on-campus and off-campus offerings by adjuncts needed to be resolved on a regular basis. Developing and retaining talented adjuncts was yet another issue. The resident faculty "owned" the curriculum, but adjuncts were expected to adopt those same objectives and delivery methods. The key to success was in the communication (or lack thereof) between resident faculty and off-campus or adjunct faculty.

In 1991 the SLIS hired a full-time person whose appointment was 50 percent in extension and 50 percent to the school. The objective of this hire was to support the growing demand and numbers of students who were beginning their graduate professional education in some location other than Columbia. The position was both an administrative appointment and a "faculty" appointment, in the sense that this person coordinated all off-campus offerings and also taught courses within the school.

In the 1993–94 academic year, the coordinator and another SLIS faculty member were awarded a grant from the federal Department of Education for the purposes of developing continuing education programs to librarians across the state of Missouri. The programs were broadcast live to a number of sites within the state, supported by an audio-video telecommunications network being assembled by the University of Missouri. The live presentations were taped for asynchronous viewing by those who were not able to connect live to the network.

In 1994 the first full three-credit hour course was offered via the same telecommunications network. A core course, Library Information Systems, was offered simultaneously to students at all four UM system campuses (St. Louis, Kansas City, Rolla, and Columbia). On-campus credit was awarded to all participants. This was a significant departure from the standard residency requirements, which were location-based. The cost to deliver the course, beyond the costs normally associated with an on campus three-credit hour course, was in excess of $10,000. Although reaching a larger audience, the telecommunications costs proved to be exorbitant, preventing further use of the real-time, synchronous, two-way audio-video system.

Thus the efforts in the 1970s, 1980s, and early 1990s are best characterized as a mix of well-intentioned but not always effective or affordable strategies to meet the distributed demand for LIS programming. Although some strategies are still employed today (e.g., an enhanced adjunct faculty strategy), a robust strategy was needed to be truly responsive to the needs of students who were at a distance.

MEETING THE DEMAND FOR LIS PROGRAMMING IN THE STATE OF MISSOURI AND WITHIN THE REGION

After the formation of SISLT in 1997, the new unit was responsible for several professional degree programs, including the MLS, a master's degree in Educational Technology, and an interdisciplinary doctorate in Information Science and Learning Technologies. The move from being an autonomous unit to being part of a larger college within the overall campus structure brought new opportunities. Though still a separate unit, the former SLIS had to deploy its distance and distributed educational opportunities through the Extension Division of the university. Unfortunately, the student head count and tuition revenue associated with such offerings did not remain with the school, even though it carried with it many administrative and curricular responsibilities. The new parent unit, the College of Education, had its own division for Continuing Professional Education (CPE). This unit was developed some time ago in response to the continuing professional development needs of teachers in Missouri. Coursework developed by SISLT that addressed distributed audiences was administered by CPE, and credit hours along with student revenue streams accompanied those offerings. The business of offering distance and distributed course offerings made the risks and investments of developing new coursework and innovative delivery systems more palatable to the school. Monies generated from student credit hours of new offerings could be reinvested directly into the development of courses and delivery mechanisms.

At the same time the university formed a new unit to support the development and deployment of distributed learning opportunities. The Distance Design Learning Center (DDLC) was initially created under the auspices of the Extension Division. DDLC was charged with administrative and technology support services associated with new and innovative delivery mechanisms. Operating on a cost-recovery basis, this unit sought to support faculty and academic units as they ventured into the uncharted waters of technology-based distance learning. CPE entered an arrangement with the DLDC in 1997 to begin offering graduate-level coursework to students distributed within Missouri and beyond. The primary distribution medium of the new offerings was to be the Web.

The first offering tested by CPE was an SISLT course. Development of a Web-based course offering began in 1996, and the first on-campus offering of a fully developed Web-based course was Library Information Systems, developed by a faculty member within the SISLT and supported by the CPE and DLDC. The course was first offered in fall 1997. Subsequent course development has followed, and currently a number of Web-based courses available to the MLS student are being offered to students in Missouri and the Midwest. Courses include a mix of LIS and Educational Technology content, with the Educational Technology courses sometimes included as electives in an LIS student's program of study.

Since fall 1997 and the Web-based debut of Library Information Systems, SISLT has developed and currently uses a variety of coursework delivery mechanisms. As of spring 2002 these include:

1. Traditional face to face, both on campus and, using adjuncts, in distance sites.

2. Web-assisted courses on campus. The majority of the coursework is delivered via the Web, but a number of face-to-face meetings are held over the semester. This eases the commuting burden on students living within a reasonable driving distance of Columbia.

3. Starburst courses. Starburst courses are developed and taught, via the Web, by Columbia-based faculty. There are face-to-face meetings, up to four a semester, at distant sites, led by an adjunct. SISLT is still experimenting with the optimum configuration for Starburst. At issue are overall student enrollment, enrollment at individual sites, number of sites, and finding qualified adjuncts. There is no doubt that in terms of cost to the school Starburst is an extremely effective delivery mechanism.

4. Purely Web-based courses.

Much of the development of innovative course delivery and enhancement of the distance program in general came as a result of a proposal to the University of Missouri System office in 1999. "Proposal to Create and Sustain

Distributed Graduate Programming in Library and Information Science" gained SISLT program enhancement funding that allowed expansion in several areas. Among those was the hire of an experienced LIS faculty member to be distance learning coordinator. Other parts of the proposal included:

1. Placing LIS clinical faculty in the St. Louis and Kansas City libraries. Clinical faculty will have joint appointments in the sense that they will work both in the campus library (in St. Louis or Kansas City) and teach in the MU LIS program. This approach addresses the isolation issue, removes the tenure and promotion problems, provides local instruction, and increases student access to LIS resources at those two metropolitan areas, each representing an area of high student demand for LIS programming. Clinical faculty may come from the existing cadre of professionals already employed by the libraries in those areas, or they may be new hires.

2. Creating educational partnerships with selected institutions of higher education within the state. Expertise and interest in LIS graduate programming is not limited to the Columbia campus. Regional institutions of higher education within the state offer graduate coursework specializing in school library media certification, for example. In different areas of the state, different models for cooperation will likely be employed, tailored to the unique situation present at each participating regional site.

3. Enhancing the quality of MA adjunct faculty by integrating them further into the life of the school and students;

4. Increasing the number of online MA courses; and

5. Expanding the existing quality assurance mechanisms

As of spring 2002, SISLT is very close to placing a clinical faculty member in the University of Missouri–Kansas City library. The faculty member will work for both the school and the library, strengthening the bonds of the system, and giving the Kansas City–area LIS students far more face-to-face opportunities than they currently enjoy.

Educational partnerships are in place with Southwest Missouri State University, and the University of Nebraska–Omaha. SISLT is currently working on establishing more partnerships, both inside Missouri and in the Great Plains region.

The SISLT faculty is deeply involved in reviewing the structure of the curriculum with an eye toward taking advantage of the Web where possible and putting into place quality control measures in the system of adjuncts and Starburst instructors.

Use of the Web as an instructional tool has certainly increased, but perhaps not in the way originally envisioned in the proposal. As outlined the school is now making extensive use of Web-assisted and Starburst course delivery models in the belief that in some cases, they are more effective pedagogy than pure Web-based delivery. Some courses that do lend themselves to a purely Web-based environment will continue to be offered in that fashion.

A distributed program such as this generates a unique set of quality assurance challenges, challenges greater than those associated with a campus-based program. The challenges include such issues as common syllabi, faculty coordination, resource availability, and course scheduling, as well as ensuring a quality educational experience. SISLT currently uses a quality assurance mechanism referred to as the LEAD (Library and Information Science Educational Access and Development) Initiative. This initiative will need to be expanded in light of the proposed developments in increasing access to the LIS program.

DISTRIBUTED LEARNING AND ASSOCIATED CULTURES

Because the University of Missouri–Columbia and thus the SISLT is essentially isolated from a major population center, they continue to face those challenges associated with the delivery of educational programs. In 1998 the MA graduate degree program implemented a move to a forty-two-hour program, a change from the previous thirty-six-hour requirement. More adjunct course offerings are being developed and supported to meet the demand for student credit hours in distributed locations. All this is taking place while the SISLT continues to develop a cadre of courses using Web-based technology as a major component.

Over the years, while the program was primarily taught in a face-to-face fashion by resident faculty, tensions have developed between two cultures within the student body: the on-campus resident students and the off-campus students. This is made more complex by the fact that more students, resident or not, are attending part-time while meeting employment and family responsibilities as well. The two groups of students (on-campus and off-campus) often represent two totally different cultures.

Resident students, whether full- or part-time, have made the decision to relocate to the Columbia campus and pursue their studies. They seek to engage themselves with the resident faculty, often participating with faculty in research endeavors and project development. They have the opportunity to collaborate face to face with their fellow students and with the resources of the university. Those resources include the faculty and staff of the SISLT, rich library resources, ready access to high-speed telecommunications systems, and the various social and educational opportunities provided in a typical residential campus setting.

Distance students often have restrictions placed on them by their employers or simply by the fact that they are remote from the residential life on campus. A number of students are employed full-time, and they are provided some release to attend classes. Transportation to and from the campus takes its toll in terms of time and cost of transport and parking. Distance students are often fully engaged in the mix of professional practice and educational opportunities and must make sacrifices to balance these demands on their time. Certain events that occur on every campus (e.g., the chance to hear renowned visitors or speakers, participate in weekend activities, and take advantage of the campus technology infrastructure) may not be the sorts of opportunities they will take advantage of, simply because it involves the hours associated with another trip to campus.

The on-campus culture also includes the resident faculty, some of whom may feel threatened by the success of certain online/distributed course offerings. There are strong feelings regarding restrictions such as residency requirements, taking courses from "regular faculty," using resources available in the on-campus environment, and related topics. On the other hand, graduate professional programs incorporate these requirements for good reason: to ensure that the student has an opportunity to interact and work with campus faculty and the research and professional activities to which they might be committed. The socialization of students into the profession is an important aspect of graduate study. The quality of instruction and presentation of learning opportunities is likewise important. These are difficult qualities to replicate in a distributed environment. This is something the SISLT faculty must keep in mind as we continue to adjust to the vast changes in higher education brought about by the development of the Web, the demands of nontraditional students, and the expectations of the field.

It is quite clear that LIS education in general is in a state of continuous revision as the schools and their student constituents make changes and experiment with new modes of both delivery and styles of learning. The SISLT experience over the past decade is unique in the sense that every LIS school has developed different ways of dealing with vast change. Yet SISLT is like many other schools in that we have adapted, innovated, changed, and been creative in meeting challenges and opportunities brought on by the demands of distance education. What is emerging, and not just in Missouri, is the realization that we may no longer be in need of the adjective *distance*. Much of what we do now is simply education using delivery methods that are not overly concerned about where a student may be physically located. The worldview of distance education has so permeated the way we look at ourselves that at the MA level that distance education is no longer unusual. It is simply what we do.

REFERENCES

Kochtanek, Thomas R. and Yuan Hua Wen. "A Multi-Dimensional Analysis of Student Perceptions on Distance Learning." National Educational Computing Conference. Atlantic City, NJ (presented June 24, 1999).

Kochtanek, Thomas R. and Karen K. Hein. "Building Student Learning Communities Based on Asynchronous Learning Networks." Presented at the 5th Annual Conference on Asynchronous Learning Networks, October 3, 1999, University of Maryland, College Park.

"Proposal to Create and Sustain Distributed Graduate Programming in Library and Information Science." Proposal by John Wedman, Director to SISLT, to the Office of the Provost, dated January 21, 1999.

13

THE UNIVERSITY OF NORTH CAROLINA AT GREENSBORO MASTER OF LIBRARY AND INFORMATION STUDIES

Beatrice Kovacs

HISTORY

Originally established as the State Normal and Industrial College (1892–1919), and then as the North Carolina College for Women (1919–32) and Women's College of the University of North Carolina (1932–63), the University of North Carolina at Greensboro (UNCG, 1963 to present) was one of the original three branches of the formally consolidated University of North Carolina system. Graduate studies were authorized in 1919, and the first graduate degree was awarded in 1922. The Graduate School was created in 1922, supporting graduate studies in the arts and sciences. In 1964, UNCG became coeducational.

A program in library education was begun by the North Carolina College for Women in 1922. "Six years later two courses of study (i.e., an undergraduate major and a minor) were instituted in library science, one for those who wished to major in library science and one for those who were majoring in another subject but wished to be part-time librarians."[1]

The Department of Library Science was fully accredited under *Minimum Standards for Library Schools* (adopted by the ALA Council in 1925) for the years 1931–33. Although the library education program was then transferred to the University of North Carolina at Chapel Hill as a result of the formation of the UNC system, the authority to provide a program of library education for the preparation and certification of school librarians was retained by UNCG. Senior-level training (for a total of twelve semester hours' credit) continued to be offered for prospective school librarians, through the Department (now School) of Education. Gradually, declining enrollment forced the discontinuation of the undergraduate library science course offerings.

Interest in reactivation of library education resulted in the appointment of a half-time faculty member to teach one graduate course and operate the School of Education's Curriculum Materials Center for the 1962–63 academic year. By 1982, faculty increased to six full-time positions; the university approved a master's degree program for library education in the School of Education; and ALA awarded accreditation to the Department of Library Science/Educational Technology's (LS/ET) MLS degree. As the program continued to evolve, the department formally changed its name to the Department of Library and Information Studies (DLIS) in 1989, awarding the master's of library and information studies (MLIS) degree.

DISTANCE EDUCATION FOR THE MLIS

Distance education efforts supported by the LS/ET Department began in the 1980s, under Chair Kieth Wright (1980–86, 1997–2001) when a number of courses were provided on site in Statesville, NC, for those interested in school media certification. Faculty members traveled to Statesville to provide many of the courses; students then completed the remainder of their coursework on the Greensboro campus.

In the late 1980s, a substantial number of students in the MLIS program were residing in Charlotte. Many of the Charlotte students worked full-time and traveled one to two hours to attend classes on the UNCG campus (a few could transfer a limited number of credits from other institutions). To assist these students in pursuit of their degree, the first Charlotte cohort was created in 1990. Because only one or two courses were offered each semester, most of the students in the first cohort took three or more years to graduate.

In an effort to provide coursework for the Charlotte cohort students in a timely and convenient fashion, the department attempted several delivery methods. Aside from faculty traveling to the site, a remote method of delivery consisting of videotapes of a required course were sent to Charlotte and the University of North Carolina at Charlotte (UNCC) provided a classroom for viewing these tapes. The faculty member who created the tapes traveled to the site four times during the semester to consult with the students and answer any questions about the course content. It was quickly determined that this was not an effective delivery method for quality instruction. As a result, faculty began broadcasting courses through interactive telelearning facilities at North Carolina Agricultural and Technical University (NC A&T) in Greensboro to the Charlotte cohort, with the Greensboro students traveling across town to NC A&T for the class.

Under Chair Marilyn L. Miller (1987–95), a formal distance education program was initiated. This was the first master's program approved by the UNC System's General Administration to offer its entire degree via telecommunications. In 1993, the LIS program received approval to offer its program to distance education sites, including Charlotte and Asheville, both in North Carolina. During the initial phase of the distance education program

(1993–95), broadcast of the courses to Charlotte, Asheville (the first cohort was accepted in 1993), and Greensboro originated in the telelearning facility at Winston-Salem State University (WSSU) in spring 1993, while a facility at UNCG was under construction (completed by fall 1993).

An additional cohort was developed in Virginia in fall 1993 and included sites at Charlottesville, Roanoke, Emory and Henry College, and Blacksburg. Originally, the UNCG Virginia program was transmitted by satellite with a telephone connection for questions and comments to sites located at Clinch Valley, Emory and Henry College, Virginia Polytechnic Institute, the University of Virginia at Charlottesville, and the Roanoke Public Library. The Clinch Valley group was eventually consolidated with the Emory and Henry and Blacksburg groups. The Virginia cohort graduated in 1995, and no additional cohort for Virginia was created. (Eventually, the University of Tennessee, working with Radford College, provided a distance learning master's program for Virginia residents pursuing a degree in librarianship.)[2]

Although selected courses are still offered by faculty on site at one or both of the distance sites, the primary mode of delivery for the MLIS program is two-way interactive television using the North Carolina Research and Education Network (NC-REN) system. Telelearning classrooms at UNCC and the University of North Carolina at Asheville (UNCA) are provided for the use of the students in the cohort, with the cooperation of the graduate centers of each of these schools. UNCG cohort members also have access to the library services at both UNCC and UNCA.

In 1998–99 the state legislature mandated that distance and extension enrollments be counted as a part of the enrollment base of each campus offering such courses. Summer courses are excluded from the enrollment base figures. As a result, previously uncounted distance students became part of the statistics used for campus funding and enabled the department to add an additional full-time faculty member. Presently, there is one coordinator at the Charlotte site (a three-quarter-time position) as well as one half-time coordinator for the Asheville site.

As the distance program evolved, many of the UNCG faculty experimented with online delivery of coursework. The first platform supported by UNCG's campus was TopClass. Workshops in use of TopClass were provided for faculty, and several mounted one or more of their courses into TopClass as Web-assisted instruction, moving eventually to fully Web-based instruction. In 2000, as the TopClass provider decided to change focus, UNCG determined to provide instruction and support for the Blackboard and/or WebCT courseware platforms. Some of the courses in the MLIS program were converted to Blackboard and provided online to all students. This change enabled distance cohort students to complete their degree requirements in a shorter period of time, if they wished. It provided more flexibility in course offerings to distance sites because the schedule for the telelearning classroom was available for only two evenings a week for MLIS offerings.

IMPLICATIONS FOR THE MLIS PROGRAM

Distance education courses frequently make additional demands on a faculty member because of large class sizes and the necessity of answering e-mail and telephone questions from cohort members. Up-to-date equipment and support personnel, including graduate assistants, are provided to each faculty member. Also, if a faculty member has a telelearning or Web-based course with sections for all cohort groups, then that person receives a course load reduction.

Benefits of the course load reduction are counterbalanced by the increase of student advisement loads. A number of resources have been developed to assist this process. Advisement loads have been equitably distributed to all faculty members, regardless of specializations. Pamphlets, brochures, and Web-based information are now available to all students via the DLIS home page. The Library and Information Studies Student Association (LISSA) provides orientation sessions for new students through an interactive real-time telelearning seminar. Also, the faculty travels to each site at least once a year to answer questions and advise and inform students of important matters. A faculty member who teaches a telelearning course originates at each site at least twice during the semester, providing opportunities for students to meet and receive advice in person.

UNCG STUDENT REACTION TO DISTANCE EDUCATION

Since 1990, graduates of the MLIS and school media certification programs have been surveyed, annually through 2000 and every five years. Questions included their reasons for selecting UNCG's MLIS program, perceptions of the value of the coursework, preparation for employment, and suggestions for changes in curriculum. It is interesting to note the responses of graduates. For example, Table 13.1 shows the number of respondents for each of the years covered by this report.

Table 13.1
Numbers of Respondents: 1990–98

Year of Graduation	Number of Respondents
1991	55
1992	41
1993	61
1994	52
1995	77
1996	37
1997	38
1998	42

It should be noted that there is a sharp increase in the number of responding graduates during the 1995 calendar year. This is the year that most of the one-time-only Virginia cohort graduated, increasing the number of UNCG MLIS graduates substantially.[3]

When they were asked to rank the UNCG MLIS program at the time when they applied, graduates overwhelmingly identified it as the first or only choice, as can be seen in Figure 13.1.[4]

Clearly the majority of the graduates felt that the UNCG LIS program was the only choice if they wished to get an ALA-accredited MLIS degree. Table 13.2 demonstrates the overwhelming number of respondents who indicated that proximity to home and/or availability of the program was the primary rea-

Figure 13.1
Rank of UNCG LIS at Time of Application

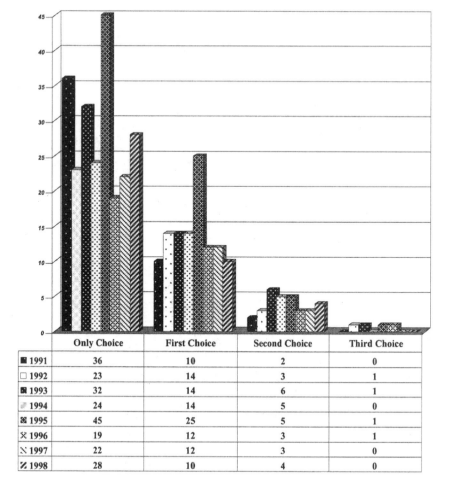

	Only Choice	First Choice	Second Choice	Third Choice
■ 1991	36	10	2	0
☐ 1992	23	14	3	1
▨ 1993	32	14	6	1
▨ 1994	24	14	5	0
▨ 1995	45	25	5	1
✗ 1996	19	12	3	1
⋰ 1997	22	12	3	0
▨ 1998	28	10	4	0

Table 13.2
Factors Important in Selecting UNCG LIS Program: 1991–98

Factors	1991	1992	1993	1994	1995	1996	1997	1998
Reputation of LIS Program	11	12	11	5	10	8	6	11
Reputation of LIS Faculty	3	1	2	4	7	0	2	2
Proximity to Home	43	34	41	36	51	28	34	29
Financial Reasons	8	9	16	16	27	17	13	16
Availability of Program	36	25	34	31	59	19	20	26
Overall Education Climate of LIS/UNCG	8	2	10	4	12	8	2	4
Recommendation by Friend/Colleague	6	9	14	8	17	6	7	6
Recommendation by Graduate of LIS	7	9	5	9	10	8	8	10
Other Reasons	5	16	10	5	9	5	3	3

sons for selecting UNCG. (*Note:* respondents to the survey could choose up to three responses, so the totals are greater than the number of respondents.)[5]

Another important aspect of the UNCG MLIS program is support of the UNCG mission to support the people of North Carolina and the region. As can be seen in Figure 13.2, with the exception of 1995, an overwhelming

Figure 13.2
In-State and Out-of-State Employment by Year of Graduation

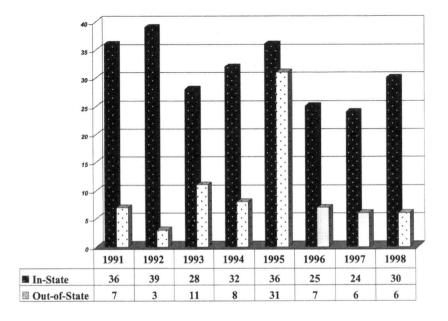

	1991	1992	1993	1994	1995	1996	1997	1998
■ In-State	36	39	28	32	36	25	24	30
▩ Out-of-State	7	3	11	8	31	7	6	6

Table 13.3
Positions Held by Graduates 1990–97 ($n = 162$)

Type of Employment	Number of Respondents
Professional Permanent Full Time	131
Professional Permanent Part Time	11
Professional Temporary Full Time	3
Professional Temporary Part Time	1
Nonprofessional Full Time	7
Nonprofessional Part Time	1
Continuing Formal Education	1
Unemployed/Not Seeking Employment	5
Unemployed/Seeking Employment	3

percentage of MLIS graduates stay in North Carolina. The graduation of the Virginia cohort accounts for the much of the rise in the out-of-state employment figures for 1995.[6]

Because a significant majority of graduates tend to remain in North Carolina (with the exception of the 1995 graduate group that included the Virginia cohort), the UNCG LIS Department can assume that the graduates are filling a need for professionals in the state. Because graduates are employed before or soon after graduation, the UNCG LIS Department assumes that employers perceive the graduates to be effective on the job. Most graduates (81 percent full-time and 9 percent part-time or temporary, as shown in Table 13.3) are hired in professional positions, so the quality of the program can be demonstrated in the employment record of the graduates.[7]

CONCLUSION

Distance education at UNCG, under the leadership of the current chairperson (Lee Shiflett), is evolving into an exciting and challenging method of delivering instruction to students in remote areas of North Carolina and elsewhere. Delivery of the MLIS to interested students is presently limited to cohorts within the state to provide maximum interaction between faculty and students. With only eight full-time faculty and the determination to limit the number of courses taught by adjunct faculty members, the DLIS has no current plans to expand beyond the current boundaries of its student base. As it is, the faculty has enough to do to provide quality education for the MLIS and school media certification programs.

NOTES

1. Elizabeth Ann Bowles, *A Good Beginning: The First Four Decades of the University of North Carolina at Greensboro* (Chapel Hill: University of North Carolina Press, 1967), p. 111.

2. University of North Carolina at Greensboro, School of Education, Department of Library and Information Studies, *Program Presentation for the Committee on Accreditation, American Library Association* (Greensboro: UNCG, 1999), pp. 2–5, 8.

3. University of North Carolina at Greensboro, School of Education, Department of Library and Information Studies, *Program Presentation for the Committee on Accreditation, American Library Association. Appendix D: Graduate Survey Summary Report, Annual Surveys of Graduates 1991–1998* (Greensboro: UNCG, 1999), pp. 299–316.

4. Ibid, p. 301.

5. Ibid, p. 302.

6. Ibid, p. 303.

7. Ibid, pp. 304, 306.

14

WHAT WE CAN LEARN FROM AUTOMATING THE CARD CATALOG? DISTRIBUTED LEARNING AT THE UNIVERSITY OF NORTH TEXAS

Philip M. Turner

INTRODUCTION

In fall 1997, the faculty of the School of Library and Information Sciences (SLIS) voted to revise the master's program core and deliver the core using distributed learning. Fourteen months and considerable efforts later, one of the faculty and I arrived together early one morning. He had been co-teaching one of the core courses to three sites using two-way video for the past month or so. I asked how the teaching was going, and he replied, "It's just like automating the card catalog." Now this faculty member is an expert on the organization of information, so I pursued this line of conversation.

"Remember when we first automated the card catalog by putting facsimiles of the catalog cards on the computer?" he asked.

I replied that I did and even remembered that some of the facsimiles had the little circle that represented where the rod went through the card.

He continued, "After a few years, we made the leap to take the information that was on the card and use the power of the computer to organize and retrieve that information in a way that was not possible before."

"Yes, and soon the automated catalogs looked nothing like a card catalog," I noted.

"Well, we are doing the same thing in distributing our courses. The first step is to take the pictures of our teaching and use the technology to distribute them," our faculty member observed. "Now, we have to figure out how to use the technology to distribute the knowledge products in the most effective way that we can."

"Ah," I concluded, "and the result will probably look completely different from the classroom!"

In fall 1996, the University of North Texas (UNT) set as a priority to increase its presence in the distributed learning environment. In May 1996, the faculty of SLIS included in their strategic plan an objective to serve as a model program for that effort. The goal of this effort is to use technology to most effectively deliver the knowledge products to our students, wherever they might be.

Prior to 1996, the school had been a leader within the university in outreach efforts and had established programs in Houston and Lubbock. These programs were delivered on Saturdays by faculty flying to the sites. In each case, a relationship was fostered with a host institution (University of Houston and Texas Tech University) to provide classrooms, library resources, and computer labs.

The school had previously pioneered offering the total program on Saturdays at the university. It was also the first to offer courses during the break between the spring semester and the summer session. Each of these efforts can be linked to a corresponding growth in enrollment.

The immediate reason for offering some of the courses electronically to Houston and Lubbock was an effort to increase the variety of course offerings to these sites. In addition, the faculty voted to restrict teaching the revised core to full-time faculty only. This requirement meant that these faculty resources would have to be distributed to the sites, especially with the advent of the cooperative master's program in fall 1998.

PROVIDING THE FOUNDATIONS FOR DISTRIBUTED LEARNING

Evolving from traditional classroom delivery to a true distributed learning approach requires a university-wide effort in many different areas. The following are some of the resources necessary and a description of both school and university support that was provided. Where a relevant Web site exists, the URL is provided.

Technological Infrastructure

During 1996–97, two electronic classrooms with videoconference capability were installed in the school's facilities. These rooms were connected to the university's new videoconference network, which, in turn, was connected to the major networks in the state and to the public switched network (www.unt.edu/cdl/untvn.htm).

In spring 1998, a university-wide faculty committee selected WebCT as the Web platform for the university. By May 1999, 210 courses were using this platform, enrolling over 4,000 students (http://courses.unt.edu/webct/studentguide/introduction.html).

In spring 1999, the university received a $1.5 million grant to support distributed learning. In addition, several million dollars in bond money was allocated for the internal networking effort. Additional videoconference rooms, and a variety of high-capacity servers for streaming video and audio were purchased and installed. The university became a member of the Internet II initiative and began to increase the size of the connection(s) to the Internet.

Faculty Support

The university created the Center for Distributed Learning in August 1998. The center provides instructional design assistance, graphic artists, media specialists, and Web production support to UNT faculty at no charge. In addition, the center awards approximately $100,000 in production grants to support faculty in the redesign of courses for distributed learning. The center also provides a year-around training program as well as crash courses for faculty. One particularly effective activity is holding monthly brown-bag lunch meetings at which faculty demonstrate their courses (www.unt.edu/cdl/consultdesign2.htm, www.unt.edu/cdl/dlcourses.htm, and www.unt.edu/cdl/brownbag.htm).

Faculty in SLIS have been very successful in obtaining university grants to support course redesign. These grants have purchased equipment, such as digital cameras, and have also enabled the faculty to hire student help to create Web materials. Each faculty member in SLIS who redesigns a course for delivery via distributed learning is provided one or two course releases. In the past two years, over fifteen course releases have been awarded.

Faculty Compensation

A very important issue that must be addressed as a program moves into the distributed learning environment is how the faculty member will be compensated for students in the class in addition to those in the on-site classroom. The faculty of the SLIS voted to adopt a formula in which a faculty member will be compensated based on the number of students in the virtual classroom. The compensation can be taken as a course release, funds for travel and equipment, or a direct task payment. As a result, some faculty teach only one semester per year!

Intellectual Property Ownership

A policy on ownership of the copyright and on educational/commercial licensing was developed reviewed by the university community. The purpose of the policy is to develop partnerships between the university and the faculty that would encourage course development.

Distributed Learning Funding Model

In spring 1999, the university adopted a funding model that returns the tuition directly to the college or school for each student in a distributed learning course who resides at least fifty miles from the campus. This first-of-its-kind effort provides the resources and incentives for programs to front the considerable resources required to distribute courses and programs (www.unt.edu/cdl/fundingmod.htm).

Advising

Distributing correct information in a timely manner is a significant challenge even when the majority of students are full-time and on campus. The challenge escalates when off-campus sites are involved and becomes truly formidable when faculty are not physically present at all class sessions. Interestingly, there seems to be a perception, common in almost every off-campus site with which I have worked, that students who attend classes at the home site are privy to all the information they need. In fact, off-campus students often create their own networks and have superior information and social contacts to those students who pursue the degree part-time on campus.

The SLIS has implemented a number of actions to assist in providing information and advising to the students enrolled in the off-campus and virtual programs. The first and most important tool is the school's Web site. One of the job duties of the SLIS Coordinator of External Affairs (a full-time staff position) is to monitor the SLIS Web site and to work with the SLIS Webmaster to keep information up to date. Links to the university's Web information pages are featured at the top of the SLIS home page.

The associate dean of the school serves as the advisor for all off-campus students, with the exception of those pursuing the learning resources endorsement. In this way, all students receive the same information and have a common contact point.

At each off-campus site, the school has worked with the host campus to install a video modem device and monitor. This technology allows for a two-way video session to be conducted over regular telephone lines. The dean and associate dean have similar devices in their offices, and the signal can be delivered to the school's videoconference rooms. In addition, the school maintains a toll-free phone number.

In March 2002, the school launched the SLIS Village, a virtual student union. Using the WebCT platform, the SLIS Village features a mail room, meeting house, library, and a very popular coffee house. The coffee house has "tables" that are correlated to topics selected by the residents of the village. These topics include Cooking and Eating, Storytelling, This Was My Week, Dean's Corner, Curriculum, Garage Sale, and many others. The Village features neighborhoods that correspond to geographical areas in Texas and sites around the country where SLIS has geographically based cohorts. The SLIS Village is a service of LISSA and has a Village manager in charge of operations.

Library and Computing Support

Library support is often neglected in creating off-campus programs, and the results of this neglect can seriously impact the quality of the educational experience. At SLIS, we include library staff in the team that makes the initial visits to off-campus sites. The library representative meets with his or her counterpart in the host institution to address collection development, reserves, interlibrary loan, and other issues. This has been a very successful procedure and, as any problems with library services have arisen during the program, the UNT librarians have a contact in place at the off-campus sites. The university has an excellent electronic library that supports a variety of instructional needs. For example, the library will assist in making licensing arrangements to duplicate instructional videotapes to place in viewing centers for Web-based courses (http://irservices.library.unt.edu).

Computing services is another necessity, one that often requires considerable negotiation to provide at the off-campus sites. SLIS has a practice of identifying and contracting with a host college or university to provide both library and computing resources. The computing lab needs to be as close to the classroom as possible. We have identified videoconference classrooms where each student station has a computer built into the desktop. These classrooms allow for the school to teach computing-intensive courses, such as Web Site Management.

Although the school provides access to high-level computing resources at each off-campus site, all students are encouraged to provide their own computing resources at home or at work. Because 85 percent of SLIS students work full-time, most find it preferable to do homework away from the site at which classes are held. The SLIS faculty have developed a recommended technology sheet that is updated each semester (www.unt.edu/slis/students/techreq.htm).

Other Student Services

Students can register by telephone and over the Web. The UNT bookstore has a special service for off-campus students. Textbooks can be ordered using a toll-free number, and the books will be shipped directly to the student's address.

THE FUTURE OF DISTRIBUTED LEARNING AT SLIS

Distributed learning continues to be a priority at the University of North Texas, and the faculty of SLIS continue to include an objective to be a model for this effort in the SLIS strategic plan.

Vision of the Future

How will distributed learning actually impact higher education in general and library and information science education specifically? Higher education has been extremely resistant to change other than to grow rapidly in the past forty years. However, a combination of rapid innovation in telecommunications and information technologies and the need for constant training in the workforce might be the catalyst for significant changes in teaching and learning in higher education. Emerging from a period in which a significant number of the LIS programs were closed or altered, those that remain have become entrepreneurial and early adopters. These characteristics, in combination with the fact that demand for LIS education tends to be widespread geographically but not concentrated, have resulted in LIS programs pioneering off-campus programs and distributed learning approaches.

What will the future hold for LIS education? In some cases course development will migrate from the traditional classroom to include synchronous but distance-independent approaches (videoconference). Many courses will continue to meet for the usual number of contact hours but use some sort of a Web-based approach to provide supplemental materials and out-of-class discussion opportunities. As these classes develop additional Web-based resources, there will be a tendency to replace some of the contact hours with asynchronous experiences, and a natural migration toward fully asynchronous classes will occur.

Some programs will immediately replace some or all of the contact hours with asynchronous learning. Many will combine on-campus introductory work with Web-based follow-up activities. The lessons learned from each experience will guide future course development.

The first tendency is to develop the entire program exclusively within an existing LIS school or department. Cooperation between academic programs and universities does not have a strong history. As LIS programs discover the costs of creating and maintaining a course that can successfully compete in the virtual university, there will be a strong motivation for several programs to cooperate in creating the coursework for specific programs of study. As an example, two or three LIS programs might cooperatively develop courses in legal information management so that each course is of premium quality. These partners could then share the courses and, if they were of sufficient quality, could license the courses to other programs. In spring 2002, we implemented a joint marketing effort with the University of Washington Information School with each program featuring the courseware for one course.

If this scenario of cooperative program development emerges, it would parallel the future of successful corporations as projected in much of the business literature. As an example, see the chapter "Leadership and Collaboration" in Miles and Miles (1999), in which collaboration is identified as the most important corporate behavior in the next century.

Challenges Remaining

Each category listed presents its own challenges. The necessary technological infrastructure is a moving target, requiring a constant infusion of money to maintain. Training and compensation of faculty will continue to require patience and creativity on all sides. Library support, especially the attempt to replicate the on-demand features available to a local student, will not be totally satisfactory in the near future.

A huge challenge for other such schools of LIS, especially because of their small size, is maintaining a "traditional" program while creating a virtual presence. What will the impact on course delivery be when faculty are given release time to reengineer courses? What will be the impact on the research programs for these faculty?

If a course, especially a required course, is offered only in a distributed mode, what is the school's responsibility to the full-time local students? Did they quit their jobs and move to campus to study full-time, only to be in a class without an instructor? If a school moves to a totally distributed environment, where will the teaching and research assistants come from? Who will perform the student government roles that are so critical to establishing the academic community?

We do not have the answers to these questions at UNT SLIS and recognize that these answers will not easily be found. We are committed to creating a distributed learning approach for those courses in which such an approach makes sense. We will continue revising and improving our approach so that both the learning environment and the academic community will be better than ever. Our goal at SLIS is to prepare professionals for the information century. Being a student in this period of rapid change in the learning environment presents a challenge in addition to that offered by the evolving course content. We at SLIS believe that meeting both challenges is necessary to prepare a student for the information century.

REFERENCES

Miles, Raymond E., and Miles, Grant. (1999) "Leadership and Collaboration." In Conger, Jay, Spreitzer, Gretchen M., and Lawler, Edward E. III (eds.) *The Leader's Change Handbook: An Essential Guide to Setting Direction and Taking Action.* San Francisco: Jossey-Bass.

15

PARTNERSHIP IN MULTISITE DISTANCE LEARNING: A COOPERATIVE PROGRAM FOR MASTER'S DEGREES IN LIBRARIANSHIP AT NORTH TEXAS

Keith Swigger and Phil Turner

INTRODUCTION

The School of Library and Information Science of the University of North Texas (UNT) and the School of Library and Information Studies of Texas Woman's University (TWU) together delivered a master's degree program in librarianship to two cohorts at seven sites in Texas using interactive video with Web supplements. This chapter reports why and how we engaged in a program in which two library schools collaborated with six other universities to offer a program across two different video networks—true multitype collaboration. Our goal was to solve the problem of providing more librarians for Texas. Our approach was pragmatic, always focused on the goal. This pragmatic cooperative design suggests possibilities for even more radical approaches to the delivery of professional education.

In its first round, the multisite cooperative program opened access to library education at four sites in Texas: Abilene (at Abilene Christian University, a private university), Wichita Falls (at Midwestern State University, an independent public university), Texarkana (at Texas A&M University at Texarkana, a campus in the Texas A&M System), and Edinburg (at the University of Texas–Pan American, a campus in the University of Texas [UT] System). In the second cohort, 1999–2002, the program was again at UT–Pan American and also at Texas A&M–Corpus Christi and at UT Tyler. When this project began in 1997, both UNT and TWU were independent public universities, as TWU still is. In 1999, the Texas Higher Education Coordinating Board, which has oversight responsibility for higher education in Texas, designated UNT as a system with campuses in Denton, Dallas, and Fort Worth. UT–Pan Am is served by the UT interactive video network. All the other universities participating in the project, including UNT and TWU, are subscribers to the TTVN interactive video network hosted by the Texas A&M System.

PROFESSIONAL LIBRARY EDUCATION IN TEXAS

Three public universities in Texas offer master's degrees accredited by the ALA: the UT-Austin, UNT in Denton, and TWU in Denton. TWU began teaching librarianship in 1918; the accredited master's program began in 1949. From its inception in 1901 until 1972, TWU admitted only women. In response to federal legislation, TWU began admitting men to its graduate programs in 1972. Men have been admitted to all programs since 1994. In 1969, citing the need for opportunities for males to study librarianship, UNT (then North Texas State University) applied for and received authorization to offer master's degrees in library science. For thirty years, we have had the anomaly of two public universities offering accredited master's degrees in library science little more than a mile apart.

We have had three decades of peaceful coexistence. UNT and TWU have a cross-registration arrangement through the Federation of North Texas Universities. The federation is a compact, an agreement rather than a bureaucratic agency, that enables student access to several regional public universities' resources in a transparent manner. Students at one university who want to take a course at another register and pay fees at their home university, and credits appear on their home transcript; interinstitutional transfer is never an issue. UNT and TWU together present the Federation Lecture and the Lazerow Lecture (funded by the Institute for Scientific Information). The two library schools have long had informal agreements about not duplicating offerings in highly specialized electives.

UNT and TWU have each developed its programs in its own way. Like plants of the same species growing in a field divided by a wall, over the years the schools' curricula and pedagogy have evolved differently, a predictable outcome of separate faculties and schools operating in different university environments. Operating within the constraints of ALA accreditation (which impose some uniformity) we have become different in some respects and similar in many others. Despite any differences, our missions overlap in an important way. Both schools are responsible for providing professional education for librarianship for the people of Texas.

It would be disingenuous to say there has been no competition in these thirty years. We go our own ways, but with a watchful eye on one another. One of our differences prior to 1997 was our approach to providing access to learners outside Denton. UNT began offering classes in Houston (at the University of Houston) in 1991 and in Lubbock at Texas Tech in 1989, flying faculty into those cities. TWU began offering classes in Dallas in 1994 and in Fort Worth in 1997 at the Fort Worth Independent School District.

cities; TWU had offered a distance education program in librarian-
interactive video to Canyon, Texas, in the Panhandle. To verify the
need and demand, we assessed the market for a program using a vari-
ools. These included:

groups, where librarians from a region attended invitational meetings to
ibe their needs for new employees;

d surveys to library directors and other employers;

of the employment market as manifest in position announcements; and

ssions with librarians at state and regional professional meetings.

tionally, we received a petition from a group of potential students in
y and invitations from several institutions to deliver library education
ns to their campuses. Finally, leaders of Texas professional associations
dly urged the deans of the schools to deliver off-campus programs.
consideration of data and discussion with the potential hosts, we set-
four sites: Abilene, Wichita Falls, Texarkana, and Edinburg.
l 1999, we surveyed Texas library employers and potential students to
ine levels of need and demand around the state. We made a series of
campuses that might serve as hosts to a new cohort, and we held
ons in various cities to discuss regional needs and the nature of the
ative effort. We selected three sites for a cohort for 2000–2002.
principal objective was to maximize opportunities for access to gradu-
ary education. Access to the video networks and the availability of a
k link between the A&M and UT networks were important consider-
n selecting sites. Geographic location was also important. We selected
at would not compete for students with existing off-campus programs
t would provide access for students in four different parts of the state.
ght partner institutions that could provide not only the appropriate
lassrooms but also the academic support required. Academic support
case includes adequate library resources, adequate computer facilities,
graduate curriculum in disciplines and professional schools comple-
y to librarianship from which our students could choose electives suf-
o fill out their degree plans. Finally, we sought partners willing to take

use we were seeking approvals at the same time we were developing
ents with host university partners, we needed partners who were com-
with contingent agreements enacted in good faith but with the
anding that ultimately things might be different than planned. To
partnership work, there has to be something in the deal for everyone.
sic agreements called for partners to provide a video classroom every
y from fall 1998 through summer 2000; in-classroom technical assis-
ibrary services, computer labs, and parking for our students; permis-
our students to enroll in graduate courses outside library science.

In 1994, TWU started a program at West Texas A&M University in Canyon
using videoconferencing through the TTVN videoconference network.

In the meantime, UT–Austin had begun offering classes via videoconferencing at UT–El Paso and San Antonio. By 1997, one or another of the three
professional schools was teaching in some form at all the major metropolitan
areas of Texas. Still, the needs for professional education were unmet.

STAKEHOLDERS AND DEMAND FOR EDUCATION FOR LIBRARIANSHIP

In Texas, graduate education for librarianship is an obvious application for
distance learning approaches because (1) the need for librarians is widely
spread but is thin in any particular spot; (2) there are many stakeholders with
varied interests in library education; and (3) the number of qualified
providers of library education is small.

Many individuals and groups in Texas have a stake in library education.
Most fundamentally, the citizens of the state deserve high-quality library services. There is a broad but thin need for librarians in this large state. The need
is broad because a wide variety of citizens in a wide range of social roles are
dispersed over a huge geographic region. In recognition of the need and
importance of the services of professional librarians, state standards require
all public libraries and all school libraries to employ certified librarians. A certified librarian for a public library is a librarian who holds a master's degree
accredited by the ALA; a certified school librarian is one who has a Learning
Resources Endorsement to a Texas Teacher's Certificate. Effective fall 2003,
school librarians will be required to hold master's degrees.

To comply with their missions of providing quality educational experiences
and to comply with specialized and regional accrediting requirements, academic libraries also seek to employ professionally educated librarians. The
services of professional librarians are also important to clientele of special
libraries of a wide variety of types—medical, business, legal, association, and
so on. Although there are some major metropolitan areas (Dallas–Fort
Worth, Austin, San Antonio, Houston) in a large state such as Texas, libraries
and the librarians who staff them are dispersed across an enormous area.

Library patrons of many kinds have a stake in education of qualified professional librarians who can provide the services they need and want. Libraries
as institutions and the institutions libraries serve, such as schools, colleges,
and businesses, have a stake in professional education. The professional community of librarians also has a serious interest. If qualified personnel are not
available to meet needs, there is a pressing danger that institutions will
employ unqualified persons, resulting not only in poor performance of librarians' roles but also a diminished public perception of librarians' capabilities.

The need is broad, but outside the major metropolitan areas, both need
and demand (the number of potential students) are low. In most cities, the

local demand for librarians is insufficient to support a fully accredited program, and the educational providers were concentrated in metropolitan areas.

The vastness of Texas makes access to accredited library education difficult. The difficulty is compounded by the nature of the student population. The "traditional" library education student is what universities call "the nontraditional student": female, in her thirties, part-time student, employed, with a family and other social ties. These students are not mobile and cannot leave home for full-time study in another city.

A COOPERATIVE PROCESS

Early discussions among the three schools about cooperation in distance learning took place in 1995. At that time, there was insufficient common commitment to interinstitutional cooperation to proceed with a united plan. Between 1995 and 1997 discussions continued, and it became increasingly clear as distance learning emerged to prominence in academia that a cooperative approach was consistent with the interests of meeting the widespread need for new librarians while meeting the public's demand for efficiency and effectiveness in programming graduate education, as expressed through the Texas Higher Education Coordinating Board (THECB).

The deans and faculty representatives from the three graduate library education programs made up a committee that began earnest discussions in January 1997 about a cooperative program. After the School of Library and Information Science at UT–Austin decided in late spring 1997 to withdraw from participation, UNT and TWU pursued the initiative together. At the time, THECB policies on distance learning were more restrictive than they are now, requiring full board approval of each distance education program. The concept of distance education was still sufficiently new that board members wanted full assurance that state funds would be well spent.

A cooperative approach makes sense for many reasons. Cooperation makes economic sense. Distance learning is expensive in terms of human, temporal, and physical resources. A cooperative program gives each partner a supportable load. By partnering, these two public universities demonstrate a commitment to make taxpayers' investment in library education as effective as possible.

Cooperation makes sense professionally. Library education, like librarianship in general, is more standardized than it is idiosyncratic. Although debates within the profession may sometimes make it appear we are at odds among ourselves, when we take a step back we see that most library schools still have much in common in terms of instructional goals and objectives. A cooperative program will produce graduates whose allegiance is to the profession they join. It will help librarians build their commitments to the profession, if not to a particular professional school.

A cooperative approach accommodates confl the conflict that inevitably lurks around progran of knowledge but also a potential market for lear ond, a cooperative program resolves many com than compete in delivering a program to east Te together to meet the need. Third, cooperation learning development among the partners. As teaching and administration of the program, w both schools and faculties grow together in the program helps us temporize differing views of the librarianship, and thus serves the interests of th engage in our internal professional debates, we public front that says, "We agree on a definition

The process of actually designing a program parallel steps, loops, and rebooting. Developm gram took place in an environment of shifting fact, many new regulations, policies, and prac were responses to policy vacuums we identified priate administrative plans, solve financial and malize partnership agreements. THECB policies what remained constant was THECB staff enco their commitment to the value of cooperation. development, THECB policies made a transition ulated monopoly (granting a particular geograp an open market model (universities now can of cally wherever they wish as long as they meet time that these regulations were evolving, we als of the Southern Association of Colleges and S university accrediting agency. SACS was in tra distance education as regular university busine change that required major oversight and reviev

Throughout the process, we held to several co (and is) real. People need good librarians. Sec here than just a library science program—the pr changes we demanded had consequences in hel ers to reconsider basic assumptions about how cation and how we define our institutions. Thi ourselves and to our university offices, "It's oka before."

NEEDS ASSESSMEI

Both UNT and TWU had been receiving campus library science programs. Both had res

various
ship vi
level of
ety of

1. focu
desc
2. mail
3. stud
4. disc

Add
one cit
progra
repeate
Afte
tled or
In fa
determ
visits t
recepti
cooper
Our
ate libr
networ
ations
sites th
and th
We sou
video
in this
and a
menta
ficient
risks.
Bec
agreen
fortabl
unders
make
The b
Saturd
tance;
sion fo

We assured the partners that UNT and TWU would provide instruction, advising, registration, and bookstore services; remote library support and remote computer support; approvals to transfer up to nine semester credit hours from the host university; a cash payment per student per course (the amount was determined by the situation at each partner site).

Through prior experiences in distance learning and off-campus classes, we had developed a common understanding of guidelines that were valuable to us in working with our new partners. The first, a guiding principle, is the importance of detailed formal agreements: every stakeholder's interests have to be served. Obviously, everybody's financial interests have to be protected. Less obvious but equally critical are staff support issues. Many of the details that have to be worked out when working with another institution concern the problem of "our" and "their" students and the problem of teaching people at the operational staff level about what is happening. It is one thing for the provost or president to say they love to partner—it is quite another for a computer lab monitor, a cashier, or a parking enforcer to say the same thing.

The second guiding principle is the importance of letting staff at the participating universities work things out laterally—librarian to librarian, telecommunications manager to telecommunications manager. Faculty had to recognize that their relations with staff at other sites have to be dealt with through administration (deans). Everybody has to respect institutional boundaries. Faculty should not call librarians at a distant site and make their own arrangements for materials for their courses, for example, as they might "at home." Rather, they must call their local distance education librarian, who then makes appropriate arrangements with librarians at the sites. It is important that lateral arrangements always include informing the dean.

Third, we anticipated, correctly, that distance education students would be deeply committed. They perceive that the distance education program is their only chance to earn a degree they need. For a professional program like library science, where the degree is the required job credential, this is a critical motivator. Distance education students develop a bond and a sense of unity, a them/us view of things. Distance education students think their troubles are uniquely theirs and that everything for the on-campus students is just great (registration, parking, computer labs, faculty access). They often envision a mythical student body of full-time students who obtain their education through a Socratic dialog interspersed with enriching social events. In fact, part-time commuting students dominate the student body in both of our programs.

The fourth guiding principle was the necessity to establish institutional routines for distance learning. Distance education providers need university-wide awareness of distance learning. Then engaging in distance learning, deans and other academic administrators must ensure that support staff at every level know there is a distance learning program and how to deal with it. One uninformed clerk in an office or an uninstructed technician can bring an

elegant enterprise to a halt. Ignorance of the university's activities is danger-
ous. Ignorance's ally is the mindset that says, "We never did that before;
therefore it's not possible." Our experiences, for example, led us to argue to
our home universities for policies to waive fees for services students could
never use (such as health services) while imposing distance learning fees, to
accept information via e-mail or fax rather than typed on forms, and to relax
the limits on transfer credits.

INSTRUCTIONAL DELIVERY

TWU and UNT delivered the multisite synchronous program to four sites
over the A&M and UT system interactive video networks. The decision to
use this medium came from prior experience in videoconference course delivery; Dr. Turner had managed videoconference learning for the University of
Alabama prior to coming to Texas, and TWU faculty had been using the
technology to teach to Canyon since 1994. Videoconference technology was
an appropriate choice because it allows for a significant amount of interaction
between students and faculty and among students at the different sites. Faculty who prefer to teach in lecture/discussion format can make the transition
from traditional classroom settings to distance learning more readily when
the shift does not require a total reorientation to their work.

Technology support is a major issue in videoconferencing. There are room
coordinators at each site for each class to provide first level technology troubleshooting and camera operation (if the faculty choose not to operate the
cameras themselves). Room coordinators also provide control of the sound
system, the most sensitive component of interactive video technology—they
mute/unmute microphones and manage question-and-answer traffic. They
also proctor exams and provide general classroom assistance. Data communication personnel are available at home sites at the beginning of each class to
ensure connections are made and are on call all day Saturday. Videoconference technicians are also on call at the TTVN and UT network offices.

Videoconferencing does not meet all the instructional needs, however. We
wanted students to be able to work independently and in groups, to work on
projects outside class time, and to have ready asynchronous communication
with each other and with faculty as well. The solution to these problems was
an agreement between TWU and UNT to adopt a common Web interface,
WebCT, for the classes. As the cohort goes through the program, they need
learn only this one interface. Although one might make strong claims for
competing systems, the important point is that we agreed on and stayed with
a common system, putting pragmatism and convenience ahead of a search for
perfection.

The WebCT platform served an important purpose outside of in-class
communication. As each cohort began, a WebCT course was created to pro-

mote the creation of a continuing learning community that would operate outside of and after the completion of each class. This communication site proved to be very valuable for communication among students, faculty, staff, and administration, and hundreds of postings were recorded during the life of the cohort.

A COOPERATIVE ACADEMIC PROGRAM: CONJOINING THE CURRICULUM

Given the hot debates with librarianship about the proper nature of library education, one might think that finding agreement between the faculties of two schools might have been the most difficult aspect of the cooperative program. In fact, it was one of the simplest problems to solve. TWU and UNT do have different curricula based on different assumptions and interpretations of librarianship. For the purposes of this program, the faculties quickly agreed that fighting curricular wars would only defeat the purpose of providing access to professional education. Three observations helped us come to speedy resolution: (1) our curricula are more alike than they are different; (2) the number of courses that can be offered in a cohort program is small, calling for a fairly generic degree program; and (3) there must be room in the program for graduate electives taken at the host universities. The cooperative curriculum is a compromise, a pragmatic agreement placing the possible ahead of the perfect. Table 15.1 lists the courses offered in the cooperative.

A master's professional paper is a university-wide requirement at TWU—the paper is a three-credit research paper or description of a professional project. At TWU a 3-credit practicum is required; at UNT, the practicum normally is a no-credit option, but for the cooperative program practicum may be in the student's degree plan. UNT requires a comprehensive exam at the end of a student's program.

In summary, these are the features of the program:

- cohort program (clear beginning and clear end, clear commitment that students must make, predictability for them and us)
- primarily videoconference, secondary WebCT, with faculty presenting from different sites
- one class taught by each school per semester, on Saturday (consistency, predictability, planned commitment of school and university resources for a fixed period of time)
- Extended transfer allowance (nine to twelve credits; minimizes load on UNT and TWU, extends flexibility for students, provides a stake for host partners)
- links three networks (TWU, TTVN, UT)
- multitype partnership

Table 15.1
A List of Courses in the Cooperative Curriculum

The Information Professions. Information and communications in society and culture. Professions and professional development. Cultural change and the history of information transfer. Librarianship in the context of evolving information professions. Access to information. (TWU)

Introduction to Information Access and Retrieval. Epistemological foundations of information use. Basic principles and techniques of information retrieval and access services. Introduction to systems access, search and retrieval skills, and collection management. Study of evaluation methods for all formats of resources, services, and user satisfaction. (UNT)

Introduction to Information Organization. Principles, concepts, and practices of information organization and presentation. Concepts and problems of human information behavior, classification, and categorization related to information organization. (UNT)

Cataloging and Classification. Standard descriptive and subject cataloging of library materials. Theory and practice of classification schemes. Technical services operations in electronic environments. (TWU)

Management of Information Agencies. Management principles and practices. Problem solving, public relations, and program development. Libraries and information centers and their social and political context. Coping with change. Facilities and equipment. (UNT)

Juvenile Literature. Survey of literature and reference materials for children and young adults, with emphasis on reading interests, professional evaluation, educational uses, and readers' advisory. (TWU)

Research Methods and Analysis. Principles, techniques, and areas of research. Basic research designs and measurement problems. Evaluation of representative studies. (UNT)

School Library Media Center. Philosophy, management, and planning of resources, personnel, programs, and facilities. Budgeting. Collection building. Instructional design. Services to students and teachers. Program evaluation. Public Relations. (TMRU)

Information Resources and Services in Culturally Diverse Communities. Seminar in information resources and services for ethnic cultural minorities. Issues in the provision of information services to ethnic cultural minority communities. (UNT)

Collection Development. Collection development, evaluation, selection criteria, and tools. Community analysis. Censorship and intellectual freedom issues. Library standards. Publishing industry. (TWU)

Capstone Seminar. Integrative seminar concerning issues and trends in librarianship. Participation in and critical evaluation of professional conferences and other learning and networking experiences. Creation of professional development plans for postgraduate careers. (TWU)

REFLECTIONS

Our collaborative approach to distance education called on us to abandon the concept of "our" program and look at our knowledge offerings as pieces or components of a learning construct that students assemble from a variety of sources. There are lots of institutions and persons offering knowledge and learning opportunities in a growing variety of formats. Many of them are very good. Some of them are as good as and maybe better than some of the units our schools can offer. The assemblage concept is particularly true of professional programs but applies as well to liberal arts programs. Some faculty resist the notion, touting the integrity and specialness of "our" own brand of education—yet if one wants a vigorous faculty debate in most schools and departments, challenge the faculty to articulate with precision what that unique, integral education is made up of.

One of the most positive outcomes of this cooperative program was that out of the seven very separate physical sites, one virtual class emerged for each cohort. In this program, the faculty and the students were not aware who was TWU or UNT. Furthermore, the relationships and bonding among students across sites was extraordinary. As an example, a student from the site in Edinburg and one from the site in Texarkana (750 miles apart!) found out that their fathers had served together in World War II. They arranged to meet at the Texas Library Association and regularly exchange correspondence. We are convinced that, although the experience of these students might not duplicate that of the mythical full-time residential student, the quality of this experience is superior in many ways to that of the commuting part-time student who arrives to class fifteen minutes before the class begins and leaves fifteen minutes after.

Our experiences in building a cooperative program helped us refine a reminder list for ourselves and anyone else involved in distance education. Here is our list:

- Good advising is critical.
- Keep the goal in mind—examine every issue in light of the goal of enabling access to education.
- Recognize that everyone involved has an interest, and that interest must be served.
- Tolerate ambiguity and uncertainty. Things will work out.
- Keep communication lines open, keep messages flowing.
- Plan for technology failures.
- Recognize that there is an adaptability scale, a fact of life with which one must deal. In order, from most adaptable to least adaptable:

  students

  university leaders

  professional community

faculty

technicians

regulators

university and other bureaucracies (by the time the first class was held, we had generated over eight pounds of paper documents.)

- Good advising is critical.

First and last, *Good advising is critical*. Students want educational opportunities. They are willing to adapt to the conditions necessary. But they feel isolated and remote, a realistic assessment. To overcome that isolation and to ensure that they survive all technological and bureaucratic system crashes, advising is critical.

Those considering entering into cooperative arrangements for distance education should understand that cooperation is enormously time-consuming. But it is also immensely popular with university administrators, academic regulatory agencies, legislators, the professional community, and the general public. Contrary to what some might expect, successful cooperation does not depend on personal politicking—it depends on and calls for the highest levels of professionalism. Finally, cooperation is productive. Together, we have provided professional education to people who otherwise would not have had it.

CONCLUSION

Technology—interactive video—was a driving force in developing our cooperative program. New instructional technology—Internet-based classes—brought the program to an end. As it became easier to move content, exercises, and even discussions out of the classroom and onto the Web, faculty migrated their courses and students enthusiastically went along. Internet-based courses offer levels of simplicity and convenience with which video-based classes cannot compete.

As our individual programs migrated to the Web, opportunities to serve students all over Texas—or anywhere—grew. No longer do we have to restrict our degree offerings to Denton or to some other particular set of cities. In Texas, where the population is dispersed and cities are so sprawled that they cannot be traversed easily, Internet programs make more sense; by offering them, each school has a greater opportunity to provide its curriculum to more people.

The TWU/UNT cooperative program ended in August 2002 when students in the second cohort graduated. The level of cooperation between our two schools will likely return to its previous form, which consisted primarily of cross-registration and easy transfer of courses between us. Now, with so many library schools involved in Web-based learning, we can look toward a more expanded model of cooperation, in which our distance education students will be able to enroll in courses at any accredited library school.

The issues we confronted as a pair of schools now confront us as an assembly of schools. The questions are the same, but they call for more sophisticated answers and for policies worked out at higher levels than those of deans. These issues—such as how many hours may be transferred from another institution, how can registration at another school be made transparent to the student, how can one institution assure itself of the quality of instruction offered by another, what does "admission" of a student mean, what is intellectual property in distance learning—will call for broad attention. Library schools can continue to be leaders in innovation in professional education by teaching their universities, their accrediting agencies (both professional and regional), and the various state agencies concerned to recognize the issues and by modeling solutions.

16

"THE SPIRIT OF LEARNING IS A LASTING FRONTIER": DISTANCE EDUCATION IN LIBRARY AND INFORMATION STUDIES AT THE UNIVERSITY OF OKLAHOMA

Danny P. Wallace

ORIGIN OF THE UNIVERSITY OF OKLAHOMA SCHOOL OF LIBRARY AND INFORMATION STUDIES

The School of Library and Information Studies at the University of Oklahoma offers the second-oldest ALA-accredited degree program west of the Mississippi River, the tenth oldest overall. Although the first degree program—a bachelor's degree—was not accredited until 1930, the stage for professional education of librarians in the state of Oklahoma was set when the Oklahoma Library Commission was created in 1919.

Oklahoma in 1919 was a young state coping with tremendous population growth and a rapidly changing economic and societal base. The land runs of the 1880s and 1890s had nearly tripled the state's population and replaced the Indian Territory and Oklahoma Territory with a transformed environment that moved rapidly toward statehood, which was granted in 1907. The oil boom that began with the state's first commercial well in 1897 brought unanticipated wealth and opportunity as literally dozens of oil companies found their homes in Oklahoma. The new population of the new state wanted the amenities of modern society, including libraries.

From the outset, the Library Commission emphasized the need for learning experiences for the state's librarians. In direct response to concerns raised in the context of the Library Commission, University Librarian Jesse Lee Rader founded a summer training program at the University of Oklahoma in 1920, only thirty years after the founding of the university. According to Ruth Janice Donnell's "A History of the School of Library Science, University of Oklahoma, 1929–1960," a paper completed for the class Library Science 401, the summer program continued for thirteen years and served a total of 412 students. The success of the summer program led to the founding of the School of Library Science in 1929. Rader continued as administrator of both the University Library and the School of Library Science until his retirement from the university in 1951.

Oklahoma's population was and is geographically dispersed. Although 2000 census data rank Oklahoma nineteenth among the fifty states in land area, the state ranks thirty-sixth in population density. Only thirteen Oklahoma communities have populations greater than 25,000; only two have populations greater than 100,000. Fourteen of the state's seventy-seven counties are associated with five metropolitan statistical areas; two of those counties—Oklahoma County and Tulsa County—accounted for 35 percent of the state's 2000 population. The Census Bureau's population density map reveals that the population is primarily distributed along a line from the northeastern corner to the southwestern corner of the state.

Rader's summer training program was intended to overcome the geographic challenges to providing effective library education for a state with substantial population dispersion by concentrating the learning experience in a short and intense time frame. The emphasis on serving the needs of students for whom a residential program at the University of Oklahoma campus in Norman was impractical appears to have been abandoned when the program was recast as a bachelor's degree. The 1949 *Bulletin* of the School of Library Science included an explicit statement that "the School of Library Science does not conduct courses by correspondence and extension." The need and demand, however, did not evaporate.

THE EXTENSION PROGRAM

The precise history of courses offered away from the Norman campus is largely undocumented. The earliest experience with off-campus instruction may have been the extension program initiated in Tulsa in 1957 as a partnership with the Tulsa City-County Library. Minutes of the March 12, 1970, faculty meeting indicate that Tulsa course enrollment averaged fifty students per semester from 1957 through 1969. By the late 1960s there was an established program of extension courses involving at least three sites—Midwest City (suburban Oklahoma City), Lawton (in the southwest corner of the state), and Tulsa (in the northeast corner of the state). The 1970 ALA accreditation self-study described courses offered in Ardmore (south central Oklahoma), Clinton (west central Oklahoma), and Chickasha (southwest Oklahoma) as well as Oklahoma City, Lawton, and Tulsa. Courses were taught by a combination of adjunct and full-time faculty and were offered in the facilities of libraries in those communities. Rules established by the Graduate College required that 75 percent of a student's instruction be provided by full-time faculty, effectively limiting the use of adjunct faculty. Additionally, the Graduate College required that half of a student's course of study be completed on the Norman campus.

The extension program was deeply enough ingrained by the late 1960s to be a topic of discussion of nearly every faculty meeting. The stresses caused by providing an active extension program resulted in a situation in which the faculty were legitimately concerned about the negative potential of extension courses. Minutes of the February 12, 1968, faculty meeting indicate that the faculty members had become sufficiently concerned about the impact of extension courses on faculty time and the quality of the overall student learning experience to impose limits on the specific courses offered at extension sites. Despite these concerns, which were a recurring theme for many years, involvement in extension courses was an established component of the curriculum that was never again far from the surface of the school's operations. That involvement coalesced into two major areas: support for the needs of the Tulsa area and the emergence of televised and video instruction systems.

THE TULSA PROGRAM

Although there is a history of flirtations with a variety of other sites, Tulsa has been a consistent force in determining the activities of the school away from the Norman campus. In addition to being the state's second-largest population center (after Oklahoma City), Tulsa is distinguished by having no publicly supported university. As a result, the city has a long history of identification as a primary market for the extension programs of the state's public universities. The University of Tulsa, a privately supported institution, offered an undergraduate program in library science in the 1960s, but the program—which was never accredited by the ALA—appears to have never been truly viable and had been abandoned by 1970. The University of Oklahoma has historically emphasized graduate programs in its efforts to provide learning experiences in Tulsa.

The school's 1957 agreement with the Tulsa City-County Library was a truly pioneering effort initiated with no university-supported infrastructure. By the 1960s, however, the university had established a formal Graduate Center in Tulsa with on-site office and classroom space. The School of Library Science, with more than a decade of independent experience in Tulsa, was well positioned to assume a leadership role in the Tulsa Graduate Center. Despite the infrastructure of the Tulsa Graduate Center, however, the school's program offerings there continued to be sporadic and apparently rather casually planned through the 1970s.

A coordinated program for offering courses at Tulsa was developed and widely advertised in 1980 and was listed in the school's *Bulletin* for 1980–81. In 1982 the Tulsa Graduate Center was reorganized as the University Center at Tulsa (UCT), a collaborative effort funded by the State Board of Regents to support public higher education in Tulsa by providing access to programs offered by the University of Oklahoma, Oklahoma State University, Langston University, and Northeastern Oklahoma State University. The School of

Library Science was one of four University of Oklahoma programs incorporated into the original UCT design.

The transfer of library science courses to the UCT did not take place immediately. The UCT, operated directly by the State Board of Regents as an administrative unit separate from the four participating universities, was perceived as being unresponsive to the needs and concerns of the School of Library Science. The UCT lacked adequate facilities to support technology-oriented courses, resulting in classes that required use of computer technology continuing to be held at Tulsa City-County Library. Library resources were also inadequate in comparison to the library science collection that had been built at the public library to support the long-standing partnership between the library and the School of Library Science. Although these problems were eventually overcome, the relationship between the school and the UCT (and its later manifestations) was one of variable effectiveness.

Prior to establishment of the UCT, the school had viewed course offerings in Tulsa as primarily a vehicle for accelerating student access to the school's offerings, with the explicit expectation that a significant portion of any student's course of study would take place at the Norman campus. A major feature of the UCT initiative was that courses offered at the UCT would carry resident credit and would therefore be exempt from the Graduate College's rules requiring that 50 percent of a degree program be completed on campus. An operating principle of the UCT design was the expectation that students would be able to complete each degree program offered at the UCT without traveling to the program's home campus. Failure of some programs—including the School of Library Science—to comply with this principle led to a State Board of Regents committee recommendation that programs not delivered in their entirety should be discontinued. Discussion at the November 5, 1984, faculty meeting centered around the nature of the Tulsa program. The outcome of that discussion was a plan for delivering the program in its entirety at the UCT on a structured cycle designed to present each required course twice every five years and each elective course at least once in every five-year period. By fall 1986 enrollment in Library and Information Studies courses accounted for half of University of Oklahoma enrollment at the UCT.

A recurring discussion item throughout the decades of the 1980s and 1990s was the potential for hiring Tulsa-resident faculty. At its September 27, 1985, meeting, the faculty of the School of Library and Information Studies reached a consensus view that a single faculty member stationed in Tulsa would be isolated from the remainder of the faculty and that to hire a single Tulsa-resident faculty member was therefore undesirable. In 1986, however, a special allocation of funds from the State Board of Regents was authorized to support hiring a Tulsa-resident faculty member, and a search to fill that position was initiated. In 1991 a faculty member whose official instructional and advising responsibilities lay entirely in Tulsa was hired. A second Tulsa faculty line was requested in 1992 but not approved. In 1993 the faculty member stationed in Tulsa was transferred to the Norman campus. Subsequent discussions of positioning a faculty member in Tulsa reiterated earlier concerns regarding the dangers of isolation. The potential for hiring one or more Tulsa-resident faculty members continued to be discussed throughout the 1990s.

In 1985, the citizens of Tulsa voted to approve a tax to support funding a new campus for the UCT. Planning in earnest began in 1988 for a new facility for the UCT. It was reported at the March 25, 1988, faculty meeting that the new facility would "have an embarrassment of equipment riches in an open lab and a teaching lab." The program moved to the new facility in fall 1988. In 1992 the University Center at Tulsa was recommissioned by the state as a full member of the Oklahoma higher education system, with institutional status comparable to that of other state universities.

A regularly scheduled review of the programs offered by the School of Library and Information Studies was conducted under the auspices of the Provost's Office during 1988. The review panel recommended that "serving the OU Norman campus programs must remain the priority of the School." This statement was amended by the provost, who reaffirmed the school's responsibility to serve both the Norman campus and Tulsa. The provost's recommendations included a statement that "offering programs in Tulsa, especially ones that are unique to OU, is and will continue to be a high priority of the University as a whole." The provost further commended the school's use of a variety of delivery methods for courses offered in Tulsa and encouraged examination of new delivery methods.

In 1996 the University Center at Tulsa and Rogers State University, a state-supported institution located in Claremore, Oklahoma, were merged to form a new entity, named Rogers University. This experiment was sustained for two years. In 1998 the two institutions were separated, and Rogers State University ceased operation in Tulsa. Oklahoma State University–Tulsa, a newly named institution, emerged in a position of substantially greater strength than the three remaining partner institutions. This was the beginning a process of dismantling the UCT that has continued through the establishment of a campus of Northeastern State University in Broken Arrow, a southeastern suburb of Tulsa and the relocation of all University of Oklahoma programs to a new site in south central Tulsa.

TALK BACK TELEVISION

In 1970 the Oklahoma State Regents for Higher Education authorized funding for a system officially named the Oklahoma Higher Education Televised Instruction system, commonly known as Talk Back Television, or TBTV. TBTV was a commercial product used in Oklahoma to broadcast live courses to studio classrooms distributed across the state. Originally available at eleven studio classroom sites, the system was expanded over time to include more than seventy sites. The TBTV system incorporated one-way video and two-way audio. The system as originally implemented allowed only for black-and-white transmission and supported virtually no use of any approach to instruction other than lecture. TBTV was described in the following terms in the school's 1978 ALA-accreditation self-study:

The talk-back television system provides studios on the Norman campus wherein courses originate. Each receiving location, and there are many spaced throughout the state, is provided with a large viewing screen and a number of desks with telephones attached by which students can ask questions of the instructor. The talk-back television system provides for the use of audio-visual materials, as well as a courier system for the distribution and collection of papers, outlines, and the like. As for resources, in its original offerings, the School was careful to choose receiving locations in areas where there was reasonable expectation of library resources.

Receiving locations at the time of the self-study included Tulsa, Chickasha, Weatherford, and Lawton.

Minutes of the May 4, 1972, faculty meeting describe a general discussion of the system, with the statement, "If there is any interest in the program, we will discuss it further at a later date." There apparently was interest: The School of Library Science first offered courses using TBTV during the 1972–73 academic year. The first year's experience appears to have been largely negative. The minutes of the October 4, 1973, faculty meeting contained the following statement on TBTV:

It was moved, seconded and passed that the Library School withdraw from continued participation in the televised course instruction which has been offered state-wide, pending improvement and clarification of such problems as campus-coordination, color and re-taping privileges.

There is no extant record of when or how the TBTV was improved sufficiently to gain approval of the faculty of the School of Library Science. By the end of the 1970s, the system was in regular use for delivery of courses to students in Tulsa, and demand was being voiced from other locations in the state. The self-study for the 1978 ALA accreditation review emphasized the use of TBTV as the school's only approach to off-campus course delivery, with a statement of the following ground rules formulated by the State Board of Regents:

1. The course will be part of the department's regular offering.
2. The faculty member teaching the course will be a regular member of the department.
3. The course will be offered in a classroom setting, before a group of students that are regularly enrolled.

The School of Library Science additionally imposed the following requirements:

1. *Suitability*. Some courses lend themselves to television production and some do not. Courses that deal in computer-based searching obviously are not suitable to television.
2. *Complexity*. Some courses require extensive laboratory work and are thus unsuited to television presentation. The school's course, Organization of Library Materials I and II are examples of such courses.
3. *Resource Availability*. Some courses require extensive library holdings. All of the school's bibliographic courses, basic and advanced, require such holdings. Although it can be assumed that the Oklahoma State and Central State University Libraries, the Oklahoma City and Tulsa City-County Libraries have such collections, these would likely be the only ones. The limited number of collections would prevent those kinds of courses being offered statewide.

The potential for delivering courses to Lawton via TBTV was discussed at the February 4, 1980, faculty meeting but was rejected on the basis of lack of resources and frequent system problems.

The November 3, 1980, faculty meeting was primarily devoted to discussion of the system with the campus coordinator of the TBTV program. Minutes of that meeting reveal substantial concern regarding the processes and prospects of the system. When asked for guidance on the use of the system, the TBTV coordinator offered the following pointers:

1. Do not attempt class discussion because it is too difficult.
2. Because the class is two and a half hours in length, variety is a must.
3. Transparencies can be adapted for use.
4. A total lecture time is not advisable because rapport with the students is not possible.
5. There should be some alternative form of testing other than the proctor type.
6. The courier system is not 100 percent perfect at the present time but will work sufficiently if material is sent to TBTV office in time to be sent out to the student.
7. Variety may be achieved by use of guest speakers, panel discussions, and the implementation of use of many media forms.
8. The instructor needs to know what he or she can expect from the system.

An evaluation of the Tulsa program conducted late in 1981 reported that major concerns regarding TBTV included the limited potential for class discussion, the lack of opportunities for students to interact with the instructor outside of class, lack of reliability of the courier service used to deliver materials to and from Tulsa, and the resulting need for faculty members teaching live courses in Tulsa to act as couriers. Although policy suggested that "no more than 15% of an instructor's time per semester shall be committed to participation in the Tulsa program," "participating faculty estimate that teaching in the program required on the average of 36.5% of their week." Furthermore, agreements regarding financial support from the College of Continuing Education for the Tulsa program had not been fully met. Nonetheless, the report on the evaluation concluded that

The Tulsa program has been successful in bringing quality library education to the state's second largest SMSA. The faculty, despite the hardships, has responded in excellent order to the needs that were set forth.

The campus coordinator for TBTV returned to the November 8, 1982, faculty meeting to answer "faculty questions regarding the effective use of talkback TV and recommended that concerns about major improvements in talk back TV should be addressed to the State Regents and the Chancellor's Office." The coordinator also suggested that most courses were amenable to being adapted for the TBTV environment. At this meeting she gave the following recommendations, mostly having to do with the use of graphic material:

1. Use horizontal layouts for the TV camera.
2. Aspect ratio (3 × 4) allows the camera room to focus on important aspects—center for information.
3. Print needs to be large enough. Use a primary typewriter (one-quarter inch). Hand lettering should be three-eighths inch.
4. Use blue tablets for hand lettering; white is too reflective.
5. Transparencies are no problem if the lettering is large enough. Projected material does not work well on TV.
6. If an instructor is planning to use sixteen-mm film, take it to the studio to have it transferred to videotape. Slides can be used but need to be planned in advance.
7. Be flexible.
8. Communicate with the students.
9. Try to relax and feel comfortable with the medium.

These recommendations clearly did not effectively address the critical concerns of the faculty. By 1985 the use of the TBTV system had been suspended due to faculty concerns about the quality and reliability of the system. Plans to improve the system were discussed frequently at faculty meetings, with use of the system deferred until such improvements became a reality. Discussion of renewed use of TBTV resumed as the new UCT facility was being planned in early 1988 with the expectation of improved TBTV facilities. At the April 29, 1988, faculty meeting it was proposed "that an ad hoc committee be established in the fall 1988 semester to develop criteria or a checklist of items provided at a site before that site would be accepted for receiving LIS TBTV courses."

INTERACTIVE VIDEO

By 1991 the TBTV program had been replaced by an interactive compressed video system—specifically a VTEL MediaMax 386 system—located in a classroom partially controlled by the School of Library and Information Studies. This system was used with mixed success until 1998, when it was partially replaced by a Grass Valley/Tektronix Videotransport J-Series system. These systems were based on the M-JPEG analog video format and required scheduling through a centralized telecommunications center—originally operated by Oklahoma State University and later operated by ONENET, Oklahoma's educational and governmental telecommunications network. Operation of these systems was sufficiently complex that a trained operator was stationed at a console located at the rear of the classroom. The instructor had no direct technical control.

In fall 1994 a Distance Education Task Force was established to draft a policy statement and planning environment for the school's distance education activities. The vision for distance education expressed in the spring 1996 report of the Distance Education Task Force entailed "delivering the master's program and courses and other educational opportunities for enhancement of the knowledge and skills of practicing information professionals throughout the state of Oklahoma" by 2000. The report called attention to the guidelines provided in the Oklahoma State Regents for Higher Education report, "Polices and Procedures Pertaining to the Electronic Delivery of Courses and Programs," which was approved in June 1995. The task force report described an impressive—perhaps nearly intimidating—array of opportunities and challenges facing the school as it moved forward with its distance education agenda.

Although the major emphasis of interactive video instruction continued to be support for the school's program in Tulsa, by 1997 planning had been initiated for interactive video courses to be offered beginning in spring 1998 at Southwestern Oklahoma State University in Weatherford, the University of Science and Arts of Oklahoma in Chickasha, the Ardmore Higher Education Center, as well as Rogers University in Tulsa. This plan was expanded over the subsequent two years to include Cameron University in Lawton, Northwestern State University in Enid, Northwestern State University in Alva, Southeastern Oklahoma State University in Durant, and a facility operated by the Oklahoma City Public Schools. The basic plan for all of these sites was to incorporate them into multiple-site interactive video courses with students also enrolled in Norman and Tulsa.

This aggressive program, which extended the reach of the school to all major sections of the state, immediately proved to be problematic. Although planning and advising sessions held at each of the cooperating institutions suggested substantial interest on the part of potential students, enrollments were small, usually no more than one or two students at a site. Additionally, the technological difficulties associated with multiple-site courses were significantly greater than anticipated, largely as a result of incompatibilities among the interactive video systems located at the various campuses. By spring 2001 the frequency of technological malfunctions had increased to a level so intolerable that the faculty of the school declared a moratorium on interactive video delivery to sites other than Tulsa.

In summer 2001 a grant from the College of Arts and Sciences made it possible to replace the aging Grass Valley system in Norman with a Tandberg Tutor series digital system operating under the H.323 packet-based multimedia teleconferencing standard. A virtually identical system was installed in a classroom controlled by the University of Oklahoma–Tulsa in fall 2001. These systems have largely overcome the technological failings experienced with the failing analog technology formerly in place while adding substantial capabilities not previously experienced. Where the analog system required an in-the-room technician to control the session, the new system is designed to be operated directly by the instructor. Although a technician is still on call and immediately available as needed, the necessity of positioning a technician in the classroom for every interactive video course has evaporated. The new system incorporates significant improvements in the areas of audio fidelity and camera control and operates in a fully digital manner, allowing for a direct system-to-system Internet connection with no need for an intermediary link through a centralized communications system.

THE WEB

The incorporation of Web technology into the instructional offerings of the School of Library and Information Studies has been a mixed environment of substantial enthusiasm and reasoned caution. The school's first entirely Web-based course was Electronic Access to Social Science Research Resources, a service course designed primarily for students enrolled in the University of Oklahoma's Advanced Programs initiative, a long-standing effort to provide global graduate education for students serving in the U.S. Armed Forces. A second fully Web-based course, Bibliographic Management in Web and Hybrid Libraries, was offered as a special topics course during summer 2000. A Web version of the Government Publications course was offered in fall 2000. A new undergraduate course was offered entirely on the Web for spring 2002.

Although the development of completely Web-based courses has proceeded relatively slowly, the use of the Web to support conventional and interactive video courses has been widespread among the school's faculty. The most commonly used course-support tools are the WebCT and Blackboard course management packages. A small number of faculty members have developed non-Web courses for which a limited number of experiences are integrated entirely via Web content.

THE FUTURE

The School of Library and Information Studies began the twenty-first century with a wealth of new opportunities, including a greatly improved technological platform for delivery of interactive video courses, growing experience with the use of the Web in instruction, two new degree programs, and a new physical facility in Tulsa.

Responding to expressions of demand from the state's information industry and the information infrastructure operations of other industry segments, the school began planning in fall 1999 for a new undergraduate degree program in information studies. Students were first admitted to the program in fall 2001 and the first new courses were offered in spring 2002. Design of the first undergraduate course, The Information Environment, was supported by a grant from the College of Arts and Sciences. This course, a required foundational course for the bachelor of arts in Information Studies (BAIS) degree program, was taught entirely on the Web in asynchronous mode.

In spring 2002 a second master's degree program supported by the School of Library and Information Studies was authorized. The master's of science in Knowledge Management (MSKM) is "designed to teach professionals how to successfully manage the overwhelming flow of information and knowledge within varying organizational settings." The MSKM program was developed in close consultation with representatives of the information industry in the Tulsa area and will be primarily based in Tulsa but also available in Norman and possibly Oklahoma City. A major commitment of funding from the University of Oklahoma–Tulsa resulted in the development of a Tulsa-resident faculty contingent to support the MSKM program.

In 2000, the University of Oklahoma acquired the former BP-Amoco Research Center in Tulsa and began the process of building a new campus, named the Schusterman Center. The Schusterman Center merges the operations of the University of Oklahoma–Tulsa and the Tulsa Health Sciences Center—formerly separate operations—at a single location with an integrated administration. By fall 2002 all University of Oklahoma programs in Tulsa were offered at the Schusterman Center. The space plan for the Schusterman Center includes office space for faculty, including two School of Library and Information Studies faculty members, office space for graduate assistants, administrative offices, classrooms (including a variety of interactive video classrooms), and computer labs.

In spring 2001 the faculty of the school formally recognized that with Tulsa accounting for between 40 percent and 55 percent of students enrolled in the master's program during any given semester, there was no longer any convincing rationale for treating Norman as a primary site and Tulsa as a secondary site for course delivery. A policy implemented in fall 2001 is designed to equalize support for students at the two sites. Following a carefully planned course rotation schedule, each course offered in a given semester will normally be offered at both campuses using a mixture of interactive video courses, Web-supported and Web-based courses, and on-site courses taught either by full-time faculty or by adjunct faculty. During academic year 2001–02, only three graduate course sections were offered in Norman that were not also offered in Tulsa.

The transition within a one-year period from a school with a single graduate program to support of three degree programs, one undergraduate and two graduate, has been somewhat breathtaking. The rethinking of the status of Tulsa, combined with the initiation of the BAIS program and the approval of the MSKM program, has resulted in a reassessment of the core needs of the MLIS program and the integration of the school's three degree programs. In April 2002 the faculty of the School of Library and Information Studies staged a day-long curriculum retreat to address the feasibility of a shared core for the MLIS and MSKM programs. The plan that emerged from the curriculum retreat will lead to new curricula for both degrees with a common origin in the basic principles of information creation, representation, organization, and use and the sociopolitical environment.

The improvements in technological capability and reliability represented by the new interactive video system installed in 2001 lead to the anticipation that the school will re-explore the prospects for extending course availability to sites in addition to Norman and Tulsa, perhaps using a more assertive mixture of interactive video and Web-based courses. At the same time, the faculty of the school recognize that there are some courses for which an on-campus experience may be fundamentally necessary.

The key strength of the extension and distance education offerings of the University of Oklahoma School of Library and Information Studies has been frequent analysis, evaluation, and assessment of the off-campus offerings, accompanied by a documented willingness to take action when the outcomes of assessment were less than positive. In some instances the result of such assessment has been withdrawal from or reduction of involvement in distance education, but in other cases the result has been a strengthened commitment to distance education and systematic efforts to improve the distance education infrastructure. In 1998–99 the school's emphasis on analysis and assessment resulted in the formulation of an explicit set of guidelines for distributed learning, which are reproduced as an appendix to this chapter. The core criteria on which distance education planning is based include educational need, technical capacity, financial feasibility, and faculty and supporting resources availability.

The school's greatest challenges in the delivery of off-campus instruction have centered in the lack of a predictable administrative and technological infrastructure. During much of the history of the school's involvement in distance education the fundamental technological infrastructure has been beyond the direct control of the school and subject to only limited control by the university. The support base for operations in Tulsa in particular has been provided by institutions other than the University of Oklahoma, with results ranging from apparent indifference to the needs of the school to circumstances that seemingly bordered on open hostility. Opportunities for effective training in either the use of distance education technology or the incorporation of distance education technology into an integrated approach to student-centered learning experiences have been rare to the point of nonexistent.

Administrative support has historically been variable. The current administrative support structure, however, is vastly more supportive. The College of Arts and Sciences, in addition to providing faculty grants for design and implementation of distance education courses, also supports an instructional technology grant program (through which the school's interactive video classroom in Norman was re-equipped in fall 2001) and offers a broad array of learning opportunities for faculty members seeking to incorporate digital technology into their course development activities. The School of Library and Information Studies is viewed positively as a leader in distance education and the use of information technology in general and benefits tangibly from that image. The move to the Schusterman Center in Tulsa has significant potential for improving both the administrative and technological infrastructures by centering the school's operations in a University of Oklahoma–controlled facility.

An important aspect of the school's approach to distance education is and will continue to be an emphasis on quality rather than quantity. Although extending learning opportunities to a broader geographic base is an important goal for the school, the programs are not in any way enrollment-driven. Master's degree courses, regardless of the mode of delivery, are normally limited to a maximum of twenty-five students per section. Limited enrollment is also a condition of the College of Arts and Sciences grants for support of Web-based course development. These enrollment limits are an explicit recognition of both the additional demand distance delivery places on faculty members' time, energy, and professional development activities and the school's commitment to a curriculum that is rich in direct human interaction and in opportunities to effectively engage students in the learning experience at the highest levels.

A LASTING FRONTIER

Outside the entrance to the School of Library and Information Studies, which is located in the original 1929 wing of Bizzell Memorial Library, stands a stone on which is mounted a plaque with the slogan, "The Spirit of Learning Is a Lasting Frontier." The origin of the slogan is unknown; for many years it appeared on the cover of the school's *Bulletin*. It is a statement that serves as a proper emblem for a state in which the frontier spirit is still keenly felt. It is also a fitting theme for a school that has continuously striven to explore beyond its most obvious boundaries for more than thirty-five years. As the University of Oklahoma School of Library and Information Studies moves forward in support of new degree programs and innovative approaches to delivering those programs, it will be in conscious pursuit of "a lasting frontier."

APPENDIX: DISTRIBUTED LEARNING GUIDELINES

UNIVERSITY OF OKLAHOMA
SCHOOL OF LIBRARY AND INFORMATION STUDIES
GUIDELINES: Distributed Learning
STATUS: Approved by SLIS Faculty, February 19, 1999

The University of Oklahoma School of Library and Information Studies is committed to expanding access to its master's program and courses through whatever means are conducive to a quality educational experience. In support of this commitment, the School endeavors to respond to requests for course delivery in a manner that incorporates attention to the elements of educational need, technical capacity, financial feasibility, and faculty and supporting resources availability. The following guidelines are used in making decisions regarding extension of course/program availability.

EDUCATIONAL NEED

An assessment will be made of the immediate and longer term potential for sustained enrollment at the delivery site. This assessment includes

- the source and number of requests for a specific course or courses
- the population base for enrollment on which the course can draw
- the projected demand over time
- any external factors influencing demand, such as changes in certification requirements
- the presence/absence of alternative educational providers to meet the need
- the pedagogical appropriateness of the proposed delivery.

TECHNICAL CAPACITY

An evaluation will be made of the technical requirements for the proposed delivery mode and the capacity of the relevant provider and support units at OU, of the distribution system for the delivery, and of the receive sites. Included in this evaluation will be assessment of technical capacity requirements for individual students to participate in the delivery as well as technical capacity requirements for faculty responsible for the course design and delivery. Other factors to be considered in the assessment are

- prior OU or OU related units' experience with the delivery mode, distribution system, and receive site
- presence/absence of technical support for the receive site
- availability of troubleshooting assistance
- effect of technical capacity requirements for students on potential enrollment.

FINANCIAL FEASIBILITY

Determination will be made of the financial implications for the School of extension of delivery. The extension of course/program access beyond sites to which the School is already committed is done on the basis of at least a financially neutral impact on previously existing delivery. If additional costs are incurred through extension of access, these additional costs must be recovered through site charges, special funding (such as a grant), substitution of delivery sites, or some other appropriate means. In order to establish a new site or delivery mode the School may wish to underwrite the delivery on a short term basis. However, in such cases, an analysis outlining the extent of the financial commitment, the source of the funds, and the time period for underwriting will be prepared prior to undertaking such a venture.

FACULTY AND SUPPORTING RESOURCES AVAILABILITY

An assessment will be made of the impact of the extension of delivery on the workload of faculty projected to provide course design and delivery. Included in the assessment will be such elements as

- consideration of additional course preparation required
- increase in numbers of students enrolled in a specific course and the faculty member's overall student enrollment numbers
- increased complexity of logistical arrangements for which faculty would be responsible.

Assessment will also be made of the increased workload in the administration of the program, including impact on office staff due to additional logistical and support needs.

Although provision of access to the classes for a course will not be presented as provision of access to all resources needed to complete a course, evaluation will be made of the availability of reasonable access provided by the various support units of OU to the resources needed. Elements to be assessed include provision of library resources and services by OU Libraries, bookstore services (either through OU or by arrangement with local area facilities), and access to any specialized software needed for completion of the course.

17

THE UNIVERSITY OF PITTSBURGH'S SCHOOL OF INFORMATION SCIENCES DISTANCE EDUCATION: PAST, PRESENT, AND FUTURE

Susan Webreck Alman, Christinger Tomer, and Kara Lizik Pilarsky

INTRODUCTION

Distance education at the University of Pittsburgh's School of Information Sciences has evolved in four distinct (and fairly typical) phases, beginning with the on-site delivery of select courses at remote locations and culminating, at least for the time being, in a master's of Library and Information Science (MLIS) curriculum offered mainly over the Web. Until recently, the development of distance education capabilities has been slow and fitful, in part because the university itself has never made a full commitment to distance education or the development of a wholly suitable infrastructure, but also because the school has focused its collective attentions largely on other initiatives, such as an undergraduate degree program in information science, a graduate program in telecommunications, and new tracks, such as archives and records management, in the ALA-accredited MLIS program.

In recent years, however, circumstances have changed. Competition in the educational marketplace is keener than ever before. As a consequence, educational programs in many disciplines and professions, including library and information science, have embraced distance education as a viable means of outreach and growth. Attitudes have changed, too, in no small measure owing to the success of the Web as a medium for communication and information exchange and the transforming effect that the Web has had on myriad attitudes, including those regarding distance education.

Today, at the University of Pittsburgh's School of Information Sciences, where the FastTrack MLIS represents the first degree offered by the university via the Web, distance education represents a new array of opportunities for growth in several areas, including post-master's certificate-based education. It also affords a set of formidable challenges in a number of areas, including curriculum design and development, technical support, and impact on faculty workloads.

A BRIEF HISTORY OF THE SCHOOL OF INFORMATION SCIENCES

The origins of the University of Pittsburgh's School of Information Sciences can be traced to 1901, when the Carnegie Library of Pittsburgh founded Pittsburgh's first library education program, the Training School for Children's Librarians. In 1905, a one-year course was added for graduates of other library programs, resulting in the matriculation of students from the New York State Library, Albany, Drexel, Pratt, Simmons, University of Illinois, and University of Wisconsin. About fifteen years later, owing to the many changes throughout the library profession and growing demands for educational training leading to an academically certified professional degree, the Training School became a department of the Carnegie Institute of Technology, and its name was changed to the Carnegie Library School. In 1934, the ALA approved the Carnegie Library School's one-year professional program. In 1948, the bachelor of science in Library Science degree was superseded by a master's in Library Science degree; one year later, in 1949, nineteen students were awarded Carnegie Institute's first MLS degrees.

The Carnegie Library School moved to the University of Pittsburgh in 1961, and Harold Lancour was appointed the founding dean. In 1962, the University of Pittsburgh Graduate Library School officially opened, with a faculty of 4 and a class of 134 students. Allen Kent introduced the first information science course in 1963, and within five years the demand for education in information science had grown so quickly and so great that the school expanded into two departments, the Department of Library Science and the Interdisciplinary Department of Information Science.

MOVEMENT TOWARD DISTANCE EDUCATION

The first steps toward the establishment of a distance education program began in the 1970s. During the 1970s (and into the 1980s), the Department of Library Science conducted summer courses at the Chautauqua Institution in upstate New York. Instructors from the department taught full-credit courses drawn from the MLS curriculum. Although many students from the University of Pittsburgh traveled to Chautauqua to attend the courses offered there, the principal aim of the program was to recruit students who would subsequently enroll as full-time students in the on-campus MLS program. The off-site program at Chautauqua was never more than a modest success, and it was eventually abandoned as overhead costs grew and the logistics of delivering the courses off-site became increasingly complicated.

In 1979, the University of Pittsburgh's Department of Library Science also implemented a joint program for agriculture information specialists, in conjunction with West Virginia University's College of Agriculture and Forestry and the Pennsylvania State University's School of Agriculture. Students in this program traveled to the participating universities to take courses and consult with faculty advisors at each institution.

DISTANCE EDUCATION THROUGH THE EXTERNAL STUDIES PROGRAM

Distance education in its more contemporary sense began in earnest at the School of Information Sciences in 1988, when Nancy Evans Weaver, then a faculty member in the Department of Information Science, taught two courses, Human Information Processing and Human Factors in System Design, through the University's External Studies Program (UESP) for the first time. (The UESP is based on self-paced instruction. Most of the work is done independently using materials prepared by university faculty.)

Early on, Evans relied mainly on extensive study guides and textbooks as the basis for these two courses. More recently, she has supplemented the study guides and required textbooks with short lectures on videotape. The videos are viewed in a classroom setting during the course of the term and are followed by group discussion typically facilitated by a graduate student assistant. Evaluation of the academic progress is determined by exams held at proctored sites and then mailed or faxed to Evans for grading; lately, the course on human information processing has begun to offer computerized testing for sections of the exams.

Now living in New Zealand, Weaver still teaches these courses through UESP. She believes that distance education alters the learning experience of students. In her experience, students are more independent and fully responsible for learning the material; therefore, it is easier for students who are naturally independent learners to succeed in this type of situation, whereas students who have difficulty budgeting time and following a set schedule may profit more from a traditional classroom setting. In addition, Weaver notes that communication and interaction with her students has been altered. She says, "I work hard to create a friendly persona that encourages students to reach me by e-mail. I work harder on that than I did in class because I think students have to take an extra step now to get to me and I want to make that as easy as possible." Some students have utilized Weaver's open line of communication for school-related discussions and also to fulfill the need of a personal connection with their instructor. Weaver's efforts have been successful enough that she regularly communicates with former students years after they have completed her courses, receiving messages from some who tell her how the course transformed their ideas about systems design as well as those who struggle with the independence and responsibility of such a class and prefer a structured classroom setting.

INTERACTIVE TELEVISION

The next step in the process of developing a distance education capability came in 1992, when faculty from the school's Department of Information Science offered two courses via interactive television (ITV). The courses, in cognitive science and telecommunications, were offered simultaneously to students at the university's main campus in the Oakland section of Pittsburgh and at its Greensburg campus, located thirty miles east of Pittsburgh. Wes Jamison taught the cognitive science course from the Greensburg campus, and the late Leon Montgomery taught the telecommunications course from the main campus.

In this initial effort, the technology available was good enough to provide a consistently clear picture, but the reliance on a single camera and the limited skills of camera operators limited what was in view to "talking heads." Audio quality was poor, however, particularly when interactive discussion was attempted. Part of the problem of audio quality stemmed from the fact that the microphones at the Oakland site were voice-activated, which meant that students at the Greensburg site could hear almost everything that was said in the Oakland classroom, whereas the Greensburg campus's microphone was activated by a push-button, thus allowing the class to engage in private discussion while leaving the Oakland campus without audio.

The first course—the class on cognitive science taught by Jamison—was regarded as a success. The biggest problem encountered was the cancellation of a class session because a student had inadvertently broken the fiber optic cable connecting the two campuses. There were other, minor issues to be resolved—for example, the video technology did not support the use of PowerPoint® presentations—but Jamison's greatest concern with the course was the lack of communication. The technology created a high level of anxiety among the students, making them reluctant to interact with one another. Jamison noted that "[the students] need to deal with technology because they will be dealing with similar situations in the workplace." He also observed that interaction is greater between campuses when the instructor visits the remote campus during the term.

Although ITV continues to be used occasionally as a medium for delivering courses to the university's regional campuses, owing to the convenience it affords, ITV has never achieved the popularity that was once anticipated. The limitations of the medium itself, particularly when production and technical support is constrained, was a factor, but the most powerful factor was the cost of offering courses using ITV. Indirect costs, especially those associated with faculty time, were considered high, and the direct costs were also judged ultimately to be onerous, in part because the unit within the university responsible for ITV is operated as a cost-recovery center and therefore passes the real costs of production and access to relevant technologies on to the academic unit offering the course.

THE EXPANSION OF DISTANCE EDUCATION

The next major step in the development of distance education occurred in February 1996, when Associate Dean Mary K. Biagini proposed a distance education partnership with Millersville University's Elementary Education Department. (Millersville University is part of Commonwealth of Pennsylvania's State System of Higher Education, located near Lancaster in the southeastern part of the state.) The plan was approved and took effect on September 18, 1997. The first of two endeavors was a workshop titled Update for Librarians Working with Children and Youth: Developing Collections for the Electronic Age. Students were able to earn one graduate credit for this workshop that consisted of five three-hour sessions held biweekly from September to November. A second workshop was held the following spring, and it focused on school library media center management issues.

Biagini and Susan W. Alman taught the first workshop from the University of Pittsburgh, and Marge Tassia, a professor in the Elementary Education Department at Millersville University, facilitated the group in Millersville. Tassia stated that having a facilitator at the "far site" (Millersville) enabled students at both sites to benefit from a third instructor.

This learning experience was enhanced for both groups of students because of the interaction among the students and instructors and the group activities that were held during the classes. Students at both sites agreed that the workshop was beneficial. One individual noted the technology experience provided through the distance education class was an added bonus to her educational experience, and she believes all instructors and librarians should experience distance education courses as students. Tassia also commented on the advantages of the experience. She felt one of the best aspects of the course was the sharing of professional experiences between the two sites. The mix of students from diverse backgrounds enabled them to share techniques and personal accomplishments and failures that could never be read in a textbook and may not have been gained without the distance education course.

At about the same time in 1996, Pittsburgh's Richard Cox and Margaret Hedstrom of the University of Michigan's School of Information developed a course exchange agreement under which access to the course on archival appraisal offered by Cox and the course on electronic records management offered by Hedstrom was shared via ITV.

According to Cox, the courses were pedagogically productive. It was clear, however, that instructors need to make significant modifications to accommodate the ITV environment. For example, Cox noted that because lecturing for fifty minutes and then entertaining questions was not an effective way to manage two classrooms separated by hundreds of miles, he divided the meetings of the course into various segments with lectures lasting for no more than twenty minutes. After a short lecture, he would incorporate a case study or discussion to ensure that all students were part of the learning process. To coordinate readings for the course, a teaching assistant at the Michigan site was responsible for ordering the textbooks and placing the required readings on reserve.

Notwithstanding the perception that the courses had been positive teaching and learning experiences, the cooperative arrangement was not continued. A principal reason was that each program was able to increase the number of faculty members teaching in the area of archives and records management in the years that followed, thus eliminating the problem—shortage of qualified instructors—that compelled the two schools to cooperate in the first place. Another factor was once again the perception that the medium made comparatively greater demands on the instructors. Cox estimated that class preparation was 25 percent greater for his distance education courses than those taught in the traditional fashion.

COOPERATION IN CONTINUING EDUCATION

In spring 1999, the University of Pittsburgh Department of Library and Information Sciences initiated discussions with other LIS organizations in Pennsylvania aimed at assessing the need for coordinated efforts in the area of continuing education and professional development. As a result, the Pennsylvania Alliance for Continuing Library Education (PACLE) was formed. PACLE was a partnership among

- University of Pittsburgh Department of Library and Information Sciences
- Drexel University College of Information Sciences and Technology
- Clarion University of Pennsylvania Department of Library and Information Sciences
- Commonwealth Libraries of Pennsylvania
- PALINET
- Pennsylvania Library Association

PACLE had two basic goals:

- Coordinate continuing education to maximize the quality of instruction and minimize unnecessary duplication of effort; and
- Promote the value of continued education, especially to library personnel who have not taken continuing education in the past.

PACLE failed not because those goals were irrelevant but because the Pennsylvania General Assembly unwittingly created a set of conditions that increased competition among continuing education providers and militated against cooperation among them. In June 1999, the General Assembly passed legislation requiring all public library directors to complete eight hours per year of continuing education, and also requiring any library employee working more than twenty hours per week to complete six hours of continuing education every two years. Unfortunately, the legislation actually undermined the respective positions of the aforementioned educational providers because it set so few explicit criteria for fulfillment.

Throughout the 1990s, the SIS faculty periodically examined issues relating to the technological requirements of distance education. The general purpose of these reviews was to determine whether the school should build its own distance education capabilities, use the limited infrastructure that had been erected by the university, outsource support for distance education, or forgo it altogether. In each instance, the same conclusion has been drawn; namely, that the technology was too costly and insufficiently standardized to warrant major investments by the school. The last of these reviews also concluded that the next generation of distance education technology would be developed primarily in the context of data transmission networks, moving away from the reliance on cable and ITV that was characteristic of distance education in the 1980s and 1990s, and that these new teaching and learning technologies would take advantage of the quality-of-service features that will form an integral part of the next-generation Internet (i.e., Internet Protocol version 6).

VISION FOR DISTANCE EDUCATION

By the late 1990s, faculty members from the Department of Library and Information Science had come to the conclusion that distance education in some form was certain to be an important part of LIS education in general, and at the University of Pittsburgh's School of Information Sciences in particular. Recognizing that in the new digital economy, the destabilization of competitive advantage is both opportunity and threat, a small group of faculty members, led by Biagini, Christinger Tomer, and Alman (who is also the SIS coordinator of professional development), developed a proposal for the establishment of a version of the MLIS degree program that combines limited on-campus educational experiences with coursework delivered primarily via the Web.

After approximately eighteen months of planning and development, and following approval at the university level, delivery of the FastTrack MLIS began in May 2001 with a group of thirty-five students undertaking two required courses, LIS 2001, Understanding Information, and LIS 2600, Introduction to Information Technologies. The members of the first Fast-Track MLIS cohort came from Delaware, Florida, Maryland, Nevada, New

York, Pennsylvania, and the District of Columbia. The thirty female and five male students ranged in age from twenty-four to sixty-two, with an average age of thirty-nine. Though many students held undergraduate degrees in elementary education or English, other students held undergraduate degrees in psychology, art history, zoology, communications, social work, urban planning, sociology, speech, biology, and mechanical engineering. Five students held additional advanced degrees. Though most members of the cohort had library experience—the average length of library work experience was five years—eight members had less than one year experience on entering the Fast-Track MLIS program.

The second and third cohorts of students that were accepted into the program in 2002 and 2003 had similar profiles. Owing to the increased applicant pool, however, the qualifying GPA for prospective students in Cohort 3 was substantially higher (3.5 or above on a 4.0 scale), and 15 students who were admitted held master's degrees in other disciplines. The geographic range of prospective students also broadened and included applicants from Hawaii, Alaska, California, Florida, Maine, Texas, Canada, and the United Arab Emirates.

A degree specialization in medical information/librarianship was added to the curricular offerings in 2003. Students in the program are evenly divided among the possible areas of specialization—school library certification program or academic, public, and special librarianship.

THE FASTTRACK MLIS

Establishing the FastTrack MLIS

The goal of the initiative that eventually came to be known as FastTrack was to extend the reach of the MLIS program. By the end of the 1990s, as the professional education market shifted demographically toward older students with more personal constraints on their time and mobility, it seemed clear that the inflexibility of traditional educational delivery was placing real and substantive limits on the audience for the core program. There was also the practical fact that the Department of Library and Science (and the School of Information Sciences) found itself in a position, financial as well as political, that placed a strong emphasis on tuition income as a basis for the generation of operating revenues.

Key Planning Decisions

Early on, several key decisions that influenced the nature and conduct of the FastTrack MLIS were made. The first was the decision to require that students in the program subscribe to broadband Internet service. This decision was based in part on the dramatic growth in the availability of broadband services and the belief that the quality of broadband connections has the effect of pushing the technology into the background and pushing the intellectual content of the courses into the foreground.[1] It was also determined that the technological basis on which students enrolled in the program operated should be as highly standardized as possible; consequently, specifications and standards relating to both hardware and software were established.[2]

The second and even more important decision was a commitment to organizing the educational experience on the basis of cohorts. This decision was predicated mainly on the idea that dealing with a community of learners, as opposed to individual students, would provide a more powerful learning experience while mitigating higher attrition rates.

The concept of the cohort was "not just a single student with a computer but rather an online community of learners." The perceived advantage of organizing student cohorts was that students would be able to draw on their peers as well as their instructors for support throughout the program. Peer interactions were expected to play an important part of the on-campus learning experience, and this interaction was also expected to extend into the online learning environment.

Under the plan that was ultimately implemented, FastTrack MLIS students begin the program as part of a cohort of peers that moves through the program collectively. Each new cohort begins with a five-day on-campus orientation in the summer term that introduces students to the program, faculty, and each other, provides hands-on computer training, and builds camaraderie and a cooperative learning network among students and faculty. The students in the cohort also spend time together with their instructors in learning experiences over a weekend each term after the initial summer term orientation.

Emergent Issues

As the delivery of the FastTrack MLIS began, several key issues emerged. The first to arise concerned the adequacy of the technological infrastructure and support system provided by the university. The computing and networking infrastructure at the University of Pittsburgh is of high quality and reliability. In addition, support for desktop computing as offered by the university is at least adequate, if not better. There is a twenty-four hours a day, seven days a week help line that, according to reports from students and faculty members, has improved steadily in responsiveness and general customer satisfaction with the quality of the assistance provided. The university also provides an array of short courses and workshops, many of them specific to the principal operating system or most widely used applications. But in the months preceding the matriculation of the first FastTrack cohort, the period during which the Napster phenomenon (downloading copyrighted material for free) was at its peak, the availability of bandwidth across the university's network was a persistent problem that degraded the quality of a number of important services, including e-mail and CourseInfo, the university's course delivery system. The problem was compounded by the university's approach, which was to meet the demand for additional bandwidth only when the shortage of available bandwidth had reached nearly overwhelming levels.

During the first term in which FastTrack students were enrolled, the bandwidth problem abated, because the university's Computing and Software Systems Development group had increased bandwidth, and because the summer term almost invariably produces a decline in student demands on the computing and networking infrastructure. However, in ensuing terms the problem of available bandwidth returned, and because the university continued to deal with the problem reactively, it remains an intermittently serious issue.

Other technical issues have emerged as the university's Center for Instructional Design and Distance Education, which is responsible for managing the course delivery system, has upgraded from CourseInfo to Blackboard® 5. In particular, problems with several key features of the Blackboard system, such as the grade book, the digital drop box, and the threaded discussions, have been sources of frustration for both students and instructors. Limitations of the Blackboard have also become more obvious through repeated use, the most important of them being that objects cannot be moved within a Blackboard course using methods such as click-and-drag or cut-and-paste, but instead must be re-created at the point of the new location.

Another area of concern has been that of faculty support. Support has been limited and qualified, in part because of qualitative concerns, but mainly because some tenured faculty members have been opposed to the additional work that distance education entails and how additional work might affect their other duties and goals, and because untenured faculty members have been reluctant to make the requisite commitments in such an environment, particularly when the implications of a commitment to teaching in distance environments are unclear where promotion and tenure are concerned. Faculty attitudes, positive and negative, and faculty support (or the lack thereof) will become even more important as the FastTrack MLIS grows and the demand for additional sections of core courses and electives grows with it.

Of the issues that emerged in the development and initial implementation of the FastTrack MLIS, none was more important or more frustrating than the problem of providing access to commercially licensed library resources. The University Library System subscribes to a substantial array of databases, electronic journals, and reference materials—in fact, the University of Pittsburgh's annual investment in such resources is one of the highest among members of the Association of Research Libraries. However, under the contracts that the university has negotiated with various vendors, access is limited to computers that have an Internet address that falls within the university's domain, pitt.edu.

To accommodate off-campus users, the university entered into an agreement with a commercial Internet service provider (ISP), Stargate, that enabled off-campus users to use a virtual private network (VPN) that Stargate developed and maintained as part of the university's network. Initially, the service was available only to users subscribing to the full array of Stargate services, and this posed a problem for a significant number of students enrolled in the FastTrack MLIS program because Stargate offered only 56K dialup service in most areas, thus forcing many students to choose between the broadband services offered by other ISPs and the greater access available via Stargate and its VPN. Subsequently, and in response to requests from many quarters, including representatives of the FastTrack MLIS program, Stargate introduced a VPN-only service that allows users of other ISPs to gain access to the university's network for a fee of 10 dollars a month

In the interval during which the university developed these services with Stargate, students in the FastTrack MLIS program lacked full access to the resources of the university's library system. However, several factors offset the effects of this problem. First, librarians at the university and elsewhere provided direct and substantive assistance. Second, a number of the students in the FastTrack MLIS program, but particularly those who reside in the Commonwealth of Pennsylvania, had access to electronic resources through the State Library's POWER Library program and their local public libraries.[3] Similarly, students were able to gain access to commercial databases and electronic texts through educational programs that a number of vendors, including DIALOG, Lexis-Nexis, Factiva, and Gale, have developed to support LIS education.

Accomplishments

Perhaps the greatest accomplishment to date is that the first FastTrack MLIS cohort has completed the first of two years of study, and with the exception of one student, the entire cohort received the MLIS degree in April 2003. A general assessment has not yet been conducted; however, the student and expert reviews of the courses offered to date indicate that the teaching and learning experiences that form the essence of the program have been largely successful.

The University's Center for Instructional Design and Distance Education (CIDDE) has been very supportive of this initiative. The CIDDE enables faculty to identify and use technology and other instructional resources available to them. CIDDE provides faculty with a primary contact point for many of the instructional services they need and also assists in developing and supporting distance education programs and courses.

When the cohort was on-campus for orientation during the midpoint of the first term, two instructional designers from the CIDDE staff conducted five focus groups to determine the students' satisfaction with the FastTrack

MLIS program. The primary goal of the focus groups was to collect data regarding the learners' satisfaction with the online program. Surprisingly, the CIDDE staff felt that the feedback could be applied to most online learning environments.

The responses from the focus groups broke down into the following five themes:

1. General program issues
2. Course issues
3. Communication/interaction issues
4. On-campus experience issues
5. Technology issues

The feedback from these MLIS adult learners reflected a strong positive satisfaction with both the courses and the program. They reflected the following perspectives, which are very common to adult learners: the need for flexibility in when and how they participate in the program, the need for clear expectations, the need for technological support, and the need for instructor–learner and learner–learner interaction.

Online focus groups were conducted in subsequent terms of study. These groups included both on-campus and online students who were enrolled in the same classes. Once again the FastTrack MLIS students expressed satisfaction with the online courses.

From the faculty perspective, the most important benefit to date is the new and occasionally powerful insights into teaching and learning that this venture in distance education has provided. There is now the expectation that these insights will enhance not only the FastTrack MLIS but the on-campus program as well.

The program has had "political" value within and outside of the university. The fact of the FastTrack MLIS has reinforced the identity of the School and the Department of Library and Information Science as units responsive to the educational needs of the library community. Within the university, the program has been acknowledged as an important initiative.

The success of the FastTrack MLIS has also engendered interest in exploring other areas in which distance education may be offered. Specifically, there are plans and proposals now under active consideration that if adopted would lead to the development of a post-master's certificate program in management and leadership aimed at the needs and interests of mid-career librarians.

LOOKING TO THE FUTURE

Looking further ahead, however, the School of Information Sciences and the Department of Library and Information Science expect to provide remote access to educational services that rely exclusively on broadband network capabilities, deliver interactive multimedia presentations in real time, and offer both instructors and students an array of adaptive features.[4]

There is evidence, including the limited evidence of the experiences at Pittsburgh, that successful learning environments can be developed within the framework of existing distance education models. Yet there are also many unresolved issues.

How do various modalities interact with identified learning styles? How do media affect instructional style and content? How does distance education's reliance on technologies influence the role of the instructor? How does it change the relationship between the instructor and the support staff? How reliable is the technology, and how much redundancy is necessary in the systems in place for course delivery and student–teacher interactions? How will distance education change the economics of colleges and universities, the composition of faculties, and the development of new programs?

A great deal of skepticism exists among educators, especially those schooled under the traditional system. Many believe that the qualitative trade-off associated with technology-based, distributed education is highly unfavorable. Others are open-minded, but they often argue that the technologies are not sufficiently refined and that the economic benefits, if they exist at all, are largely undocumented.

Changing the attitudes and behaviors of instructors will require changes in the incentive system of parent institutions. Within institutions that reward innovation and excellence in teaching, it may not be difficult to convince significant numbers of instructors to convert their syllabi and course materials into digital formats, or to begin to rethink the approach to teaching and delivery of course content at the most basic levels. But research-oriented universities that place far more emphasis on research and publication will be much slower to respond, because the current system of incentives for faculty will have to be altered significantly before they begin to respond in substantial numbers. More to the point, unless and until significant numbers of instructors are willing to adapt their course development methods to the digital environment, large blocks of instructional material will continue to be delivered in traditional forms.

The interest in distance education is also an outgrowth of a broader debate over the economics of knowledge transfer within education settings. Over the last several decades, colleges and universities have been forced to adopt new, more business-oriented models of operation, as budgets have grown less elastic and the competition for students has grown more acute. In the process, educational policy makers have examined the teaching mission of their institutions in terms of service delivery models, focusing to a significant degree on the fixed costs of course production and delivery. The idea of using an amalgam of communications and information technologies to deliver courses remotely is one of the principal products of this process.

This process of economic assessment has had other effects, too, perhaps the most notable being an increasing emphasis on the notion of markets for educational programs and services and the role of marketing in maintaining revenue streams. As a result, many educational institutions have begun to view program development, the renewal of infrastructure, and various other activities, in terms of new, external markets, as well as the traditional settings. As the interest in distance education has grown, several general points have emerged. First, distance education requires a significant capital commitment. Second, the element of risk is significant, because it is not clear whether many of the markets for distance education, even when viewed on an aggregate basis, are large enough or lucrative enough to recover these investments. Finally, it has become clear that the market for distance education is highly segmented, with segments differing substantially by degree of capitalization, technologies in use, and the demographics of specific markets. Which means, in this context, that it may not be fair or reasonable to compare the approach to distance education taken by the MBA program at Duke University, which charges a premium of $32,000 over and above the regular tuition and fees of approximately $50,000 to participate in the distance version of its executive MBA program, to, say, the approach taken by the School of Information Studies at Syracuse University, which charges no premium and in fact effectively uses its distance education program to discount the cost of the MLS program.

Even within the colleges and universities that have made a major commitment to distance education, there are serious questions about its merits. Powerful technologies are being applied to the tasks of teaching and learning in distributed environments in the interests of economy, but these technologies are costly and require large numbers of students or extraordinary tuition charges to justify their use. Not surprisingly, there is a considerable reluctance on the part of many institutions to commit resources to the business of developing an infrastructure for distance education. In fact, a 1997 study published by the National Center for Education Statistics indicated that among the factors keeping institutions from starting or expanding distance education programs, the most powerful were program development costs (43 percent), limited technological infrastructure to support distance education (31 percent), and equipment failures and costs of maintaining equipment (23 percent).[5]

In the specific context of LIS education, it seems clear that the broadest and most powerful commitments will be made by programs affiliated with universities that have already made major capital commitments to distance education. Where such a commitment has not been made, it seems reasonable to imagine that LIS programs will enter into distance education on a much more limited basis, owing to their inability to capitalize more ambitious projects on an independent basis and the limited economic potential of their natural markets. In the short run, this means that the performance of low-cost, asynchronous delivery systems supported by the Web will be of critical importance in determining the success or failure of the distance education initiatives mounted within LIS education.[6] It also means that the capabilities of the software for Web-based instruction are a key factor in the short-term success of distance education efforts.

Today, many of the Web-based instructional software packages are based on proprietary development models that sharply limit efforts to make them better. Equally problematic is the fact that these proprietary designs inhibit sharing among institutions or across technical environments. Therefore, efforts to develop technical standards for the software used to create and deliver courses via distance education are of critical importance.

The work of the Instructional Management Systems (IMS) Project is likely to be particularly important in the development of platform-independent courseware. In November 1994, EDUCAUSE (then EDUCOM) launched an initiative called the National Learning Infrastructure Initiative (NLII). The NLII identified a common need among educational institutions for nonproprietary, Internet-based strategies for customizing and managing the instructional process and for integrating content from multiple publishers in distributed- or virtual-learning environments. As a result, the IMS was established to serve "the development of a substantial body of instructional software, the creation of an online infrastructure for managing access to learning materials and environments, the facilitation of collaborative and authentic learning activities, and the certification of acquired skills and knowledge."[7] Its goal is to establish a specific set of "higher-order standards and tools that enable teachers, learners, software developers, content providers, and other parties involved in the learning process to create, manage and access the use of online learning materials and environments."

As it has evolved, the IMS Project has attempted to address three barriers to providing effective online materials and learning environments:

- Lack of standards for locating and operating interactive platform-independent materials;
- Lack of support for the collaborative and dynamic nature of learning; and
- Lack of incentives and structure for developing and sharing content.

It is difficult to assess the success of the IMS Project at this stage. It should be noted, however, that the IMS Developers' Network now has more than 200 participating organizations, including corporations, publishers, and universities.

The continued development of such standards is critically important, especially from the perspective of LIS education. Open technical standards produce a technological and economic environment in which undercapitalized organizations have a chance to make substantial and important use of information technologies and networked services. Unhappily, the commitment to open technical standards for distance education is not particularly strong, despite the vastly instructional experience of Internet development. There are many reasons for this state of affairs, most of them credible, but the fact remains that the success of distance education will depend largely on the continuation and success of standards-making efforts like those of the IMS.

In the long run, two trends will reshape distance education. First, data networks will be refitted with the bandwidth and the management infrastructure necessary to support real-time, multipoint interaction incorporating data, audio, and video. Second, highly adaptive learning systems capable of modulating knowledge, as well their own functionality, to the need of learners will emerge. Adaptive learning systems will offer high degrees of flexibility and scalability—content and courseware will be reusable, interoperable, and easily organized at many different levels of complexity throughout the instructional environment. These systems will be able adaptive enough to support just-in-time learning. Perhaps more to the point, adaptive learning systems will be a key component of a new learning economy, where learning experiences are pulled by demand rather than driven by any supply.

But achieving this level of adaptability will require advances in a wide range of intellectual technologies, including authoring systems, multisensory interfaces, search technology, and network middleware. Continued progress will also be required in software reusability and interoperability, especially for high-bandwidth applications. All of this will depend squarely on the emergence of relevant standards and the development of tools that address the real requirements of teaching and learning.

NOTES

1. The commitment to the use of broadband Internet services was eventually complicated substantially by a university agreement with an Internet service provider, Stargate.Net, under which external access to certain university resources, such as access to the licensed databases, electronic journals, and online reference works of the University Library System, was limited to Stargate customers only. Because Stargate offers broadband services on a limited geographical basis, the agreement places significant limits on the access available to students who elect broadband service offered by another ISP. Students with a Stargate account are provided access to a virtual private network gateway that enables them to use the full resources of the university's computing network on a remote basis. Students who live in areas where Stargate provides DSL services are required to subscribe to those services. Students who live in areas where Stargate provides dial-up service only and where other ISPs provide broadband connectivity are advised to subscribe to both services.

2. FastTrack MLIS students trade the expenses of on-site housing, transportation, and parking for the expenses of computing equipment and connectivity. Students are required to own a computer capable of running Microsoft Office 2000 or Office XP, and a Web browser with Java support. Software is available at no or minimal charge to students, including the Student Toolkit CD and Microsoft Software Campus Software Suite. The system should be based on an advanced microprocessor, such as the

Intel Pentium 3 or 4 microprocessor, the Intel Celeron, the AMD Athlon or Duron, and the Macintosh PowerPC G3 or G4. In the case of computers using the AMD or Intel processors, a clock speed of 600 MHz or higher is recommended; iMac and PowerMac computers should run at clock speeds of 400 MHz or higher. Intel and AMD systems should have no less than 128 MB RAM; iMac and PowerMac systems should have at least 64 MB RAM. Computers based on the Intel or AMD micro-processors should run under Microsoft Windows 98, Windows ME, Windows 2000, or Windows XP. Windows 2000 and Windows XP are recommended, owing to their greater stability. Apple computers should be running Mac OS 8 or higher. Operating systems such as UNIX, Solaris, or Linux are not recommended because there is no suite of office applications available for any of these platforms that is sufficiently com-patible with Microsoft Office 2000 or Office XP and because we are not prepared to offer support for such operating systems. The computer should be equipped with a high-speed CD-ROM (or DVD-ROM) drive, a graphics adapter capable of support-ing streaming video, and a sound system capable of supporting audio input and out-put.

3. The POWER (Pennsylvania Online World of Electronic Resources) Library is offered as a service of Pennsylvania's public libraries, school libraries, and the State Library. The POWER library enables users to access thousands of full-text periodical articles, newspapers, a major encyclopedia, plus photographs, pictures, charts, maps, and reference materials.

4. There are many signs that the market for broadband educational and learning services will emerge rapidly. For example, according to the International Data Cor-poration, households accounting for about two-thirds of the purchasing power of the U.S. economy have Internet access. According to a 1998 report by Forrester Research, 16 million homes in the United States will have broadband access to the Internet by the end of 2002, owing to the consumer-oriented deployment of cable modem and DSL services.

5. National Center for Education Statistics. *Statistical Analysis Report: Distance Education in Higher Education Institutions.* October 1997 (NCES 98-062).

6. In the long run, implementation of the quality-of-service features of IPv6 will make it possible to use the Internet as a medium for the distribution of multimedia content and real-time interactions. Related implementations, such as multicasting and network-based caching schemes, should eventually help lower the cost of high-bandwidth services to a point of comparatively broad affordability. But reaching that price point will take years, because implementing the basic components of these new services will require upgrading the general network infrastructure. In the meantime, the success or failure of most distance education efforts will be dependent mainly on the performance of low-end technologies.

7. See IMS Background Statement, available online at www.imsproject.org/background.html.

18

THE UNIVERSITY OF RHODE ISLAND REGIONAL PROGRAM DISTANCE EDUCATION IN NEW ENGLAND

C. Herbert Carson

Since its inception, a primary goal of the Graduate School of Library and Information Studies (GSLIS) at the University of Rhode Island (URI) has been to provide an ALA-accredited program to the citizens of the New England states. Discussions regarding the need for a library school at one of the state universities began between the presidents of the New England Land Grant Universities in the late 1950s.

A certificate program in librarianship was being offered through URI's Extension Division in Providence. Courses were first offered in this program in 1957. The enrollment in this program had been successful, and URI planned to have a new library completed for the 1963–64 academic year that could support a library science program. The presidents of the New England Land Grant Universities agreed that URI was the logical site for a library science program in New England. It was also agreed that the school would be placed under the New England Board of Higher Education (NEBHE) compact. Under the compact at that time, students from New England states would be allowed to take courses at URI and pay in-state tuition and fees.

In March 1961 President Frances H. Horn recommended to the Board of Trustees of State Colleges in Rhode Island that the Graduate Library School (GLS) be established. In October 1962 the Board of Trustees voted to establish the school, effective July 1, 1963, with students to begin enrolling in the fall term of 1963.

Because distance education has revolved around a regional program that was intended to provide an accredited master's degree in library science to the residents of New England, the evolution of distance education will be embedded in a brief history of GSLIS. The history will be followed by a description of recent distance education accomplishments. Finally, future goals regarding distance education at GSLIS will be outlined.

A BRIEF HISTORY OF GSLIS

Jonathan Ashton was appointed as the first dean of the GLS in 1963. He was charged with fulfilling the administrative duties as well as teaching classes. Ashton and three adjunct faculty members taught library science courses during the 1963–64 academic year. The school was housed and the classes were taught at the extension campus in Providence.

E. J. Humeston Jr. was appointed dean in summer 1964 following the resignation of Ashton. After having received the approval of the necessary bodies of the university, a full-time program was begun in September 1964. Three full-time faculty members, Lucy Salvatore, Helen Geer, and Benjamin Page, were also appointed at this time.

In 1965 the school began offering one class per semester at the Kingston campus. Courses were first offered outside of Rhode Island during the 1967–68 academic year when classes were taught in Hartford, Connecticut. This marked the beginning of the regional program in that URI courses were being taught outside of Rhode Island within the New England region.

The Regional Program Officially Begins

GLS moved to the Kingston campus in June 1969. The administrative and faculty offices were located in Home Management House on Lower College Road. Classes were held at various classrooms as assigned by the registrar. Registration for classes under the NEBHE compact officially began in fall 1970. The Committee on Accreditation (COA) of the ALA accredited the school for five years in June 1971.

The regional program was expanded to include courses offered at the University of Connecticut at Storrs and at the University of Massachusetts at Amherst in fall 1970. These classes, as well as those being offered at West Hartford, Connecticut, were taught by adjunct faculty members and administered by a faculty committee made up of full-time GLS faculty members Lucy Salvatore and Jonathon Tryon. Full-time faculty members from Kingston began teaching courses in the region as early as fall 1972.

In the early 1970s the dean made an agreement with the University of Vermont (UVM) allowing students to transfer courses from a program that lead to a master's of education degree in the School Library Media Education in the College of Education at UVM. These courses were usually core courses in the MLS program at URI. Students from Vermont usually completed the courses for the MLS during summers. This agreement was discontinued in the mid-1970s because GLS faculty believed they should have greater control of the core courses.

Only one core course was taught each semester at each of the regional centers from fall 1970 through spring 1973. The only exception to this was that an elective course was also offered at Amherst in addition to the core course during spring 1973. Classes began to be offered at the University of New Hampshire (UNH) in Durham in fall 1973. Two courses began to be offered at Amherst, Storrs, and Durham each semester beginning in spring 1974. A rotation of at least one core class and one elective was eventually developed for the fall and spring semesters at the each of the regional centers.

The Ad Hoc Committee on the Extension Program recommended that courses be offered only at the university centers at Storrs, Amherst, and Durham (Tryon, 1974). Regional classes were last taught at West Hartford, Connecticut, in spring 1974.

In July 1973 the Joint Operations Committee (JOC) of the Land Grant University of New England was formed to coordinate planning and collaborative academic activities among the Land Grant Universities of New England. The presidents of the New England state universities felt that NEBHE was not responding to certain needs, including the need for improved cooperation in the provision of graduate and professional education and the need for better sharing of faculty and other educational resources (Nicoll, 1973). Bergen (1974) noted that Nicoll apparently envisioned a variety of coordination possibilities, one "possibility may be the regionalization of the instructional and advisory activities of the Graduate Library School with central administration from Kingston, Rhode Island."

Healey (1973) noted that courses offered in the region started with basic courses and had grown to ten courses. He pointed out that it was possible for a student to take the entire MLS degree away from the URI campus by transferring six credits in from another institution. He suggested there was little coordination of the regional program, minimal faculty input to the selection of extension faculty, and a need to give the regional program direction and cohesion. Following is a summary of his suggestions to formalize the regional program.

1. Offer the program only on the main campus of the state universities in the five New England states. In addition to providing the program to regional students at the main university, they would be able to participate in elective courses at that university, and library and administrative support would be ensured. He pointed out that this policy would prevent courses being taught in West Hartford or at the University of Massachusetts in Boston.
2. Two new faculty members should be appointed. One of these new positions would have the part-time responsibility of coordinating the regional program.
3. The universities participating in the regional program would agree to build library collections that would support the program. He suggested that the main campuses in the other states had libraries that were probably at least as large as URI's and at least a third to 40 percent of the courses could be supported.
4. Regional students would be required to meet the same admission standards as those admitted in Rhode Island. Grades and degrees would be awarded by URI.

In his report to the faculty of GLS, Bergen (1974) also pointed out that GLS must be in accord with the requirements of the COA. It required that schools offering course work at outlying locations must ensure that the offerings are:

1. integral to the program of the library school;
2. subject to the same academic standards; and
3. supported by adequate instructional (including library) resources.

Bergen suggested that the missions of the Extension Division and GLS were incongruent. He saw the interests of the Extension Division as providing "course work for persons who are interested only in a license to practice school librarianship (not the MLS), continuing education, and so on." He suggested that the GLS should have complete budgetary control of the regional program. Discussions between the Extension Division and the faculty of GLS apparently eased this concern. Dean Humeston (1975) reported that the GLS was inclined to see less incongruence between its mission and the Extension Division's than was originally thought. GLS wanted to fully cooperate with them in developing a regional program.

In 1976 a survey was taken of fifty students in Durham, thirty-four in Amherst, and forty in Storrs. Thirty-seven percent of those surveyed had been admitted to the program. Fourteen percent of those not admitted had made application for admission, and 87 percent of those who had not submitted an application intended to apply. Most were taking two courses per semester and took courses at only one regional center and Kingston. The area of specialization of most interest was school library media (51 percent), public library (23 percent), academic library (15 percent) and special library (11 percent). Seven percent were interested in school library certification only. Twenty-five percent reported that they had received counseling from faculty members.

The GLS was not awarded accreditation by the COA in 1976. Among the recommendations of the COA visiting team were that the school should evaluate its goals for serving the New England region and to have a more stringent review of part-time faculty. Humeston retired in 1976, and Nancy Potter, professor of English, served as acting dean for one year. In 1977 Bernard Schlessinger assumed the position of dean.

Regional Coordinator Appointed

Patricia Jensen was appointed to coordinate the regional program and the school library media program in January 1978. Guidelines for the regional program were prepared that included:

1. Policy recommendations for the Regional Program are developed by the Regional Program Committee and submitted to the faculty for consideration.
2. Coordination of the Regional Program is carried on by a faculty member.

3. Library resources at the Regional Centers appropriate to graduate study in librarianship are surveyed and evaluated by the Regional Coordinator with assistance by the GLS's full- and part-time faculty.

4. a. The number of off-campus hours allowed in the Regional Program is twenty-four.

   b. The remaining twelve hours in the program must be taken in library science courses offered and taught on campus in Kingston.

5. a. Each semester a maximum of two courses is offered at each of the Regional Centers.

   b. No courses are offered at any regional location in the summer.

6. Courses in Regional Centers are taught for two and a half hours on weekday evenings. The option may be exercised by the individual faculty member of teaching ten three and three-quarters hour sessions, either on an evening or on Saturday.

7. a. Full-time faculty participate in teaching in the Regional Program on a voluntary basis, with a limit of one course taught per year. The method of compensation for such teaching is elected by the individual faculty member.

   b. Part-time faculty in the Regional Program are selected from a core that includes those persons who have successfully taught for the school or who have indicated interest in such teaching. On the basis of résumés, teaching experience, and interview, the Regional Program Committee recommends appointments to the full-time faculty and dean, who make the final decision.

8. Evaluation of regional instructors is accomplished by use of the standard campus SET (Student Evaluation of Teaching) forms. These are forwarded through the dean to the appropriate center for analysis.

9. Admission applications from students in the Regional Program are treated in the same manner as all other applications to the GLS. The same rules for advanced standing and transfer of credit apply.

10. Advisement of students in the Regional Program is carried on in the same way as that for all other students accepted into the GLS program. Informal counseling is arranged each semester for all students enrolled at each Regional Center.

These guidelines have been updated regularly to reflect appropriate changes in policy affecting the regional program.

F. William Summers, dean of the College of Library and Information Science at the University of South Carolina, served as a consultant to the school and visited GLS in January 1978. The school was moved to Rodman Hall in spring 1978. The COA visiting team had recommended that a more permanent space be found for GLS. As a result of meeting this and other recommendations, accreditation was awarded in January 1979.

The Regional Program Expands to Boston

The University of Massachusetts at Boston Extension Division asked to extend the regional program to its Harbor Campus in 1983. Courses were first offered at the Harbor Campus of the University of Massachusetts at Boston in the fall semester 1983. On the approval of the Massachusetts Board of Regents for Higher Education, the regional program in Boston officially began in fall 1984.

On the resignation of Schlessinger, Lucy Salvatore began a term as acting dean in 1983. The name of the school was changed to the Graduate School of Library and Information Studies (GSLIS) in 1983 to reflect the inclusion of information science in the curriculum. Lea M. Bohnert was instrumental in introducing information science courses to the curriculum, and Leena Siitonen joined the faculty in 1984 to add expertise in information science and technology.

Walter A. Crocker Jr. was appointed dean of the College of Continuing Education (CCE) in 1984. CCE had changed its name from the Extension Division in 1981. Under Crocker CCE has managed to amass and allocate resources in an entrepreneurial way that has served GSLIS very well.

In December 1984 GSLIS asked the COA to postpone the scheduled visit for the fall of 1985 until the 1986–87 academic year. This request was denied. Thomas J. Galvin, dean of GSLIS at the University of Pittsburgh, was hired as a consultant and visited URI in early 1985. He recommended, among other things, that the regional mission of the school should be highlighted in the report.

As early as 1982 both Schlessinger and the vice president for Academic Affairs had suggested that GSLIS should be repositioned within a larger unit of the university. They felt that GSLIS, the smallest school at URI, had become somewhat isolated, and were it to be positioned within one of the colleges, GSLIS would have greater exposure and involvement within the greater university community. Various options were discussed, but the College of Arts and Sciences surfaced as the best place. In July 1985 GSLIS maintained its name but became a department in the College of Arts and Sciences. The position of dean of GSLIS was changed to that of a director.

There was also discussion to discontinue GSLIS by the administration at URI in the mid-1980s. However, because of very strong support from the library community at both the state and regional levels, the administration decided to maintain the program and pursue accreditation. A COA visiting team visited the campus in September 1985.

Enrollments at the University of Connecticut at Storrs campus began to decline in the mid-1980s. These classes failed to meet the required minimal enrollment in spring 1986. Courses were discontinued at the Storrs campus beginning in fall 1986.

Elizabeth Futas was hired as the director of GSLIS in January 1986. GSLIS learned that it was denied accreditation in February 1986. Over the following two years Director Futas

fostered improvement in the School through curricular changes, scheduling changes, and better administrative procedures. She argued for and received permission to fill vacant faculty positions, increased the School's holding of computer hardware and software, and oversaw renovations to the School's facilities. (Tryon, 1996).

She and her colleagues on the faculty became involved in the library communities in Rhode Island and the other New England states. She was a strong advocate for libraries and librarianship throughout the region and incorporated the concerns of practitioners into her vision for the school. GSLIS was accredited in July 1988, following a site visit in March 1988.

Professor Jensen retired from the faculty in December 1991, and Fay Zipkowitz became the coordinator of the regional program with the new title of assistant to the director for Regional Studies. The faculty voted to change the MLIS requirement from thirty-six credit hours to forty-two credit hours in January 1992. Under this new requirement, regional students were required to take eighteen credit hours in LIS courses in Rhode Island.

On the untimely death of Director Futas in February 1995, Zipkowitz served as interim director until September 1995, when Jonathan Tryon was appointed director for the next three years. GSLIS was scheduled to have a visiting team from COA on campus in spring 1996, so it was agreed that Gale Eaton would coordinate the program presentation to provide continuity during this time of leadership changes. The team visited the campus in March, and the school was notified that it had been awarded accreditation in June 1996.

GSLIS has continued to grow since its last accreditation. The number of applications received each year and the number of matriculated students tends to grow slightly larger for Rhode Island residents, regional students, and students outside the New England region.

When Zipkowitz retired in December 1996, C. Herbert Carson became the assistant to the director for Regional Studies. Tryon stepped down as director at the completion of his three-year term, and Carson served as interim director from June until December 1998. The eighteen credit hours taken in the region by regional students was reduced to fifteen credit hours in September 1997. The regional guidelines were updated and approved by the faculty in spring 1985, fall 1988, spring 1991, and spring 1994. The most recent revised version of the guidelines is shown in the appendix to this chapter.

Professor Siitonen was responsible for creating a computer lab for GSLIS in Rodman Hall in the mid-1980s. She maintained the facility until 1991, when Carson assumed its operation. Recognizing the GSLIS's need for more adequate information technologies, Paul B. Gandel, vice provost for Information and dean of Libraries, provided space and equipment for a new computer lab in the library that opened in fall 1998. University computer staff with aid from GSLIS graduate assistants maintains the new computer lab.

Michael Havener became the director in January 1999 as the result of a national search. With over ten years of experience working in distance education at the University of Oklahoma, he shares the GSLIS faculty's interests in expanding in this area.

DISTANCE EDUCATION AT GSLIS

With Jensen coordinating the regional program, the regional centers at Amherst, Boston, and Durham became an established part of the GSLIS program. At least one core course and one elective have been offered at each of the three campuses during both the fall and spring semester since spring 1974. The core courses are rotated so that all of them will have been offered at least once at each of the regional centers. Continuing students in Rhode Island and at each of the regional centers are surveyed regularly to determine the courses that would be preferred. For example, continuing students were surveyed in December 1998 concerning courses to be offered in summer 1999. Demands for LSC 529, Theory and Production of Library Media Communications, were low, but interest was shown that indicated an additional section of LSC 597H, Internet for Librarians, was needed. LSC 529 was dropped from the summer schedule, and another section of LSC 597H was added.

Cooperation from the libraries and the continuing education divisions at all of the campuses has allowed GSLIS to offer courses of comparable quality to those being taught in Rhode Island. Some courses have not been offered in the region because of insufficient facilities or the lack of a qualified instructor in the area. Such courses would then be scheduled in the summer in Kingston or in the late afternoon, evening, or on Saturdays during the fall or spring semesters in either Kingston or Providence. To help ensure quality meetings of the entire faculty, both full-time and adjunct faculty members are scheduled each semester. These "meetings often feature guest speakers and workshops such as adult learning, assigning grades, or integrating research into the classroom" (Tryon, 1996). There appears to be no significant difference between the SET scores of courses taught in the region and those taught in Rhode Island.

Regional courses have been coordinated through Virginia Nardone, director of Special Programs at the CCE. GSLIS's working relationship with CCE has been outstanding over the years.

The states of Vermont and Maine have both expressed interest in having the GSLIS offer the MLIS program in their states. The GSLIS was first approached by the University of Maine to open a regional center in Maine as early as 1981. GSLIS courses have not been offered in either of these states. One reason why courses have not been offered has been a concern by the faculty regarding access to adequate facilities to support the courses. The full-time faculty members want to have a presence at each of the regional centers, and the number of faculty in GSLIS would be stretched to the limit if they were to be traveling to two additional remote sites. The distances to Burlington, Vermont, and Orono, Maine, are also considerably farther than to the other regional centers.

Two courses were offered for the first time at the Colleges of Worcester Consortium facility in Worcester, Massachusetts, in spring 2002. Worcester's central location in New England provides an ideal location for students in most states to gain access to GSLIS's program. It is anticipated that at least two courses will be offered at the Worcester location each fall and spring semester in future years.

Until recently the GSLIS faculty accomplished distance education by traveling by automobile or train to teach the classes. In their positions as assistant to the director for Regional Studies, both Zipkowitz and Carson stressed the need to use newer technologies such as e-mail, online discussion lists, two-way video, and the Internet to offer courses throughout New England.

E-mail and Online Discussion Lists

Several faculty members have used e-mail and online discussion lists in support of their courses taught in traditional classroom settings. The first to use these technologies as the primary communication mode was Gale Eaton. She offered LSC 531, Reading Interest of Young Adults, to students at the UNH campus via e-mail and online discussion in fall 1996. She taught LSC 597G, Nonfiction for Children and Young Adults, in spring 1997 to students at the University of Massachusetts at Amherst and LSC 531 in fall 1997 at URI in Kingston. All of these courses were presented in the same basic format: four classes—the first, two in the middle for student presentations, and the last— were held in a classroom on campus. The rest of each course was accomplished via e-mail and online discussions.

Two-Way Video

PictureTel, a two-way video technology, became available on the Kingston and Providence campuses in 1998. Cheryl McCarthy volunteered to teach the first GSLIS course to be presented using two-way video. She taught LSC 502, Library Management, using Picture Tel between the CCE campus in Providence and the University of Massachusetts in Boston in fall 1998. She taught one class at the beginning of the course, one in the middle, and one at the end in Boston. The other classes all originated in Providence. When McCarthy was at one campus, graduate assistant Deborah Rich, a former student in the class, was present at the other campus to provide technical support and aid students.

McCarthy continues to teach LSC 502, Management of Library and Information Services, using PictureTel during the fall semesters. In fall 1999 she taught it between Providence and UNH with Linda Smart, a recent graduate of URI with her MLIS, assisting at the UNH campus. Charles Schiller, a student nearly finished with his MLIS and possessing a very strong technology background, assisted at the University of Massachusetts at Amherst campus during the fall 2000 semester, when McCarthy taught LSC 502 from the Providence campus.

Professor Eaton taught LSC 530, Reading Interests of Children, between Providence and UNH during spring semester 1999 using PictureTel. She used Providence as the main source of origination for the course and taught from UNH for four classes with one at the beginning, two in the middle and one at the end. Linda Smart assisted at the campus opposite Eaton each week.

During the fall 1999 semester, Carson presented LSC 508, Introduction to Information Science and Technology, between Providence and the University of Massachusetts at Amherst. Schiller assisted in Amherst. WebCT, an interactive Internet-based resource that integrates class management tools such as e-mail, bulletin boards, online chat, and others into the courses, was used to encourage communication among the students at the two locations.

Yan Ma taught LSC 505, Organization of Information, between the URI campus in Kingston and the University of Massachusetts at Boston during spring semester 2000 using PictureTel. Renee Pomerville, a former student in the class, assisted at the Boston campus. Donna Gilton used PictureTel between the URI–Kingston campus and UNH to teach LSC 597I, Multiculturalism in Libraries. Linda Smart assisted on the UNH campus.

WebCT

WebCT was first used by Professor Eaton to teach LSC 535, Public Library Youth Services, in Kingston during fall 1999. One class was taught at URI at the beginning of the course to introduce the course, and two were held in the middle so students had the option of giving their presentations during a classroom session. The impetus for offering the class this way was that several students in the region asked to have other options for courses during this semester. This course had never been offered in the region or during a summer session, so Eaton wanted to make it available to regional students.

Carson taught two sections of LSC 508, Introduction to Information Science and Technology, via WebCT in the ten-week summer session of 2000. Ma taught two sections of this same course using WebCT during fall semester 2000. During each of these semesters both sections met together during the first week of class for students to be introduced to each other and to WebCT. The following classes were all held online. All entering students in the MLIS program were required to take LSC 508 in their first semester in the program beginning in the fall 2000 semester. Carson taught LSC 508 in this same format during spring 2001. Beginning in summer 2001, all sections of LSC 508 began meeting for a day and a half during the first week of classes for orientation to the course followed by use of WebCT for the rest of the course. He also taught LSC 548, Internet for Librarians, using WebCT during the ten-week summer session of 2001.

Eaton taught LSC 521, Public Library Services, using WebCT during fall 2000. The first session and two subsequent sessions during the semester met on the Kingston campus. She also taught LSC 535, Public Library Services to Youth, in this format during the spring 2001 semester.

WebCT tools are also used by some members of the GSLIS faculty in support of classes held in traditional classrooms. Students are encouraged to use the e-mail, bulletin board, chatroom, and presentation features to increase communication with the instructor and other members of the class. WebCT courses continue to be presented each semester with three to six courses being offered entirely on WebCT and several other courses that use WebCT as a supplement to the traditional classroom.

THE FUTURE OF DISTANCE EDUCATION AT THE GSLIS

The faculty of GSLIS plan to expand the use of new technologies to provide more flexibility for regional students in earning their MLIS degrees and for providing continuing education for professionals in the library and information services. They plan to use a variety of media, including technologies such as PictureTel, WebCT, the Internet, and others as they become available. The traditional format of traveling to regional centers will continue to be used for courses that lend themselves to such an approach. Integrating the new technologies with this traditional approach is becoming more prevalent as faculty become more comfortable with the new approaches.

The GSLIS plans to begin discussions with Maine and Vermont with the intent of opening regional centers in each of these states. The availability of resources on the Internet and through interlibrary loan systems now allow students to have better access to support materials than just a very few years ago. Multiple sites can be reached using two-way video technologies, so courses can be taught by originating at one site and reaching other sections of the same course at one or more other sites. WebCT can be used to offer courses asynchronously, so students throughout the region or the world will be able to have access to those courses that lend themselves to this format.

Director Havener has been working with Winifred Brownell, dean of the College of Arts and Sciences, in increasing the GSLIS's ability to meet its goals by adding staff support and expanding the faculty. In 2002 the number of tenure-track faculty equaled the largest number (nine) in the history of the school. With the combination of increased personnel, availability of new technologies, and unprecedented support from the university's administration, GSLIS plans to expand its program to the New England region using distance education in the future.

APPENDIX: REGIONAL PROGRAM GUIDELINES

1. Coordination of the Regional Program shall be carried on by a full-time faculty member designated Assistant to the Director for Regional Studies.

2. Policy recommendations for the Regional Program shall be developed by the Assistant to the Director for Regional Studies in consultation with GSLIS faculty.

3. Within the forty-two (42) credit-hour MLIS degree program, fifteen (15) credit hours must be taken in library and information studies courses offered and taught on the Kingston campus.

4. Of the nine (9) credit hours required for the School Library Media Practicum, three (3) credit hours may be counted toward the fifteen (15) on-campus credit hours due to attendance at the bi-weekly seminar on the Kingston campus.

5. Up to three (3) credit hours of Independent Work and/or Professional Field Experience may be counted toward the fifteen (15) on-campus credit hours; all work is to be done under the supervision of a GSLIS faculty member and with the approval of the student's advisor.

6. Each semester at least two (2) courses will be offered at each of the Regional Centers; no courses will be offered at any regional location in the summer.

7. The core courses (LSC 502, 503, 504, 505, 507, and 508) will be offered, on rotation, at each of the three regional centers where sufficient computer laboratory support is available.

8. In addition to the core courses, a selected list of electives will be offered at the three regional centers. Low-demand electives and those requiring computer support may not be offered at the regional centers.

9. Advisement of students in the Regional Program will be carried on in the same manner as that for all other students accepted to GSLIS. Informal counseling will be arranged each semester for all students enrolled at the regional centers by the Assistant to the Director for Regional Studies.

10. Students taking courses at the regional centers who elect to withdraw from a course during the semester shall follow the procedures of the respective center and notify, *in writing,* the course instructor *and* the Assistant to the Director. Failure to follow such procedures could mean a failing grade.

11. Persons holding the baccalaureate degree and wishing to take graduate level courses at URI may do so through admission as degree candidates or by enrolling as non-matriculating students on a space available basis. Admission applications shall be submitted to the GSLIS (see *Graduate Student Manual* 3:10 and 3:20 for specifics and 18 below*).

    For regional status and tuition, residency forms must be submitted to URI, and a letter granting approval must be received by students before registration. Students are responsible for beginning this process in a timely fashion to allow for processing and approval.

12. Non-matriculated students are persons holding the bachelor's degree who desire registration with credit in courses during a regular academic year, but who are not candidates for an advanced degree. If non-matriculated students later wish to be admitted to a degree program, they must complete the regular admission procedures. This should be done as soon as possible due to the limitations on advanced standing and transfer credit. (See *Manual* 3.30 and 7.20.*)

13. Credits earned by a non-matriculated students before admission to a degree program may be used toward degree requirements only upon recommendation of the

student's major professor (advisor) and with the approval of the Dean of the Graduate School. The usual form for this approval is the Program of Study (see 15 below). Not more than a total of six (6) credits of work taken through the University of Rhode Island by a Non-Matriculated student may be applied towards degree requirements in a master's degree program. Transfer credit for courses taken elsewhere also must fit within a twelve (12) credit limitation as well as within the limitation of one-fifth of the total master's programs as provided in 7.20 and 3.33 of the *Manual**.

14. A degree candidate may request credit for work taken at another accredited institution of higher learning not exceeding one-fifth of the credits required in the program. Transfer credit is granted only when the request is endorsed by the student's major professor (advisor) and approved by the Dean of the Graduate School (*Manual* 7.21)*. Conditions for the transfer are provided in the *Manual** and should be read carefully.

15. Each student enrolled in a master's program shall submit a Program of Study to his or her advisor for approval by the end of the first semester (or nine credit hours). Forms to be used for reporting the Program of Study are available at GSLIS (*Manual* 7.43). Petition for Change in the Program of Study shall be submitted, if necessary, through the advisor, and must be approved before the student registers for a course which is not on the original Program of Study.

16. It is recognized that circumstances do arise which necessitate the interruption of graduate studies. When students must interrupt their programs by not registering for a single semester before they have completed their course work, they may be permitted to do so without loss of graduate status. A "Leave of Absence" form (available at the GSLIS) must be submitted to the Director of GSLIS as soon as the need becomes apparent. Registration materials will be sent directly to the students from the Registrar for the term in which they are scheduled to return (*Manual* 4.31)*.

17. Only students admitted to degree status will be granted tuition benefits under the New England Regional Student Program. These benefits currently apply to residents of Massachusetts, Maine, Vermont, and New Hampshire.

*The Graduate Student Manual can be seen on the World Wide Web at http://www.uri.edu/gsadmis/TOC.html or can be purchased at the URI Bookstore or Kinko's in the Kingston Emporium.

REFERENCES

Bergen, D. (1974). *A Regional Profession School.* Unpublished manuscript. University of Rhode Island, Graduate Library School, Kingston.

Healey, J. S. (1973). *The Extension Program—Some Suggestions.* Unpublished manuscript. University of Rhode Island, Graduate Library School, Kingston.

Humeston, E. J. (1975, February 6). Memorandum to William R. Rerrante, vice president for Academic Affairs. Unpublished memo. University of Rhode Island, Graduate Library School, Kingston.

Nicoll, D. E. (1973). *Cooperative Program Planning for the New England Land Grant Universities.* A report to the Presidents of the University of Connecticut, the University of Maine at Orono, the University of Massachusetts, the University of New Hampshire, the University of Rhode Island, and the University of Vermont. Unpublished manuscript.

Tryon, J. S. (1996). *Program Presentation for ALA Accreditation*. Kingston, RI: School of Library and Information Studies, University of Rhode Island.

Tryon, J. S. (1974). *Recommendations Concerning Extension*. Unpublished manuscript. University of Rhode Island, Graduate Library School, Kingston.

19

THE TORTOISE MAY BE RIGHT: THE MOVEMENT TOWARD DISTANCE EDUCATION AT RUTGERS UNIVERSITY

Kay E. Vandergrift and Karen Novick

While many of our colleagues in other institutions have taken a "hare-like" stance and jumped ahead in the race toward distance education, we at the School of Communication, Information and Library Studies (SCILS) at Rutgers University are betting on the slower but steady and consistent pace of the tortoise to win in the end. Of course, this is a faulty analogy because LIS programs are not racing against one another. Each institution is attempting to keep pace with changing technological and educational needs and to develop its own strengths for professional education in the twenty-first century.

The SCILS movement toward distance education originated in our Professional Development Studies (PDS). This self-supporting continuing education office has a strong history of delivering professional education to those beyond the walls of the university and has embraced new opportunities and new technologies to accomplish this goal. Currently, PDS offers a series of individual online courses for professional development (see http://scils.rutgers.edu/ac/pds) and as one online advanced certificate program. The Library and Information Science (LIS) Department has been participating in the movement toward distance education by increasing online components to campus-based courses over the past several years. Some of the courses in the online certificate program have also been approved for MLS credit; and beginning in fall 2001, other MLS courses were offered online.

A number of factors at Rutgers and SCILS converged to create this pattern. Strong leadership and innovative adjunct faculty in PDS recognized that the average PDS student is a forty-nine-year-old so-called sandwich generation woman with a full-time job and a family who must fit coursework into a busy and complex life schedule. Another factor has been the university's emphasis on technologically enhanced campus-based courses and the grant support provided to individual faculty to encourage them to participate in this initiative. Joseph J. Seneca, University Vice President for Academic Affairs, has been instrumental in supporting funding for innovative school or department uses of instructional technology. These initiatives, along with the building of a strong infrastructure to support them, will encourage various units of Rutgers University to build on these experiences and move toward distance education in the next few years.

Because is impossible to consider Rutgers LIS programs and decisions separate from the larger contexts of the school and the university, we will summarize the history of some of these developments at Rutgers and SCILS and then analyze issues facing LIS faculty as we consider our future in distance education.

HISTORICAL CONTEXT: LIS AND PDS

When the Graduate School of Library Service (GSLS) was established at Rutgers University in 1956,[1] the faculty began almost immediately to offer continuing education classes. These programs included some one-day workshops held on campus and a larger number of graduate credit courses held at locations around the state of New Jersey. The credit courses were offered in conjunction with the University Extension Division and were designed as continuing education classes, not applicable to the MLS degree.

In 1972, Dorothy Deininger assumed the title director of Professional Development Studies, and the new entity began to offer continuing education classes on a more systematic basis. Deininger served as director until 1977; Ilse Moon then held the position until 1979, and Jana Varlejs provided leadership from 1979 to 1993. During these years PDS staff offered a steady schedule of fifteen to twenty off-campus credit courses each year, plus noncredit workshops that, under the direction of Varlejs, increased from a handful to about two dozen each year. In 1982, GSLS merged with the School of Communication Studies at Rutgers to become the SCILS. PDS continued as a unit within the new school and eventually began to broaden its interests beyond LIS to include professionals in communication, journalism, and media studies.

As the financial climate in higher education changed in the early 1990s, Rutgers instituted policies requiring continuing education programs to be totally self-supporting. A new director, Karen Novick, was hired on a staff (rather than a faculty) line, and new marketing strategies were undertaken to enable the department to remain self-supporting. Over the next few years additional noncredit workshops were offered, and enrollments in departmental programs increased significantly. In spring 1996, SCILS PDS began to offer a limited number of asynchronous distance education courses via the Internet.

This historical relationship between LIS and PDS has undoubtedly helped shape the thinking of LIS faculty in respect to responsibilities for distance education. Traditionally, regular faculty offered campus courses within the MLS and doctoral programs, and PDS took courses out to practicing professionals away from the university. PDS is now a self-supporting unit within SCILS, but it is also one of three dozen continuing education programs with an additional formal relationship to the Office of Continuous Education at Rutgers University. Nonetheless, the relationship with SCILS, and especially with LIS, remains intact.

RUTGERS UNIVERSITY AND DISTANCE EDUCATION IN THE 1990S

Rutgers, the State University of New Jersey, as one of the original land grant institutions has always been concerned with distance education, with serving the needs of various constituencies throughout the state. Although members of the Rutgers University administration were tracking contemporary developments in distance education, they did not jump on the bandwagon at an early stage of development of electronic or Web-based forms of distance education. In September 1995, Francis L. Lawrence, president of Rutgers University, issued the *University Strategic Plan, A New Vision of Excellence*.[2] Although this document did not specifically call for distance education programs, it did recognize the strategic importance of increasing visibility and market presence throughout New Jersey and, by implication, beyond the state. In October 1995, Richard J. Novak, then the assistant provost, New Brunswick campus, called together a group of faculty identified as DE experts to form an online discussion list for discussion on this topic. On July 1, 1996, Raphael J. Caprio became the first Rutgers University vice president for Continuous Education and Outreach, and on July 5 his office distributed a draft document titled "Continuous Education, Distance Learning and Outreach."[3] This document proposed six task forces, one of which was the Electronic Teaching Policy and Procedures Task Force.[4] Novak became executive director, Continuous Education and Distance Learning.

Until very recently, Continuous Education and Outreach concentrated on synchronous interactive television, primarily among campuses of Rutgers University. In fact, until 1999, SCILS was the only school within the university offering any asynchronous distance education, largely due to the lack of infrastructure support for such endeavors. In spring 1999, under Caprio's leadership, Rutgers signed a contract with a commercial vendor to support online education. This vendor supports online administrative functions and provides technical support for faculty and students, as well as software for mounting courses. Within the next five years, the university anticipates offering graduate-level and professional degrees online.

TECHNOLOGICALLY ENHANCED CAMPUS-BASED COURSES

As technology became increasingly important in higher education, Rutgers University focused its emphasis on technologically enhanced campus-based courses rather than distance education. The Teaching Excellence Center on the New Brunswick campus (TEC) (see http://teachX.rutgers.edu), directed by Gary A. Gigliotti, became the leader of innovations in teaching by granting funding for individual faculty members to develop new uses of technology for their classrooms. More important, the TEC provides a center for the sharing of information about teaching and technology through workshops, seminars, summer institutes, discussion groups, online tutorials, guest lectures, and the training of teams of students who provide private technological assistance to faculty.

The TEC was also instrumental in drawing together an assemblage of units in the university into the Rutgers New Media Center as a member of the New Media Centers Organization. "The function of the New Media Center at Rutgers will be to help educate faculty in the use of the World Wide Web, graphic packages, presentation packages, distance education tools, digital video, and digital audio to improve and innovate in their teaching. The New Media Center will also provide support to students using new media to enhance learning" (see http://teachX.rutgers.edu/newmedia).

In addition to the Office of Continuous Education and Outreach and the Teaching Excellence Center, several other units of Rutgers offer technological support for teaching and learning. The Office of Print and Electronic Communications offers technical assistance, including digitizing materials for delivery via the Web. Media Services, a division of the Rutgers University Libraries, provides instructional support, media collections, and equipment services and has been instrumental in converting large class meeting rooms to smart classrooms to facilitate the use of a variety of educational media.

Rutgers University Computer Services provides the technological backbone for all these activities, provides specialized training for students and faculty, and supports courseware packages, such as WebCT. Of course, the Rutgers University Libraries, especially the Scholarly Communications Center (SCC), is central to technologically enhanced education. The SCC provides "a work and demonstration space where electronic resources can be taught in hands-on classrooms, demonstrated in a state-of-the-art auditorium, and manipulated in the Data Center. It is a fully networked facility with over 70 workstations, with software for accessing information and creating new information products" (see http://scc01.rutgers.edu/SCCHome).

The RU Net 2000 Project, nearing completion at Rutgers (see http://runet2000.rutgers.edu), is the first of its kind for a major university in this country. It addresses the total infrastructure of the university to develop an advanced technological environment to foster the mission of teaching, research, and public service in the information age. The fiber optic backbone network connection to 500 academic and administrative buildings will accommodate high-speed data transport, interactive video transmitting, improved voice applications, and facilitate high bandwidth connection to Internet2. A private university-wide video network will support instruction and outreach, increase the speed and capacity of linkages among the university's three campuses, and increase connectivity with other educational institutions.

These and other offices and centers within Rutgers University offer rich resources and support to faculty who wish to use technology in their teaching and research. Individual faculty members, however, must still invest a great deal of personal time and energy to get to a point where they can make effective use of these resources.

TECHNOLOGICAL ENHANCEMENTS AND DISTANCE EDUCATION AT SCILS

Meanwhile, back at SCILS, several faculty were already developing their own technologically innovative strategies to enhance their teaching. In fall 1993, then LIS faculty member Kathleen Burnett, with Nancy Roth, a colleague in the Communication Department, received funding from TEC to develop CommuniStation, a hypermedia tutorial to supplement education in communication research. In 1997–98, Kay Vandergrift received a TEC teaching fellowship to continue her development of Web-based materials for the education of youth librarians. During the 1998–99 academic year, she received another TEC grant to develop TECHSOS, an online resource for students entering the MLS program to administer a self-assessment test of technological competencies essential for success in SCILS. Vandergrift and Jenny Mandelbaum also received another major university instructional technology grant for the enhancement of the introductory course in the SCILS Communication Department.

SCILS is fortunate to have its own servers and its own Computing and Network Services (CNS) with two full-time staff to assist faculty and students. The SCILS building was one of the first buildings to be rewired as a part of RUN2000, and the three computer labs are regularly upgraded with the latest hardware and software appropriate to professional education at SCILS. Jon Oliver, the director of CNS, is the assistant dean for Network and Information Technology. He, along with Alex Daley, manager, Information Technology Services, and a staff of TAs and work-study students provide technical support and troubleshooting and a regular series of in-depth workshops for faculty and students, and ensure the availability of the computer labs seven days a week. This proximity of service enables SCILS faculty to experiment with a variety of Web-enhanced developments because of the special accommodations of server space and personalized technical assistance. This support system also functionally provides the current infrastructure for the distance education components of campus-based courses.

Richard Budd, dean of SCILS from its founding in 1982 to 1997, anticipated the university administration's interest in distance education. In January 1995, he appointed Todd Hunt of the Communication faculty as the
school's first director of Distance Education and mandated that the first distance course be delivered beginning in September of that year. Budd also
appointed a faculty committee to work with Hunt on school-wide issues
related to distance education. During summer 1995, Hunt visited colleges
and universities around the country experienced in the delivery of distance
education. He also worked on the production of ten hours of videotaped
course materials that, along with a student manual and handbook, were the
basis for his Public Relations Management course. A course homepage was
launched on the Web, including the class syllabus, information on assignments, and a databank of abstracts of academic and professional articles.
Although the major portion of this course was asynchronous, students did
meet three times for discussion, exams, and student presentations. In subsequent offerings of this course, the face-to-face meetings were deemed unnecessary, but students did assemble on campus for a final celebratory sharing at
the end of some courses. As the students in these classes became more geographically distributed, face-to-face class meetings became impossible. Additional courses were developed to establish a twelve-credit Communication
Management Certificate, which, unfortunately, was discontinued in 1999
due to lack of support by the Communication faculty after Hunt's retirement. This experience confirms that broad-based support for distance education courses and/or programs must exist if they are to survive the changing
interests, burnout, or retirement of those vested in their success. This program also evolved from combined video and Web-based courses to exclusive
delivery via the Web. Now when we refer to distance education at SCILS, we
include only Web-based courses.

With Budd's departure in 1997, Hunt was appointed acting dean of
SCILS for one year and Vandergrift became director of Distance Education.
At that time, SCILS was still the only school within the university offering
any asynchronous distance education courses. Nonetheless, aware of the lack
of support for the existing Certificate in Communication Management, Vandergrift slowed the pace and spent a great deal of time that year just talking
with colleagues in all three departments of SCILS in support of the Rutgers
emphasis on technologically enhanced campus-based courses. She also
expanded Web-based support for distance education to include a variety of
resources to assist faculty in their teaching, either in their classrooms or in
distance education. Vandergrift, who became chair of LIS in summer 1998
and then associate dean of SCILS in 1999, also worked on the LIS Web site
and encouraged faculty to post syllabi and other course and faculty information on that site. Clearly, she believes that the future of distance education is
on the Web, and that for many faculty the move toward teaching an online

class will be in a natural progression from the technologically enhanced classroom-based course.

Gustav W. Friedrich, the current dean, arrived at SCILS in summer 1998 and brought a new brand of leadership to the school. He also brought a realistically grounded concern for teaching and a belief in the power of instructional technology to empower teachers and students. Friedrich is concerned with creating commitment to a shared vision and concentrating resources to make that vision a reality. This view of leadership matches the movement of the university toward distance education, and his support of that movement enables SCILS to remain in a key position in this area at Rutgers.

The LIS model of evolution from technologically enhanced campus and classroom-based courses to distance education may not be as speedy or as showy as more dramatic moves to online education, but it has a number of advantages. First, both faculty and students have time to become comfortable with and work out some of the bugs in the technology before the entire delivery of course content is dependent on it. Second, there is time to polish the development of particular course components because everything does not have to be done at once. Third, there is opportunity to verify the strength and reliability of the technological infrastructure before having to rely on it totally. This evolutionary approach is also more likely to encourage versatility and a variety of personal educational designs precisely because it does not require institutions to decide on and train faculty to use a particular set of electronic resources. One of our recurrent nightmares is that the wide range of educational possibilities that attract us to the Web will be lost in a cookie-cutter mentality resulting from the too-early adoption of particular courseware. This is not to say that standardized course delivery packages will not be necessary sometimes, but the experience in the evolutionary translation from classroom to the Web makes faculty more critical consumers in the process of selecting courseware that offers more freedom than limitations to those who use it.

Of course, there are disadvantages to this process as well. There may be elements of trial and error in selecting appropriate software to accomplish specific tasks. For instance, in setting up online class discussions, one faculty member started with the shareware Nicenet, then used WebBoard before experimenting with portions of Lotus Learning Space, WebCT, and the eCollege courseware. Naturally, this was time-consuming, and the learning curve remained high for some time; but ultimately the process was very useful in understanding what is really important for teaching and learning. The knowledge and experience gained from the process also enabled SCILS faculty to request modifications, at least to some degree, in the program of a commercial vendor negotiating with the university. Unfortunately, the amount of time and the degree of commitment required of faculty engaged in this process may take them away from other pursuits and can lead to a belief in a false dichotomy between techie and scholar.

During the 1997–98 academic year Vandergrift worked with PDS to develop a new online fifteen-credit, advanced certificate program, the Youth Literature and Technology Certificate (see http://scils.rutgers.edu/ac/pds/litandtech.jsp), which offers two courses each semester. The program was announced in spring 1998 and the first course offered in summer 1998. This summer course was the only one in the program not offered entirely on the Web. The Art of the Picturebook began with a one-week intense seminar at the Zimmerli Art Museum on the Rutgers New Brunswick campus. It was the finalization of a grant that Vandergrift received in 1997–98 from the Mellon Foundation/Zimmerli Art Museum for research on children's book illustration. Students worked with original children's book art and with a staff of artists, museum experts, and faculty during that week and subsequently completed course requirements with online faculty mentoring and collaboration among students.

In the subsequent year, one course was offered each semester. In 2001 the program had eleven courses rotating through a three-year cycle, with plans to add new courses in the coming cycles. Five students completed the certificate program in fall 2000, and several more fulfilled all requirements in 2001. The interest in and demand for the certificate demonstrates that professionals do want a cohesive program that allows them to gain expertise beyond the master's degree without enrolling in a doctoral program.

These and other distance education course offerings continue to grow in the SCILS Professional Development program. Eighteen different online courses were taught from spring 1996 to fall 2000. Topics include integrating technology into educational settings, creating Web sites, and understanding issues related to the uses of technology in libraries and schools, as well as the literature courses of the youth literature and technology certificate program. Novick sees this as a niche operation and consciously does not offer the same things that are offered elsewhere. For instance, PDS provided a great deal of hands-on Internet training before others in the area picked up these kinds of programs. Now the regional library consortia do almost all of this training, and PDS is providing other educational opportunities to an audience consisting primarily of practicing librarians, media specialists, and teachers.

Despite limited marketing outside of the New Jersey area, 15 percent of the students in these online courses come from outside the state, including those from Hawaii, Georgia, North Dakota, Massachusetts, Pennsylvania, and New York. Although this is a small percentage, it is important to note that the PDS regular off-campus program has only about 1 percent out-of-state participation. Initially, many of these courses had one class meeting at the beginning of the semester to introduce students both to each other and to technological requirements. As face-to-face class meetings were eliminated, the number of out-of-state course registrations increased. Plans to market to a wider geographic audience will undoubtedly cause the number of out-of-state students to continue to increase.

UNIVERSAL FACULTY ISSUES IN DISTANCE EDUCATION

There are a number of issues to be considered by higher-education faculty before embarking on distance education. The two major concerns are time and technologies. Any new venture takes time, and there are often few incentives for faculty to invest the time and energy to learn and manage new technologies and to develop the materials necessary for teaching on the Web. In fact, there is often a disincentive. Untenured faculty especially may be perceived as putting teaching before the research necessary for tenure or as courting favor with students or administrators rather than concentrating on serious scholarship. There is no question that developing a successful Web-based course is far more time-consuming than preparing for classroom teaching each week. It is not only the content that must be prepared; it is the display and presentation of that content and the planning for collaboration and interactivity. Therefore, schedules, expectations, and limitations must be made clear at the beginning of the course.

Another time constraint is the amount of turn-around time if a faculty member is dependent on technical personnel to load content on the Web. This is especially important at the time of initial mounting of the course because inevitably one will notice formatting difficulties, typos, and other errors on seeing the content on the site. Unfortunately, not all of these identified errors will be spotted at the same time. It is very frustrating if, after waiting several days for corrections to be made, one discovers additional problems with the site, especially if those problems have immediate implications for the conduct of the class. This kind of technical dependency also makes it very difficult to immediately introduce a very current professional issue or a pertinent new publication.

Another faculty concern with this kind of technical dependency is the lack of control over the look and feel of the course presentation on the Web. We acknowledge the value of having some commonality that immediately identifies the school and the university but believe that faculty should have the freedom to express their own style at the course level. It seems reasonable that a youth literature course might—and probably should—look quite different from an advanced database searching course. In fact, one might argue that the same basic course taught in different LIS programs should, in its Web presence, reveal some of the flavor of the course and faculty as well as the content. This will enable distance education students to select the courses most appropriate to their own interests and needs. The concern about sameness of appearance may be especially a problem when a university has a contract with an outside vendor. It would be absolutely ironic if, in a rush to embrace electronic media that allow for personalization and individuality, we settle for courseware that relies on templates to generate uniform-looking Web pages regardless of course content or faculty preferences. Our approach at SCILS is to encourage faculty to learn the necessary protocols to upload their own courses, thus giving them more control over both design and time factors.

A very basic technological concern is the need for confidence in a secure, adequate, and well-managed infrastructure and in readily accessible technologies or courseware that do not restrict teaching creativity. Too many such products implicitly impose a linear structure on a nonlinear medium or seem to assume that there is one right way to teach or to learn. Participants in distance education are ordinarily serious about testing alternative teaching scenarios based on current research on new learning approaches and processes. Those who perceive distance education as just an electronic correspondence course or a new version of independent study are neither examining what exists nor considering the possibilities of what might be.

UNIVERSAL IMPEDIMENTS IN DISTANCE EDUCATION

There are a number of impediments to distance education that are imposed, or at least amplified, by the nature of the Web. Copyright and the ownership of intellectual property (see www.scils.rutgers.edu/special/kay/copyrightissues.html) are closely intertwined but are sometimes thought of as opposite ends of a continuum by those involved in Web-based teaching. Most often, one worries about copyright in relation to the use of someone else's material and intellectual ownership in relation to one's own work. It is unlikely that anyone is totally clear on how questions surrounding the Digital Millennium Copyright Law will be resolved. On the Web, as in the classroom, one of the most difficult questions is that of fair use. Generally we assume that reasonable quoting and placing materials for a limited time period in a closed, password-protected file complies with the spirit of the law.

The concern about protecting one's own intellectual property should be treated similarly. Some faculty seem to be dominated by a belief in the ownership of ideas, separate from published materials, and fear that others will steal what they make available on the Web. Password-protected Web sites available only to registered students, however, are probably no more accessible to theft than classroom presentations and handouts. Of course, many of us believe in the university as a place for the free exchange of ideas and in student use and reshaping of a teacher's ideas and materials to be one of the most desirable outcomes of the educational exchange.

A serious dilemma for university faculty working on the Web is that Web publishing is often not recognized as scholarship. One needs to distinguish between course publication and other electronic publication. Even refereed electronic journals are not always valued equally with other peer-reviewed publications. Web teaching itself may not be considered as seriously as classroom teaching because colleagues are often uncertain about what one actually does in a virtual classroom, and distance education students often do not submit evaluation forms. (All PDS students do submit course evaluations.) Faculty, especially untenured faculty, who spend large amounts of time in Web teaching must build into that work additional time for a research component.

RESEARCH AGENDA

Before professional education becomes any more invested in distance education, we must step back and establish a solid research agenda as an underpinning for this work. This is essential if these new designs and delivery systems are to be taken seriously and if we are to develop them to their fullest possibilities. In research universities also, it is important to acknowledge that research dominates personnel and other decisions. If we want to be free to encourage the best and the brightest young faculty members to participate in distance education, we must be certain they are entering into an established and respected research community.

There are at least three categories of research that are essential, and we have set forth a series of research questions to facilitate the planning of future investigations. The first focuses on the design and construction of Web-based courses.[5] Can we draw on solid theoretical frames from information science, cognitive development, communication, education, and aesthetics to assess and evaluate distance education? For instance, we believe that the aesthetics of a course are important both in conveying meaning and encouraging involvement and would like to see the use of aesthetic theory to investigate both the effective and affective results of course design.

Several decades of scholarship extrapolating various models of teaching from theory in different disciplines has been expanded through research in higher education.[6] How are these models enacted in virtual classrooms, or can we identify unique models of teaching in electronic environments? What theories of higher education or adult learning are especially informative for hypermediated course construction? Of particular interest to some Rutgers faculty involved in distance education is the degree of structure that must be built into course design to allow students the freedom of navigation that encourages them to create their own learning paths. How do we structure courses to allow students to go beyond learning to the personal and social construction of knowledge?

The second category of needed research focuses on the nature and degree of faculty and student involvement, interaction, and collaboration in distance education. How do students navigate within the electronic environment to shape their own personal and collaborative meanings? What can we transfer from the analysis of gaming environments on the Web that will inform our understanding of student engagement and interaction with Web-based courses? Can we build on Brenda Laurel's work on the computer as theater to provide space for creative drama and student improvisation within the educational stage settings and scripts provided by faculty?[7] Also, how do students feel about online education, and how are affective responses influenced by various aspects of Web-based courses?

The third category of potential research deals with the relationship between the perceptions and the realities of distance education for all the stakeholders. This is especially important in professional education, where the relationship with practicing professionals is vital. What are the attitudes of supervisors and potential employers toward distance education programs and their graduates? How can distance education faculty effectively respond to the differing attitudes and expectations of students in relation to the balance between theory and practice and between learning specific content and exploring alternative ideas and approaches to the content?

Some forms of research could cut across all three of these categories. For instance, feminist scholars might examine how gender affects course design, student engagement in online courses, and attitudes toward the results of distance education.

Obviously any of a number of research methodologies can be employed in the study of distance education. To date, we at Rutgers have concentrated on two. The first is the use of the case study. Vandergrift's "The Anatomy of a Distance Education Course: A Case Study Analysis"[8] uses Michael Moore's[9] theory of transactional distance to analyze her spring 1999 course Gender and Culture in Children's Picture Books. In that article, she departs from Moore's work to propose the concept of "restrained presence" as an aspect of the role of faculty in distance education. Case studies of additional distance education courses, designed and taught in very different ways, should yield useful data in both the design and execution of future courses.

Other research projects at Rutgers focus on the design and creation of Web sites for graduate and undergraduate education. The first of these, Project Eclipse, funded by the Rutgers University Information Science Council, involved the collaboration of faculty and graduate students from information science, communication, and library studies, as well as a rare book expert and a museum curator to develop a scholarly Mother Goose site and a shadow site that documents the design and decision-making process in the development of the original site. The second project, the development of a virtual habitat built to support learning and teaching in the new undergraduate Information Technology and Informatics (ITI) program at SCILS,[10] includes a wide range of resources for both faculty and students and has its conceptual base in the work of Chuck Hoberman and the Hoberman Sphere. This expanding and contracting sphere serves as a metaphor for the kind of flexibility necessary to provide for alternative organizations and designs of content, alternative teaching and learning styles, and alternative modes of delivery. Careful monitoring of design and development costs as well as student and faculty use are embedded in the project.

THE FUTURE OF DISTANCE EDUCATION

The immediate future of distance education at LIS/SCILS still resides primarily in PDS. PDS will continue to expand its online offerings and begin conducting more out-of-state marketing to fill those courses. PDS will also consider the development of additional multicourse certificate programs to fill other needs of practicing professionals. We doubt that LIS will offer an online degree program in the immediate future. As student demand increases and as faculty become more experienced and more comfortable with electronic delivery systems, however, individual sections or courses within the MLS program and the undergraduate major in Information Technology and Informatics will become available online. New faculty with online teaching experience are already beginning to propose new distance education courses.

To make significant changes in distance education, universities as well as individual schools and faculty members will need to shift their focus from an emphasis on providing education to a serious consideration of student needs. Of course, administrators are concerned with the financial possibilities of distance education, but education and economics need not be in conflict. Quality programs pay. New markets, such as targeted international populations, busy professionals, and high school or college advanced placement students, deserve new educational configurations. If students are able to select from a variety of educational options and are empowered to be more self-directed and self-paced as learners, there is certainly going to be more competition for students, both among traditional educational institutions and commercial vendors.

Perhaps cooperation among institutions will also result from such student options. It should be possible for a student enrolled in one school to take a course not offered in that school at another institution through distance education. Ultimately this might lead to cooperatively planned student-centered programs that build on the strengths of more than one institution. This does, however, raise myriad institutional concerns. Some of these are financial, especially when different tuition structures are in place. Other critical issues include the determination of the degree-granting institution and procedures for assessment and accreditation. An additional factor to be considered is whether or not students can receive credit for outsourced courses from professional associations, museums, and commercial vendors.

The future of distance or distributed education may ultimately turn the whole educational enterprise on its ear. We do not believe that new technologies for teaching and learning will replace traditional schooling any more than radio, TV, or the computer replaced the book. Those communication media that provide alternatives to books, along with new electronic conceptual tools for learning (building personal knowledge) and knowledge building (expanding the knowledge base through theory and research), will offer students and faculty more options for personalized, multidimensional designs for constructivist education.

What of the slightly more distant future? Although we have faith in the tortoise-like model of the gradual move from technologically enhanced classrooms to distance education, we are also mindful of the need to break with traditional patterns of thought. The range of available technologies and electronic resources can truly be transformative if educators are willing and able to think outside the boxes and beyond the walls we have grown accustomed to in education. To begin, we must shift our thinking from instruction to construction. Instruction confines our students to what we already know; construction challenges them to use conceptual tools and cognitive amplification tools to find, evaluate, and organize information; to interpret personal knowledge; and to reflect on what they now know in new and personally meaningful ways. This kind of personal sense making requires commitment, the consideration of multiple perspectives, and the ability to communicate and to work collaboratively with others in the social construction of knowledge. Students make connections among diverse individuals and communities, integrate disparate data and ideas, and contextualize their work to bring a variety of real-world professional experiences and concerns into the virtual community. This active, collaborative, and constructivist learning in which one can feel the closeness-at-a-distance of having a mind at home in the virtual presence of other minds leads to confidence in the development of competencies for personal enrichment, professional achievement, and the satisfactions of life-long learning. It also begins the process of integrating students into professional scholarly and research communities.

One way to begin designing distance education courses and programs that will accomplish such ends is to study the best gaming software that is so compelling to users. Essentially, computer games put players in a virtual situation or environment in which they must actively seek information and develop competencies to be used in the acquisition of personal goals. This notion, along with Laurel's image of computer environments as theater, holds great promise for helping educators break with tradition to provide a kaleidoscopic array of alternatives for distance education. Laurel writes:

Designing human-computer experience isn't about building a better desktop. It's about creating imaginary worlds that have a special relationship to reality—worlds in which we can extend, amplify, and enrich our own capacities to think, feel, and act.[11]

What better way to think about the future of distance education?

NOTES

1. Library education at Rutgers University actually began in 1927 when the Library School of the New Jersey College for Women (now Douglass College)

offered its first library courses. In 1929 this program was fully accredited as a senior undergraduate library school by the ALA Board of Education for Librarianship. From the unpublished manuscript "The Library School of the New Jersey College for Women, 1927–1952: A 'Type III' School in Historical Perspective," by Ethel M. Fair.

2. Francis L. Lawrence. *University Strategic Plan: A New Vision of Excellence.* New Brunswick, NJ: Rutgers, State University of New Jersey, 1995.

3. "Continuous Education, Distance Learning, and Outreach." Internal memo, Rutgers University, July 5, 1996.

4. "Part 2: Identification of the Process: Specification of the Recommended Task Forces," in "Continuous Education, Distance Learning, and Outreach." Internal memo, Rutgers University, July 5, 1996, pp. 5–8.

5. Anthony G. Picciano. "Developing an Asynchronous Course Model at a Large, Urban University." *Journal of Asynchronous Learning Networks* 2, no. 1 (March 1998). Available online at www.aln.org/alnweb/journal/vol2_issue1/picciano.pdf.

6. Joyce, Bruce, and Marsha Weil. *Models of Teaching,* 5th ed. Boston, MA: Allyn and Bacon, 1996.

7. Brenda Laurel. *Computers as Theatre.* Reading, MA: Addison-Wesley, 1993.

8. Kay E. Vandergrift. "The Anatomy of a Distance Education Course: A Case Study Analysis." *Journal of Asynchronous Learning Networks* 6, no. 1 (2002). Available online at www.aln.org/publications/JALN/v6n1/v6n1_vandergrift.asp.

9. Michael G. Moore. "Learner Autonomy: The Second Dimension of Independent Learning," *Convergence* 5, no. 2 (1972): 76–97; "Independent Study," in R. Boyd, and others, eds., *Redefining the Discipline of Adult Education.* San Francisco: Jossey Bass, 1980, pp. 16–31; and "Editorial: Distance Education Theory," *American Journal of Distance Education* 5, no. 3 (1991). Available online at www.ed.psu.edu/acsde/ajde/ed53.asp.

10. The Technological Habitat, funded by Rutgers University's Instructional Technology Initiative II, is built on existing resources in SCILS and in the university and models a cyberspace that encourages and facilitates a wide variety of technological activities and experiences to serve the ITI curriculum. The habitat also provides for the development of additional resources essential for student success in the information marketplace and with sound grounding in social, cultural, and political fundamentals of information technology.

11. Laurel. *Computers as Theatre,* pp. 32–33.

20

DISTANCE EDUCATION AT SAN JOSE STATE UNIVERSITY

Blanche Woolls and David V. Loertscher

The California State University system is made up of twenty-three campuses located throughout California. In 1989, with substantial support from southern California's professional community, administrators at one of the campuses, California State University at Fullerton (CSUF), asked another member, San Jose State University's (SJSU) School of Library and Information Science (SLIS), to expand our program in LIS to southern California. This inaugurated our distance program, and it has evolved into a fully functioning branch campus with full-time faculty, office staff, and computer laboratory facility housed in the Pollock Library on the campus of CSUF. From the beginning, a full program of courses was offered with many of the courses taught by part-time faculty.

As this distance program continued, librarians in other locations requested that we bring our program to their sites and not all of these were on a CSU campus. Classes were scheduled in Pasadena and San Diego in the public library as well as on the CSU at San Marcos campus.

Demand continued as opportunities for LIS education in California decreased. The LIS program at Berkeley had been reopened with a focus on business and industry and with the news that they did not intend to apply for accreditation from the ALA. The program at the University of California at Los Angeles (UCLA), more focused on their doctoral program, remained a two-year full-time master's degree, making it difficult for students who were working to attend.

One consideration for offering the program was that the Fullerton program was offered through Continuing Education, a cost-recovery option. That is, all expenses for the program must be covered by revenues generated from the program. The faculty, staff, and facilities at Fullerton as well as part-time instructors became "overhead" to be charged against the tuition generated. In addition, the Continuing Education office and the chancellor's office each took a part of the tuition charged as overhead costs for their offices. Adding full-time faculty on this location was not a viable option. We remained more dependent on part-time faculty.

The SLIS has been and is very lucky to have many practitioners in the Fullerton area and doctoral students in the program at UCLA who have been willing to teach in our program. They and other excellent practitioners across California provide our students with excellent instruction. The array of opportunities for practicum experiences is also a bonus to students in the program. However, as the program expanded, it became clear that the full-time faculty in Fullerton could use some support from the full-time faculty in San Jose.

Further expansion of our distance program meant a rethinking of the way that our courses would be offered. It was obvious that faculty on both campuses needed to share responsibilities for teaching at each location as well as to provide instruction at other CSU sites. One way to offer the program at a distance was through the use of interactive communication technologies. During the early 1990s, Stuart A. Sutton, director of SLIS, secured a large grant from Pacific Bell. The project supported the installation of asynchronous transfer mode (ATM) technology. Funds were allocated to upgrade one interactive television classroom on each campus (SJSU and CSUF) with appropriate sound systems, large-screen monitors, and other required hardware and software. Classes began to be transmitted between the two campuses. While teaching, faculty members used computers to demonstrate anything that could be done with a computer, such as online searching, a PowerPoint slide show, a document, or an Internet site, supplementing the lecture format of instruction. An overhead camera allowed the instructor to use video, telephone interaction, and conversation among many sites.

At each interactive classroom site, technical help is on-site the entire time the class is in session. Scheduling interactive rooms in the CSU system dictated to some extent when classes could be taught. Although the mode of teaching was innovative, these classes were taught in the traditional format of three-hour classes over fifteen weeks. As other faculty members decided to use the interactive classrooms, they chose to teach longer sessions on Saturdays and Sundays to meet the needs of the students who worked at least part-time, including many who worked full-time. Sites were opened at CSU Sacramento, Sonoma State University, and San Francisco State University. Faculty were now using one of three methods to offer this instruction:

- Teach all classes from one location, and the students in the distance location saw the instructor only on camera.

- Move from site to site throughout the course. One faculty member who did this found that several of his students chose to drive from site to site to be in the room with the instructor during the class.

- Provide a mentor in a distance site to answer questions, distribute materials, and represent the instructor during the class meeting.

When grant funds ran out in 1997, the CSU system accepted the costs of the ATM switching (approximately $12,000 per month), and this continued for one year. At that time, SLIS seemed to be one of the few units within the system using this technology, and the system wished to use the higher speed for data transmission rather than teaching. We were switched back to 4cNet and Codec technology to transmit our classes. For one year, the difficulties encountered in teaching over this slower system and the problems caused with lack of technology assistance on the weekends so discouraged faculty that many began to refuse teaching with interactive television.

The demand for classes on other sites continued. Faculty members found an alternative to interactive television in the ability to use the Internet for instruction, and they began transferring much of the content of their classes into digital resources. The challenge of this was the time required to make the change from lecture in front of a classroom or a TV camera to this new design requiring change in methodology. The University of Illinois had overcome this difficulty by providing faculty with a semester off before teaching and assigning the faculty member a single class the semester they taught the new class. Because this option was not available to SJSU and or to other schools with similar budgets and teaching assignments, a grant was written and submitted to the Institute for Museums and Library Services. This grant made it possible for participants from state library agencies, state education agencies, national library associations, and public library staff development personnel as well as LIS educators to come to San Jose for two weeks and work with experts in instructional development, transforming one course into an online experience and beginning to develop a second course.

Participants were asked to bring an already developed course with them rather than create a totally new course. Each person was given the software program used during the institute so that the programs they developed could be taken away on the system they used for development. A server was purchased from independent funding to ensure that ownership of the creative work remained with the developer.

During the two weeks, instructional design and other information presentations were followed immediately by hands-on opportunities to transform the teaching into application. Students had their work critiqued by each other as well as by the institute staff. Other lectures covered projections for future developments, and participants also visited Silicon Graphics to learn what this company had available immediately and what they were planning for the immediate future. All these experiences made it possible for participants to take away most of a course, and one participant began teaching an online course the last Saturday of the institute.

Two follow-up sessions were offered for participants to share what they had learned in conducting their classes and to show their courseware as it had evolved. These were held at the same time as the ALA summer conference in 2000 and 2001 to minimize travel schedules and arrangements. Instructors from the institute were available to report their analysis of new software available for online course development and to offer their predictions for the future.

The success of this training suggested that something similar, but obviously not as long, be offered to part-time faculty who taught in our program. We have had two weekend sessions, one in December 2000 and one with a larger audience in August 2001. The December session was held in San Jose and two instructors, one from Kansas and another from Texas, as well as two instructors from Fullerton spent three days planning their courses for offering in spring 2001. They were given Real Presenter software and a microphone so they could develop audio lectures.

At the August session, one of the institute participants came to share her expertise and other participants came from Kansas and Missouri, as well as the part-time instructors teaching in Sacramento and the Fullerton area. For this session, explaining the technology assistance available from the school and providing the necessary software and hardware to instructors has proven invaluable.

Another aid to teaching in this format was found in management software. The university supports one brand of management programs, WebCT, whereas the SLIS has purchased its own license to Blackboard, the choice of all but one of the faculty. All students must register themselves on this program, and it is used for chatrooms, interactive discussion, giving and receiving assignments, and maintaining grades. Faculty members quickly learned that students needed instructions for registering on this system, and simple instructions were placed on the SLIS Web site. In addition, the opportunity for a two-hour workshop was offered at orientation. This will be continued each term for incoming students.

More part- and full-time faculty members are moving more of their courses into Web-assisted formats. When they request it, they are provided with Real Presenter, allowing them to add audio links to their PowerPoint lectures. Faculty members find that transforming their lectures and editing them for the next semester takes no more time than revising their lecture notes and giving their lectures. They keep the modules shorter so that students need not stay on the computer for more than fifteen or twenty minutes to listen and view the contents. As the bandwidth for communication widens, it will be possible to video stream as well as audio stream.

One discussion at faculty meetings has been their expectations for student competencies for admission to our program and for the level of hardware they must have available if they are to be successful in our program. These requirements change yearly, if not semester by semester, and are posted on our Web site so that students who are applying can explain how they meet these competencies. Although using Blackboard requires them to have computer skills, they must also be able to download and read documents sent from student to student and also to access materials in an instructor's virtual library. Skills with various systems and software continue to increase in sophistication.

As an additional aid, instructors have created virtual libraries of information to be shared among the students. Often this information is quite lengthy, and if students do not have high-speed access, the downloading process can be quite frustrating. Students may complain that it takes longer to download the material than it takes to read it once it is on their screens.

The school continues to provide technical assistance as needed to help in the creation of courses and in the transmission. A full-time network specialist and a Web person help mount the programs on instructor courses on our Web site. The network specialist also helps field problems students have with their technology. This means more virtual interaction between the network specialist and students. At the same time, it has radically changed the need for on-site labs for students. With the decrease of numbers of classes taught in the traditional format, the numbers of students who come to campus to use the labs has decreased to the point that access to computers in the student lounge serve the students who need them on site.

At this time, courses are taught in time frames that go from the traditional three-hour courses over fifteen weeks to seven weekly sessions that are six hours in length. Instructors teach weekends (eight hours both Saturday and Sunday) or Saturdays only. Some choose to teach one full day at the beginning of the term or one day at beginning, middle, and end of the term. Others teach half-days on Saturday for three Saturdays throughout the term. The remaining classes are on the Web.

Students grumble about their desire to have face-to-face interaction with both instructor and other students, but when class schedules are posted, those classes with fewer meetings fill more rapidly than classes with more face-to-face meetings. Some of their reluctance is due to the problems of traffic while driving to class and problems finding parking spots after arriving on campus. However, as stated earlier, most of our students work either part- or full-time, and the ability to spend time at home rather than driving to and from class is very appealing. To provide for interaction, group assignments are made with students who may be attending at four different locations in California with the driving distance from one student to another seven hours, or in the case of our student from Alaska, a long flight. We were pleased to hear Rick Luce from the Los Alamos Laboratory Library, who told the audience at the Lazerow Lecture that one skill he looked for in hiring librarians and information professionals was the ability to conduct and participate in virtual group sessions.

The school faculty plans to continue expanding their distance program using the current array of formats and time frames. With a program so dependent on part-time faculty, the quality of each person hired must be very high. When the numbers of applicants to our program were increasing, we advertised through the *Chronicle of Higher Education, Library Journal,* and *American Libraries* to add to our part-time faculty. This was extremely successful, and we had excellent responses from faculty located in other schools of LIS who would like to teach one class each year in the distance mode. They are given the choice of coming to campus to meet with their students one or more times or meeting them only virtually.

This brings us to the question of our full-time faculty and their ability to teach in a virtual setting. Our distance program with its two-site location requires new methods of management in a highly bureaucratic setting. A system with twenty-three independent campuses is a challenge when one small program headquartered on one campus with full-time tenured faculty and staff with a full-time program is located on a second campus. The movement of faculty between campuses and the possibility of faculty members living some distance from both campuses because of the high cost of housing in San Jose and Fullerton are two very real matters. Other schools of LIS have had one or more of their colleagues who were not on campus as often as others. With the ability to teach, have office hours, and carry out their research and publishing from their homes, the question surfaces of how much time in a campus office is really necessary. Actually, faculty members appear to be *more* available to their students online than when they had designated office hours. When students aren't interested in coming to campus to attend class or to meet with their faculty members, it opens the question of where faculty should spend their time. It also raises the question of how course content will be prepared.

What was apparent at the institute was that instructors need help with the pedagogy surrounding their courses. Although students say they prefer face-to-face interaction, they also prefer not to travel. Pure lecture courses are seldom as effective as courses that have projects, and the implementation of project assignments in the virtual setting requires careful planning and execution. Students must be able to converse with small groups and with everyone in the class, and some of that conversation must be real-time.

As mentioned earlier, instructors can be reached more often online. Some of the SLIS instructors have been forced to set virtual office hours or their students seem to expect an answer to a message placed at 3 A.M. by 5 A.M.

Finally, students must enter these programs with a high degree of competence in technology. They must be prepared to have at their disposal minimum requirements and be prepared to add the upgrades necessary if they are to be successful.

Were you to ask the SLIS faculty if they wanted to return to the way it was before 1990, the answer would be a resounding "no." The real success of our distance program has been in the options it offers to both instructors and students. If an instructor likes one particular method of instruction and wishes to offer it within a specific time frame, our program accommodates this. Students who want classes in a particular time frame and using a particular method of instruction find it available for them. This ability to offer a win-win teaching/learning situation makes distance education at the SJSU SLIS an appealing option for California.

21

OPENING THE DOOR TO DISTANCE LEARNERS IN SOUTH CAROLINA: THE COLLEGE OF LIBRARY AND INFORMATION SCIENCE STORY

Daniel D. Barron

THE FIRST YEARS: FULL-TIME TO PART-TIME AND FACULTY ON THE ROAD

Nancy Jane Day, library science educator, supervisor of Library Services for the South Carolina Department of Education, and then president of the South Carolina Library Association, began an effort to create a graduate library science program in 1961 (see www.libsci.sc.edu/History/mom1.html). Her strong ally was University of South Carolina (USC) President Tom Jones, who joined her and many in the professional community to pursue a program of library studies that would serve the unique needs of the people of South Carolina. After nearly a decade of hard work and political maneuvering, funds and approval were obtained, and the new college was conceived.

Dean Wayne Yenawine began recruiting faculty for the new college in 1970, a process that took a year to accomplish. He wanted "responsive, pioneer-spirited, imaginative" individuals who might never "teach courses as they have taught before" and those willing to "contribute their special competencies and talents to a team effort." This new faculty was to help students "be prepared to use information and modern technology to fulfill our community's needs," and were "very conscious of its obligation to serve our community." These same qualities in faculty have contributed to the success of the college on many fronts, especially in the area of distance education.

In fall 1971, the new faculty began its work with an academic year set aside for them to craft a new curriculum. They named it the College of Librarianship and began the first course with eight faculty and forty-seven full-time students on Monday, September 11, 1972. The ProSem, as it was called, was a twelve-hour block of integrated learning activities that involved the faculty and students working together.

Minutes from the early planning meetings indicate that the faculty were well aware of the professional education needs of those with full-time jobs, families, and other circumstances that made full-time student status an impossibility. Although they were sympathetic with those situations, they felt that the initial testing of the program required full-time students only; however, from the beginning the faculty affirmed their own commitment to address later the needs of part-time students. The first discussions related to the possibility of rescheduling the ProSem took place in spring 1974, but action was deferred in preference to seeking additional funding for full-time students. Although it was possible for those working in elementary and secondary schools to complete the ProSem full time (in the summer session) or as a part-time student as early as summer 1973, other courses were not available until the faculty agreed in fall 1974 to offer Friday evening and Saturday morning courses.

Responding to an increasing voice of need from the professional community unable to attend courses on the Columbia campus, the faculty voted in fall 1975 to offer courses off campus. This decision was based also on a year-long study sponsored by the university and the Lucy Hampton Bostick Residuary Charitable Trust and included the recommendation for intensive weekend courses, which the faculty again agreed to offer beginning in 1976. At the first faculty meeting of the 1976–77 academic year, the faculty confirmed by one vote their commitment to offer courses off campus, one each semester in Greenville and Charleston.

One of the major areas of critical need established prior to the founding of the college and used as an argument for its creation was the lack of school librarians in the state's public schools. In 1979, the position of coordinator of the School Library Media Program was established. Almost immediately following the announcement of that appointment, district supervisors, principals, and representatives of the South Carolina Association of School Librarians began an unrelenting plea for the college to expand its efforts to meet the needs of part-time students who could become school library media specialists. Their efforts were matched with those of the USC Graduate Regional Studies Coordinators. This group, often with offices at one of the eight regional campuses of the university, had close working relationships with the schools in the areas served by the Regional Campus system and were strong advocates for those communities. At that time, there were some nine academic preparation programs for school librarians, most of which were staffed by local university librarians with a large adjunct faculty made up of practicing school librarians. Though their intentions were good, the lack of depth did not contribute to the overall improvement of library services in the state's schools. The professional community called upon the College of Librarianship to reach out and help overcome this problem.

OPENING THE DOOR WIDER TO THE PART-TIME AND DISTANT LEARNERS: THE 1980 TV DECADE

Based on the feedback from a systematic needs assessment undertaken in fall 1979, a five-year projected off-campus schedule was proposed in spring 1980 that would take most of the courses for the school library media program, including the required or foundations courses, to within forty miles of everyone in South Carolina. At that time, it also opened the door to those close to the borders in neighboring states of Georgia and North Carolina. With no out-of-state tuition hike, this was a very attractive plan for them. The new sequencing began in fall 1980 with faculty driving to Greenville, Charleston, Florence, and Aiken. It was proposed in fall 1980 and approved in spring 1981 that a site in Rock Hill, later called USC at Carowinds by the faculty, served a growing number of students from the Charlotte area as well as the growing population in that part of South Carolina. Also in 1981, again at the request of a wide range of persons in the public school community, a number of adjunct faculty in the area of media production and media hardware management were identified around the state who could implement a course required by the State Department of Education for certification. The course was developed by a regular faculty member in the college, monitored by the faculty member who met with the adjuncts prior to and during the course, and evaluated as were all the courses offered by the college. A total of ten sites was selected, and over 200 students participated in the courses. The evaluations were universally positive and the faculty approved the continuation of hiring adjuncts under these conditions to teach the course again.

In summer 1980, the South Carolina State Department of Education approached the college with a proposal to allow a South Carolina Educational Television (SCETV) crew to videotape a children's materials course as it was being taught in the classroom in the fall semester. Recent legislation required that candidates for a degree in early childhood education take a course specifically related to books and other materials in that area. The college had developed such a service course for the College of Education; however, it was delivered only on the Columbia campus in a traditional classroom format. After much discussion related to the merits of providing a course like this to those unable to come to Columbia and the importance of taking full advantage of the media of television, the college negotiated a grant to create a broadcast-quality course in collaboration with SCETV, which was called "Jump over the Moon: Sharing Literature with Young Children." Work began on the fifteen-part series in the fall 1980 and was field tested with over 100 students across the state in spring 1982.

As faculty followed the development of "Jump," the potential of TV for delivering courses became apparent. Using TV, live and interactive as well as on videotape, had been pioneered by the Colleges of Engineering and Business Administration in the late 1960s. At that time, the College of Social Work was using TV to deliver a portion of their required courses. In December 1981, a proposal was submitted to the faculty to offer one of the required courses using the live one-way video and two-way audio system that covered the state. After nearly a semester of investigation, including consultation with faculty in units already involved with television delivery, and of course a great deal of often emotional debate, approval was given to offer CLIS 703, Information Sources and Services, in fall 1982 with a team of two faculty members responsible for it. The spring of 1982 also marked the beginning of a core of five three-hour required courses replacing the ProSem block. Both events are indicative of the faculty's willingness to take the needs of both the profession and those who aspire to enter it into consideration as they continued to create a credible academic program.

Before the first course was offered, the faculty had to verbally commit to teaching a course in spring 1983 or lose the slot to another unit. With CLIS 703 still a week away from the first class in which over sixty students had registered statewide, the faculty agreed to offer at least one other course in the spring. The concept of planning this far in advance and having to compete for air time was a significant learning experience that continues to challenge faculty patience and sense of humor.

The first course offered over TV, as it began to be labeled, perhaps was the most studied course ever offered by the college with the possible exception of "Jump over the Moon." The two faculty who teamed to offer CLIS 703 met with the students on a weekend prior to the beginning of the course, thus beginning a tradition of bringing members of the class together for a general face to face session before the weekly televised sessions. Precourse, midterm, and end-of-term surveys were administered to the students. Grades of part-time, full-time, distance, and home campus students were compared. The general consensus was that there were not significant differences among the variables compared with the exception of some full-time students resenting being in a class without the "full-time" attention of the instructor. This feeling is one that surfaces periodically; however, most students share the same feelings as the faculty in that we are all involved in an effort to help the profession grow and strengthen. Reaching out to those who cannot attend a full-time traditional program is as important as attending to the academic and social needs of those who come to the campus for a more traditional learning experience.

Although there continued to be studies and debates, emotional exchanges among faculty, and honest agreements to disagree regarding policy and procedures, the use of television to deliver courses in South Carolina continued throughout the 1980s. This usually meant that one or two courses were offered during any one semester. "Jump" was the only scripted video used; however, some faculty taped lectures that were delivered either by satellite or by videotapes to the students' homes. The live courses usually met one day each week in a lecture/demonstration format using one-way video and two-way audio communications. Most TV courses required students to attend at least two full days on campus, usually on Saturdays during the semester. Assignments were mailed in by students and back by faculty with the assistance of Distance Education and Instructional Support staff taking on the responsibility for checking assignments in and mailing them back. Some faculty elected to have all assignments mailed directly to them in an effort to decrease the time students had to wait for feedback.

A major milestone in the history of the college generally, and especially in its efforts to develop a distance education program of positive distinction, came with the reaccreditation of the college's master's degree program in 1986. The visiting team paid particular attention to the distance education program and concluded that it was of a high quality and that the college should be commended for its efforts in this area.

During the February 1987 faculty retreat, distance education was given a major time slot for the entire faculty to discuss issues, concerns, and directions. Although the decisions related to the college's investments to this point in distance education had always been influenced by if not approved in an open faculty forum, this meeting marked the beginning of a full faculty commitment to the distance education program. Everyone, including the dean, from this time forward is expected to participate in the distance education effort.

In spring 1987, representatives from the professional community in Georgia contacted the college and later met with the full faculty during the summer requesting that a degree program be offered through the telecommunication system that was in place similar to that in South Carolina. Their argument was that Georgia did not have a publicly funded master's degree program accredited by ALA nor did the existing program offer distance education alternatives. This began a very long (five years) and involved process that included a great deal of negotiation with the Georgia Board of Regents, which did not appear to support out-of-state distance education programs regardless of the expressed needs within the professional community.

It was in fall 1987 that the college adopted the terms *distance education, home campus,* and *on site* to describe the program and the distinction between students participating in classes on the Columbia campus and on other campuses. These replaced the terms *extended classes* and *off campus,* which carried a great deal of negative interpretation by students and other members of the university community and, most important, did not describe the efforts of the faculty to provide the same quality of education for distance learners as those able to attend more traditional classes on the home campus of the program being offered.

The faculty adopted the first five-year proposed course sequence also in 1987. This was a direct outgrowth of the faculty consensus commitment to make distance education an ongoing effort of the college.

OPENING THE DOOR WIDER AND TO OTHER COMMUNITIES: THE 1990 COMPLEMENTARY TECHNOLOGY DECADE

In December 1990, a proposal was submitted to the faculty that the college consider offering courses outside the state. Representatives from West Virginia and Georgia contacted members of the college faculty with such a request, it was considered by the faculty, and they agreed to explore the various possible approaches to taking the master's degree to those states. After a number of visits to the states and many conversations with members of the professional communities in Georgia and West Virginia, the faculty unanimously agreed to purse a project that would provide opportunities in those two states for individuals to complete the entire master's degree program. A proposal was presented to the faculty at the July 1991 faculty meeting to begin the program in fall 1992. The faculty unanimously accepted the proposal with the stipulation that applicants meet fully all of the entrance requirements of the college, that the courses be delivered as they had been in South Carolina with live TV and weekend on-site classes for each course, and that the professional communities in the two states be given the opportunity to provide input prior to the beginning of the program.

The proposals to take the program to Georgia and West Virginia took nearly eighteen months. Lengthy documents were required for the approval process by the University Board of Trustees, the South Carolina Commission on Higher Education, and the governing bodies for higher education in the respective states. After receiving permissions from all, members of the faculty and administration conducted a series of town meetings in Georgia and West Virginia to meet with potential students and members of the professional communities. The first course began in fall 1992 with students in all three states, in addition to a few others from neighboring states who attended class sessions in public libraries, technical colleges, and other institutions of higher education. Some enterprising students attended class in such unique locations as a church, a county jail, a satellite dish communications firm, a health care facility, a research center, and in the homes of three individuals who purchased satellite dishes to participate in the degree program.

In 1993, representatives from the professional community in Maine approached the college with a request to consider bringing the program to their citizens. After exchanges of visits with faculty, members of the professional community, and potential students, the faculty agreed to begin offering the master's degree program to the people of Maine in fall 1994.

At the request of the professional communities, based on the faculty's success in their first efforts and the continued needs in the states, second cohorts of students were formed in West Virginia in 1997 and Maine in 2000. Also at the request of the professional community in Georgia, a cohort of students who wanted to complete the specialist's degree was formed along with a corresponding cohort of students in South Carolina.

THE NEW CENTURY: LESSONS LEARNED AND MODELS FOR THE FUTURE

As the college entered the new century, the second Maine cohort was in midstream and the second West Virginia cohort was nearly ready to graduate. The college renewed its commitment to distant learners in those and other states for two reasons. The first is the continued belief that the strength of the profession depends on quality preparation, which is not immediately available to people and communities who need better library and information services. The second is the continued growth and development of the college that depends on income that a "state-subsidized" (a term used in financially challenging times instead of "state-supported") appropriation has not been able to provide.

Reaching out to those beyond the state has provided a positive benefit for the people of South Carolina. For example, prior to the faculty decision to take an entire degree program to other states, TV airtime and faculty travel time restricted the number of courses available to students in the state. Instead of the one or two time slots given the college for TV broadcasts per semester in the 1980s students have access to over eighteen courses per semester.

The stress of larger classes and learning new delivery systems and techniques have raised concerns among faculty including reduced scholarly productivity, physical and mental stresses associated with twenty-four-hour-a-day, seven-day-a-week access by students, and a feeling of losing personal contact with students. At the same time, faculty have learned how to use the various technologies and techniques to the learners' advantage in both distance and distributed (on campus use of technology) environments. Just as students are admonished to accept change and new technologies as a regular and ongoing aspect of being in this profession, the faculties also have committed themselves to meeting those challenges with their students. When they first began using TV, faculty members developed an increased awareness of and began using more visuals during lecture/demonstration presentations. As the various technologies became available to their students, the faculty began incorporating them into their distance education courses and most into their more traditionally delivered courses on the home campus. CLIS faculty were the first to use compressed video for course delivery in 1991. They were the first to use online discussion software for course information and support. They were among the first to create Web-linked CD-ROMs for course delivery and offer totally Web-based courses. From syllabi and handouts available on Gopher to the full suite of services available through the current university-wide Web course development software, Blackboard, CLIS faculty continue to be among the first in the university to embrace new technologies—not for technology's sake but for the benefits to the students.

A few numbers suggest the commitment of the faculty over the years. They have offered 374 courses using televised delivery since 1982 with 22,668 enrollments. There has been an 80 percent graduation rate for the cohorts of students in other states. As the distance education efforts expanded so have the numbers of full-time students on the Columbia campus as well as an increase in the numbers of students coming from outside the state.

The South Carolina model includes the following elements:

- All faculty, including the dean, participate in distance course delivery.
- Admission requirements are the same for all students entering the degree programs.
- The same syllabus and assignments are used for each course offered regardless of type of delivery or student location.
- The same course that is offered via distance delivery includes students that semester who are full time students on the Columbia campus.
- All courses are offered in what has become the popular term, a blended format (e.g., live face-to-face for each, online discussion list, Web support, usually video components, and e-mail for assignments and communication).
- The entire degree may be completed via distance delivery.
- Ongoing assessment for each course taught, periodic surveys of students, and in depth assessments for self-studies provide faculty and the Distance Education Committee with regular feedback. (Two dissertations have been written and one is under way focusing on the college's distance education efforts.)
- Access to university library and information services via the Web and with the support of a specifically designated person, the Distance Education Services Coordinator, are essential.
- Collaboration with state library agencies and institutions of higher education, and having a designated contact person within each state are essential.
- The local team that includes the college's Distance Education Coordinator and the University's Distance Education and Instructional Support unit is a critically important factor in the success of the distance education effort.

PARTING THOUGHTS

In 1937, Professor of English Havilah Babcock said, "If you can't come to the university, the university will come to you." This has been an inspiration for many faculty in the university, including those in CLIS, who believe that reaching beyond the traditional confines of the home campus is important for the people of the state and nation, their professions, and their communities. Beginning in the 1960s, the Colleges of Engineering and Business began offering master's degree programs to distant learners by videotape and using the South Carolina Educational Television network. Over the years, every professional school has begun to offer courses or degree programs to distant learners. The college was fortunate to have this rich tradition and infrastructure in place, and we have taken full advantage of it. In fact, since the 1980s the college has taken a leadership role in promoting the effective uses of information technology for distance and distributed learning in the university. Technology and communications systems doubtless will change many times in the next decade; however, one constant will remain. The faculty of the college will embrace those changes and continue in their commitment to provide the highest-quality professional education possible to as many people as they can reach.

REFERENCES

The majority of the information presented herein came from an unpublished work by a former faculty member, the minutes of faculty meetings as recorded by Virginia Patterson (1976–85) and Gayle Douglas (1986–2002), and annual reports provided by Gayle Douglas.

Pope, Elspeth. (1981) *History of the College of Library and Information Science.* Unpublished manuscript, University of South Carolina.

22

DISTANCE EDUCATION AT THE
SCHOOL OF LIBRARY AND
INFORMATION SCIENCE,
UNIVERSITY OF SOUTH FLORIDA

James O. Carey and Vicki L. Gregory

HISTORY OF THE SCHOOL

The University of South Florida (USF), headquartered in Tampa, was created by the Florida Legislature in 1955 and formally opened for students on September 26, 1960. In the first year approximately 2,000 students were enrolled in the four original colleges: Basic Studies, Business, Liberal Arts, and Education. The USF Library and Information Science Program had its beginnings in academic year 1961–62 in the School Library/Audiovisual Certification Program in the university's College of Education. (At that time, all Florida universities were allowed to have such a certification program without specific state authorization.)

In its original management configuration, the USF College of Education was not departmentalized, and joint upper-level undergraduate programs were arranged within the curriculum areas of the college, and if necessary in conjunction with various discipline areas of other USF colleges. An undergraduate program, composed of two tracks, combined dual majors of English Education and Library Science/Audiovisual Education. Graduates of these programs were certified as secondary teachers of English and as K–12 librarians. In 1964, the Library Science courses were taught by Florence Cleary, the former chairperson of the Library Science Department at Wayne State University, and by a number of adjuncts. In 1965, Alice G. Smith was appointed as the first chairperson of the Library Science Program, and the Library Science/Audiovisual Education program became a department within the College of Education with an authorization for two and a half faculty members, offering an undergraduate program for school library certification. A master's program in school librarianship only was first offered in 1965–66, with seventeen students enrolled. In April 1970, the Florida Board of Regents approved the establishment of a comprehensive, across-the-board graduate library science program at the master's degree level. In 1975, the program was accredited by the ALA.

When first organized in 1965–66, the department was housed in a windowless former storeroom (with only one door and a single electrical outlet) on the fourth floor of the Physics Building. In fall 1966, the department was moved to the new Physical Education classroom building, where it enjoyed its first faculty offices, a small switchboard, and a reception area for students. By 1968, the department had five full-time faculty members and was moved yet again to a suite of offices located on the top floor of the business building.

For a number of years after 1968, the department shuttled from the business building, to the Faculty Office building, to the top floor of the library, to the Human Resources building, and finally to its current specifically constructed quarters in the Communication and Information Science building in January 1993. That same semester, on April 1, the Division of Library and Information Science became a part of the College of Arts and Sciences and was attached to the Department of Mass Communication for the first year. In 1994, it obtained independence from Mass Communication and became the School of Library and Information Science.

DISTANCE EDUCATION

The USF School of Library and Information Science was a pioneer in the distance education arena. By 1980, classes were being offered by the school at various distant sites away from the Tampa campus, including on the University of South Florida–Bayboro campus at St. Petersburg; at the USF–Ft. Myers campus in Orlando at both the downtown Orlando Public Library and at facilities of the University of Central Florida; and in Boca Raton at a building located on the Florida Atlantic University campus. Initially, all classes were traditional, face-to-face classes with an instructor traveling to a central site at the distant location to teach students from the surrounding area. With an early commitment to a branch campus infrastructure and a concomitant perceived lack of necessity for other innovations, the use of distance teaching technology was slow to develop for USF generally.

Beginning in 1989, however, some televised courses were offered with an instructor in a studio in Tampa and students at such receiving sites as Lakeland, Sarasota, Palm Beach County, and St. Petersburg. Fred Pfister taught the first such offering, the collection development course, which was offered to five sites, including the local Tampa class in the broadcast studio. Practicing professionals were hired at each distant site to act as associate instructors for purposes of guiding discussions, answering students' questions, distributing materials, and so on. Pfister met with the associate instructors frequently to coordinate the course. The next semester Robert Grover and Bahaa El-

Hadidy team-taught the basic reference course to the same sites with about fifty students. The courses were delivered in one-way video coupled with a two-way audio mode.

Generally, students had a single televised course available to them in any one semester, so student utilization of course offerings by television was never extensive. Course offerings were limited due to faculty concerns about the lack of a university policy dealing with faculty compensation and work-loads for such courses. (At that time, the College of Education viewed a class of fifty or more students at various distant sites as a single course assignment.)

East Coast

The USF School of Library and Information Science has provided a Florida East Coast master's program continuously since 1978 with students being able to take all program requirements for their master's degree through site-based classes delivered at East Coast locations. In the past, many students traveled to Tampa to take elective courses; currently many take site independent courses by Internet to supplement those taught face-to-face on the East Coast.

The first East Coast classes were held in fall 1978 on the campus of Florida Atlantic University (FAU) in Boca Raton. Initially, to ensure a quality pro-gram, all courses were taught by regular USF faculty without any adjuncts. The same faculty member would teach the same course or courses in both Tampa and in Boca Raton. For the first two years, USF offered one or two organized courses per quarter plus independent study and fieldwork. Classes had very large enrollments, usually between forty and sixty-five students, who came from throughout the areas of Broward, Palm Beach, and Dade Coun-ties, as well as more distant locations. Various patterns were used in teaching the classes to meet adult learning needs. A Tampa-based faculty member would usually fly to West Palm Beach and sometimes teach two sections of the same class, one section Friday evening and the other Saturday morning.

A few years later, the program was moved to the Commercial Boulevard campus of FAU located in the northern area of Ft. Lauderdale, to accommo-date the numerous requests of students from Ft. Lauderdale and Dade County. Most courses were offered at the FAU campus, but a few were offered at other libraries, such as the main Broward County Public Library. In 1988, Florida Atlantic University changed the function of its Commercial Boulevard building, turning it into a research center instead of a classroom building. Therefore, USF found need for another location, which was met at the main Broward County Public Library. Some classes were still held in other locations, such as a public high school or the University Tower of FAU-FIU (Florida International University) located adjacent to the main Broward County Public Library. From 1985 to 1993, Henrietta M. Smith, a full-time regular USF faculty member, was designated the coordinator of

USF's East Coast Program and both advised students and taught classes, mostly in Broward County but occasionally in Ft. Myers and Tampa. She retired in 1993 but has continued to teach as an adjunct on a regular basis in the East Coast Program.

By 1986, USF was offering between four and six classroom courses per fall and spring semester plus the opportunity to do fieldwork and independent studies in Broward County. At this point, the school had necessarily begun using adjuncts, who were credentialed in the school's regular process.

Ft. Myers

The School of Library and Information Science began offering coursework on a continuing basis on the USF–Ft. Myers campus in fall 1989. During the 1989–90 academic year, one course per semester was offered. In view of the demand for additional courses due to the need in USF service counties for public librarians and school media specialists, the school began offering two courses per semester to enable students to complete a degree program within a two-year period. The coursework offered in Ft. Myers included all four core courses required in the master's program as well as additional courses required for state certification as a school media specialist.

Central Florida

Courses have been offered in several central Florida sites, including Orlando, Gainesville, Cocoa Beach, Satellite Beach, and at the USF campus in Lakeland. Orlando, the most populous city in central Florida, is located approximately eighty-five miles northeast of the USF–Tampa campus. Students have regularly commuted this distance for coursework. Sensitive to the needs of working adults, the faculty began offering courses, usually one per semester, in the Orlando area. Offering course work at the USF–Lakeland campus, located about forty miles from the main campus, has enabled central Florida residents to travel shorter distances to take classes in library and information science. Since the time course offerings began in Lakeland, they have been a mix of televised and live instruction. Gainesville, located 120 miles northeast of the Tampa campus, is also an off-campus site in central Florida. As a response to a petition from the Alachua County Public Library staff, course offerings began in Gainesville in summer 1994.

Because courses for media certification are taught in a National Council for Accreditation of Teacher Education (NCATE)–approved program at the University of Central Florida (UCF), the school cooperates with that university to transfer appropriate credits. Thus, residents of central Florida, if carefully advised, can complete the degree without the need to attend any classes at the main campus in Tampa by taking a mixture of courses taught in

Orlando, at USF–Lakeland, in the libraries of Brevard County, in Gainesville, by Internet, and by transfer from the UCF media program.

St. Petersburg Bayboro Campus of USF

From time to time the School of Library and Information Science has offered courses at the USF–Bayboro Campus in St. Petersburg. The entire program has never been available there, but some coursework was provided up to 1989. Beginning in 1989, a few courses were offered using instructional television fixed service (ITFS) with one-way video and two-way audio. The Bayboro campus received these telecasts, but about that time it was decided to discontinue face-to-face classes there due to an inability to work out financial details between the Tampa and St. Petersburg campuses. Currently, there is some discussion of offering one course a semester through the USF–St. Petersburg campus, and, in fall semester 1999, a Web-based section of foundations was offered through the Bayboro campus.

BOARD OF REGENTS REVIEW OF EXTERNAL SITES

The Board of Regents report of 1984 recommended more funding and staff, including support of off-campus programs. One result of the review was that the Board of Regents mandated that both USF and Florida State University be responsible for LIS education throughout the state, with special attention to southeast Florida, which at that time had more than 4 million people but no accredited LIS program. The additional funding was never forthcoming, but the need was so great that the USF LIS faculty continued to teach on the East Coast as part of their regular teaching load.

As a result of the first Florida Board of Regents review done in 1984, USF was no longer mandated to seek approval from FAU and FIU to teach in southeast Florida, nor from UCF to teach in Orlando or east of there. An unwritten agreement was that USF would offer courses in Broward County only and that Florida State University would offer courses in Dade County only (this was reconfirmed as a formal directive in the 1988–89 Board of Regents recommendation). This arrangement continued until 1993 when Florida State University began offering courses in Broward County. There was some attempt to coordinate courses, but such coordination did not last beyond that academic year.

A PERIOD OF TRANSITION

During the time period from fall 1992 through spring 1995 the school was immersed in transitions that included an organizational move out of the College of Education into the College of Arts and Sciences; a physical move into new facilities; a discontinuation followed by a quick reinstatement of the East Coast Program in Ft. Lauderdale; and the start of new undergraduate course offerings. Staffing at the school was also in transition from 1992 to 1995. Two interim directors were followed by a new director, and five faculty were hired, two retired, and one resigned. These transitions consumed the interests and energies of the faculty and it is not surprising that the only outreach to off-campus students during this period was by one televised class and the traditional face-to-face delivery of courses at the USF regional campuses, the Ft. Myers site, and the East Coast site. During this same period the university's distance-learning infrastructure was also in transition. Campus Audiovisual Services was merged with several other administrative units to form Distance and Technology Mediated Learning (DTML), with subsequent displacement of formerly key distance learning support personnel. Coming out of this period of transition, the school was in a growth mode and ready to renew its efforts to reach distance students by technological means.

FROM TELEVISION TO THE INTERNET TO THE WEB

In spring 1994 faculty delivery of courses by television began again, but even as faculty members were preparing courses for TV, the information technologies that were changing the content of many of our LIS courses began to change the way we thought about delivering those courses to our students.

A Renewed Television Initiative

Instructional TV at USF had taken two forms. USF's Open University used WUSF-TV, the public TV affiliate station, to broadcast mass-enrollment undergraduate and graduate offerings to Tampa and the surrounding communities; the closed-circuit ITFS system was used to "distribute" courses taught on campus in Tampa to classrooms equipped to receive the signal on the regional campuses at Lakeland, Sarasota, and St. Petersburg. The ITFS signal could also be passed along by fiber cable to receiving sites in Lake Wales and West Palm Beach. Open University courses were produced along the traditional instructional television (ITV) model with extensive preproduction planning and development, studio taping, and postproduction editing and assembly. On the other hand, the ITFS system was dubbed the "candid classroom" because courses originated with an instructor and students in a TV studio classroom on campus and were distributed live over the system. The ITFS system was designed for signal origination from either Tampa or Lakeland; regardless of point of origin the system only had one-way capability that was supplemented by a telephone bridge on the Tampa campus that allowed students from remote sites to dial an access number and ask questions of the professor or report comments or observations. The candid classroom concept was sold to faculty with the promise that the instructor could prepare and teach a traditional class with minor accommodations for the distance students. The staff of DTML, where ITFS services were housed, would advertise the course, enroll the students, duplicate and distribute course materials, proctor exams, and collect and deliver student products to the instructor. All televised classes taught by the school were over the ITFS system.

From spring 1994 through fall 1996, the school offered seven televised courses by three regular faculty and three adjunct faculty. One reason for the renewed interest in television was that student demand for classes exceeded faculty resources, so faculty members were televised to regional campuses rather than being sent by automobile. A second reason for the renewed interest in televised courses was that DTML had begun offering a $2,000 per course incentive to departments and faculty on campus for using the ITFS system. The incentive was typically used to help pay for a graduate assistant who worked with the instructor to manage the large enrollments in distance classes. A third reason for TV courses was that two new faculty members had previous experience with televised instruction and were willing to try it at USF. The television classes were successful in extending the school's program, but the candid classroom was not without its problems.

The Television Dilemma

Managing the candid classroom was simply not as easy as it looked, and eventually a faculty member in the school was assigned to provide internal support for colleagues using TV. Only one teacher involved in televised courses became a repeat user, and all faculty struggled with pedagogical, technological, and institutional support problems.

Pedagogical Problems

The distance education literature is equivocal on the relationships among levels of active student participation, student motivation, and student achievement. Some researchers have concluded that student performance is not related to the level of student interaction; critics point out that performance measures are often of low-level skills. Negative attitudinal factors often linked with lack of active participation include difficulty communicating with the other students and the professor, lack of group affiliation, and the impersonal nature of televised classes. Even if student participation does not predict performance, faculty members in the school who enjoyed the ready give-and-take of a traditional classroom were uncomfortable with the artificial, solicited participation from students at multiple remote sites and were dismayed by the amount of class time given to managing remote student participation. The

candid classroom technology at the same time enabled and inhibited spontaneous student participation. Several strategies were tried in the school's televised courses to ensure student participation and to foster remote students'
affiliation with the larger class group. They included

- getting students signed up for computer accounts and establishing student-to-
  student and student-to-professor communication by e-mail;
- videotaping student introductions at remote sites and playing back over the network for all class members to share;
- small-group "break-out" sessions during class time with reporting back to the
  entire group;
- very tight course organization and management with complete, detailed handouts
  to substitute for office hours and face-to-face question-and-answer time;
- direct, immediate telephone contact with students when unanticipated technical or
  scheduling problems arose;
- small-group, team projects to encourage cooperative, personalized learning; and
- when technically feasible, originating class broadcasts from remote sites to introduce remote students to the professor and the technology, and to broadcast group
  project reports.

Limited research conducted in two of the TV classes indicated that there were
no differences in achievement on projects and the final examination between
students in the Tampa TV classroom and students in the remote receiving
sites; however, students' attitudes in the campus-based group were far more
positive. Review of students' anecdotal comments on end-of-course evaluations indicated that technical problems and infrastructure limitations flavored
their attitudes about the course even though their performance did not suffer.

Technological Problems

None of the candid classroom courses escaped technological problems.
They included everything from lightning strikes that wiped out signal transmission equipment to unexplained loss of the video feed to persistent, annoy-
ing audio volume, echo, and feedback problems in the remote site call-in
system. Faculty understood the technological nature of the delivery system
and the inevitability of failures but were frustrated by the unpredictability of
the problems and the lack of personal control over the teaching/learning
process. Another frustration for faculty was the nature and level of institutional response when problems did occur.

Institutional Support Problems

The support structure on campus for ITFS distribution was modeled on a
system designed to support small groups of high-tech engineering students
receiving video signals over fiber optic cable in conference rooms in host

companies, such as Honeywell, Martin-Marietta, and Florida Power. This support structure was largely driven by a set of print guidelines for faculty, distance site coordinators, and student participants. The problem with the print guidelines was that there was no way to anticipate and set up rules for managing all the contingencies that occurred in the loosely structured regional campus ITFS system at USF. When technological failures occurred there was a reporting procedure to follow, but staff were not available to make phone calls to students before they drove sixty miles to a receiving site that had no video signal. Those supporting the ITFS system did not seem to share a faculty member's level of urgency for student needs. Rather than being left unattended, student service needs were often done by faculty, graduate students, and office staff in the school. Other institutional support problems included the following things.

- Many technical support functions were performed by hourly student workers, thus resulting in low job continuity and high turnover rates.
- Regional campus receiving sites had widely varying standards for the level of support services that they provided.
- Regional campus personnel who supported ITFS services had functional lines of responsibility to Tampa DTML that did not parallel the administrative lines of authority at the site in which they worked.
- Communications among sites and coordination of distribution and collection of materials was slow and sometimes erratic.

Although televised courses presented problems for faculty, several precedents were set during this time regarding faculty assignment of duties that were later adopted as part of the school's approach to teaching load for Internet courses. One faculty member was given credit for two teaching assignments when she taught a young adult literature class to fifty-eight students distributed among the Tampa TV classroom and five remote sites. Two other faculty members each received a full teaching assignment when they split responsibilities for fifty-two students in a televised foundations class. The two shared student grading equally, but one did the majority of the classroom presentations while the other did the majority of the preparation of support materials for the televised class sessions and managed communications with the receiving sites and distant students.

Television served the purpose for a few years of allowing a faculty member to be in more than one place at the same time and thus met a real programmatic need at the school. This mode of distribution, however, still required students to drive to a central location for a synchronous event that was available in only a fraction of the geographic area served by the school.

The Lure of the Internet

When the school moved to its new facilities in early 1993, all faculty had new networked computers on their desks. Faculty were on the Internet, and e-mail became the mode of communication. The school set up an automated electronic mailing list and encouraged all faculty and students to sign up. The role of electronic communications grew as computer prices came down and Internet service providers proliferated. By 1996 dependence on the Internet for all kinds of information had grown to the point that it was natural that one of the faculty who had been a longtime computer user decided to try delivering a children's literature course by Internet e-mail. Her first course was essentially a correspondence class, but it was immediate and interactive. She posted a syllabus, assignments, and weekly "lectures" to a class mailing list and students responded and "conversed" with each other by the mailing list. She was assigned two sections of the class and taught a combined total of sixty-six students. The course was not without logistical and technological problems, but to a large degree many of the limitations of the ITFS system were diminished. Sophisticated technological infrastructure was required, but the instructor managed it from her home or office desk; she set standards for student participation; she distributed and collected her own course materials; and she delivered the course to students all over the state.

Table 22.1 is a summary of the number of class sections taught by TV and Internet for academic years 1993–94 through 2001–02. The table illustrates how briefly television was used and how quickly faculty adopted the Internet as the preferred method of course distribution to distance learners. Six faculty members taught by television and only one of them was a repeat user; whereas by fall semester 1999, nine of eleven graduate faculty had taught or co-taught by Internet and the other two faculty members taught by Internet in 2000.

The Web and Growth of Internet-Based Distance Learning

Although one faculty member continued to use e-mail with an automated mailing list as the method for course delivery through summer 1998, other faculty members quickly picked up the Web for formatting and delivering courses. Table 22.2 provides a view of the growth of Web-based distance learning in student credit hour (SCH) production and percentage of graduate program productivity for school years 1994–95 through 2000–2001. Although there was a 55.1 percent growth in total graduate SCH production over the time period, Internet-based graduate SCH increased from 0 to 2,250 and at the end of 2000–2001 and represented almost a third of total graduate SCH.

Web-based coursework has been a natural choice for distance learning both for faculty and students. There are a variety of reasons for the growth of Web-based courses in the school, ranging from (1) student demographic characteristics to (2) the nature of traditional professorial roles and (3) the development of institutional infrastructure for support of distance learning.

Table 22.1
Number of Distance Learning Class Sections Taught by Television
and Internet

	Television	Internet	Total
1993–94	1	0	1
1994–95	0	0	0
1995–96	4	3	7
1996–97	2	6	8
1997–98	0	16	16
1998–99	0	22	22
1999–2000	0	25	25
2000–01	0	26	26
2001–02	0	36	36

Student Demographic Characteristics

One obvious factor that explains the growth of Web-based courses is the
way that students have responded to the format. The typical student in the
school's graduate program is a mature, working female with family responsibilities who must commute to a campus or off-campus site for traditional
face-to-face coursework. The availability of Web-based courses allows many
USF students to solve a number of problems by managing the time and place
of some of their learning experiences.

Table 22.2
Graduate-Level Student Credit Hour Production by Internet-Based Distance
Learning

	Internet-Based Graduate SCH	% of Total Graduate SCH	Total Graduate SCH
1994–95	0	0	4365
1995–96	429	9.2	4666
1996–97	885	17.1	4998
1997–98	1191	24.7	4810
1998–99	1410	28.2	5106
1999–2000	1798	32.2	5571
2000–2001	2250	33.2	6771

Note: Total graduate SCH includes all students taught in all courses and is slightly higher than
funded SCH due to inclusion of some exercising staff tuition waivers.

- Site-independent, asynchronous instruction allows the scheduling of learning time around job and family responsibilities.

- Mature students who have "learned how to learn" can manage, and often prefer, independent learning.

- The need to travel to and from class is largely eliminated, so for some students, Web-based instruction enables course and degree enrollments that otherwise would be impossible due to time and distance constraints.

- Web-based courses allow greater breadth and variety in course selection for students statewide.

Traditional Professorial Roles

Cost and convenience factors for students certainly drive the popularity of Web-based courses, but there are also characteristics of the traditional professorial role that have enabled quick growth of instruction by the Web.

- Change is easiest when it is incremental, and the Web allows ready adaptation of old pedagogical styles for delivery by new telecommunications technologies. The traditional professor-centered teaching role of choosing and organizing content, delivering content, and managing discussion is easily carried out in Web-based courses.

- Delivering instruction by the Web allows a professor to function in the role of independent professional that is hard to maintain in broadcast TV or interactive videoconferencing. Both forms of televised instruction require preplanning and active, real-time participation with teams of technicians, whereas technical support for Web-based instruction is remote and largely invisible. Faculty in some cases appreciate the same freedom that students cite to conduct class and work with students outside the time and place constraints of a traditional class schedule.

- Most faculty members in the school were making extensive use of Web-accessible resources for their personal research and their face-to-face classes, so it was an easier step into Web-based courses for SLIS instructors than for faculty with less Web knowledge in disciplines with less developed Web resources.

- Most SLIS faculty view the Web as a tool of their trade, so development of Web-based instruction requires refinement of regular, desktop work skills in a familiar technology rather than development of new technological skills.

Institutional Infrastructure

Any initiative in Web-based distance learning would be difficult to develop and sustain without a strong institutional infrastructure. USF has been a leader in recognizing and acting on support needs for faculty and students in distance programs.

- Support efforts for early Web-based courses at USF were centered in College of Arts and Sciences Computing and campus Academic Computing. Both provided the e-mail accounts and server space for supporting distance education. Campus

Academic Computing subsequently began to provide commercial course management software (Course in a Box, WebCT, Top Class, and Course Info), Web authoring tools, a digital audiovisual production lab with staff support, and dedicated servers for distance learning. In 1999 Academic Computing began studying the feasibility of campus-wide management software that would integrate an instructional interface with other online student and faculty services. That led to the adoption of the Blackboard system, described later in this chapter.

- As distance learning became a more prominent feature of USF's academic program, the central administration authorized the hiring of a dean of Educational Outreach with centralized authority for off-campus credit and noncredit programs. That office provides: (1) program marketing and publicity, (2) registration and student support services, (3) instructional design and Web design services, and (4) personnel and technical infrastructure for ITFS and videoconferencing.

- The campus Center for Teaching Enhancement instituted competitive technology grants, summer stipends, and graduate assistant support for faculty beginning development of distance courses. The center also runs regular workshops for faculty in pedagogical issues in distance learning.

- The Florida Center for Instructional Technology is housed on the USF campus and offers training for faculty in commercial course management software and Web authoring software.

- The USF Library has been one of the most visionary supporters of distance learning. The Virtual Library provides remote Web access to the entire array of database resources that are available to a student on campus. The library has developed a password-protected electronic reserve system for professors teaching local and distance courses, and the USF Library housed the Florida Distance Learning Reference and Referral Center that provided 106 hours per week of toll-free telephone access to library services for all students enrolled in Florida public universities and community colleges. The center ceased operation in December 2001 when legislative funding for the statewide services ended; but the center established models for distance student library services that have been adapted by the USF Library for provision to its patrons.

- A campus-wide working group named VITAL was organized to coordinate technology and service initiatives among the agencies listed (Academic Computing, Educational Outreach, Center for Teaching Enhancement, Center for Instructional Technology, and USF Libraries) and WUSF-TV and the Health Sciences Center for Information Services. The mission of VITAL is to support applications of technology in instruction at USF in both campus-based and distance teaching. Resource sharing and eliminating duplication of effort are high priorities, and VITAL members have collaborated in areas such as policy development, faculty and staff training, software support, and hardware and software purchasing.

- Because of the growth in distance SCH productivity, the College of Arts and Sciences authorized the school to hire a Webmaster in the 1999–2000 school year to provide direct technical support for faculty developing or offering Web-based courses. This staff addition has reduced some of the production and maintenance burdens associated with online course development and management.

ISSUES AND CONCERNS

The rapid growth of the school's distance learning program has many positive aspects, but issues remain that are still of concern to the faculty as the future of the program is considered. These concerns lie in the areas of student outcomes, faculty work life, institutional infrastructure, and distance learning program development.

Student learning from traditional versus technology-mediated instruction has been studied in classroom and distance settings. The literature in this area generally concludes that significant differences do not exist. Recent research at the school confirms those findings, concluding that Web-based distance learning is a satisfying experience for students, and is perceived as equivalent, and in some regards superior, to comparable face-to-face classroom experiences. Among faculty who have taught by the Web, there is not undue concern for student learning outcomes; however the issue of affective outcomes remains. In a sequence of research at the school that included televised instruction, e-mail/online discussion list instruction, and Web-based instruction, a consistent result has been that students in traditional face-to-face classes report more interaction with classmates and stronger feelings of group affiliation than distance students. This research needs to be expanded to determine (1) the value that students place on interaction and group affiliation, (2) whether these course-related findings affect overall programmatic outcomes, and (3) whether interventions are warranted to promote interaction and group affiliation in Web-based courses.

Perhaps the most troublesome aspects of distance learning for faculty at the school relate to work life issues. Faculty concur that both development and management of Web-based courses are more time-consuming than for traditional courses. Recognition and reward within the university setting for distance teaching efforts are dependent on three factors. First, the promotion, tenure, and merit systems must value the faculty teaching role, including efforts in innovative, technology-based distance learning. Second, current methods for evaluating teaching effectiveness must be investigated to determine their appropriateness for Web-based teaching and learning. Third, the extraordinary time demands of online course delivery must be accommodated through such steps as enrollment considerations, differentiated staffing plans, and faculty load assignments. At USF, a policy is in place that addresses the reward structure for teaching; research is in progress on evaluation of distance teaching effectiveness; and the director works with faculty in the school on multiple strategies for equalizing the impact of distance teaching load. The work life concerns remain, however, because Web-based teaching is relatively new and faculty across the university who are still the core of the peer review and reward system do not uniformly share the school's vision, commitment, and understanding of distance teaching and learning.

Although the institution has made tremendous strides in support for distance learning, there are still troublesome aspects regarding infrastructure. Currently a per-course distance fee is added to tuition for supporting distance services that otherwise would have no funding base, including marketing, promotion, student recruitment, course-related travel, and site-based management and student services in Ft. Lauderdale. The distance fee is a convenient add-on that pays necessary bills, but the overall approach to funding distance education services needs to be investigated more systematically for long-term stability, efficiency, and equity.

USF has begun to address the needs of distance programs in a manner that allows student interface with a single, uniform services system. The system that became available in January 2002 is a university Web portal titled "my.usf.edu" that provides a one-stop shop of online services for faculty, staff, and students. Students are automatically enrolled in a Blackboard online class for each course for which they are registered, and a class roll and instructional tools are automatically created for each course on the Blackboard platform. Faculty may then use as many or as few of the available course management tools as they choose to enhance the courses that they are teaching. Course tools include content spaces for syllabi, documents, presentations, Web links, and so on; course bulletin board; chatroom; group project management; assessment and grade management; homework drop box; announcements; and e-mail. Although an innovative solution to many problems, the my.usf.edu infrastructure with its Blackboard course management solution is raising concerns among faculty about the one-size-fits-all assumptions that accompany its implementation and the inevitable decrease in university support for other course management systems.

Another infrastructure issue that continues to be a concern is the need for sufficient personnel and technological redundancy in critical Academic Computing support areas to ensure twenty-four hour a day, seven days a week service access for students taking Web-based courses. This priority has been voiced campus-wide, and funding is being sought for solutions.

The final issue concerning the faculty is an underlying concern that the evolution of the distance learning program be in directions that will meet the needs of remote students while maintaining the integrity of the master's degree program. The faculty concur on the view that many student learning outcomes cannot be taught to desired levels of mastery and/or assessed adequately using current online tools to which most distance students have access. There is no doubt that this view will change as broadband access proliferates and instructional delivery technologies continue to evolve in Web-based courses. The needs of distance students and educators will be well served by change as long as the focus remains on the outcomes of instruction rather than the technologies that enable instruction. As practices evolve, the faculty must continue investigations of whether new combinations of learning outcomes, course structures, scheduling options, and delivery modes can provide suitable avenues for better meeting the needs of distance students.

THE FUTURE OF DISTANCE LEARNING AT USF

The school's plan for delivering distance education includes (1) maintaining strong programs in the school's branch campus and off-campus sites, (2) solidifying infrastructure for continued growth in Web-based course delivery, (3) developing programs for cooperative delivery of the school media certification program with other universities in the Florida State System, and (4) investigating opportunities for expanding distance learning through new delivery technologies.

Maintaining Branch Campus and Off-Campus Sites

The school's historical focus on its statewide mission has emphasized the branch campus programs in Lakeland, St. Petersburg, and Sarasota and off-campus program sites in southeast Florida, Ft. Myers, Gainesville, Orlando, and Pasco County. The school continues to get requests for and positive response to site-based courses, and the careful coordination of these programs will continue. Course offerings by traveling faculty and adjunct professionals have increased, and now those face-to-face courses have been supplemented by Web-based classes. This increase in availability of courses provides students in branch-campus and off-campus programs with greater flexibility in scheduling and additional latitude in planning programs of study that match career interests.

A recent approach for the school in site-based course delivery is cohort groups. Agreement was reached in 1999 with Miami–Dade County to provide a complete master's degree for two cohorts, each of thirty students, through a combination of site-based and Web-based courses. The school has implemented cohort programs in two additional counties and will continue to pursue this promising approach to solving the critical shortages of certified school media professionals in Florida.

Solidifying Infrastructure for Technology-Based Course Delivery

As we monitor the school's ongoing use of distance technologies to deliver academic programs, we find that many of the efficiencies claimed for distance learning are still achieved only through management and logistical costs that are borne by the faculty and the school's support staff. The school will continue to pursue solutions for some of the burdens imposed by distance education, including:

- working with the College of Arts and Sciences, with various support services on the USF–Tampa Campus, and with internal school resources to configure the most productive professional, technical, and logistical support structures for offering courses by distance learning; and
- working to create seamless personalized service for students taking courses by distance technologies.

Our experience in distance learning in the school over the past decade or so has convinced us that addressing personnel, technical, and logistical infrastructure requirements is critical to maintaining the momentum that has developed in distance learning and expanding student and faculty buy-in.

Developing Cooperative Programs with Other Universities

In the past, three factors have tended to limit the number and variety of course offerings in distant sites: (1) limited availability of school faculty for travel to off-campus locations, (2) limited availability of qualified adjunct faculty in off-campus locations, and (3) limited availability and access to specialized facilities for course meetings in off-campus locations. The delivery of courses over the Internet has helped, but in the school media certification program there is still the problem of availability and access to specialized facilities, and several of the required courses are laboratory-based with extensive hands-on production skill requirements.

A review of programs offered in other state universities shows that in addition to the ALA-accredited program in information studies at Florida State University, several other universities offer coursework that is approved for media certification by NCATE and the Florida Department of Education. The school has a formal working agreement with FAU (Boca Raton), an informal working agreement with UCF (Orlando), and has initiated discussions with University of Florida (Gainesville) and Florida Gulf Coast University (Ft. Myers) for exchange of course syllabi and identification of appropriate courses in specialized areas of school media certification for transfer toward their master's degree at USF. This kind of interuniversity cooperation in conjunction with our traditional off-campus program and newer Internet-based coursework provides enhanced access to the school's ALA-accredited degree for a broader population of students.

Investigating New Distance Learning Technologies and Pedagogies

Although challenges in providing distance learning often preoccupy our thoughts, there are also exciting possibilities that await exploration. The school is in the business of educating professional managers of information, and in this capacity we must be poised to incorporate new technologies as both content and delivery methodology in our courses. The faculty see possibilities in distance learning that arise from new digital technologies and from combinations of digital technologies with established methods of distance and traditional learning. Some of these possibilities include:

- broader outreach through hybrid combinations of distance learning that combine a limited number of traditional class meetings with alternative methods of digital distribution and student interaction;
- broader outreach through enhanced bandwidth options and compression technologies that will support computer-based, desktop learning communities interacting in synchronous or asynchronous time with full-motion multimedia;
- new course management software that will enable more personalized, real-time interaction with students in their sites of choice;
- new routes of access to underserved and unserved student populations; and
- the emergence of new pedagogical methodologies that accommodate the teaching/learning needs of professors and students in distance learning environments.

CONCLUSIONS

Models of distance learning in higher education have come and gone, and for many reasons the role of nontraditional delivery of instruction in higher education has remained modest; but in the past few years the creation, management, packaging, and distribution of information has become a cottage industry with distribution channels to its customer base as ubiquitous as the twin copper wires that carry phone messages into our homes. The question is not whether new models of distance learning will flourish, nor is it whether distance learning will replace traditional methods of higher education; rather, the question is how distance learning can be balanced in varying degrees with traditional methods to meet the range of needs of a diverse student population. With almost a third of its current SCH productivity generated through distance learning and steady growth in the proportion of total SCH attributable to distance learning, the school must work from year to year to assess students' changing needs and find the right balance of traditional and distance strategies to meet those needs.

23

THE UNIVERSITY OF SOUTHERN MISSISSIPPI SCHOOL OF LIBRARY AND INFORMATION SCIENCE DISTANCE EDUCATION HISTORY AND PROGRAMS

M. J. Norton

HISTORY AND DESCRIPTION OF THE SCHOOL

The School of Library and Information Science at the University of Southern Mississippi (USM) offers programs at the undergraduate, graduate, and post-graduate levels. The programs are the bachelor of arts Library and Information Science major and the bachelor of arts with School Library Media Class A licensure; the master of Library and Information Science, the master of Library and Information Science School Library Media Class AA licensure, a dual master's with the MLIS and either History or Anthropology; and the specialist in Library and Information Science and the specialist in Library and Information Science with School Library Media Class AAA licensure.

Courses in library science were first offered at USM in 1926. In 1957, the program in library science became a department in the College of Education and Psychology. The master's degree was initiated in 1963–64, and the School of Library Service was established July 1, 1976, as a professional school. The graduate program was accredited by the ALA in 1980, and accreditation has been continued after site visits in 1987 and 1995. USM is accredited by the Commission on Colleges of the Southern Association of Colleges and Schools, the National Council for Accreditation of Teacher Education, and a wide variety of other discipline-accrediting agencies.

On July 1, 1988, as a result of university-wide reorganization, the School of Library Service became the School of Library Science in the College of Liberal Arts. To demonstrate administrative, curricular, and faculty responses to current trends in the profession, the name of the school was officially changed to the School of Library and Information Science in fall 1993.

DISTANCE EDUCATION OVERVIEW

Since its beginnings, the School of Library and Information Science under all its many names has offered classes in residence at the Hattiesburg and Gulf Coast campus in Long Beach. Face-to-face student faculty classes were and will continue to be a mainstay of the programs offered. The need to serve place-bound students has been perceived as a critical and essential responsibility of the school since its inception. Influenced by available transportation, previously the university had its own plane service; until the early 1990s classes were taught off-campus in face-to-face student faculty situations. Faculty traveled to remote sites to conduct classes. Plane service was terminated as a cost-saving measure for the university, but faculty continued to travel via car and train. In the early 1990s other technology and resources became available, such that there was a decrease in the number of classes involving faculty travel to remote sites. Transmission of classes via a statewide Interactive Video Network (IVN) allowed classes to be taught at remote sites without requiring faculty to travel for every class, though each faculty member taught from each of the sites throughout the semester to ensure faculty–student connection. The IVN is still used to conduct classes. As Internet technology and computer resources has become more readily accessible, class formats changed, permitting classes to be conducted in either hybrid or totally online mode. Even as the school launched a totally online master's degree program in fall 2002, face-to-face student–faculty classrooms will still be offered by the school as required to provide the full spectrum of educational experiences to interested students. The extensive involvement of the School of Library and Information Science in meeting the needs of the students of the region demonstrates its investment and commitment to both local and distant education modes.

HISTORY OF DISTANCE EDUCATION

Mississippi covers 47,233 square miles. It is 340 miles north to south and 180 miles east to west. The interstate highway system includes parts of I-55, I-59, I-20, and I-10. I-55 extends the length of the state from south of Memphis, Tennessee, near the northwestern corner of Mississippi through Jackson, the capital of Mississippi, to the border of Louisiana near Kentwood. Two-thirds of the state is north of Jackson and has only the westerly lying I-55 as an interstate highway. Extending from the western border at Vicksburg across the state, I-20 merges with I-59 near Meridian. On the eastern border of the state, roughly parallel with Jackson, I-59 extends from east of Meridian, southwest through Hattiesburg, to intersect with I-10 two miles into Louisiana in Slidell. The coastal area of Mississippi is served by twenty-six miles of I-10 crossing from Louisiana to Alabama, rarely more than twenty miles from the Gulf of Mexico. The state is still rural, with population centers dispersed and usually measured in thousands. The total population of the state is approximately 2.7 million. The largest city is Jackson, the capital. The majority of roadway is rural, fifty-five mph or slower, with many unlit roads with towering pine and magnolia forest in the southern portion of the state and long stretches of flat, nearly treeless roads in the northern section, where cotton is still an important crop.

Although it is a beautiful state with many enchanting and historically important areas, Mississippi's rural road systems may discourage travel and make what might be a short trip by interstate a lengthy one by two-lane routes. People tend to be place-bound, whether as a result of the road systems and little intrastate transportation or due to family and business responsibilities. It has been and will continue to be critical to provide educational access as convenient to the populace as possible.

A consortium of Mississippi universities previously used a facility in Jackson to offer courses in the metropolitan area that were not offered by Jackson State University. The higher education system in Mississippi grants universities regional governance of course offerings within a fifty-mile radius. Mississippi universities cooperate in providing access to disciplines, or specialty programs not normally offered on their own campuses, but generally discourage offering courses typically taught by the regional institution. Recognizing a large place-bound populace, the Mississippi university system has consistently attempted to make diverse program offerings reasonably available across the state via cooperative arrangements.

As the only ALA-accredited library school in the state of Mississippi, the USM program has borne the responsibility of providing access to its program throughout the state. Prior to the advent of the current distance learning technologies, the program offered courses throughout the state by hiring qualified local adjuncts and/or sending regular program faculty to off-campus sites. Participation in the consortium and university cooperation has enabled the offering of LIS courses across Mississippi.

Through the consortium arrangement the School of Library and Information Science (SLIS) offered much of its curriculum, one or two courses at a time, at the center in Jackson. In 1995, there were changes in the management of the shared location, and it was no longer possible to offer SLIS courses from that site. Since that time, however, other sites in Jackson have been arranged and are operated with the cooperation of the consortium. Efforts continue to develop new cooperative ventures in and around Jackson.

DISTANCE EDUCATION WITH TECHNOLOGY

IVN

The use of regional adjuncts to support the SLIS program in those areas continues, but sending program faculty to remote sites has almost ceased due to the availability of a variety of technological alternatives. Started in 1993, using space formerly employed by the SLS, an IVN classroom was constructed on the Hattiesburg campus. A similar room was constructed seventy miles south, on the Long Beach campus of USM. This permitted classes to be taught from either site sending to the other site. In spring 1994, USM became the first university in Mississippi to offer interactive video classes.

Each room is equipped with four video broadcast cameras. One camera is directed toward the instructor and another toward the students. These cameras have nearly 180-degree rotation potential. Camera three is a graphic display unit for overhead projection to data screens or monitors, and the fourth camera has a VCR connection. A CODEC computer codes and decodes the camera and audio signals sent over telephone lines. The computer also permits management of the cameras and audio from a control panel. Four large, ceiling-mounted TV monitors are installed in each room, two in the front of the rooms and two in the back. Students can view the remote sites, overhead display, or video on the front screens, and the instructor can view the remote sites on the back screens. One of the front TV monitors has been replaced with a larger data display screen in the largest IVN room on the USM campus. The control stations are equipped with remote-control VCRs, a computer for presentation and instructor use, black-and-white monitor to preview the graphic display, keyboard, and control tablets. Each student desk has a touch-activated microphone. The instructor may use a touch-activated microphone, or a lavaliere microphone with power pack. Each of the USM rooms is also outfitted with a fax machine with phone, a copy machine, and whiteboard or chalkboards. Decisions about the design of the rooms and the complementary equipment were based on extensive investigative work of the Teaching Learning Resource Center staff, and faculty committees concerned with the anticipated needs of the students. USM also determined that the control stations would be managed by a staff member, freeing the instructor to focus on the students and course content.

Prior to the completion of the construction of the rooms and the initiation of the program, a number of committees studied the viability and the liabilities of engaging in such a program. Among the issues studied were the impact on the learning environment, academic quality of course offerings, educational support at remote locations, faculty support mechanisms, ensuring compliance with copyright laws, responding to intellectual property concerns, development of regulations for the selection of faculty and courses as well as scheduling, the Mississippi fifty-mile radius rule,[1] impact on compensation for institutions and faculty, and formulation of policies to guide the growth of the system. Anticipated learning environment issues, such as making the space and technology serve the student, were addressed by educating faculty about the limitations of the technology. Faculty members were reminded of the need for extensive reinforcement, adjusting the speed of presentation, eye contact via the cameras, and use of support technologies as well as local resources.

It was determined that academic quality had to be maintained regardless of the medium employed or the environment involved. To ensure this, courses offered via IVN must have requirements and standards comparable to the same courses offered on campus and must comply with the Southeastern Association of Colleges distance learning guidelines. Furthermore, any other appropriate accrediting body standards dealing with distance education have to be addressed.

To deal with resource support at remote locations, cooperation with the local libraries and universities was sought, contact persons identified, and textbooks or related resources shipped to the remote sites. In some cases it has been necessary to use postal or express services to ensure that materials are received at the remote sites in a timely fashion.

Issues of copyright and intellectual property concerns were studied by a number of committees and legal experts. Guidelines and compliance criteria were provided to the faculty and are periodically updated. Discussion of the examination and attention to be paid to these issues is frequently a case study in SLIS classes.

Concern that there would be significant competition for course time slots led to the creation of an approval and scheduling plan. The Institutions of Higher Learning (IHL) and the chief academic officers of the system developed the policies and criteria for the implementation of distance learning programs for the IHL members. Specifically, the policies were designed to prevent unnecessary duplication of programs and the demise of ongoing programs offered in the traditional campus mode. Most important, however, the intention of the policies was to maximize educational opportunities for the people of Mississippi. The policies govern the criteria and procedures for offering distance education programs. Development of such programs requires an assessment of need, identification of locations of offerings, methods for ensuring and evaluating quality, and specifications of the arrangements made with other institutions for technology and resources.

A system of priorities for using the IVN rooms was devised that gives highest priority to graduate courses, followed by advanced undergraduate courses, then highly specialized undergraduate courses, non-credit academic activities, and lowest priority to administrative activities. Additionally, courses with enrollment at multiple campuses have higher priority, as do courses with higher enrollment. Departments or schools wishing to offer classes via the IVN submit requests for slots with course titles and appropriate syllabi and related documentation approximately one year in advance to facilitate the coordination of the multiple sites. As site arrangements are made and schedules confirmed, the departments are notified of approval, or conflicts, or lack of sites. The long lead time allows for readjustment in planning to compensate for conflicts and opportunities to change a proposed schedule to an available time slot or location.

Faculty support was and is a critical component of the success of the IVN system. To encourage that support the university provides funds to the departments offering courses via IVN. For each course offered and enrolled with a specific number of students, departmental budgets receive $1,000. These funds to departments are typically used by the faculty member who teaches the IVN course. The faculty may also receive an additional separate honorarium if the enrollment exceeds a given number related to student status.

The SLIS began offering courses via the interactive video method in fall 1995 after conducting a statewide survey and extensive discussion among the faculty. The SLIS offers only upper-level undergraduate and graduate courses, qualifies as a specialized program, and therefore has priority when petitioning for course time slots. Like all other participants in this distance education method, SLIS faculty participated in several hours of classroom training with the equipment, as well as attending several workshops on how to modify existing instructional material to be useful in this environment. The University provided funding for creating or modifying curricula for the new environment and for retooling overheads, classroom aids, computer presentations and such.

The SLIS has offered fifty-two classes via interactive video network since fall 1995, employing the initial network as well as three other interactive networks developed since. USM expanded its own network to include two IVN rooms on the Hattiesburg campus and six rooms on the coast campuses.

Other Mississippi universities also constructed IVN rooms, creating what is known as the IHL interactive video network. The community colleges of the state also created an IVN system, actually preceding that of the universities. A third network is the STARS system, which placed an IVN classroom in each school district. The three network systems can operate interactively and have been used to supply courses to remote sites at other universities, community colleges, and schools. Though the other network systems work with the USM equipment, not all the sites have fax, copy machines, or computers. Each site makes arrangements to have these resources available for course support.

Beginning with the initial class offerings until fall 2000, USM conducted evaluations of the IVN system by soliciting evaluations from students and faculty for each course each semester. The results of the surveys have been used to identify environment, technology, and course problems. Usually situations have been addressed as soon as USM has become aware of a problem, such as installing larger display systems in the bigger IVN classrooms, changing the computer system at the instructor stations and upgrading the CODEC. The evaluations have also informed faculty of student perceptions and expectations related to this method of teaching.

The long-term statistical studies of student performance indicate no significant differences in student grades between students taking courses in traditional mode versus the IVN mode or between student grades at the sending site versus the receiving sites. Over the life of interactive video at USM, the majority of negative comments from students and faculty have been related to equipment failures. Accessibility to courses has been cited as the most desirable aspect of the system, often making the difference for students whether or not they would be able to pursue or complete a program of study.

The Gulf Coast to Hattiesburg IVN sites have been the easiest connections to use, as far as resources for SLIS courses because there is a shuttle to those campuses three times a week. This permits easy distribution of course resources. Using connections to sites without shuttle service has typically involved having a local librarian act as liaison to secure or arrange to transport resources. The technical capacity for multiple sites has allowed SLIS to offer classes to as many as seven sites at once. However, the lag time created by the signal speed to distance, the line capacity in use, and other technical problems make transmission to more than four sites uncomfortable and sometimes trying. Mississippi has extreme thunderstorms and unpredictable winds, which have a negative effect on any transmission technology. The majority of students have been positive and very responsive to the use of IVN; however, it has not been a unanimous finding, and work continues to improve both the technology and organization used in the SLIS courses. As of fall 1999 every required course as well as a number of electives had been offered via IVN to western, northern, and southern sites, using all of the available networks. SLIS has transmitted courses to Cleveland, Ruleville, Greenwood, Oxford, Pontotoc, Tupelo, Jackson, Natchez, Summit, McComb, Long Beach, and Gautier, employing all of the available IVN systems.

Internet-Based Distance Education

The SLIS pioneered the use of the Internet in education at USM. Students were required to use e-mail, threaded news readers, and electronic sources as a complement to IVN courses as well as other SLIS courses. When SLIS reached out to Delta State University in Cleveland, Mississippi, one of the primary considerations in sending IVN to the site was based on their complete willingness to provide computer access and support to the students who would be using Delta State facilities to take USM courses. Working closely with computer services and IVN staff, courses offered at the Delta State University campus have been very rewarding. As more sophisticated Internet resources were available, more was required of the students. However, separate from the IVN system, the school offered Internet-enhanced courses in spring 1996 and 1997. Several courses were taught in traditional classroom format, conducted on site at Hattiesburg for approximately half of the semester with the second half taught using online software. The interactive multiuser object-oriented (MOO) site of Diversity University provided virtual classroom space for the course offerings.

After getting classes started in the classroom and training students in the use of the computer software, the classes moved to the virtual campus. Meetings were held at the usual class time but were conducted in the enhanced environment of the MOO. Students interacted with each other and the instructor via the text screens from wherever they could connect via computer. Class discussions were "recorded" and e-mailed to students after the class to use as a method of taking notes and permitting students to interact more spontaneously. Once students were comfortable with the software, usually after one class meeting, students were extremely responsive and excited by the method. Class attendance was 100 percent during the virtual portion of the classes. Students who were too ill to go to campus attended class from home; several students attended classes even when they were out of state on conferences or other business.

In fall 1998, USM began offering several hybrid, face-to-face class meetings supplemented by online classes and fully online courses with no face-to-face contact, using WebCT software. The SLIS offered its first fully online course using WebCT during summer 1999. The content of the course and management of the environment was the instructor's responsibility, though the department of Continuing Education and Distance Learning was available to advise and assist in the initial stages. The course, Introduction to Information Science, involved students connecting from Louisiana, Canada, West Virginia, Maryland, Mississippi, and one student who seemed to be in a different state each week.

The class had two required and scheduled chat meetings each week. One was a class with instructor chat meeting, and the students attended another chat on another day to chat without the instructor. The class chat was a combination of prepared notes, lecture, questions and answers, and what often was usually lively discussion of the readings and topics. All the chats were recorded and posted to the course bulletin board so students had later access to all the chats even if there were power outages or other problems. This was critical because serious lightning storms disrupted these sessions on more than one occasion; as long as the server did not go down in Hattiesburg and the storms were not local, all chat participation was recorded. The only way to reach the postings, bulletin boards, and chat areas was via a password assigned by the instructor. Readings were posted to a content area. Outside readings were also assigned, and some interlibrary loan services were employed to access the necessary resources. Students were required to post brief analyses of assigned readings, and additional related readings they identified to a threaded bulletin board. This permitted students to look at others' interpretations as well as share resource information.

As the course was being run in the traditional campus meeting mode for another section, the two sections were asked to meet in the Web space for a class and a student chat. The discussion was extraordinary but extremely difficult to moderate. The combined sections created a class size too large for the software to handle, and some students were unable to connect. After reorganizing by splitting into two sections so they could have smaller discussion groups, the result was more satisfactory. Students reported enjoying the exchange in smaller groups and not liking the larger group because the speed of the discussion was too fast to follow. There was some dismay about never actually meeting the instructor or the other students, though by the conversations with the students one would not recognize that they were physical strangers. Some displeasure resulted from some students mistakenly thinking that a totally online course would be "a come when you please and do what you want" affair. There were serious grumbles about the stringent attendance, participation, and work requirements, which mirrored those for the on campus section.

Another issue involved the various confidence levels of students related to the technology. Despite having examined the technological requirements for participation, and having actually managed to get into the software, several students expressed great anxiety about their skills with the system. Despite attempts to demystify the technology, students had the incorrect expectation that everything should work exactly as anticipated regardless of whatever else happened. When there was a server failure, students convinced themselves that their own systems had failed. When incorrect commands were used in posting to the bulletin board, students refused to accept that the cause was their own actions. Overall, the course was well received, the students did ultimately perform very well, and most reported their willingness (even eagerness) to attempt another course using the online system.

During summer 2000 the same course was taught without any face-to-face contacts and no campus sections. Students participated from Montana, Tennessee, Louisiana, Florida, Alabama, and several locations within Mississippi. Chats were structured such that a student leader was responsible for keeping the discussion on task, as well as managing the order of speakers. Students were asked to keep to the order established at the opening of the chat as a way to ensure that everyone had an opportunity to comment. Some students found the structure to be restrictive, but most reported that it did improve a person's ability to comment on everything said.

In fall 2000 the SLIS offered seven hybrid courses and one completely online course. Information Ethics, taught fully online, and one of the hybrids, Libraries in American Society, used Blackboard. The Blackboard hybrid course was taught by a faculty member who had never used any Web or online instruction system. The online course was taught by a faculty member experienced with WebCT. Another hybrid course was taught using WebCT by another faculty member who had never used any Web software. The software enrollment process for the courses was easier using Blackboard, even for novice users. Loading documents and other course content involved far fewer steps in Blackboard then in WebCT, thought the internal e-mail system of WebCT was reported to be especially useful. Both novice users were competent computer users but had to have support in learning how to use the software. The training required for WebCT involved significantly more time. The experienced user preferred Blackboard, but the free version of Blackboard did not permit recording or logging the chat meetings, which was a significant handicap in an online course. (Blackboard 5, currently in use, does have a chat archive feature.) Both faculty new to the online course environment reported very favorable experiences, and enjoyed the versatility of being able to conduct classes even when attending conferences. Student comments were primarily satisfied with the online class structure. Students who had experienced both software packages were unhappy with the inability to record chats in Blackboard, but felt it was less difficult to use. SLIS determined in summer 2002 to rely on Blackboard for online course software but will continue to review emerging online or supplemental courseware systems.

In spring 2001, seven hybrid courses and one fully online course were taught. Two of the courses employed Blackboard, and the others used WebCT. The version of Blackboard in use for the spring had several powerful archival features and was less complex as to enrolling students and loading content compared with WebCT. Two courses were taught using a combination of IVN and online to extend the hybrid course to include physical meetings via IVN rather than entirely on site in Hattiesburg or entirely online. Combining hybrid courses with IVN permitted visual contact, which may diminish some of the student discomfort and possibly aid in building student confidence. At the same time, the number of physical contacts was reduced, minimizing travel requirements and allowing for the maximizing of time spent on task, rather than on the road.

During summer 2001, one totally online course and one hybrid course were taught, both using Blackboard. In fall 2001 one totally online course, as well as four hybrid courses were taught, all using Blackboard. Unfortunately, in fall 2001 Blackboard's free software system was overwhelmed by more than 100,000 new free courses added to their systems. Connecting to the free course sites became problematic due to the traffic. Although Blackboard's immediate response to put up more systems resolved the connection crisis before the end of September, it did not fully address the traffic impact on the chat features. Fortunately, the discussion board feature worked well, and most class business was conducted using the discussion board as well as the digital drop box and was supplemented by e-mail. Unlike WebCT, which resides on a server on the USM campus via a typical contractual license, SLIS was using only the free side of Blackboard, meaning the software was resident only on the Blackboard systems, not any of our campus machines. Blackboard has since modified its free course agreements, and offers a single-course one-year license for a fee or a sixty-day free course agreement. SLIS determined until it could afford to obtain a full site license for Blackboard we would test other systems, and instructors who elected to use Blackboard would receive funding per course.

During spring 2002 one fully online class used the fee-based Blackboard with no technical problems. Four faculty tested the Yahoo! course system and Yahoo! groups for chats with hybrid courses. There were mixed results for the Yahoo! instructors and students. Students with a preference indicated that Blackboard or WebCT were easier to use, though they could not be specific about why.

The school is seeking collaboration with other members of the College of Liberal Arts in hopes of funding a full site license for Blackboard. Other online classroom software will be examined as it becomes available. Key features that will be expected will include easy registration of students, ease of content construction or importation, reliable service, documentation, discussion board, e-mail, and especially the capacity to record chats.

SUPPORT ISSUES

The university has several committees examining support and policy issues related to all forms of distance education. Distance education impacts all the stakeholders in different ways. The faculty involved in developing IVN, hybrid, and online courses are faced with the challenges of modifying presentation formats, adapting their teaching style to the medium, as well as ensuring appropriate content and rigor of the courses. For the IVN format this entailed learning camera-oriented skills—how to engage the remote sites using camera image and continuing verbal contact while keeping the students involved on site; modifying presentations to fit the display systems and planning class time differently—the pace of IVN classes by nature of the medium is slower than traditional face-to-face. This training and revision of syllabi and classroom planning is time-consuming and occasionally labor-intensive. The university has provided small grants and preparation assistance for the modifications but these activities still demand time. The hybrid and online classes demand many of the same changes, but also much more detailed planning on the part of the instructor; the free flow of the classroom that can help move topics along is not easily achieved online.

Additionally, unlike the IVN classroom, where the technology surrounds the student, online and hybrid courses require that the student be actively engaged with the technology. Many students still do not possess basic computer skills or are not aware that there is more to operating a computer and working online than point-and-click behavior. Ultimately, the task of helping students master the technology to participate in online or hybrid courses falls to the instructor. Various online help sites have been created, but these have not yet proven to be sufficient to the task, especially if the student does not reference them. The hybrid course instructor has the advantage of having several face-to-face classes where hands-on instruction can be undertaken. The totally online course does not have this potential. USM does not yet require students to attend an orientation on campus for online courses. SLIS has posted and informs students of the minimal skills necessary to be successful at online or hybrid courses, but this still relies on the student's self-evaluation.

Committees examining the impact on faculty productivity and the effect on related issues of tenure and promotion are concerned about the time investment in dealing with the technological problems and the investment of time in developing these courses. Faculty involved in online and hybrid courses are concerned with how the involvement in these types of courses will influence their future evaluation. Though most schools and departments may set internal tenure and promotion criteria within the framework of the university, that does not necessarily mean that the larger evaluation bodies or the colleges and the university review committees will recognize the value of this type of service and teaching involvement.

A critical component of distance education is supplying services to students that support their basic educational needs as well as the ones generated by being distant students. University committees interested in the student support side of the problem are examining ways to improve online services to students. USM's Cook Memorial Library has made significant contributions to making online courses possible via the extent of their support and services. Students have access via the library to a wide variety of databases, including full-text and international sources. The library has developed an electronic reserve site, accessible only to registered students, to provide for reserves at a distance. A document delivery service ranging from faxing materials to obtaining materials from alternative sources is in place and operating successfully. The library maintains tutorials, help pages, links to resources, and e-mail reference services. The students need only avail themselves of these resources. Continuing to expand the resources available for distance students will be a challenge but is absolutely essential. In the long run, additional technical staff and faculty support will have to be obtained to provide continued support for students.

FUTURE DISTANCE EDUCATION

The SLIS at USM has long been committed to providing access to its programs at distant locations, serve the place-bound, and expand the opportunities of the people of Mississippi. Ever increasing inquiries into our online offerings suggest significant interest from outside of Mississippi and the United States. Based on a history with IVN and the ongoing work with online computer systems, the school plans to continue offering courses, on site, on site at remote locations, via IVN, and via online systems. Online courses or hybrid courses will continue to be offered, and improved online classroom software sought, including streaming video. Work continues to provide more online reserve materials via the library as well as through resource support via Web pages connected to the course, links directing students to related or associated sites, password-protected course content areas, and e-mail. Faculty will be available at class times, and have both physical and virtual office hours. It may be useful to expand the number of hybrid courses, including their physical meetings via IVN rather than entirely on site in Hattiesburg. The underlying premise is that the personal contact may diminish some of the student discomfort, allow the instruction of appropriate tools, and even aid in building student confidence. At the same time, the number of physical contacts will be reduced, minimizing travel requirements, and allowing for the maximizing of time spent on task rather than on the road.

As new technology becomes available, there will continue to be changes in the methods used to provide access to education. The same technological evolution will require more people to return to the educational theater to maintain and upgrade their skills. A cycle of increased opportunity and increased demand will require the continuous upgrading of educational resources. The SLIS at USM plans to continue to develop and expand with the technology as quickly as is feasible.

NOTE

1. Mississippi higher education authorities grant the universities authority over course offerings within a fifty-mile radius of each institution. One university may not offer face-to-face courses within a fifty-mile radius of another university without permission of the local university. Permission to offer courses is usually related to whether the proposed course duplicates an offering of the granting university.

SUGGESTED READINGS

Additional information about any of the University of Southern Mississippi programs can be found online at www.usm.edu.

Additional information about the School of Library and Information Science can be found online at www-dept.usm.edu/~slis.

Additional information about Diversity University can be found online at www.du.org.

Additional information about WebCT can be found online at www.webct.com.

Additional information about Blackboard can be found online at www.blackboard.com or http://coursesites.blackboard.com.

Additional information about Yahoo! can be found online at http://courses.yahoo.com and http://groups.yahoo.com.

24

A TRADITION OF INNOVATION: THE SYRACUSE UNIVERSITY EXPERIENCE

Ruth V. Small and Barbara Settel

To transform the information field through leadership in research, development, and education.
— Mission of the School of Information Studies, Syracuse University

"In recent years, there has been a growing interest in providing graduate distance learning programs in library and information science.... Exciting new opportunities are increasingly available to students separated by time and space from gaining professional library and information science credentials."[1] The School of Information Studies at Syracuse University has a long and rich history of leadership for innovation and change in the information fields. This chapter describes the school's history, the development of its interdisciplinary structure, and the emergence and evolution of its innovative distance learning programs, which have provided a model for other schools throughout the country.

HISTORY OF THE SCHOOL

Syracuse University, founded in 1870 in Syracuse, New York, has an undergraduate student body of approximately 12,000 and a graduate enrollment of close to 5,000 students. Syracuse University's ALA-accredited and nationally ranked School of Information Studies (IST) is one of thirteen schools and colleges located on the university's sprawling 200-acre campus. As a result of the university's encouragement of cross-disciplinary study and collaboration and its vision as a "student-centered research university," IST participates in programs and projects with such other nationally ranked schools on campus as the S. I. Newhouse School of Public Communications and the Maxwell School of Citizenship and Public Affairs.

The IST was founded as a library science program in 1896. Currently, the school is housed in the university's Center for Science and Technology, a high-tech facility that fosters interaction and cooperation among faculty and students in information studies, computer engineering, computer science, and chemistry. IST cultivates an innovative academic environment, priding itself on its interdisciplinary faculty, programs, and courses.

The background and expertise of IST's faculty represent the fields of management, communications, computer science, education, cognitive psychology, economics, and library and information science, thereby offering an intellectual diversity that enriches both teaching and research at IST. IST faculty and doctoral students have won numerous awards for teaching (e.g., Syracuse University's Professor of the Year, ASIS Outstanding Faculty) and research (e.g., ALA's Carroll Preston Baber Research Award, AASL/Highsmith Award for Innovative Research, and ASIS Outstanding Dissertation Award).

In addition to intellectual diversity, the faculty and administration have identified five other common values, including:

- dedication to exploration and innovation, promoted through discovery, development, application, integration, and active learning.
- commitment to and respect for the individual, valuing individual differences.
- an adaptive environment that promotes risk-taking and entrepreneurship.
- a "faculty of one" philosophy.
- enduring contributions to our field.[2]

In the spirit of these values, the school has an innovative structure that reflects its philosophy. Unlike other schools of its kind (and other schools within Syracuse University), IST has chosen to have *programs* rather than *departments,* thus eliminating competing entities and the partitioning of loyalties. IST has an undergraduate program in information management and technology, three master's programs (library science, information resources management, and telecommunications and network management), and a doctoral program in information transfer. Faculty teach across all programs, functioning as a whole, not as individuals or groups who represent any one specific program. Students representing all five academic programs may be found studying side by side in many of the school's elective courses.

IST's tradition of innovation makes it a school of many firsts. In 1974, it became the first school with an MLS degree program to use the word *information* in its name. In 1980, it was the first to offer a master's degree program in information resources management, a program that prepares sophisticated information systems managers, able to respond to four basic challenges confronting organizations today: (1) increasing the productivity and creativity of managers and executives who work with information resources, (2) planning the effective use of information and communication technologies within organizations, (3) developing corporate and government policies to maximize the benefits resulting from the widespread use of these technologies, and (4) improving the strategic use and management of information resources in business, government, and nonprofit organizations.[3]

In 1987, IST became the first school to offer an undergraduate program in information management and technology, which prepares students to understand the value of information to society, organizations, and individual professionals. Last but not least, it was the first school to offer Internet-based, limited-residency distance learning programs in library science (1993), information resources management (1996), and telecommunications and network management (1998).

DEVELOPMENT OF NONTRADITIONAL PROGRAMS

IST has a long tradition of offering programs to meet the needs of working adults and part-time students. Prior to 1987, the school was solely a graduate school and more than half of the graduate students attended classes part-time. In conjunction with the university's division of continuing education, IST established evening, weekend, and short, intensive summer classes to enable students to complete their degree programs while maintaining full-time jobs.

DISTANCE LEARNING PROGRAMS

Though IST had always been sensitive to the needs of part-time students, it wasn't until the 1980s that the school began to experiment with distance learning programs. At first, IST developed some regional extension site programs to extend its reach into other sections of New York. Later, IST recognized a larger issue—a need for quality distance learning programs that addressed the needs of (1) students living in remote areas of the country where no information studies programs existed and (2) students with jobs or other responsibilities that precluded them from traditional part-time study, requiring commuting to and from a specific site at a specified time.

EXTENSION SITE PROGRAMS

Despite offering campus-based alternatives for part-time study, it soon became clear that some students could not easily travel back and forth to Syracuse for classes. In 1985, a group of prospective MLS students based in Ithaca, New York (about fifty miles from Syracuse), approached the school to consider offering extension classes there. The school soon began to offer one course a semester, and about ten to twenty students took classes taught mostly by adjunct faculty. Library access and classroom facilities were cooperatively arranged with the help of Cornell University librarians, many of whom were IST alumni. Students enrolled in the extension program were still required to complete a component of their degree on the main campus. They were also expected to come to campus for faculty advising, career counseling, and all other administrative business. In 1988, extension classes for students in the information resources management (IRM) master's degree program were offered in Endicott, New York, where Syracuse University already had established continuing education engineering and computer science classes for IBM employees.

Although the extension classes were certainly convenient for these regional populations of students, the educational experience proved less than satisfactory. Students were isolated from other students in the on-campus program; it was difficult to keep them informed of events and activities in the school; and the schedule of extension classes was too limiting. Competition for students from other MLS programs led to declining demand in Ithaca. In Endicott, changes in the workforce at IBM led to decreased demand. Both programs were short-lived.

THE WASHINGTON PROGRAM

Despite the eventual demise of these two extension site programs, today IST maintains a successful extension program in Washington, D.C. The Washington, D.C. program offers both a thirty-credit master's degree in IRM with a Specialization in Government and, for those unsure (or unable) about pursuing a full master's program, a certificate in strategic information resources management (SIRM) in the federal government. The master's program builds on Syracuse University's eighteen-credit graduate certificate. The certificate can later be applied toward the master's degree or used as a post-master's degree credential.

The SIRM program takes advantage of Syracuse University's Greenberg House, a facility containing meeting and reception rooms, located in the heart of Washington. Typically, courses are taught in Washington over several weekends by IST faculty (both full-time and adjunct) at the Greenberg House. This allows the school to draw from the rich resources (both human and technical) in the Washington area. Often, SIRM courses incorporate officials in strategic government positions as instructors and guest lecturers, providing the richest and most relevant teaching and learning environment.

Students in the Washington program are encouraged to take some of IST's Internet-based distance courses, described later. In addition to taking classes tailored to their special needs and interests in Washington and some of the more general Internet-based courses, these students also have the option of traveling to Syracuse to participate in IST's Summer Institute courses.

SUMMER INSTITUTE

The school created its Summer Institute on Leadership and Change in an Information Society in 1991. Originally designed to target the school media community, the institute 's enrollments quickly soared, quadrupling in the first two years. This caused both students and faculty to demand a broadened scope of institute offerings. By 1993, IST's Summer Institute offered a wide variety of two-day workshops and five- or seven-day intensive courses over a three-week period. The institute allowed the school to be able to offer a mix of traditional courses and "hot topics," such as data mining, information security, and Webcasting, appealing to both current IST students and practitioners in the field who want or need to update their knowledge and skills. The increased importance and relevance of some of these Summer Institute courses have motivated the school to transform them into regularly offered courses.

Most Summer Institute courses have integrated enrollments from IST's three master's degree programs. This integration creates an enriched learning environment for both faculty and students. Dean Ray von Dran, who teaches regularly in the Summer Institute, describes his first class: "Part of the thrill of this class was the great intellectual and philosophical diversity present, and how it played out in discussion. Students learned from one another at every level and the class came away transformed! Nowhere else do I know this happening in the information field."[4]

By 1999, the Summer Institute had grown to twenty-nine separate courses to appeal to a wide audience, representing topics as diverse as Business Information for Strategic Intelligence and Marketing Your Library, Wireless Industry Global Economics, and Storytelling. With the creation of the Summer Institute, the school established a vital and necessary cornerstone for the establishment of its innovative Internet-based limited residency distance learning program that emerged two years later.

LIMITED RESIDENCY DISTANCE LEARNING PROGRAMS

Encouraged by the success of its extension programs and the potential of its Summer Institute, the school began discussions in 1992 to develop an integrated distance learning program that would give students living in remote or distant locations access to IST's curriculum and faculty. In July 1993, the school launched a "student-centered," one-on-one, many-to-many model of distance education for LIS using mainly distributed networked communications (Internet, Web) to deliver instruction.[5]

The program was originally designed to generally follow the format of Syracuse University's Independent Study Degree Program (ISDP). ISDP, offered through the university's continuing education division, is one of the three oldest such programs in the United States. Begun in 1966, ISDP sought to meet the needs of nontraditional students who could not attend traditional classes on campus. ISDP programs have combined two elements: a short on-campus residence and self-paced study that students complete at home. The first Syracuse ISDP students were enrolled in a bachelor of arts in Liberal Studies. These fifteen students completed a three-week residency on campus each summer, taught by an interdisciplinary team of full-time faculty. The rest of the year the students completed their courses at home, working independently with periodic communication with faculty via phone and mail. Since 1966, ISDP has changed considerably in size and format. Today, over 1,000 students are enrolled in the undergraduate program in Liberal Studies and the eight master's degree programs in schools and colleges across the campus.

But from the very beginning, IST made a conscious decision to develop an innovative distance learning program, incorporating the most current information technologies. Thus the first Internet-based limited residency distance learning program at Syracuse University and the first such program in LIS in the United States was born.

The Syracuse MLS distance learning program, like its campus-based counterpart, offers a thirty-six-credit, ALA-accredited program for part-time students. Its curriculum parallels that offered to local resident students. Only students matriculated into the distance program could enroll in distance format courses.

The MLS distance program has entailed shorter campus residencies (i.e., two days in length) than other distance programs at Syracuse University. Residencies are usually held at the beginning of each semester. Residencies allow students to receive necessary technology training, hands-on labs, and some group activities while facilitating bonding of cohort groups, face-to-face networking with faculty and staff, and becoming familiar with the school and university. IST's Dean von Dran believes the residencies are "the critical element for this program because the students already have a social bond when they get online together."[6]

Following the limited residency, courses continue via the Internet once students return home. As von Dran states, "What is unique in the Syracuse model is the combination of residency and non-residential interaction throughout the academic year. In some ways, students in IST's distance program receive nearly the full classroom interaction of a traditional residential program *and* fifteen weeks of academic interaction after the residency."[7]

In 1993, e-mail was the primary medium of communication for instructor–student and student–student interactions, and online discussion groups served as the main method of group communications. Students could also communicate via postal mail, telephone, or fax.

That first summer in 1993, thirty-seven students arrived on campus as the first MLS distance learning cohort group, lived in a university residence hall, and took a one-week introductory course that introduced them to the faculty, campus, and curriculum as well as the issues and literature of the field. The intensity of that first week caused the students to dub the experience "library boot camp," and that nickname has stuck to this day. During the week, social events such as picnics and ice cream socials were sponsored by the school to help relieve some of the inevitable stress students felt (caused by being in a new place, among strangers, returning to higher education, living in a dorm, etc.) and to encourage bonding and personal interactions. On the last day of boot camp, students were introduced to the instructor of the fall semester course and provided information and materials they would need to begin work on that course before they returned to Syracuse in September.

Following completion of the introductory course, students had the option of remaining on campus for one or more brief, intensive elective courses offered in the Summer Institute. These students then returned to their homes, where they soon received additional course material for their fall semester core course. When they returned to campus in the early fall they had already completed independent assignments and interacted online with the instructor and other students. They repeated this process for the spring semester. The first cohort group proceeded through the program together for two years, taking core curriculum courses in distance mode (Internet-based, with a brief on-campus residency) in the fall and spring semesters and completing electives through the Summer Institute, independent studies, and internships in their local communities.

IST faculty and staff learned a lot in that first year. They learned to provide a list of necessities to bring to campus in the summer (such as fans and comfortable walking shoes) and in the winter (such as boots and thermal underwear). They learned about the importance of providing mini-fridges and Internet connections in dorm rooms. They learned to communicate regularly with students about their learning progress so they don't feel they have been left hanging in cyberspace. Over the past years, many changes have been made to IST's distance learning programs; the most dramatic changes have occurred in the use of distance learning technologies.

DISTANCE LEARNING TECHNOLOGIES

As technologies evolve, so has distance learning at Syracuse, inspiring several research studies and dissertations. A study conducted in 1995, comparing the experiences of distance and resident students at IST, revealed that less than one-half of all respondents had computers at home. A 1999 follow-up study found that over 80 percent of all students now have home access and a greater number have access at work than they did in 1995.[8]

Sensing this shift in access and recognizing the emergence of more powerful distance learning technologies, IST's faculty began to experiment with text-based, asynchronous group communications software packages (e.g.,

Lotus Notes, HyperNews) to deliver instruction to distance students. In 1996, some faculty developed a graphic interface to group communications using Palace, "a unique virtual world chat software program that allows people to communicate interactively via the Internet, with the added value of pictures and sounds."[9] This graphical environment included classrooms, discussion, and other special purpose rooms, and personal avatars, simulating the face-to-face traditional classroom. Although students found this software easy and satisfying to use during the residencies, the synchronous nature of this software presented some limitations for distance use.

In 1998, IST's faculty adopted a standard yet versatile Web-based learning environment called WebCT, changing the way much of the instruction is delivered at IST. Over the past two years, WebCT, originally developed at the University of British Columbia, has been incorporated into many distance and on-campus courses for everything from posting assignments and syllabi to incorporating group work, interactive lectures, synchronous discussions, and self-paced learning modules.

WebCT is described as "an easy-to-use environment for creating sophisticated WWW-based courses."[10] It offers a wide variety of tools and features, such as online chat, student progress tracking, group project organization, grade maintenance and distribution, e-mail, course calendar, and automarked quizzes. With WebCT, courses can now be delivered in distance mode to *all* students. Faculty could teach and students could learn from anywhere in the world—for example, one student completed his IRM degree while serving aboard a U.S. Navy submarine in the Pacific.

CURRENT STATUS

Distance learning at Syracuse University's School of Information Studies continues to grow and evolve. To date, IST's distance learners are diverse, representing more than thirty states and ten foreign countries in four continents. "This diversity," von Dran comments, "makes all the difference!"[11]

The following statements describe the current status of distance learning at IST.

- There are currently approximately 250 students pursuing one of the three Internet-based distance learning programs at IST.
- The MLS distance learning program has grown to over sixty students in two cohort groups each year.
- Distance learners range in age from their twenties through their sixties.
- The name "independent study" is no longer used by our programs because it conveys the notion that students are studying in isolation and without formal structure.
- The school has hired a full-time director of distance learning, who oversees all of the programs and the Summer Institute.

- Faculty regularly build distance learning-type experiences into the structure of both distance and on-campus courses.

- The school has hired a full-time coordinator for instructional resources who builds and maintains all course sites on WebCT and offers a training program for students and full-time and adjunct faculty on a regular basis.

- Ongoing technical support is provided by the school's director of IT services and coordinator of instructional resources.

- Opportunities have been provided for faculty who have used WebCT creatively in their teaching to share their techniques and ideas with their colleagues.

- Many courses still follow the format of the original courses, combining brief residencies with Internet-based communications; however, residencies are now limited to two days.

- All distance students begin their programs on campus in July with an introductory course.

- Some courses are offered completely over the Internet using WebCT and can be taken from home or office without ever traveling to the main campus or one of the extension sites.

- Most of the Internet communication for distance courses is asynchronous and does not require students to be connected at a particular time.

- Some courses are offered to both distance and resident students in distance format only.

- Students can take elective courses in a variety of formats including brief, intensive on-campus summer courses, online courses, independent studies, and internships.

- Distance students may complete internships in their local communities.

THE FUTURE

Distance learning at Syracuse continues its tradition of innovation into the future. The school is exploring the possibility of holding residencies in locations other than Syracuse. One possibility is working with its international programs to hold residencies in Europe and Asia. Von Dran explains, "I see the potential to have a multitude of sites for our residencies to further enrich the learning experience. At this time we have a site in Washington, D.C. Our University also has facilities in New York, London, Madrid, Florence, Strasbourg, and Hong Kong. In the future we may wish to take advantage of these venues as well."[12]

A new program for a cohort of school media students from New York City will combine a variety of distance formats. These formats include courses with residencies in Syracuse and New York City; brief, intensive courses; courses held over a series of weekends in New York City; and totally Web-based courses.

Experimentation with new and emerging technologies continues. For example, one professor is experimenting with the use of instant messaging technology to simulate the common physical spaces in learning environments that facilitate social connections and informal communications.[13] Another professor is creating an experimental, multimedia "virtual" residency where students will log onto their computers at the same time and proceed through a sequence of activities together over a two-day period. Those activities include independent reading, synchronous activities (e.g., role plays), asynchronous discussions, CD-ROM-based video vignettes, and live Webcast sessions.

Through campus organizations such as IST's Information Institute of Syracuse and the Center for Digital Literacy, faculty, undergraduates, and graduate students work together to design creative learning environments and apply information technologies to instruction in new and different ways. This experimentation will help IST expand its values to include "a student body of one."

> The school is very careful to connect its distance education students to life on campus and is committed to turning out superior librarians.
> —Susan Winch, 1993 MLS-ISDP student

NOTES

1. Small, Ruth V. "A Comparison of the Resident and Distance Learning Experience in Library and Information Science Graduate Education." *Journal of Education for Library and Information Science,* 40, no. 1 (winter 1999), p. 28.

2. "Graduate Study Syracuse University: Master of Library Science." Graduate catalog. School of Information Studies. 1998–99, p. 1.

3. School of Information Studies Web site, http://istweb.syr.edu.

4. Online interview with Ray von Dran, dean of the School of Information Studies, Syracuse University, August 26, 1999.

5. Small, 1999.

6. Von Dran interview.

7. Ibid.

8. Small, Ruth V., and Stephen Paling. "The Evolution of a Distance Learning Program in Library and Information Science: A Follow-Up Study." *Journal of Education for Library and Information Science,* 43, no. 1 (winter 2002), pp. 47–61.

9. Gibbons, W. J. "From Dungeons to Degrees." In *Trends and Issues in Online Instruction,* Proceedings of an on-line conference sponsored by Kapiolani Community College, Honolulu, Hawaii, March 1997. Available online at www.kcc.hawaii.edu/org/tcc_conf97/pres/gibbons.html.

10. "World Wide Web Course Tools: WebCT." Available online at www.webct.com/webct.

11. Von Dran interview.

12. Nelson, Corinne O. "Susan Winch: Librarian on the Cusp." *Library Journal,* October 15, 1996, p. 31.

13. Nicholson, Scott. "Socialization in the 'Virtual Hallway': Instant Messaging in the Asynchronous Web-based Distance Classroom." Unpublished manuscript, 2002.

SUGGESTED READINGS

A number of publications have been written about the Syracuse University program. They include the following.

Gibbons, W. J. "From Dungeons to Degrees." In *Trends and Issues in Online Instruction,* Proceedings of an online conference sponsored by Kapiolani Community College, Honolulu, Hawaii, March 1997. Available online www.kcc.hawaii. edu/org/tcc_conf97/pres/gibbons.html.

Land, Mary. "Virtual U." *Quill and Quire,* July 1966, pp. 10–11.

Linden, Julie. "The Loneliness of the Long Distance Learner." A poster session presented at Educom '98. Available online at www.library.umass.edu/linden/educom.

Nelson, Corinne O. "Susan Winch: Librarian on the Cusp." *Library Journal,* October 15, 1996, p. 31.

Small, Ruth V. "A Comparison of the Resident and Distance Learning Experience in Library and Information Science Graduate Education." *Journal of Education for Library and Information Science,* 40, no. 1 (winter 1999) pp. 27–47.

Small, Ruth V., and Stephen Paling. "The Evolution of a Distance Learning Program in Library and Information Science: A Follow-Up Study." *Journal of Education for Library and Information Science,* 43, no. 1 (winter 2002), pp. 47–61.

Zhang, Ping. "Distance Teaching a Graduate Course on Information Systems Analysis and Design." *Journal of Education for MIS,* 5, no. 1, 1998.

Zhang, Ping. "A Case Study on Technology Use in Distance Learning." *Journal of Research on Computing in Education,* 30, no. 4 (summer 1998).

25

THE *ENTERPRISE* CONFRONTS THE *NIMITZ*: DISTANCE EDUCATION AT THE SCHOOL OF INFORMATION SCIENCES, THE UNIVERSITY OF TENNESSEE

Gretchen Whitney and George Hoemann

The University of Tennessee was founded in 1794, two years before statehood, as Blount College. After several additional name changes, it became the University of Tennessee in 1872, and acquired Land Grant status under the Morrill Act at this time. With the recognition of the state government came a pledge of mutual support between the state government and the university, and a commitment by the university to service for the entire state. This commitment forms part of the foundation on which the University of Tennessee as a whole pursues the extension of its campus and learning activities to the state.

The present School of Information Sciences at the University of Tennessee looks back at a long history of incarnations, first as a series of undergraduate courses offered for school librarians in 1928 in the College of Education, then as the Department of Library Service, which offered an undergraduate major in instructional materials in the College of Education (1944), a program leading to a master's degree in instructional materials within the college (1958), a revised program leading to a master's degree in school library service (1964) within the college, and finally an ALA-accredited program as an independent unit—the Graduate School of Library and Information Science—in 1971. While continuously updating and revising the curriculum to meet the needs of students and the profession, in 1992 and 1993 a team-based planning process resulted in a wholly new curriculum, degree program, and name for the school—the School of Information Sciences—in 1994. In the midst of these changing administrative structures, the school reached out to its constituency in its distance education program.

The school has continued to grow from its modest beginnings. In 1984, the student headcount was 175 individuals, which grew to 223 five years later, and to 312 in 1993–94. The full-time equivalent student count was 92 in 1984, and 150 in 1993–94. In 1998–99, the headcount was 162, and the full-time equivalent was 106, in part reflecting the graduation of the distance education cohort that began in 1994. The opening day faculty count for the school was five plus the director; it is now eleven plus the director, plus a vacant director position for the Center for Information Studies, who also serves as a faculty member.

Within the university, the school has established itself from the beginning of its efforts in distance education as an innovator and leader in the exploration of new technologies in taking the collective knowledge of the school to the profession in the state and now beyond. Since the 1980s, the school has had a collective will (if not the resources) to expand its reach and not only serve individuals and groups of students but to raise the level of the profession in the state as well.

In developing its distance education initiatives, the school has been guided by the principles of (1) a commitment to making the distance experience as much like the residential experience as possible, and not creating a distance group as a different class of students; (2) using the latest technologies available on campus to deliver the program; and (3) maintaining the curriculum (and associated activities) designed for the residential students in the distance environment.

Efforts to implement distance education in the state are necessarily influenced by the geography of the state and its infrastructure. Tennessee is divided into three parts: east Tennessee, dominated in the Tennessee Valley by Knoxville and Chattanooga in the mountains to the south; middle Tennessee, with Nashville high on the Cumberland Plateau; and west Tennessee, with its flatlands and Memphis. These three areas are culturally distinct areas, with historical roots: in the Civil War, east Tennessee sided with the North, whereas the rest of the state sided with the South. Its history is exacerbated by the length of the state (430 miles) and its width (about 120 miles), and two time zones (east Tennessee being in Eastern time, the remainder of the state in Central). Air service between the major cities of the state is expensive, and the highways are crowded north–south and east–west trucking routes, which makes driving exciting at best. At this writing there is no direct air service between Knoxville and Nashville. All of these elements contribute to the relative isolation of the three parts, and the relative difficulty of bringing them together.

Furthermore, Tennessee is a relatively poor state in per capita income, ranking thirty-third in the nation in 1997 (U.S. Bureau of Economic Analysis) or forty-fourth (Bowker) and has chronically underfunded its libraries and higher education. For 1998–99, for example, the increase of 4 percent of spending on higher education ranks it thirty-fifth in the nation. (Schmidt). The issue of resources has been a constant barrier to the intentions of the program. At the start of the new century, the state is in economic crisis, with a legislature that is entirely unable to figure out how to raise sufficient revenues to meet the state's health needs, and higher education is threatened with massive cutbacks.

The state as a whole has been very conscious of the need for distance education, particularly for its many rural and remote areas. In 1993 the state implemented EdNet, a statewide interactive video network and intranet that connects institutions of higher education and state research facilities across the state. Interactive classrooms around the state can hold between four and seventy-five students, with most in the eighteen to twenty-five seat range. In a given year, about 200 credit and noncredit courses are offered to almost 4,000 students. The state also maintains a series of teleclassrooms and other resources for distance learning and outreach.

THE EARLY YEARS

The School of Information Sciences experienced its first pressure to offer educational opportunities in remote locations before the doors were even opened. In 1968, enthusiastic librarians in Chattanooga lobbied the school for courses to be taught in their area, about 100 miles south of Knoxville. They were successful, and seven courses were taught there by part-time faculty between 1972 and 1974. Seven additional courses were planned for the next two years, but these never materialized. Insufficient enrollment and quality concerns ended the effort. In 1981, a course was developed as the result of a survey of needs; again, insufficient commitment to enrollment ended the fledgling program. There was some concern about competition from the Department of Library and Information Science at Peabody College of Vanderbilt University in Nashville, which had two distance education programs. However, Peabody was private and relatively expensive.

Offering courses in a different city was not the only effort the school made to experiment with alternative formats to meet the needs of the profession in the state. In fall 1978, the school decided to increase its offerings in evening and late afternoon time slots. This was directly in response to a decline in enrollments. The school deliberately decided to seek part-time students.

THE MEMPHIS PILOT PROGRAM

Competition from other schools prompted reconsideration of distance education in 1987. Louisiana State University, for example, is as close to Memphis as Knoxville is. And Memphis was a promising location for a variety of reasons, not the least of which was the Academic Common Market agreement, which would enable students from Arkansas (just across the Mississippi River) to take courses at in-state Tennessee tuition rates. Arkansas, without an accredited school, was an attractive expansion venue. A further pressure came from the closing of the Peabody program (1988) and the need to not just think like but act like a statewide program. Television and optical disk technology were considered as delivery methods, but the university was not ready to mount these technologies, and such efforts would not be rewarded by the university as well as research and publication.

Serious planning for distance education proceeded in early 1988 with faculty attendance at conferences and visits to Memphis institutions to gauge interest and encourage participation. Distance education was perceived as a mechanism not only for meeting enrollment needs but also for upgrading the profession in the state and building support for the school. It was also perceived as part of an overall move for the university itself to be a genuine state university. Another benefit of the program was to enable the Memphis public library to provide educational opportunities to many of its African American paraprofessionals, to enable them to raise their professional status.

The benefits to launching distance education were several. The first was financial. Enrollment is of particular importance to the university, because the university's budget is based on a formula that is tied to full-time enrolled students. If sufficient students are not enrolled, funding according to the formula falls. And this is not only at the university level but is passed on to colleges and schools. Distance education made it possible, bluntly, to meet—and exceed—quota. The second benefit was statewide visibility: the school was not just for east Tennessee, it was for the state as a whole. The university has had a historical tradition of being a regional university and was trying hard to gain the statewide recognition that it had earned in programs and educational opportunities. Finally, the effort would upgrade the profession as a whole in the state, which clearly would benefit both the profession and the school.

In fall 1988, the school launched the Memphis pilot program with two core courses, with substantial (forty-five students) enrollments. The program was offered in cooperation with the University of Memphis. It was intended as a six-year cohort-based program—in line with the University Graduate School requirements of the maximum time allowed to complete a graduate degree. Two courses were offered in the spring, and the pattern continued for the life of the program. The courses were taught on site, with faculty flying to Memphis for two three-hour sessions over the weekend every other weekend for each course. The contribution of the University of Memphis, under the direction of Les Pourceau, dean of the Libraries, was significant both in administrative details as well as support services, such as library borrowing privileges.

Teaching in the program was voluntary, and thus the teaching load fell heavily on one faculty member (William Robinson) and the site coordinator in Memphis. No additional resources were given to faculty other than added compensation.

Advising was considered to be a major component of the program, and that was a challenge. It was handled by the early arrival on site of the faculty member, via telephone and, increasingly, by electronic mail. In the early 1990s, e-mail became crucial for student support in the program.

In 1989, the issue of distance education still not was resolved. Requests had come in from Chattanooga and Nashville for a Memphis-type program. There was clear demand from the school's students. The faculty felt that students from Chattanooga were close enough (about 100 miles) to make the trip to Knoxville to classes. And, Nashville, for a variety of political reasons, was an exceedingly complex situation in which to offer classes. However, repeated requests for university support yielded naught.

As a part of its continual planning process, in 1992–93 one of the goals of the school was to expand the distance education program. Also as a part of this planning process, attention was paid to the school's participation in the university's emerging technology and telecommunications infrastructure. The school identified as one of its four goals a position of leadership in technologies in general.

In the fall semester of 1993, the Memphis program changed its mode of delivery to compressed video technology over T1 lines through the states video network (EdNet). This preserved the traditional classroom model of interaction, with simultaneous video and audio exchanges. This was a new technology for the campus, and the school was one of its early adopters. It is interesting to note that this will be the start of a pattern: first, the tail end of one program being used as an experiment for the next technological wave, and second, the school's early adoption of innovative technologies on campus. The School was the first program at the university to be involved in the delivery of an entire degree program via the latest technologies, whereas other units (such as engineering) had been experimenting with individual courses.

The pilot program was completed in spring 1995 and saw the graduation of thirty-four new information professionals for the Memphis/northern Mississippi/Arkansas area. Twelve of these students took additional classes in Knoxville and completed their programs early.

On July 1, 1992, Jose-Marie Griffiths became director of the school. In August of that year, a process for continual planning and improvement was set in place, with the development of teams addressing specific issues and meeting frequently to address issues of continuing education, research agendas, subject specializations, and the like. Distance education was set aside, given the pressure of other issues. However, financial pressures and enrollment changed this priority.

THE 1994 COHORT PROGRAM

Demand continued to grow for the accredited master's degree from potential students unable to relocate to the Knoxville campus. As a result, in the early 1990s—even before the completion of the pilot distance education program to the Memphis area—the school began investigating the possibility of offering the degree program to students in other areas of Tennessee. At the same time representatives of the school and the Virginia Library Association (VLA) began discussions to explore the demand for the degree in the Commonwealth of Virginia (Virginia having no in-state accredited degree program). Inherent in these preliminary explorations was the commitment to use the "new technologies" as the primary method of efficiently and economically making graduate-level education available to off-campus students. In the early plans, faculty from institutions such as the University of Virginia would contribute to the curriculum by offering electives that would be made available to the entire program. This was a grand idea that, unfortunately, never materialized.

Developmental planning began in earnest on the Knoxville campus in 1993 when the school entered into a close collaboration with the university's distance education office (now, the Division of Outreach and Continuing Education). Initial thinking contemplated one-way TV satellite delivery to specified delivery points with conference telephone lines for interactivity. In June 1994, given the interest expressed unofficially from members of the VLA, representatives of University of Tennessee at Knoxville (UTK) and the University of Virginia began what would become a series of meetings aimed at a collaboration between the two universities, with the long-range goal of providing residents of Virginia with the opportunity to receive the UTK degree while remaining in Virginia. The working group set fall 1995 as the target for beginning the new distance education program.

As of July 1, 1994, the school assumed the new name of the School of Information Sciences. In fall 1994, a new curriculum was put in place, with a sixteen-hour core course component and a series of concentrations such as Scientific and Technical Information, Youth Services, and Information Systems and Technology. The existence of the core—and the school's commitment to it—has determined, in part, the scheduling and admissions process beyond the initial cohort. The core is not a series of required courses that can be completed before graduation; rather, it is a series of courses that must be completed before attempting electives. This does constrain the scheduling of courses, with a small faculty, when one attempts to bring in new classes of students on a routine basis. But at this point in time, the faculty remains committed to the core as it stands.

A needs assessment survey distributed to residents of both Tennessee and Virginia suggested a possible thirteen-site delivery plan (eight sites in Virginia and five in Tennessee). At the same time, the school faced the somewhat daunting task of gaining administrative approval not only from its parent university as well as the University of Virginia but also from the higher education agencies of both states (the Tennessee Higher Education Council and the State Commission on Higher Education in Virginia). Both agencies approved the distance education program in 1995.

An unanticipated problem occurred when, for a series of reasons, the cost of satellite delivery increased beyond the budgetary guidelines adopted by the sponsoring institutions. Consequently, planning shifted to land-line–based compressed video technology (the University of Tennessee's T-1-based EdNet and dial-up ISDN connections to the Virginia sites). Although the compressed video technology was decidedly a back-up delivery modality (as the description suggests, the video/audio feed is digitized and compressed, resulting in less-than-cable-quality picture and sound), it nonetheless allowed full interactivity; that is, both video and audio would be would be sent between the Knoxville-based classroom and the remote sites. Costing models assuming compressed video delivery suggested that eight was the optimum number of sites, and the decision was made to set delivery sites accordingly. Students in Tennessee would be able to attend classes at four sites (Memphis, Nashville, Chattanooga, and Kingsport), and Virginia students could attend classes at four sites in their state (Roanoke, Charlottesville, Falls Church, and Virginia Beach). Additionally, Virginia students who were physically closer to Kingsport, Tennessee, than to Roanoke, Virginia, were allowed the option of taking classes at the Tennessee site.

By this time, however, the fall 1995 start date was no longer a realistic goal. Accordingly, the launch date was delayed one semester, until spring 1996. Unfortunately, a series of administrative changes at both sponsoring institutions put further pressure on timetable. In 1994 Jose-Marie Griffiths, director of the school, had been named interim vice chancellor for the university's Division of Information Infrastructure. Although Griffiths retained her role at the school, day-to-day administration of the distance education initiative had been assigned to John Tyson, former Virginia State Librarian, and a faculty member at the school since 1994. Shortly after his arrival in Knoxville, Tyson's health began a decline that led to his death in November 1995. Thereupon, the school's associate director, Glenn Estes, assumed responsibility for the distance initiative. Estes's own health deteriorated quickly, however, and he succumbed to pancreatic cancer in July 1996. George Hoemann of the school's administrative staff became the coordinator for the distance program. Moreover, a change in leadership at the University of Virginia's Division of Continuing Education also occurred during this period. These changes in administration at both institutions and the attendant slowdown in planning between the two partners caused the start date to be set back yet again, to fall 1996.

The agreement between the University of Tennessee and the University of Virginia specified that tuition from one state's students would not subsidize the operating expenses incurred in the other state. Target enrollments were set at fifty students for each state. The decision of the Southern Regional Education Board that Academic Common Market status would not apply to Virginia students receiving the degree through distance education prompted the sponsoring institutions to set a contractual rate for Virginia students that would be less than full out-of-state tuition but more than the in-state rate. The University of Virginia agreed to provide registration processing and library support for residents of Virginia; the University of Tennessee would provide similar support for Tennessee students.

Applications for the program were strong both in quality and numbers; in August 1996, the school offered its first interactive class simultaneously to students in Knoxville and eight remote site classrooms. Total distance enrollments for both states numbered 83, slightly lower than the goal of 100. From the beginning, the school had adopted a cohort model, that is, students would begin the program together and take the same classes during the time required for completion of the degree. Results from the needs assessment instrument indicated that the vast majority of potential students would be employed at full-time jobs. Other data from the survey instrument indicated a strong interest in certification for school library media centers. Hence, courses were scheduled to take advantage of the full six-year period allowed by UTK for completion of a master's degree and to include those classes necessary for school library certification. In the first semester students enrolled in two of the six required, core curriculum classes, IS 530, Information Access and Retrieval, taught via interactive television, and IS 504, Electronic Information and Communications Laboratory, taught by adjunct instructors at the remote sites. Thereafter, students enrolled in one or two interactive classes per semester through spring 1998 when the core curriculum was completed.

As noted, interest in and application for the master's degree had been very strong. However, there was a significant difference between the number of students accepted into the program and the number who actually began attending classes in fall 1996. Attrition between admission and matriculation of students is common for all graduate education but particularly so for distance education. Costing models set the optimum number of students at 100. Thus, the sponsoring institutions quickly agreed to extend the admission period for one more semester, allowing qualified potential students who had not yet learned of the program to take advantage of the extended admissions period. Response was very strong; by spring 1997, the cohort had surpassed its goal of 100 students. Because the new entrants had missed the classes offered in fall 1996, the school arranged for the late entrants to make up the missed classes during spring and summer 1997 using video delivery and Internet-based discussions as supporting technologies. This in part laid the base for multiple formats of delivery within a single program.

With the initiation of this new program, fundamental cultural issues began to change and be addressed. First, participation in the initiative was no longer voluntary. It was simply a part of faculty responsibilities. Second, the workload issue was raised, and it was decided by the faculty that during the semester that a distance course was offered, no other teaching responsibilities would be assumed by the faculty member for that semester. It was recognized early on that a class size of 100 students or more was sufficient. Third, the issue of intellectual property of the course, in this case ownership of the stored videos of classes, was in the hands of the individual faculty member. The faculty member could decide on distribution of taped classes and retained control of them. This remained a hazy issue at the university level. Fourth, support for the faculty member was provided in the form of a doctoral student at ten hours per week. One doctoral student was provided for all faculty, and she (Kendra Jones) provided various support functions as each faculty member required.

The school continued to receive significant numbers of inquiries about the distance education program. Due to the cohort nature of the program, the school's faculty decided to delay reopening admissions until the first cohort had completed a significant portion of the master's program. Also, given a relatively small faculty (vis-à-vis the size of the cohort), both temporal and financial resources were limited, and it would have been virtually impossible to launch a new set of core courses and at the same time maintain the elective program on campus.

In its evolving traditional pattern, the school takes up the end of a program in the exploitation of new technologies in preparation for the next program. In fall 1999, the first asynchronous Web-based course is being offered through the CourseInfo software, not only for the school but for the campus (Blackboard). This approach has its own set of challenges, both for the instructor (the first author of this chapter) and the students. But it raised new cultural issues in the demands on preparation: The instructor was granted a course reduction in the semester preceding the course offering for course preparation. If scaled up to each course offered, the financial commitment could become quite serious.

THE MILLENNIUM PROGRAM

In March 1999 the faculty unanimously decided to reopen admission to a restructured distance education program in fall 2000. In this initiative, the school has maintained its leadership position on campus in exploiting new technologies in support of both faculty and student work. With the greater variety of technologies available faculty can turn their attention to exploiting the technology (video, Web-based instruction, in synchronous as well as asynchronous modes) required pedagogically by a subject area and the needs, skills, and interests of individual faculty members. Since 1994 faculty have been exploiting various course support mechanisms by creating varying degrees of a Web presence for their courses. CourseInfo, a Web-based course management package, was first used in spring 1999 by faculty of the school to deliver syllabi and related materials.

The Millennium Program will not be cohort-based; rather, new admissions will be accepted each year—albeit not at the volume of the previous program.

The goal will be to have approximately 100 students at any one time, accepting 30–40 each year. The new program will also require a one-week residency period before the Fall term begins to offer socialization, introductions, and work on computing skills. The curriculum, including the core, will remain structurally the same.

The heart of the restructuring, however, is only partly based on new technologies. It is also based on the concept put forward by Griffiths implicitly and more fully articulated by the second author of this paper, that distance education is no longer a stepchild of the program; rather, it is simply an integral part of what we do. Every course in effect has—or can have—a distance component. By definition, our students may reside wherever they wish. This will indeed be a challenge for both faculty and students, both pedagogically as well as administratively, as the school tries to maintain its initial principles.

With the advent of Web-based instruction, the school—and the university—must deal with the thorny questions of the shift from the chalk and talk–type instruction to technology-based instruction. These include the intellectual property of faculty-produced teaching materials, faculty workload issues (the teaching workload for the semester before the class is offered, as well as the teaching workload during the semester the class is taught), promotion and tenure issues, library support issues (particularly for remote areas), and faculty support issues. The university has yet to come to grips with these problem areas, although it does recognize them. But the school is moving ahead to making its own decisions.

THE FUTURE

The early phases were just that—phases—as distance education began as a special activity in the late 1980s, as a separate and different activity apart from normal teaching activities, to, in its latest incarnation, simply a part of what we do. The University of Tennessee has transitioned from a distance education program that was a stepchild to an integrated, normal part of our teaching activities. We accept it as normal that our students may be located anywhere. And they may be getting their education at any time. The term *distance education* was but a brief articulation of what is to become our current way of doing business: Our educational community is flung now across the southeastern United States, but we are poised to offer our program to our national, if not international, community. This is not an easy transition, but we will make it, as we always have.

The sociocultural issues of intellectual property of class materials, the role of distance education in the promotion and tenure process, workload implications for faculty teaching in this mode, issues of technical support and faculty roles in the emerging teaching environment, and the roles of the various technologies themselves are issues that need to be addressed not only at the departmental or college level but at the university level as well. Although they are receiving attention by various groups around campus, they are still very much in debate and discussion. The School of Information Science faculty committees are also working on these issues in this very fluid environment, although decisions have been made on a case-by-case basis.

Over the past eleven or so years, the school's faculty and administration have learned a great deal about the problems—and opportunities—connected with distance education. We plan on learning a good deal more.

FROM THE PERSPECTIVE OF 2002

In fall 1999, Gretchen Whitney offered the first Web-based course for the school to the 1996 cohort. The course, IS 567, Information Network Applications, was partially about the Internet, so it was a logical choice as a first effort in this new medium. It was taught to 120 students in the cohort and in Knoxville. In part it was a success: All of the students completed all of the requirements for the course and passed. The medium of Blackboard—plus online discussion lists and chats—were successful. The instructor handled several thousand e-mail messages. In part it was not successful: the Knoxville students resented being treated as distance education students because they wanted an on-campus experience (though they did appreciate not having to come to class all of the time). There were simply not sufficient resources to maintain frequent group chats. Other faculty began using Blackboard to deliver syllabi and course materials while maintaining the in-class experience for Knoxville students.

It had been the intention throughout the distance education program to use the medium most appropriate for an individual course, and faculty continued to use combinations of videotape, e-mail, chats, and other technologies as needed and appropriate for the subject matter and class activities.

In fall 2000 and 2001, approximately forty students were admitted each year as the start of an ongoing annual distance education process. The students were comparable in quality and background to the Knoxville students. The novelty at this time was to introduce the Centra software, which implements telephony over the Internet in such a way that the instructor can deliver an audio lecture to the students and the students can press a button to indicate that they wish to speak to ask a question or offer a comment. The software has advantages: The students like to be able to hear the teacher. The lecture can be recorded for replaying later if a class is missed. It also has its disadvantages: The bells and whistles, like application sharing, don't really work very well.

Faculty now have a variety of technologies to work with—from video through standards-based Blackboard and Wintel-based Centra. We will continue experimenting with technologies as they become available.

We would like to close this update with a few observations about the experience.

First, the students have proven to be remarkably adaptable in the use of new technologies. They have had to relearn some lessons, in particular that faculty do not all teach the same way in the classroom. After sixteen years of schooling, they know very well that teachers combine classroom activities, such as lectures and demonstrations, in different ways. The new technologies, however, seem to exacerbate these differences for both the students and the instructors: Both are highly aware of how different these variations can be. The technologies are both confining and liberating, and we continue to explore these differences.

Second, the issues of how to develop and nurture distance communities with local communities of learners remains a challenge. In fact, the social issues surrounding these groups may be more of a challenge than the technologies themselves. The distant students have one set of expectations about their learning experience and accept certain activities like virtual community building as a part of that experience. The local students have a different set of expectations and are less likely to be enthusiastic about virtual communities as standard fare. One way to balance these needs is to provide needed information in their own spaces twice. We will continue to explore others.

Third, we as a faculty will continue to educate ourselves in the issues surrounding distance education, through sharing thoughts and ideas, experiences, and tips gained on campus and in the real and virtual classroom. This process for ourselves reflects both our past experience and our awareness of the need to continually expand and improve our offerings. The students can expect no less of us; neither can we expect any less of ourselves.

REFERENCES

Blackboard corporate Web site, www.blackboard.net. Accessed September 15, 1999.

Bowker Annual. New York: R. R. Bowker, 1998.

EdNet, www.outreach.utk.edu/EdNet. Accessed September 15, 1999.

Schmidt, Peter. "State spending on higher education rises 6.7% in 1998–99 to a total of 52.8 billion." *Chronicle of Higher Education,* Nov. 27, 1998, pp. A26–A29.

U.S. Bureau of Economic Analysis. *Survey of Current Business.* 1998.

For further information, please visit the school's Web site at www.sis.utk.edu. Last accessed April 1, 2002.

26

❖•❖

DIMENSIONS OF STUDENTS' INTERACTIVE VIDEO-BASED DISTANCE LEARNING EXPERIENCES: A QUALITATIVE STUDY CONDUCTED AT TEXAS WOMAN'S UNIVERSITY

Patricia Jackson Edwards

INTRODUCTION

The increased availability of technology-facilitated distance learning courses is evident throughout the realm of higher education. The availability and rate of change in technology have a major impact on the popularity and cost-effectiveness of distance learning. Administratively, competition for student enrollment and generation of income are key factors contributing to the endorsement and promotion of distance learning courses. There is a push to extend beyond existing physical boundaries and reach a wider audience of students.

A variety of learning opportunities must be available in different formats to fulfill the continuous learning needs of our population. "The nation's most important educational goal must be to produce learners adequately prepared for life and work in the 21st century" (Glennan and Melmed 1996, xxiv). Employers will continue to escalate their requirements for new skills and competencies, and consumers will be looking for ways to maintain currency and improve their marketability.

The use of modern technological innovations allows us to span distances and cultures almost instantaneously. Students will be able to pursue educational opportunities with a high degree of independence. As higher education moves toward a more client-centered model of course delivery, institutions must examine the critical factors that are important to the success of their programs. One of the difficulties often faced by these institutions is obtaining a thorough understanding of their clients' individual needs. Personal factors such as background, learning styles, prior learning and experience, students' expectations, skill levels, and motivation may have a significant impact on the current distance learning experience (Eastmond 1995).

> In order for distance educators to develop programs which serve individual learners most effectively, the individual learner must be understood within his or her context. By context is meant the complex of situational factors—social, economic, psychological—which can positively or negatively affect the learning experience and how the individual creates meaning. (Granger 1990, 164)

Recent trends and development within the area of instructional technology have resulted in increased emphasis on instructional theories, cognitive psychology, learner interaction, instructional psychology, and instructional design (Silvey and Cochenour 1995). Educators and technology professionals recognize the importance of bridging learning theories and the behavioral sciences to promote the effective use of instructional technology. The development of a more theoretical foundation for how technology affects a learner's cognitive processes and maximizes learning processes is required. There is a need to get beyond simply understanding how to use a piece of equipment or how to troubleshoot technical difficulties. The equipment should become an integrated part of the educational delivery system.

Statement of the Problem

Although institutions are developing and offering courses utilizing distance learning technology, generally there are no special distinctions or prerequisites noted to prepare students for the new learning environment. The time frame allotted for teaching the course may not differ from conventional courses, and thus little time is committed to incorporate an adjustment period for students to become acclimated to this classroom environment. Much of the research to date has examined the use of new technologies for teaching and the effectiveness of distance learning programs and has been predominantly based on quantitative methodologies (Jeffries 1997). Typically, studies focus on instructional methods, dropout rates, and comparisons of delivery mechanisms. With academic priorities targeting social and economic factors of enrollment, questions regarding the human experience are often left untouched. There is limited research on the impact of technology on the outcome of a distance learning program (Westbrook 1997), and there is a scarcity of attitudinal research with regard to student satisfaction and distance learning (Biner et al. 1997; McHenry and Bozik 1997). Behavior and attitude, environmental factors, perceptions, emotional maturity, self-concept, acceptance of technology, and response to change all impact the distance learning experience. James (1993) confirms that individuals' attitudes toward technology "have been identified as important to a number of aspects of their levels and types of technological involvement" and "thus an understanding of processes involved in shaping attitudes toward technologies is important" (p. 57). Because the distance learning experience is an integration of multiple physical, behavioral, technical, and cognitive factors, a more holistic research approach is needed. Morgan (1984) wrote that "studies adopting qualitative methodologies are under-represented in distance education" (p. 255) and Minnis (1985) calls for qualitative approaches borrowed from sociology and anthropology to obtain meaningful cross-cultural or comparative perspectives. Thompson, Simonson, and Hargrave (1995) state that naturalistic research paradigms are needed to examine, qualitatively, the interactions between learners and the technology.

Significance of the Problem

There are a number of elements that can impact how an individual perceives and reports on his or her distance learning experience. Some of these are emotional state of the individual going into class based on what is going on in his or her personal life, emotional reactions to those who are present at the individual's location, emotional reactions to the instructor or the institution, attitude toward course content or subject matter, attitudes toward the technology in use or the processes aided by technology, and anxiety resulting from a lack of experience in this learning environment. All of these elements may contribute toward a preconceived attitude about the distance learning experience.

Purpose

This study was conducted to examine students' responses to interactive video–based distance learning technology at Texas Woman's University (Jackson 1999). Particular attention was given to how interaction among individuals and between the individuals and the technology impacted the distance learning experience. Recent research on learning in complex environments has emphasized the importance of understanding the influence of the environment in which learning takes place (Anderson and Garrison 1995). The instructor or facilitator in a distance learning environment has the power to influence participants' attitudes toward the technology in use (Cochenour and Rezabek 1995). Entwistle (1991) believes it is the students' perceptions of the learning environment that are important to the learning process. Fulton (1988, 48) estimates that about 75 percent of learning is accounted for by motivation, meaningfulness, and memory and that the remaining 25 percent of learning is dependent on the effect of the physical environment.

REVIEW OF THE LITERATURE

With academic priorities targeting social and economic factors of enrollment, questions regarding the human experience are often left untouched.

The ability to humanize or personalize the experience is important. Failure to recognize and address the human issues surrounding the use of technology may lead to negative distance education experiences (Cowan 1984; Daly 1991; Moore and Kearsley 1996; Nickerson and Zodhiates 1988; Ostendorf 1994).

Perhaps the greatest threat of technology in this information age is that it continually asks us to give up our uniquely human nature, that part that telecommunications cannot replicate. One student told me that the harm in not receiving face-to-face feedback—nods, sighs, animation, interruption, and body language—is not in our inability to know whether the other person understood the content of our message. Instead, because that expression is missing, we fail to learn vital information about ourselves—how likable, persuasive, helpful, cogent, sympathetic, articulate, convincing we are—in ways that reinforce our own view of self-worth. By expressing our views to others, we learn about ourselves. Delaying or eliminating that information in our communications reduces us on a personal level. (Eastmond 1995, 182)

Technology as a Delivery Mechanism

Technological innovation often introduces change into an existing environment. Change has been described as "the ultimate stressor," although its effects can be either positive or negative (Nelson and Kletke 1990). Stress involves the interaction of the individual with his or her environment. Stressors are the objects, events, or situations that are perceived by individuals as disruptive. Humans exhibit a natural reaction to stressors that has sometimes been referred to as the "fight or flight response" (Nelson and Kletke 1990). Typically, the common stress response of individuals to technology is linked to the ideas of fear and loss of control and may be exhibited as resistance or reluctance to adopt technological innovation. Successful application of technology in an educational setting is dependent on a good implementation strategy (Glennan and Melmed 1996).

Many educational technologists believe that distance education is "inexorably linked to the technology" (Garrison 1987) and is therefore different from other forms of education. The emphasis on modes of delivery and physical barriers may contribute toward difficulties with course development and design as well as reluctance of faculty and students to accept this mode of education. On the other hand, equipment reliability, camera placement, and instructor and student behavior can also affect the success of a distance learning experience (Cowan 1984; Moore and Kearsley 1996). Misunderstandings and unrealistic expectations can often lead to academic difficulties and dissatisfaction with the educational experience. How individuals respond to the technology affects the outcome of the experience. The ability to humanize or personalize the experience is important. Failure to recognize and address the human issues surrounding the use of technology may lead to negative distance education experiences (Cowan 1984; Daly 1991; Moore and Kearsley 1996; Nickerson and Zodhiates 1988; Ostendorf 1994).

Environmental Variables

Each distance learning setting brings with it unique dynamics that either add to or distract from the communication process (Cowan 1984; Eastmond 1995; Glennan and Melmed 1996; Moore and Kearsley 1996). It is generally acknowledged that the physical environment has an effect on the learning process (Fulton 1988; Hayward 1994; Niece 1988). Sommer (1969) claims that "the distribution of students within the room represents an accommodation to their environment that goes on to influence subsequent behavior" (p. 110). Size of the learning group may affect the interaction between and among instructors and students. Physical surroundings, furnishings, and layout impact the classroom environment. Poorly planned seating arrangements and room design can have a negative impact on interpersonal communication patterns. Individuals' reactions to particular settings may be reflective of the effects of elements, such as formality or informality of settings or familiarity or strangeness of situations (Altman 1975).

Environmental psychologists recognize that the environment surrounding an individual affects his or her behavior. Research studies in this area often investigate the effects of physical settings on various aspects of behavior (Krasner 1980). The reciprocal interaction between the person and the environment are important factors to consider when investigating environmental influences on human behavior.

Determinants of Behavior

An individual's behavior is guided by the goals he or she seeks as well as by the way he or she reads, interprets, or imagines his or her environment. The interpretation and meaning applied to an individual's environment is based on how the environment is perceived (Proshansky, Ittelson, and Rivlin 1972). Perception aids in clarifying environmental elements. It depends upon memory or past stimulation; in other words the past lays a foundation for current perceptions (Gibson 1950). When elements are considered unknown to an individual, they may become barriers to the interactive process. Perception can supply the understanding needed by an individual to overcome these barriers. Occasionally, something may interfere with an individual's perceptual activity, thereby impacting the interactive process as well.

Communication Processes

Individuals' responses to situations are influenced by other people and by the elements of their own personal experiences. All participants in a communication event use communication processes to attain their goals and to fulfill their individual needs. In a speech-communication event, each person relates what is happening to his or her own frame of reference and experiences. It is possible, however, that an individual's goals will include the satisfaction of others' goals and needs. When this happens, more sharing between individuals can occur. A speech-communication event between individuals cannot occur unless there is some form of relationship between them (Keltner 1973).

Differences in spoken language and the meanings of words can impede interpersonal dialog. Factors such as regional dialects will influence the communication process. Individuals who share a common native language are more likely to interact together. This may also be said of shared cultural norms and experiences (Hall 1959, 1966; Suchman 1987). In his research, Hall (1996) states that "man and his environment participate in molding each other" (p. 4).

The ability to see what someone else looks like assists the communication process. Providing a visual image of others and their physical environment often decreases anxiety levels. Making an effort to exchange personal information and sharing those human qualities that set us apart from each other help increase familiarity and opens the door to further interaction (Cowan 1984).

Some researchers have found that particular emotional elements and attitudes are directly linked to specific body movements and body orientation. The actual manner of physical movement may relay significant information. For example, relaxation may be exhibited through reclining and sideways leaning angles. Ekman (1965) suggests that the head and face area carry information about the affect being experienced, such as anger and joy, whereas the body cues communicate information about the intensity of the affective experience. In his study of posture and position cues, Ekman found that although some affect information may be communicated through body cues, they are infrequent and difficult for observers to perceive. Specifically, Ekman says that facial expressions and body movements of some duration communicate specific emotional states, whereas body position and head orientations usually communicate only general affective states and not specific emotions. He further states that body acts can show moderate to high intensity of emotion, and body positions portray a full range of intensity cues. Similarly, Hall (1959) states that "what people do is frequently more important than what they say" (p. 24). Hall explains that people are constantly communicating their real feelings through what he calls their "silent language" or "the language of behavior" (p. 15).

Nonverbal communication typically includes gestures, movements of the body, limbs, hands, head, feet, facial expressions, eye behavior, and posture. Some nonverbal cues have a direct verbal translation and in fact may be used to substitute verbal messages. Diekman (1982) says that the actual meanings of most messages do not reside in words but in the nonverbal packaging that surrounds the words. Nonverbal behavior may also be tied directly to or accompany speech and can modify or elaborate on verbal messages (Keltner 1973; Knapp 1972; Mehrabian 1972). In some instances, nonverbal behavior has a regulatory effect. Changes in posture, eye contact, or position may indicate that an individual is about to make a new point, is assuming an attitude regarding several points being communicated, or that he or she wants to remove him- or herself from the communication event (Mehrabian 1972). Spontaneous and automatic responses are often evoked without thinking.

Nonverbal communication cues may be very specific or general. Some cues are delivered with the intent to communicate something, whereas other cues are expressions of information or emotions. Facial expressions are the primary means for communicating emotional states.

METHODOLOGY

Three graduate courses offered at Texas Woman's University were selected for observation using qualitative research methodology. The participant observation method, survey questionnaires, and informal, unstructured interviews were used for data collection. The courses were from two different academic disciplines and were taught by three different instructors. All classes were offered from the same originating location; there were two different connecting remote sites. Subjects were students enrolled in the three courses. A total of fifty-five students participated in the study.

Field observation for the three courses took place in the same classroom during the summer and fall semesters 1997. The interactive videoconference system at Texas Woman's University (TWU) is a two-way, fully interactive educational delivery system linking the main campus in Denton, Texas, to its three satellite campuses located in Dallas and Houston. The system utilizes full motion compressed video to transmit. It requires digital phone lines and a codec (compression decoder) at each location. A telecommunications network provides two-way audio and video interaction between and among all sites. Additionally, TWU is connected to the Texas Education Telecommunications Network and the Trans-Texas Videoconference Network networks, allowing access to a number of other educational institutions throughout the state.

The classroom used for observation is equipped with an instructor podium, an instructor PC workstation with Internet access, an ELMO display device for document and three-dimensional object display, VCR, fax machine, telephone, two cameras, and three thirty-seven-inch television monitors.

The most prominent piece of equipment is the video monitor. The room in which all classes met has two monitors located adjacent to the instructor podium at the front of the classroom and another monitor located on the left side of the classroom across from the instructor's podium. On one of the monitors in the front of the class, it is possible to see an image of the instructor, object, or document from the display device, an image from the computer workstation, or the local classroom. In summary, this monitor serves to provide outgoing images or display graphics. On the second monitor, it is possible to see the remote site or the incoming picture. The third monitor also shows the remote site and is the one facing the instructor so that he or she may have visual contact with the students at that location from his or her position at the podium.

FINDINGS

The data analysis process and integration of synthesized data resulted in a theoretical model depicting the dimensions of students' responses to interactive video–based distance learning technology. The local students' distance learning experience can best be described in terms of multiple dimensions. The interactivity of these dimensions is constant and dynamic. The interplay between and among the various elements of these dimensions defines the local students' total experience.

Dimension I: The Local Students' Physical Setting and Interaction Events

There is an exchange process between and among elements within the local students' physical setting that results in interaction events. Fellow students, the instructor, the technology, the environment, and the situation each represents an element of interaction found within the local students' physical setting. These elements may generate, alter, or influence behavior and communication patterns and are interactive as well as reactive. The process of interaction between and among these elements with the local student is constant and may be repetitive, simultaneous, or cyclical (see Figure 26.1). The relationship between the local student and these elements help define and shape the local students' responses to distance learning technology.

Observation: The instructor hears a background sound but not realizing what it was, tries to respond to the remote student. As she begins to respond she realizes that it is an echo. She asks the remote students if they are also experiencing an echo problem. They say no, but that the sound keeps cutting in and out.

Instructor: Oh, well. We can't do anything about the cutting in and out.

This brief exchange between the instructor and a remote student demonstrates the input received by the local student regarding audio transmission. The local student receives information from at least three elements: the audio experience or the situation itself, the remote students' input, and the instruc-

Figure 26.1
The Local Student's Physical Setting and Interaction Events

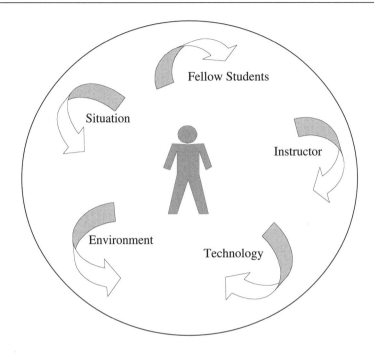

tor's response. As a result of this interaction event, the local student is aware that there are at least two different audio problems present and that the instructor feels one of them cannot be resolved. Whether this is an accurate assessment of the technical problem is not relevant. What is relevant is that the local student will now develop a series of responses regarding audio problems that will become a part of her current distance learning experience and may affect her future experiences. Similar interaction events can occur between and among the other elements within this physical setting. They may involve all, some, or only one of the elements at any given point in time.

Dimension 2: Local Students' Attitudes Toward Remote Students

Local students' attitudes toward the remote students may be defined by and/or shape the local students' interaction events. Findings from the research data of this study resulted in the identification of the primary attitude conditions that local students displayed toward the remote students (see Figure 26.2). They are the attitudes of friendliness, sympathy, detachment, and resentment. These attitude conditions may exist alone, overlap, or be in a state of flux and are affected by the elements of interaction the local student expe-

Figure 26.2
Local Students' Attitudes Toward Remote Students

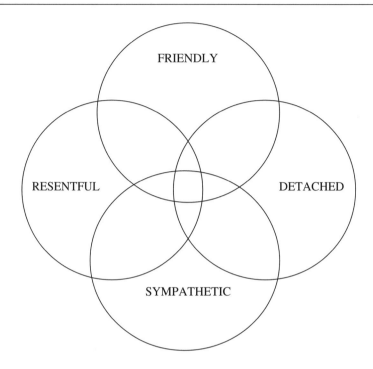

riences. Additionally, they encompass other feelings as well. Friendliness and sympathy imply an open attitude toward remote students and a positive awareness of their presence. Thoughts and gestures of caring or concern may express this attitude. In contrast, detachment and resentment imply a closed attitude toward remote students and a negative awareness of their presence. Thoughts and gestures of anger or aloofness may express this attitude.

Typically, the relationship between the local student and the remote student does not reach a depth that allows a true connection with the individual. Rather, the relationship is more general in nature and is descriptive of the remote students as a group. To move beyond the relationship level representative of the group requires the removal of distance barriers that inhibit the communication process.

Often, as individuals are first introduced to one another, the feelings and attitudes they have toward one another are not very deep. It is only through the process of developing relationships and bonding that individuals begin to get to know each other. Physical and psychological barriers must be overcome for effective communication to take place (Keltner 1973).

Current technology enables communication events to occur even across physical distances. However, the psychological distance between individuals is a more complex matter. Keltner says that there is a psychic distance between people that prevents them from communicating with one another. Breaking through the barriers of this psychic distance requires willingness and an effort from all parties to initiate and maintain communication. Keeping the barriers away requires "unlocking of the self" and "revealing the self" to others (Keltner 1973, 59).

Even with the technological communications capabilities available within the interactive video–based distance learning environment, it is extremely difficult to overcome the psychological distance between the local students and the remote students. In some cases students are able to break through the psychological distance barriers. The observations from this study confirm, however, that this is not the norm. Typically, students will develop relationships with the students around them, within their own physical setting. Although communication between settings does occur, it is at a level that rarely becomes personal. The physical settings that represent the groups of students tend to overshadow the individual students thereby creating a sense of "them." The use of the phrases "remote students" and "local students" are representative of this categorization.

As local students become involved in different situations in their distance learning environments, their attitudes toward the remote students may undergo change. The local students' awareness of the remote student shifts continually throughout the distance learning experience.

The following brief exchange is an example of one local student's friendly attitude of concern for the remote students.

Observation: During class the instructor was lecturing but had forgotten to put herself on camera. A local student called out to her to switch the image. After class the instructor asked the student, "Why do you want me to change the camera to me?"

Local Student 1: For the Canyon students. They hear your voice but they see us and it's distracting.

These students are clearly pleased about having the remote students present.

Local Student 2: The concept is neat—classmates many miles away learning with me!

Local Student 3: It was nice to get to meet those other ladies. It was like getting extra classmates.

In contrast, these students are unhappy and express resentment toward the remote students.

Local Student 1: There's another negative. I felt like the distance learning class of three kept the entire group from going to the lab when appropriate.

Local Student 2: Having two students remote disrupts the flow of the Denton class, I feel that the teacher is unable to fully connect to us because "they" are watching.

Local Student 3: The other classroom distracts also. I believe there should only be one camera in the room, focused on the instructor. Why do the two classes need to see each other? We can each see our own class, which is the norm.

These students share their experiences of mixed feelings of detachment and sympathy.

Local Student 1: For this class, I often felt disconnected from them. I would really feel bad when they would have to keep repeating themselves, or eventually just give up.... Even with e-mail, which technically would provide equal access to all students, whenever I had a question about something, I would email people I knew from the home site. The two sites just don't interact or become involved with each other like the individuals do at one site or the other.

Local Student 2: I'm pretty much indifferent to them. Just sort of tolerate their presence and feel sorry for their educational situation and the circumstances under which they have to have class.

Local Student 3: I often forgot about the students in Canyon and I'm sure others in the class did, too. This is rather sad, forgetting and thus ignoring the other classmates because they were not physically present.

Dimension 3: Stages of Local Students' Responses to Distance Learning Technology

As local students encounter the various technology components within the distance learning experience, they are exposed to a multitude of stimuli that can be categorized into stages. As students pass through these stages they are ultimately led to a point where they define their responses to distance learning technology (see Figure 26.3). These stages contain components that are both stable and dynamic. Students may go through these stages repeatedly throughout their distance learning experience.

The development of local students' responses to the distance learning technology begins with their expectations. Initially the local students bring with them an expectation of their experience with distance learning technology. These expectations may be a result of their own previous experiences or the experiences of others. They may be realistic, or they may not. Even students who say they have no expectations are indicating that there is indeed an expectation of "no effect." The levels and types of expectations the students have will affect them as they enter the next stage of their experience.

Here are examples of two local students' expectations based on previous experiences. The first student's experience leans toward the positive side; the second student's experience is a little more negative. It is important to note that the outcome of their expectation is reported here as part of their

Figure 26.3
Stages of Local Students' Responses to Distance Learning Technology

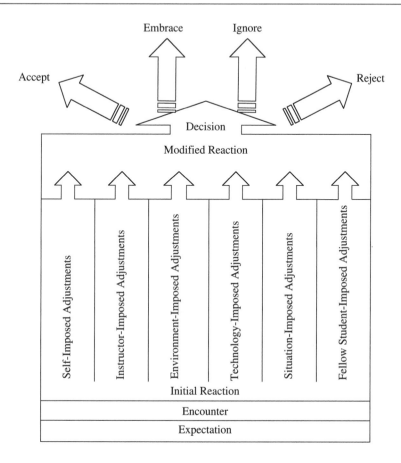

response; however, their perception of the outcome is only available because the students provided feedback at the end of their distance learning experience.

Local Student 1: Better than expected. There were not as many technical difficulties as the last class I took.

Local Student 2: It was about the same as I expected—I have yet to have a professor who has mastered the distance learning technology.

The following response from a local student not only describes her recent experience, but demonstrates the impact of this experience on her future plans.

Local Student: I feel horrible about my experience—hoped to never have to take another telecourse! It was much worse than I expected.

Local students enter the encounter stage at the point where they first experience distance learning technology. It is the time when the local students discover the reality or nonreality of their expectations. In this stage they are receiving stimuli that might support or contradict their expectations.

This local student's comments demonstrate the process of going through the expectation stage and entering the encounter stage.

Local Student: Based upon previous experience with distance learning, I was optimistic the class management and content would be well presented; however, that was not the experience.

Local students experience an initial reaction after their first encounter with the distance learning technology. The initial reaction is an immediate response to the encounter with the technology and may or may not be a true indicator of how the local student will ultimately respond. Typically, the reaction at this level is founded on a particular event or incident and its impact. The reaction will most likely be somewhat superficial until the student has an opportunity to further explore his or her experience.

Responses indicating initial reactions were typically brief.

Local Student 1: Interesting.

Local Student 2: Intrigued.

Local Student 3: Technology is an amazing thing.

Moving through the initial reaction stage the local students will enter a realm of six potential stages that will affect their responses to distance learning technology. These six stages are (1) self-imposed adjustments, (2) instructor-imposed adjustments, (3) technology-imposed adjustments, (4) situation-imposed adjustments, (5) environment-imposed adjustments, and (6) fellow student–imposed adjustments.

As the local student moves beyond the initial reaction stage, a series of events may take place to alter his or her responses to the distance learning technology. An incident with the use of the technology may result in the student modifying his or her initial reaction. Some students' experiences and perceptions of need fulfillment may cause them to self-impose adjustments in the way they respond to the distance learning technology. In the same manner, adjustments may be imposed on students by the instructor, the technology itself, the situation, the environment, and fellow students. These stages may be experienced in any order and may be reiterative. Depending on the experiences encountered in the distance learning environment, some stages may last longer than others. Some stages may not be experienced at all.

The following local student's comments imply the various stages she went through in her experience with the distance learning technology. She appears to have gone through the instructor-, technology-, situation-, environment-, and fellow student–imposed adjustment stages. It is impossible to confirm the involvement of other stages from these data alone.

Local Student: It's hard to do a presentation or group work. You have to learn the technology and do the presentation and reach both audiences.

After one, all, or some of the imposed adjustment stages have been experienced, the student enters the modified reaction stage. This stage represents a transition from the initial reaction stage that was altered by various imposed adjustments. These adjustments can produce positive or negative effects. The modified reaction represents a change in the students' feelings toward the distance learning technology.

This student expresses a modified reaction in her comment:

Local Student: When everything works well, it has been a good learning experience.

The final stage that local students experience is the stage of decision. This stage results in outcomes that define the students' responses to the distance learning technology. James (1993) reports that results from other research studies indicate that psychological reactions influence individuals' appreciation of, willingness to become involved with, and ability to master modern technologies. More specifically, James states that the theory of reasoned action is applicable to the study of psychological reactions. He explains that this theory indicates that attitudes are determined by the combination of beliefs about the characteristics or outcomes associated with a target and the value placed on those characteristics or outcomes. He further states that the values associated with characteristics or outcomes depend on perceptions of the good or ill they would yield for an individual. The data from this research study confirms James's assertions. Students' outcome decisions toward the distance learning technology are the combined result of their total distance learning experience.

Local students will define their responses to the distance learning technology after they have come through the previous stages outlined. Based on their "travels" through the various stages, the local students will make outcome decisions to (1) accept the technology, (2) embrace the technology, (3) ignore the technology, or (4) reject the technology.

Acceptance of the technology implies that the student has acknowledged its presence and uses the technology as required. The students' behavior will exhibit both negative and positive reactions, but the intent to cope and adjust will prevail.

Students who embraced the technology exhibited a desire to use the technology, were pleased with the concept of delivering education to other locations, were interested in new learning opportunities, and offered assistance to fellow students and the instructor. Some students even expressed a desire to facilitate the development of new distance learning programs and partnerships.

Local Student 1: I truly believe distance learning is going to be the best innovation to come along in a while. I live in a rural area and would love to take advantage of such a situation.

Local Student 2: I feel distance learning is the next generation in higher education. Nothing about the experience bothered me. I would hope we would not give up on distance learning, but rather extend it. With picture telephone coming of age I see a bright and interesting future for this type of instruction.

Local Student 3: Jefferson's isolation and need for continuing education has excited me to become involved to make it happen. I would love to get assistance to establish the TWU distance learning experience in Jefferson, TX at Cypress Valley Alliance.

Students who chose to ignore the technology worked to pretend it was not there. These students would avoid looking at the monitor, were inclined to participate less in class, and tried to sit or position themselves so the camera could not focus on them. They often found the technology intrusive.

Local Student 1: It hinders my ability to participate in class because I'm self-conscious about being on TV.

Local Student 2: As for the technology, I just try and ignore it, but that's not always easy.

Local Student 3: I didn't like seeing myself in the other screen. I've learned not to look.

For the purpose of this study, rejection of the technology refers to those efforts the students made to separate themselves from it. In this case, rejection is a self-imposed method of isolation. Students moving or covering microphones, changing their seating choices, and physically moving out of camera range are examples of technology rejection. The following two comments imply rejection of future experiences with distance learning technology. One local student's comment in response to the question of what she would like to change about the technology was, "Not have distance learning!" Another student responded, "I would not take a distance learning class again if given a choice."

The students who reject the distance learning technology do so because they become overwhelmed with their reactions to the technology. They are unable to become comfortable or their threshold of tolerance is exceeded, thus forcing them to withdraw from it. Feelings precipitating this rejection often include intimidation, hostility, frustration, and self-consciousness.

Dimensions of a Local Student's Distance Learning Experience

This study found that local students' responses to distance learning technology are defined within the context of the local students' distance learning experience. Responses to the individual technologies may differ across students, environments, and situations, but the processes leading to responses remain consistent.

The dimensions within the local students' distance learning experience contain the interaction events, the attitudes toward remote students, and the stages of response to technology. Each dimension contributes to the whole distance learning experience for the local student. The following theoretical model identifies the elements that exist within a local student's distance learning experience. This model may also be used to trace the process of local students' distance learning experiences.

All of the elements that make up the students' distance learning experiences are interactive and affect one another. The interplay between the dimension of interaction and the dimension of attitudes (as well as the interplay between the dimension of interaction and the dimension of responses to the distance learning technology) take place within the system of the local student's distance learning experience. A change in one dimension affects another dimension as well as the student's total experience. An examination of this entire interrelation depicts the "wholeness" of the local student's distance learning experience (see Figure 26.4).

CONCLUSION

The purpose of this study was to examine students' responses to the interactive video–based distance learning technology. Examination of the patterns and processes that emerged resulted in the development of a model depicting the dimensions of students' distance learning experiences. Although the model represents what takes place within the environments studied, it only reflects the dimensions involved in the students' relationship to the distance learning technology. No attempt was made to examine the complete role of the instructor or the remote students or the students' actual learning processes and experiences. This study confirms that the students' responses to the distance learning technology is an intricately woven series of interactions between the environment, the situation, fellow students, the instructor, and the technology. These interactions represent the "wholeness" of the students' experiences. These experiences may be defined as the end result of the interactions between and among the various dimensions identified.

To help ensure the success of an interactive video–based distance experience, it is important to acknowledge the needs and attitudes of the students entering into the experience and develop means to provide positive support

Figure 26.4
Dimensions of a Local Student's Distance Learning Experience

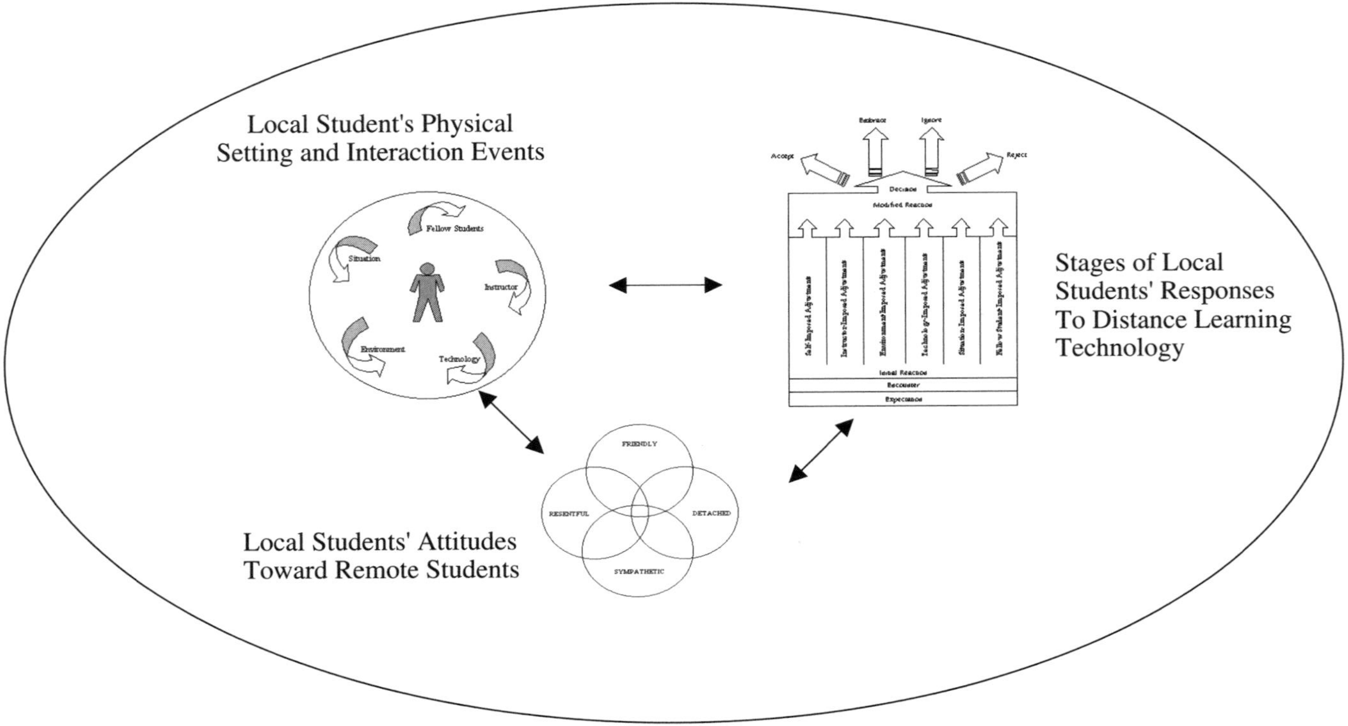

Local Student's Physical
Setting and Interaction Events

Stages of Local
Students' Responses
To Distance Learning
Technology

Local Students' Attitudes
Toward Remote Students

mechanisms. Individuals responsible for the instructional delivery of the distance learning experience must be proactive and engage students through the encounter process with the technology. New experiences can be frightening and overwhelming to some students, and they need adequate information, opportunities for exploration, and time to adjust. A planned approach in support of the students' discovery process can help ensure that the experience is positive and that negative incidents do not overtake the students' overall perceptions of their experiences.

The interaction between and among the instructor, the fellow students, the environment, and the situation affect how a student feels toward the remote student and also help shape the technology encounter process. The interaction process is an important part of the evolution of students' responses to their distance learning experience.

REFERENCES

Altman, Irwin. 1975. *The environment and social behavior: Privacy, personal space, territory, crowding.* Monterey: Brooks/Cole.

Anderson, Terry D., and D. Randy Garrison. 1995. "Transactional issues in distance education: The impact of design in audioteleconferencing." *American Journal of Distance Education* 9 (2): 27–45.

Biner, Paul M., Kimberly D. Welsch, Natalie M. Barone, Marcia Summers, and Raymond S. Dean. 1997. "The impact of remote-site group size on student satisfaction and relative performance in interactive telecourses." *American Journal of Distance Education* 11 (1): 23–33.

Cochenour, John J., and Landra L. Rezabek. 1995. "Distance education: A framework for compressed video." In *Compressed video for instruction: Operations and applications,* eds. Barbara T. Hakes, John J. Cochenour, Landra L. Rezabek, and Steven G. Sachs, 1–10. Washington, DC: Association for Educational Communications and Technology.

Cowan, Robert A. 1984. *Teleconferencing: Maximizing human potential.* Reston, VA: Reston Publishing.

Daly, Edward A. 1991. *We've got to start meeting like this: A primer on video conferencing.* Atlanta: KJH Communications.

Diekman, John R. 1982. *Human connections: How to make communication work.* Englewood Cliffs: Prentice-Hall.

Eastmond, Daniel V. 1995. *Alone but together: Adult distance study through computer conferencing.* Creskill, NJ: Hampton Press.

Ekman, P. 1965. "Differential communication of affect by head and body cues." *Journal of Personality and Social Psychology* (2): 726–35, cited in Mark L. Knapp, *Nonverbal communication in human interaction* (New York: Holt, Rinehart and Winston, 1972), 102.

Entwistle, Noel. 1991. "Approaches to learning and perceptions of the learning environment." *Higher Education* 22: 201–204.

Fulton, R. 1988. "The physical environment in adult learning." *Adult Literacy and Business Education* 12: 48–55.

Garrison. D. Randy. 1987. "The role of technology in distance education." *New Directions for Continuing Education* 36: 41–53.

Gibson, James J. 1950. *The perception of the visual world.* Boston: Houghton Mifflin.

Glennan, Thomas K., and Arthur Melmed. 1996. *Fostering the use of educational technology: Elements of a national strategy.* Santa Monica, CA: Rand.

Granger, D. 1990. "Bridging distances to the individual learner." In *Contemporary issues in American distance education,* ed. M. G. Moore, 163–171. New York: Pergamon Press, quoted in Daniel V. Eastmond. *Alone but together: Adult distance study through computer conferencing* (Creskill, NJ: Hampton Press, 1995), 58.

Hall, Edward T. 1966. *The hidden dimension.* Garden City, New York: Doubleday.

Hall, Edward T. 1959. *The silent language.* Garden City, New York: Doubleday.

Hayward, Pamela A. 1994. "When novelty isn't enough: A case study of students' reactions to technology in the classroom." *College Student Journal* 28 (3): 320–325.

Jackson, Patricia A. 1999. *Dimensions of the local students' interactive video-based distance learning experience: A qualitative study.* PhD diss., Texas Woman's University.

James, Keith. 1993. "Enhancing the perceived self-relevance of technology to influence attitudes and information retention." *Journal of Applied Behavioral Science* 29 (1): 56–75.

Jeffries, Michael. "Research in distance education." Online document available at www.ind.net/IPSE/fdhandbook/resrch.html. Accessed on September 24, 1997.

Keltner, John W. 1973. *Elements of interpersonal communication.* Belmont, CA: Wadsworth.

Knapp, Mark L. 1972. *Nonverbal communication in human interaction.* New York: Holt, Rinehart and Winston.

Krasner, Leonard, ed. 1980. *Environmental design and human behavior: A psychology of the individual in society.* New York: Pergamon Press.

McHenry, Lynnea, and Mary Bozik. 1997. "From a distance: Student voices from the Interactive video classroom." *Techtrends* 42(6): 20–24.

Mehrabian, Albert. 1972. *Nonverbal communication.* Chicago: Aldine.

Minnis, John R. 1985. "Ethnography, case study, grounded theory, and distance education research." *Distance Education* 3 (2): 1–6.

Moore, Michael G., and Greg Kearsley. 1996. *Distance education: A systems view.* Belmont, CA: Wadsworth.

Morgan, Alistair. 1984. "A report on qualitative methodologies in research in distance education." *Distance Education* 5 (2): 252–267.

Nelson, Debra L., and Marilyn G. Kletke. 1990. "Individual adjustment during technological innovation: A research framework." *Behaviour and Information Technology* 9 (4): 257–271.

Nickerson, Raymond S., and Philip P. Zodhiates, eds. 1988. *Technology in education: Looking toward 2020.* Hillsdale, NJ: Lawrence Erlbaum Associates.

Niece, Richard. 1988. "The impact of environment on teaching." *NASSP Bulletin* 72: 79–81.

Ostendorf, Virginia A. 1994. *The two-way video classroom.* Littleton, CO: Virginia A. Ostendorf.

Proshansky, Harold M., William H. Ittelson, and Leanne G. Rivlin. 1972. "Freedom of choice and behavior in a physical setting." In *Environment and the social sciences: Perspectives and applications,* ed. Joachim F. Wohlwill and Daniel H. Carson (Washington, DC: American Psychological Association), 29–43.

Silvey, Lawrence, and John J. Cochenour. 1995. "Distance education: A framework for compressed video." In *Compressed video for instruction: Operations and applications,* eds. Barbara T. Hakes, John J. Cochenour, Landra L. Rezabek and Steven G. Sachs (Washington, DC: Association for Educational Communications and Technology), 23–36.

Sommer, Robert. 1969. *Personal space: The behavioral basis of design.* Englewood Cliffs, NJ: Prentice-Hall.

Suchman, Lucy A. 1987. *Plans and situated actions: The problem of human-machine Communication.* New York: Cambridge University Press.

Thompson, Ann D., Michael R. Simonson, and Constance P. Hargrave. 1995. "Educational technology: A review of the research." In *An in-depth analysis of presentation styles, information technology usage, questioning strategies, and teacher and student evaluations in interactive telecourses,* Ted C. Jones. Ph.D. diss., University of Alabama, 6.

Westbrook, Thomas S. 1997. "Changes in students' attitudes toward graduate business instruction via interactive television." *American Journal of Distance Education* 11 (1): 55–69.

27

DISTANCE EDUCATION AT THE UNIVERSITY OF WISCONSIN–MADISON SCHOOL OF LIBRARY AND INFORMATION STUDIES

Jane Pearlmutter

As the University of Wisconsin (UW) celebrated its sesquicentennial in 1999, one topic that was discussed in official papers and public speeches was reinventing the Wisconsin Idea. Developed a century ago, the Wisconsin Idea proclaimed that "the boundaries of the university are the boundaries of the state"—the inspiring notion that the resources of a great state university should be applied to the needs of the state and its citizens. Although originally applied to agriculture, the Wisconsin Idea was behind the formation of UW-Extension and its expansion to programs, services, and continuing education in numerous disciplines. In 1921, the Wisconsin Teachers Association announced that 700 teachers lacked minimum requirements in subject matter and methods. In response to the association's concerns, extension correspondence courses were expanded to provide a variety of teacher education courses, including training for school librarians. Out of this background the distance education program in library science began in the 1960s under the direction of Muriel Fuller, who held a joint appointment in Extension and in the UW Library School. Originally housed in an interdisciplinary Extension department, the library continuing education program was transferred to the School of Library and Information Studies at UW–Madison in 1987.

From 1968 to 2002 the program included offerings via the Educational Teleconference Network (originally the Educational Telephone Network)—ETN. ETN sites existed in each county in Wisconsin, now primarily in county courthouses. At its peak there were many more sites: in hospitals, UW campuses, county extension offices, and in eleven public libraries around the state. Sites rarely gave exclusive space to ETN, however; they usually consisted of a room that could be quickly set up with a few chairs, a speaker, connection box, and microphones for the participants. This dedicated audio-only telephone network seems very low-tech today, but that also meant relatively low-cost—an important consideration for its clientele. Bridging capability at the main studio on campus also meant that guest speakers could be connected from outside the network, from phones anywhere in the world for the price of the phone call.

Almost all of the courses have been noncredit, but an occasional graduate course from the Library School/SLIS has been offered. The primary audience was public library staff (mostly in small communities) and school librarians. In the 1970s credit and noncredit courses on Medical Librarianship and Basic Library Management for Health Science Librarians were also given, as were programs for library trustees.

For over twenty-five years, public librarians were offered a monthly series called at first Continuing Education for Public Libraries, later called Timely Topics for Small Public Libraries. The sessions provided not only the means to convey new information on a variety of library issues but also a way for librarians in small towns, who often worked alone, to share experiences, tips, and questions. From the mid-1970s through the 1990s, twelve to twenty programs for librarians were offered each year on ETN. When Darlene Weingand became director of continuing education in 1982, she initiated a period of considerable growth in programming.

The small-town librarians served by these courses rarely had any formal library education, so in cooperation with the state Department of Public Instruction, the course Basic Library Management for Public Libraries was developed. Prior to 1968 the course was taught in regular classes, but in various locations whenever there were enough students in the area to meet extension enrollment requirements. In 1968 the decision was made to try this course on ETN so students would have access within their county each year. The course was still given through 2001 on ETN and now continues in a correspondence format.

In 1971, certification for public librarians became mandatory. Different grades of certification are required for different sizes of communities, and only the highest grade requires an MLS. The other grades do have varying educational requirements, including the basic Library Management class for Grade 3 and four core courses in library science (Reference, Cataloging, Collection Development, and Administration) for grade 2. All these courses were offered regularly on ETN.

In the 1980s UW–Extension also tried visuals on the telephone network, in a format called SEEN. Although a visual medium, SEEN pictures transmitted slowly and were more like a slide show than a full-motion video. With far fewer sites than ETN and a format that seemed primitive to a generation used to TV, SEEN was used sparingly by the library science program and was eventually discontinued by Extension. Compressed video technology seemed more promising, but was again limited to fewer sites around the state, so it has been used only infrequently for library classes.

By the mid-1990s, ETN programming by the library continuing education program was decreasing. Fewer sites in the state (the public library sites long since discontinued), a decrease in state support for continuing education, the demand for UW programming outside of Wisconsin, and other options in distance education were all contributing factors. In a decade of self-support (the UW continuing education programs operate on a cost-recovery basis) and increased programming, ETN revenues declined from 26.3 percent of the SLIS continuing education budget in 1991 to 3.3 percent in 2001–2. Meanwhile, in this period, correspondence course versions of several of the core certification courses were developed. These courses have featured taped lectures, textbooks, workbooks, and written discussion questions that are submitted to the instructor by mail. Many librarians from outside Wisconsin have enrolled in the correspondence courses, but they also appeal to those who cannot get to ETN sites to work on state certification because of distance or scheduling.

At the same time—1995—the continuing education services unit (now called SLIS/CES) began to look into online options for distance education. Two surveys were done to assess the clientele's distance education needs and interests. One survey was sent to students in the correspondence courses, asking primarily if they would prefer the existing cassette and workbook format or an online course. Sixty percent indicated that they preferred the existing format, and 40 percent were interested in online courses. Almost all of the respondents had Internet access at work, but most did not have it at home—the cost cited as a continuing problem in rural areas—and finding sufficient time at work for an online course was considered difficult by most respondents. Others indicated that they preferred cassettes because they could listen at home, at work, in a car, or even outdoors. Different learning styles were also mentioned. Some preferred cassettes because they felt they learned better by listening than reading; others thought they learned visually and were therefore interested in certain online formats. The response indicated a need to continue to update and offer traditional correspondence courses while beginning to develop new formats.

The second survey was conducted in 1996 in preparation for a grant-funded project to deliver library continuing education via the Internet. Continuing education coordinators at Wisconsin's seventeen library systems were interviewed by phone and asked about the current state of Internet access in their system's libraries and about possible course topics and levels. Various formats were also described (asynchronous with unlimited time; asynchronous but paced; or real-time/chat function) and participants were asked for their preference. The results from this small survey group were considered along with evaluation of other distance education programs and examination of various courseware options.

The grant proposal that was developed from this needs assessment stated:

The SLIS/CES Strategic plan specifically targets "courses...designed to assist library workers to become both comfortable and competent with new technologies as they emerge....As the UW Regents target distance education as the top priority for the next biennium, it becomes politically imperative—as well as critical for meeting client needs—to be able to offer continuing professional education via technological delivery systems. Further, the need for affordability is a foundation block to which SLIS/CES must pay attention.... The major outcomes desired are the improvement of learning and the extension of existing curriculum, efficiency of costs, sharing of resources and technical expertise, and access to materials not otherwise available due to the economic or geographic isolation of the student. Electronic classrooms focused on educational goals should make possible greater contact and sharing among students who can be anywhere in the world."

The course development grant, funded by a UW–Extension Curriculum and Program Development Initiative, was awarded to Jane Pearlmutter (currently director of SLIS/ CES) and began in fall 1997. Although some UW departments were looking to convert existing print-based correspondence courses to an online format, Pearlmutter chose to develop an entirely new course, Virtual Collection Development, as a topic that could make particularly good use of the medium.

An asynchronous paced format was chosen. The asynchronous model would provide flexibility for students who would be able to connect at any time of day, but pacing the course would give it structure and a time frame for the students' discussions and assignments. UW–Extension requested that grantees use LearningSpace courseware, which they were supporting. LearningSpace is a Lotus Notes–based courseware that can be delivered via the Web through a Domino server. It offers five databases to support the content delivery: a schedule database, which could be organized by modules or time frames and linked to readings and assignments; a MediaCenter database, containing articles, written "lectures," and links to external sites; a virtual CourseRoom for interactive discussions among participants and with the instructor, and to enter assignments or complete team tasks; a profiles database, in which descriptions, contact information, and photographs of participants could be entered; and an Assessment Manager database for quizzes or other evaluation tools.

Although the general structure of LearningSpace was excellent for instructional design and course development, there were drawbacks—at least to the version in use at that time. These included frequent problems with the translation from Lotus Notes to Web pages and a cumbersome setup in the CourseRoom that made it time-consuming and difficult for students to read each others' comments. Although interaction between instructor and students was good, there was little interaction between students, and if students did not post messages in the CourseRoom, there was no way to tell if they had logged on. When UW–Madison announced a pilot project using WebCT courseware in 1998, the Virtual Collection Development course was converted to that format.

WebCT, now in use on many campuses, offers a similar structure with many additional features. A path for course content can be designed to the instructor's specification, and may include readings, lectures, and links to other Web sites. A discussion area/bulletin board can be easily set up with multiple forums going on different topics, and the threaded discussion is easy for students to follow and respond to. Although the course content section and the discussion area provide the main substance of the course, other features that enhance it include a calendar, help files, a chat option, a space for student presentations and Web pages, private e-mail between participants, the ability to quickly compile image databases, tools for creating and administering quizzes and surveys, and tools for student management and tracking participation for both the amount of time spent and the distribution of hits among the course materials.

As of spring 2002, three courses were offered by SLIS in this format. The first course, Virtual Collection Development, has been offered twelve times since May 1998. To date, over 600 students have enrolled, from 47 states and 22 countries. This noncredit course runs for six weeks, and each week features a new topic, readings, and discussion. With a focus on selection and delivery of electronic resources that a library provides access to without physical ownership, the class examines such topics as the evolving responsibilities of a collection development librarian, writing new collection development policies, budgeting and reallocating from print to electronic resources, new selection and acquisition tools, licensing agreements, delivering electronic resources to patrons, and copyright. Readings are included in the password-protected course Web site or provided as links to other sites. The courseware provides the means to post assignments, do readings, discuss the topics with other students, and contact the instructor. The only software requirement for the student is a Web browser. Because students are using an electronic classroom to examine and discuss electronic resources, this course has been a marvelous marriage of message and medium.

In 2001, two more online courses were introduced: one of the required certification courses and Decision-Making for Digitization. In the next few years, there are plans to offer more topics in this format. It appears to provide the best level of interaction and accessibility for the reasonable cost—although course development time is considerably higher than in a format in which the instructor can just show up and speak. The traditional correspondence courses will also be offered (including a new course in collection development) because that format is still more convenient for some. In correspondence courses students are also now given the choice to submit assignments via e-mail. The future of ETN, however, rested on decisions made by UW–Extension. As it has been phased out, its most promising low-cost replacement may be WisLine Web, which combines an audio conference call with Web-based visual materials.

Although the ETN format has passed the thirty-year mark, the rate of change in computer technology has been so great that there will inevitably be many changes in delivery of distance education in the next thirty years. However, the things that have remained constant are the need to reach those in remote areas, to provide flexibility for those who have demanding or highly structured work schedules, to accommodate different learning styles, and to promote significant interaction with the instructor, and with other students when possible. ETN was geographically based and had no competition. That's certainly no longer true in distance education, so each library school should be examining its strengths regarding content and audience.

It has been particularly interesting and gratifying to now have the participation of many students from other countries. As UW–Madison seeks to reinvent the Wisconsin Idea, its chancellor, David Ward, has pointed out that "it is no longer enough to define the boundaries of the University of Wisconsin as the boundaries of the state. In a world with 24-hour stock markets, 24-hour cable news, and 24-hour instant communications, the boundaries of the university have become the boundaries of the world" (Kettl 1999).

REFERENCES

Blackshear, Orilla T., and Jane Younger. "ETN: New Approach to Continuing Education," *Wisconsin Library Bulletin,* 67, no. 3, May–June 1971.

Fuller, Muriel. "ETN: A tool for continuing education in Communication Programs," *Status of the Telephone in Education: Second Annual International Communications Conference.* Madison: UW–Extension, 1976.

Kettl, Donald F. *Reinventing the Wisconsin Idea.* The LaFollette Institute's Sesquicentennial Paper Series. Madison: University of Wisconsin–Madison, February 1999.

Rosentreter, Frederick M. *The boundaries of the campus: A history of the University of Wisconsin Extension Division, 1885–1945.* Madison: University of Wisconsin Press, 1957.

UW–Extension Chancellor's Office. *Highlight History of Extension in Wisconsin 1862 to 1999.* Available online at www.uwex.edu/exthist.html. Accessed August 26, 1999.

28

THE EVOLUTION OF DISTANCE
LEARNING AT THE SCHOOL OF
INFORMATION STUDIES,
UNIVERSITY OF
WISCONSIN–MILWAUKEE

Wilfred Fong, Judith Senkevitch, and Dietmar Wolfram

INTRODUCTION

Distance learning has provided individuals the opportunity to pursue educational advancement in environments where a lack of geographic proximity to educational institutions would otherwise make this impossible. The problems associated with geographic proximity have been particularly evident in library and information science, where a comparative dearth of programs due to program closures and the nonuniform distribution of programs throughout the country have made on-site access to education in LIS difficult. This is especially true in the upper Midwest and northern plains states, where only a handful of ALA-accredited programs exist north of the forty-second parallel. Yet demand for qualified professional librarians and school library media specialists remains quite strong.

The University of Wisconsin–Milwaukee (UWM) School of Information Studies (SOIS) has been a leader in the provision of distance learning in LIS in the upper Midwest for two decades. In this chapter, we provide an overview and history of the school, the development of its distance learning opportunities, and plans for the future.

OVERVIEW OF THE SOIS

UWM exists as part of the University of Wisconsin System. The system has been the traditional advocate for higher education to Wisconsin residents. There are a total of twenty-six campuses across the state that comprise the UW System, consisting of two-year and four-year campuses. The distribution of UW campuses throughout the state has made it easier for students who reside in the remote rural areas of the state to access postsecondary education. Access to graduate-level programs, however, is more limited, particularly to residents in the northern parts of rural Wisconsin. To meet the need for additional programs, several private colleges and UW campuses in these parts of the state have relied on a variety of distance learning technologies to facilitate student access to degree programs.

The UWM SOIS is one of the two schools in the UW System offering an ALA-accredited master's degree program in LIS. The SOIS is located on a residential campus in the largest metropolitan area in Wisconsin. The school is one of the twelve colleges and schools in the UWM organizational structure. In 2001, the campus enrollment was approximately 24,000 students, many of whom attend UWM part-time. Because of the diverse population UWM serves, there has been a long-standing recognition of the importance of flexibility in offering students access to courses and degree programs. The UWM SOIS, in keeping with its urban mission, has striven to accommodate part-time students who work full- or part-time, as well as full-time students. Many of the SOIS classes are scheduled on evenings and weekends and at off-campus sites, to allow greater access by working adults.

Although the UWM can trace aspects of its beginnings back to 1901 as part of the Milwaukee State Normal School, the SOIS program emerged during the 1970s. The school's master of Library and Information Science (MLIS) was initially accredited in 1976 by the ALA and was most recently reaccredited in 1997.

The school's curriculum is continually being refined to respond to recent and anticipated changes in the field and in society. SOIS courses provide solid grounding in more traditional information services areas, but the MLIS program has always given high priority to keeping students abreast of current information technologies and resources. The excellent education received by the school's graduates helps them respond to the growing need for library and information specialists. Most SOIS graduates find professional positions within several months of graduation. SOIS graduates are continually sought out by the country's leading institutions for their expertise in new areas of information technology.

The SOIS has also been on the forefront in distance education offerings for credit toward the MLIS degree, as well as for postgraduate work. Because of this and its reputation for state-of-the-art information technology with excellent faculty and facilities, the SOIS attracts out-of-state and international students in addition to Wisconsin residents.

One of the strongest and most unique features of the SOIS is the wide array of degree programs and certificates it offers to its students. At the graduate level, the SOIS has been a pioneer in introducing, implementing, and administering multidisciplinary and cooperative degree programs. It has been in the forefront with its offerings in information technology and in providing for-credit learning opportunities for distance students. The current list of programs includes:

- MLIS
- Coordinated master's degrees (with seven disciplines: Anthropology, English, Foreign Language and Literature, Geography, History, Music, and Urban Studies)
- Certificate of Advanced Studies in Library and Information Science (post-master's)
- Program leading to state certifications for school media specialists
- Focus in information science within the campus-wide multidisciplinary doctorate program
- PhD specialization in Education and Media Technology within the Urban Education doctorate program
- Bachelor of science in Information Resources
- Undergraduate minor in Information Resources
- Undergraduate certificate in Library and Information Science

SOIS has enjoyed tremendous growth during the 1990s. This growth is expected to continue, with the addition of one or more new programs. The SOIS is proud of its positive learning environment, which fosters closer interaction between faculty and students. The retention and graduation rates of SOIS students have been consistently high.

DISTANCE LEARNING OPPORTUNITIES AT SOIS

Initial SOIS efforts in the 1980s to provide for-credit graduate education in library and information science located outside of the Milwaukee area involved faculty travel to several sites in the state. Classes were held at UW campuses in Eau Claire or River Falls in western Wisconsin and attracted students from the northwest part of Wisconsin and eastern Minnesota. Classes were also held in the Fox Valley/Green Bay areas for students residing in the northeast part of the state and the western upper peninsula of Michigan.

Due to the travel time for instructors and students (sometimes exceeding five hours one way), classes were held in a compressed format, with an intensive three-credit course meeting on Fridays, Saturdays, and sometimes Sundays from three to six weekends spread out through the semester. Winter weather posed the only major obstacle on some weekends, requiring that a "snow date" be included in the schedule in the event of inclement weather.

Audiographics

By the early 1990s experiments began with the use of audiographics to offer selected courses. During the spring 1993 semester, SOIS offered several courses using audiographics technology. Audiographics allows for audio and visual interaction using two conference telephone lines between two or more sites. One phone line is used to carry audio signals between the sites, and the other is used to send and receive computer-based graphics (slides). A shared space permitted each site to annotate slides or to draw. Use of audiographics was supported by a statewide audiographics network (WISVIEW) maintained by the UW System's central hub with all sites tapping into this node.

Courses were broadcast from the SOIS Information Technology Lab to a number of UW sites, including Sheboygan, Wausau, Rice Lake, Marinette, Manitowoc, and Rhinelander. Offering the course using audiographics provided the students a recursive learning experience, whereby technologies discussed in the course were used to convey the course content (Wolfram, 1994). Student attitudes toward the technology were positive overall for both local students in the room with the instructor and particularly for distant students. Occasional line drops (where one or more of the telephone lines was dropped) required that the class be halted until the problem was solved but did not pose a major problem. During this time, Instructional Television Fixed Service, involving two-way audio and one-way video, was also available to sites within approximately 100 miles of the UW–Milwaukee campus but was not explored by the SOIS due to the limited areas of its coverage.

Compressed Video

By 1995, the SOIS began using compressed video over Integrated Services Digital Network (ISDN) lines. The compressed video signal, usually broadcast to no more than three sites within the state simultaneously, was often supplemented with resources available over the Internet. This allowed instructors to remain in the Milwaukee area but still required students to travel to sites supporting the video broadcast. The technology permitted a real-time interaction among the students and instructor in Milwaukee and the students situated at the remote sites. Often, instructors would make at least one visit to one or more of the distant sites. Although the technology allowed real-time interaction, not all artifacts of distance were removed. Personalities of students (and the instructor) could appear wooden without the benefit of face-to-face meetings.

SOIS has continued to offer off-campus programs in the northern region of the state, although much of the school's efforts have recently shifted toward offering Web-based courses.

International Distance Education

In addition to its statewide program, the school has extended its program to the international level. During the 1990s, the school established agreements with the Chinese University of Hong Kong and the Institut Technologico y de Estudios Superiores de Monterrey in Mexico to educate groups of information professionals from these regions. Students completed the program as part of a peer group. In both cases, SOIS faculty visited Hong Kong or Mexico to present compressed, on-site classes. During the summer, students would travel to UWM to take a series of courses. Students were able to complete the MLIS program in approximately two years. Thirty-two students from Hong Kong and twenty-six from Mexico have graduated with the MLIS through these programs.

Web-Based Courses

Costs associated with compressed video can be quite high when compared to other formats. Telecommunications fees, site rental, and site facilitation charges make the use of compressed video a costly venture. In addition, access to broadcast sites is still a limiting factor for many students who may still have to travel several hours to reach the site. In summer 1997, the school began to incorporate Web-based courses into its graduate curriculum. These courses were initially mounted using standard Web-page development tools and interpersonal communication software for discussion. After experimenting with several products, the school choose to use the WebCT management courseware to mount its Web-based courses. An instructional technology specialist was hired to work with faculty to help in the development of course materials. The WebCT environment provides a framework in which to mount courses and includes utilities for discussions (real-time and messaging), access to course materials, and additional Internet connections to various resources, such as reserve materials from the UWM Library. WebCT was selected over similar products because of its low cost, the variety of tools it provided, and relative ease of use for both resource development and access.

Since late 1998, the SOIS has also integrated streaming audio and video components into a number of the Web courses. To facilitate real-time dialog, the school has installed a Real Server to process real-time broadcast of streaming video signals over the Internet for presentations and guest speakers. Students log into the SOIS Web-based course site and may interact with the speaker/guest by posting questions via e-mail or the class chatroom. The processing and propagation delay of ten to twenty seconds has not been problematic.

The university library's electronic reserve system, which provides remote access to the full text of articles and other materials on library reserve, has made access to course materials easier for both distant and local students. The SOIS was one of the first units on campus to participate in the project. The use of electronic reserve has grown to the point where most of the SOIS courses now use this service. It has become so popular that many local students express annoyance if course materials are not available via electronic reserve.

The SOIS has been a campus leader in the area of Web-based distance education. As a result, the SOIS obtained a three-year special grant from the university to develop a Web-based curriculum, including the development of Web-based courses leading to the MLIS degree and to state certifications for school library media specialists. As a result of the recent shortage of school library media specialists, the SOIS Web-based program will provide more opportunities for students to obtain the appropriate licenses and to meet the demand for school library media specialists.

When students first enrolled in these Web-based courses, their initial expectation was that a Web-based course was similar to a traditional correspondence course but operated with the use of technology, for example, e-mail correspondence instead of regular mail. However, the SOIS Web-based course offerings surprised many students because the courses require students' active participation through the system's bulletin board and the required chatroom interaction. In addition, students discovered that because of these advanced features, a Web-based course could be even more beneficial and interesting to many students in terms of the learning environment. For example, guest speakers from outside the metropolitan Milwaukee area could be invited to present to the students using telephone and RealAudio broadcasting sessions and could participate in a chatroom discussion with students. This would not have been feasible in an on-campus section where costs associating with bringing speakers in from afar would have been prohibitive.

Instructors of the Web-based courses have observed that the development of a Web-based course takes longer than a regular classroom course, particularly the first time an instructor offers such a course. Due to the nature of the Web-based technology, a Web-based course is available twenty-four hours a day. At any time of the day, a student or the instructor may access the course site and post messages or discuss topics. Therefore, students are also expected to be self-disciplined and to check on the course site on a regular basis.

The SOIS maintains its own Web server to host the WebCT courseware. The SOIS Web server runs on a high-end computer system that was built in-house at the SOIS. To accommodate continuing developments in technology, such as live audio and video streaming and the growth in the number of students taking Web-based courses, the system is upgraded on a regular basis with additional processing and storage capacities.

As with any new technology, there is always a learning curve. When the SOIS first launched its Web-based courses, students had occasional problems in accessing the system due to not only computer hardware problems but also Internet service provider connection issues. Interestingly, the Web browsers Netscape and Internet Explorer behaved differently with the WebCT program, especially with the chatroom features. The WebCT company has been helpful in resolving some of the technical issues surrounding the program that the SOIS would not have been able to resolve. This greater dependence on technology to mount courses makes good relationships with software vendors essential.

RESEARCH ISSUES

Due to the relative newness of Web-based education, there have been few studies evaluating the efficacy of Web-based learning. In 1999, the school received a grant for a study investigating Web-based versus traditional classroom instruction. The project, funded by the UW System, systematically compared the student learning outcomes and perceived effectiveness of SOIS courses offered via the Internet with traditional on-campus sections of the same courses. The study resulted in a greater understanding of (1) the appropriateness and effectiveness of Internet (Web-based) courses for LIS education, (2) which technologies and approaches work best from both the students' and instructor's perspectives, (3) how students can best be prepared to participate in Web-based classes, (4) how faculty can best be encouraged and aided in developing and implementing such courses, and (5) cost and time issues related to developing and delivering Web-based courses. Findings of the study have been integrated into the design and implementation of Web-based courses at the school (Buchanan, Xie, Brown, and Wolfram, 2001).

FUTURE PLANS

The UWM SOIS is now expanding the Web-based MLIS program to national and international audiences. Although the SOIS presently has several international students taking Web-based courses from Japan, Hong Kong, and Germany, the SOIS would like to expand this opportunity to students in other countries.

To expand the Web-based offerings, the SOIS is now expanding its network infrastructure to ensure that it will support the increasing numbers of users in addition to supporting the streaming video technology. The SOIS Web server is now linked to a gigabit-bandwidth connection. In addition, SOIS is considering the installation of digital phone lines or DSL to make faster Internet connection available to students.

Beginning in fall 1999, the SOIS began to charge a special distance education course fee for all the Web-based courses. This special course fee has been used to support the further development and support of the SOIS Web-based course offerings.

CONCLUSION

In an era of increased competition for student enrollment, distance learning has become a fact of life for many institutions. Programs in LIS have often been leaders within their respective institutions in providing course access to distant students. UWM's SOIS is no exception. The past two decades have seen an evolution in the way the school has reached out to the learning community, first through on-site visits to remote sites, to audio-graphics, to compressed video over ISDN lines, and to Web-based delivery of course content. Most of these methods are still used and are often comple-mentary. The future looks bright for expanding delivery of courses using these and newer technologies. Many of the technologies used offer supple-mental learning experiences where the tools used to access course materials and to interact with one another will also be used by the students in their careers as information professionals.

REFERENCES

Buchanan, E., Xie, H., Brown, M., and Wolfram, D. (2001). "A systematic study of Web-based and traditional instruction in an MLIS program: Success factors and implications for curriculum design." *Journal of Education for Library and Information Science, 42*(4), 274–288.

Wolfram, D. (1994). "Audiographics for distance education: A case study in student attitudes and perceptions." *Journal of Education for Library and Information Science, 35*(3), 179–186.

INDEX

academic support, 190

access to computers, 319

adaptability: in cooperative programs, 195; in learning systems, 230

adjunct faculty: at Kentucky, University of, 123; at Louisiana State University, 136; at Missouri, University of, Columbia, 162, 163, 165; at Oklahoma, University of, 200; at Rhode Island, University of, 234, 240; at Rutgers University, 247; at South Carolina, University of, 272, 273; at Southern Mississippi, University of, 301; at South Florida, University of, 281, 284; at Syracuse University, 316; at Tennessee, University of, 332

administrative infrastructure, 210–11

administrative support, 211

admission criteria, 8, 64, 113, 117, 120, 267, 278

advising, 59, 82, 172, 180–81, 195, 196, 237, 244, 328–29

advisory councils, local, 26

afternoon classes, 89, 240

agreements, formal, 191

Alabama Council on Higher Education (ACHE), 2

Alabama, University of, 1–3

anxiety, 91, 92, 218, 307, 339, 342

archives management, 129

Arizona, University of, 5–11

assessment of distance courses, 49, 58, 210

assignments, 42, 44, 47, 266, 275, 278, 294

assumptions, challenging, 38–42

asynchronous formats: at Florida State University, 46–47; at Louisiana State University, 138–39; at Missouri, University of, Columbia, 164; at North Texas, University of, 182; at Pittsburgh, University of, 229; at Rutgers University, 248, 249, 252; at San Jose State University, 264; at Syracuse University, 319–20, 321; at Tennessee, University of, 333; at Wisconsin, University of, Madison, 362

attitudes, student, 91, 258, 288, 338–39, 342, 345–48, 353, 368

audiographics, 136–37, 367–68

audio-only telephone network, 360

audio streaming, 9, 266

bandwidth, 223–24, 266, 298

barriers, geographic, 26, 105, 326

behavior, determinants of, 341–43

Blackboard, 171, 208, 224, 266, 278, 295, 307–9, 333, 335

Bowling Green State University, 103–4, 106

bridging hubs, 78

British Open University, 36

broadband Internet service, 222–23, 225

bulletin boards, 242, 243, 295, 306, 370

candid classrooms, 286–87

Carnegie Library School, 216

case studies, 258

Centra software, 335

certification, 360

challenges, 277

change, 292, 340

chatrooms, 242, 243, 266, 295, 370. *See also* chats; discussion groups; online discussion

chats, 41–42, 306, 307, 335. *See also* chatrooms; discussion groups; online discussion

Chicago, University of, 17, 66

choice, directed, 43

Cincinnati, University of, 104, 106

classloads, 172, 294–95, 333

classroom pedagogy, 45

cohort groups: at Florida State University, 30; at Hawai'i, University of, 59; at Kent State University, 118; at Kentucky, University of, 123; at North Carolina, University of, Greensboro, 170–71; at North Texas, University of, 180, 190; at Pittsburgh, University of, 221–22, 223; at South Carolina, University of, 277; at South Florida, University of, 296; at Syracuse University, 318; at Tennessee, University of, 328, 332

collaboration: between Dominican University and College of St. Catherine, 16–20; at Hawai'i, University of, 54; in Indiana, 78; in Ohio, 103, 105, 110; in Kentucky, 122, 123; in South Carolina, 273, 278; at South-

ern Mississippi, University of, 309; at Syracuse University, 313; in Texas, 185. *See also* cooperation

collaborative (pedagogical) model, 44–45

College of St. Catherine (St. Paul, MN), 13–22

commitment, of faculty, 275–76, 278

communication, 17, 25, 47, 80, 163, 195, 217–18, 242, 243, 341–43

community, sense of, 41, 72

compensation, faculty, 179, 183, 237, 283, 302, 328

competency, technological, 268–69

complexity, 205

compressed video: at Alabama, University of, 1, 2; at Kentucky, University of, 123, 124; at Louisiana State University, 130, 137; at South Carolina, University of, 277; at Tennessee, University of, 329, 331; at Texas Woman's University, 343; at Wisconsin, University of, Madison, 360–61; at Wisconsin, University of, Milwaukee, 368

compression technologies, 298

computer literacy, as entrance requirement, 8

computing services, 181

conflict, 189

Connecticut, University of, Storrs, 234, 235, 236, 238

Connecticut, West Hartford, 234

consortia, 19

contracts, 43, 44

cooperation, 182, 188–89, 220–21, 235, 259, 297, 301, 303, 328, 360. *See also* collaboration

coordination, 110, 111, 235

coordinators: instructional resource, 321; regional, 236–37

copyright, 256, 302, 303

correspondence courses, 359, 360, 361, 363

costs, 218–19, 228, 369

counseling. *See* advising

courier services, 205

Course Administration Utility, 48

course assessment, 49, 58, 210
CourseInfo software, 333
course interfaces, 33–36, 37
course load reductions, 172, 294–95, 333
course management software, 293, 295, 298, 333
course projects, 58
creativity, 256
cultures, student, 167–68
curricula, cooperative, 193–94

data communication personnel, 192
data transmission networks, 221
Delta State University (Cleveland, MS), 305
discussion groups, 24, 42, 44, 46–47, 85, 308. See also chatrooms; chats; online discussion
distance, barriers of, 18–19
distance fees, 295, 371
diversity, 85, 219, 317, 320
doctoral programs, 27, 72, 122
Dominican University (River Forest, IL), 13–22

economic assessment of distance education, 227–28
EdNet (Tennessee), 327, 329, 331
educational need, 212
Educational Teleconference Network (ETN), 359–60, 363–64
electronic reserve, 369
e-mail: at College of St. Catherine, 24; at Florida State University, 32; at Indiana University, 85, 93; at Kent State University, 119; at Rhode Island, University of, 241, 242, 243; at Southern Mississippi, University of, 308; at South Florida, University of, 290, 292, 295; at Tennessee, University of, 329, 335; at Wisconsin, University of, Madison, 363
emoticons, 42
emotions, 339, 342
employment records, 174
Emporia State University, 23–27
enrollment: at Connecticut, University of, Storrs, 238; at Florida State University, 31, 41; at Hawai'i, University of, 57; at Kent State University, 102; at Louisiana State University, 128; at North Carolina, University of, Greensboro, 169, 171; at North Texas, University of, 178; at Oklahoma, University of, 202, 207, 211, 212; at South Carolina, University of, 278; at Southern Mississippi, University of, 300; at South Florida, University of, 294; at Syracuse University, 317; at Tennessee, University of, 325, 327–28, 332; at Texas Woman's University, 337
environment, 91–92, 302, 339, 341
equipment, 78, 228
evening classes, 2, 15, 18, 89, 237, 240, 315, 327, 366
expectations, 226, 348–50, 370
experts, 85, 93
exploration, directed, 43
exploratory (pedagogical) model, 43
extension programs, 315–16

face-to-face communication: at Florida State University, 39–42; at Illinois, University of, 68; at Indiana University, 80, 81, 91–92, 94; at Kentucky, University of, 123; at Missouri, University of, Columbia, 165; at Rutgers University, 252; at San Jose State University, 267; at South Carolina, University of, 274; at Southern Mississippi, University of, 300; at South Florida, University of, 282; at Syracuse University, 318
facilities, 240
faculty: commitment of, 275–76, 278; compensation of, 179, 183, 237, 283, 302, 328; course load reductions, 172, 294–95, 333; training of, 183, 293; work life issues, 294; workload of, 213, 224, 283, 332, 334. See also traveling faculty
faculty support, 179, 224, 302, 303–4, 334
FastTrack MLIS (University of Pittsburgh), 221–26

feedback, 44, 58, 59, 80–81, 226
fees for distance courses, 295, 371
field interviews, 93
financial feasibility, 213
Flanders, Ned A., 92
flexibility, 24, 37, 124, 137, 171, 226, 230, 243, 258, 296, 362, 364, 366
Florida State University, 29–51
"flying" faculty. *See* traveling faculty
focus groups, 225–26
Fridays Only (University of Illinois), 66–67
funding, 110–11, 180, 295, 328

gaming software, 260
General Extension Division (Florida State University), 30
geographic barriers, 26, 105, 326
Georgia, 276–77
goals, 195, 233
grade management, 266, 295
graduation rates, 278, 367
grants: at Kent State University, 104, 111; at Kentucky, University of, 124; at Louisiana State University, 129, 138; at Missouri, University of, Columbia, 163; at North Texas, University of, 179; at Oklahoma, University of, 211; at Rutgers University, 248, 251; at San Jose State University, 264, 265; at South Carolina, University of, 273; at Wisconsin, University of, Madison, 361–62; at Wisconsin, University of, Milwaukee, 370, 371
group affiliation, 294
group work and projects, 68
guidelines, 210, 212–13, 236–37, 239, 243–45, 303

hall talk, 40, 41
hardware requirements, 267
Hawai'i Interactive Television System (HITS) Services, 54–55, 56–57
Hawai'i, University of, 53–61
Haythornthwaite, Caroline, 71
health sciences, 135
help files, 48

high-tech/high-touch, 25–26
Hogan, Sharon, 66
human interaction, 25–26
hybrid courses, 298, 306–10

Illinois Board of Higher Education (IBHE), 66
Illinois, University of, 17–18, 63–73
incentives, 227
income generation, 337
Independent Study Degree Program (ISDP) (Syracuse University), 317–18
Indiana Higher Education Television System (IHETS), 78–80
Indiana University, 75–99
individualized (pedagogical) model, 43–44
Information Interaction Styles Model, 44–45
infrastructure: administrative, 210–11; institutional, 248, 293; requirements of, 297; support, 249; technological, 178–79, 182, 210, 211, 223–24, 228, 256
institutional support issues, 288–89
Instructional Management (IMS) Project, 229
Instructional Television Fixed Signals (ITFS), 54, 55, 368
instructional television (ITV) model, 286
intellectual property ownership, 179, 256, 302, 303, 333, 334
intelligences, multiple, 44
interaction: assumptions regarding, 39–42; categories of, 92–93; in distance education, 217–18, 339, 355; and Educational Teleconference Network (ETN), 364; and instructor site visits, 218; in LearningSpace (Wisconsin, University of, Madison), 362; research issues, 294; and student performance, 287; students' need for, 226; styles of, 44–45; at Summer Institute (Syracuse University), 319; in telelearning vs. compressed video, 137; and videoconferencing, 192
interactive classrooms, 264, 327

Interactive Classroom Studios (ICSs), 75–76, 77–79
interactive discussions, 266
interactive (pedagogical) model, 42–43
interactive telelearning facilities, 170–71
interactive television (ITV), 32–33, 39, 53, 54–55, 58, 77, 218–20, 264–65, 332
interactive video, 17, 19–21, 24–25, 190, 196, 207–8, 210, 344
interactive videoconference system, 343
Interactive Video Network (IVN) (Southern Mississippi, University of), 300, 301–5, 308
interactive video networks, 2–3, 185–86, 192, 327
Intercampus Interactive Telecommunications System (IITS), 1
interfaces, course, 33–36, 37, 50
interlibrary loan services, 243, 306
international distance education, 368–69
international experiences, 24
Internet: at Alabama, University of, 3; at Emporia State University, 25; at Hawai'i, University of, 53; at Indiana University, 78; at Kent State University, 119; at Kentucky, University of, 123, 124; at North Texas, University of, 179; at Rhode Island, University of, 241, 243; at Rutgers University, 248; at San Jose State University, 265; at Southern Mississippi, University of, 305–9; at South Florida, University of, 283, 289–95; at Wisconsin, University of, Madison, 361
Internet-based classes, 68, 196, 318
Internet-based technology, 76
Internet service providers (ISPs), commercial, 225
Internet Web boards, 85
interviews, 81, 85, 93
isolation, 38–39, 59, 196, 203
ITFS system, 286–87

Kent State University, 101–20
Kentucky Commonwealth Virtual University (KCVU), 124
Kentucky, University of, 121–25

land grant institutions, 63, 161, 233, 249, 325
lateral arrangements, 191
LEAD (Library and Information Science Educational Access and Development) Initiative, 167
learning communities, 39, 40–42
learning outcomes, 49, 371
LearningSpace, 362
learning styles, 364
LEEP program (University of Illinois), 67–72
library staff, 181
library support, 181, 334
licensed library resources, access to, 224–25
live digital video, 24
logistics, 59, 163
Lohrer, Alice, 64–65, 66
Louisiana State University, 127–60

mail delivery, 7–8
Maine, 276–77
management software, 266, 369
markets, 228
Massachusetts, University of, Amherst, 234, 235, 236, 240
Massachusetts, University of, Boston, 237–38, 240
materials collections, 30
media, multiple, 43
Memphis (Tennessee) pilot project, 327–29
Millennium Program (University of Tennessee), 333–34
Mind Extension University, 6–7
Minnesota, University of, 15, 16
Missouri, University of, Columbia, 161–68
multiple sites, 67, 136–38, 207–8, 243, 305
multisite synchronous programs, 192
multi-user object-oriented (MOO) sites, 305–6

National Learning Infrastructure Initiative (NLII), 229
needs assessment, 189–92, 273, 330, 362

networking, 58
network links, 190
network specialists, 267
New Hampshire, University of,
   Durham, 234, 236, 240
New Mexico, 5–6
New Pathways—Electronic Access to
   Weekend College, 16
North Carolina Research and Edu-
   cation Network (NC-REN), 171
North Carolina, University of, at
   Greensboro, 169–76
Northern Illinois University, 17, 66
Northern Kentucky University, 123
North Texas, University of, 177–83,
   185–97
Northwest Ohio Program, 103, 108

off-campus centers, 2
OhioLEARN: goals of, 105, 111;
   implementation of, 108; memo to
   prospective MLS students, 119–20;
   MLS program, 107, 113; MLS team,
   108; model, 109–15; objectives of,
   105–6; overview of, 111–13; press
   release, 116; priorities of, 106–7;
   recruiting brochure, 116–19
OHIOLINK, 104
Ohio University, 104, 106
Oklahoma Higher Education Televised
   Instruction system, 203
Oklahoma, University of, 199–213
O'Melia, Pauline, 30
one-way video, 80–81, 204, 274, 275,
   283, 368
online chat. See chatrooms; chats; discussion groups; online discussion
online courses, 171, 247, 254, 259,
   307, 308, 309, 310, 361
online discussion, 59, 93, 241, 277,
   318, 335. See also chatrooms; chats;
   discussion groups
online systems, 77
on-site visits, 82, 94
OPLIN, 104
orientation, 41, 86, 118, 120, 172,
   266

participation, student, 370
partnerships, 166
pedagogical issues, 287–88
Pennsylvania Alliance for Continuing
   Library Education (PACLE),
   220–21
perceptions, 343
personal visits, 82, 94
PictureTel, 241–42, 243
Pittsburgh, University of, 215–31
point-to-point microwave signals, 54
policies, 189
Portable Document Format (PDF)
   files, 48
practice, hands-on, 87, 88
preparation, course, 59
presentations, 243
priorities, 303
producers, 59
professional development, 93–95, 247
professorial roles, traditional, 292
program evaluation, 49
protocols, 82
psychological distance, 347

qualitative research methodology
   (Texas Woman's University), 343–44
quality assurance, 166, 167, 303

Real Presenter, 266
regional coordinators, 236–37
regional programs, 233–46
regulations, 189
research, 48–50, 257–59, 371
reserve materials, 87, 220, 310, 369
residency requirements, 17, 19, 56,
   162, 163, 164, 168, 318, 334
residency, virtual, 322
resident faculty, 202–3
resources: assessment of, 50; availability
   of, 205, 326–27; on course Web
   sites, 46; at outlying locations, 236
resource support, 303
responses, student, 348–52
Rhode Island, University of, 233–46
risk, 228
Rogers University, 203

room coordinators, 192
Rosary College, 13–14
Rutgers University, 247–61

San Jose State University, 263–69
satellite TV networks, 78
scalability, 230
scheduling, 123–24, 303
scheduling/local arrangements contacts, 108
school librarians, 128–29, 169, 187, 272, 296, 359, 370
Schusterman Center (Tulsa, OK), 209, 211
SEEN, 360
self-efficacy, 90–92
self-identity development, 49
server space, 292
sharing. See collaboration; coordination
Sharp, Katharine, 63, 64
Shores, Louis, 29, 31
shuttle service, 305
site-based classes, 283, 296
site coordinators, 25, 328
sites (geographic), 6–7, 24
skepticism, 227
Smith, Linda, 70, 71
software, 266, 319–20
South Carolina, 271–79
South Carolina Educational Television (SCETV), 273
Southern Mississippi, University of, 299–311
South Florida, University of, 281–99
spontaneity, 82
standards, 229–30, 236, 303
Starburst courses, 165, 166
Stargate, 225
streaming audio, 48, 179, 369
streaming video, 24, 179, 310, 369
student demographics, 291
students: learning outcomes of, 295; participation of, 287–88; performance of, 304–5; satisfaction of, 90–91, 226, 338
suburban locations, 19
suitability, 205

summer classes, 89, 234, 240, 315, 316–17
Summer Institute on Leadership and Change (Syracuse University), 317, 319
support, 87, 172, 252, 309–10; academic, 190; administrative, 211; assessment of, 50; faculty, 179, 224, 302, 303–4, 334; infrastructure, 249; institutional, 288–89; library, 181, 334; of local staff, 70, 108, 213; at remote locations, 302; resource, 303; technical, 249, 251, 264, 293, 321; technological, 192, 226, 250
surveys, 172–74, 236, 274
syllabi, 46, 58, 59, 87, 278, 295
synchronous chatrooms, 47
synchronous courses, 136–38
synchronous interactive television, 249
Syracuse University, 313–23

Talk Back Television (TBTV), 203–7
technical assistance, 267
technical capacity, 212–13
technical contacts, 108
technical dependency, 255
technical standards, 229–30
technical support, 249, 251, 264, 293, 321
technicians, 59, 208
technological infrastructure, 178–79, 182, 210, 211, 223–24, 228
technological issues, 288
technological requirements, 221
technological support, 192, 226, 250
technologies, distance learning, 319–20
technology, 91, 351–52
telelearning, 137, 170–71
televised courses, 278, 282–83
television, 6–8, 273–75, 286–89, 290
Tennessee, University of, 325–36
Texas Education Telecommunications Network, 343
Texas, University of, Austin, 9–10
Texas Woman's University, 9–10, 185, 337–57
textbooks, 181, 220

theoretical frameworks, 48–49
TopClass, 171
touch, 25–26
transition, 285–86
transportation issues, 18–19
Trans-Texas Videoconference Network,
    343
traveling faculty: at Arizona, University
    of, 6; at Illinois, University of, 65; at
    Louisiana State University, 137; at
    Missouri, University of, Columbia,
    162; at North Carolina, University
    of, Greensboro, 170; at North
    Texas, University of, 178, 186, 189;
    at Rhode Island, University of, 241,
    243; at Southern Mississippi, Univer-
    sity of, 300; at South Florida, Uni-
    versity of, 282, 283; at Tennessee,
    University of, 328; at Wisconsin,
    University of, Milwaukee, 367. *See
    also* faculty
TTVN interactive video network, 186,
    187
tuition reciprocity, 123
Tulsa, University Center at (UCT),
    201–3
212 Program, 36–37
two-classroom model, 20–21
two-way audio, 91–92, 204, 274, 275,
    283, 343, 368
two-way interactive television, 171
two-way video, 81–82, 86–87, 91–92,
    241–42, 343

undergraduate minors, 72
UT (University of Texas) interactive
    video network, 185

Vermont, University of, 234
video classrooms, 190
videoconference networks, 178, 190
videoconference technicians, 192
videoconferencing, 19–21, 182, 187,
    192
video interviews, 81, 85
video streaming, 9, 266
videotaped instruction, 2
videotapes, 59, 170, 217, 335

Video Teleconferencing Classrooms
    (VTCs), 75
Virginia, 330
virtual classrooms, 305–6
virtual community, 72
Virtual Indiana Classroom (VIC):
    benefits of, 76; components of Video
    Conferencing Network, 75–76;
    Network, 82, 90–95
virtual libraries, 267
virtual private network (VPN), 225
virtual residency, 322
virtual student union, 180
visits, faculty, 82, 94, 218

Washington, D.C. (Syracuse University
    extension program), 316
weather, 33
Web-assisted courses, 165, 166, 171, 266
Web-based courses. at Hawai'i, Univer-
    sity of, 60; and institutional infra-
    structure, 293; at Louisiana State
    University, 139; at Missouri, Univer-
    sity of, Columbia, 165, 166; at
    North Carolina, University of,
    Greensboro, 171; at North Texas,
    University of, 182; at Oklahoma,
    University of, 208, 210; at Pitts-
    burgh, University of, 229; at Rut-
    gers University, 252, 255; at South
    Carolina, University of, 278; at
    South Florida, University of,
    290–95; and student demographics,
    291; at Tennessee, University of,
    333, 335; time constraints of, 255;
    and traditional professorial roles,
    292; at Wisconsin, University of,
    Milwaukee, 369–71
WebCT: at Alabama, University of, 3;
    at Arizona, University of, 9; at
    Emporia State University, 24; at
    Hawai'i, University of, 60; at North
    Carolina, University of, Greensboro,
    171; at North Texas, University of,
    178, 180, 192–93; at Oklahoma,
    University of, 208; at Rhode Island,
    University of, 242–43; at Rutgers
    University, 250; at San Jose State

University, 266; at Southern Mississippi, University of, 306, 307–9; at Syracuse University, 320, 321; at Wisconsin, University of, Madison, 363; at Wisconsin, University of, Milwaukee, 369, 370

Web development, 50

Web-linked CD-ROMs, 278

WebMC, 36

Web sites: content areas, 46–48; design and creation of, 258; functions of, 48; school home page, 48

Web-supported courses, 210

weekend classes: at Alabama, University of, 2; at College of St. Catherine, 15; at Dominican University, 18; at Emporia State University, 24; at Indiana University, 89; at Rhode Island, University of, 237, 240; at San Jose State University, 264, 267; at South Carolina, University of, 272, 274; at Syracuse University, 315, 316; at Wisconsin, University of, Milwaukee, 366, 367

Western Interstate Commission for Higher Education (WICHE), 6

West Virginia, 276–77

Wisconsin, University of, Madison, 359–64

Wisconsin, University of, Milwaukee, 365–72

Wisconsin Idea, 359

World Wide Web, 8–11, 32, 33–34, 208, 256–57

Yahoo!, 308–9